Teaching and Learning in the Digital Era

Issues and Studies

Teaching and Learning in the Digital Era

Issues and Studies

Editor

Jun Xu

King's Own Institute, Australia

NEW JERSEY · LONDON · SINGAPORE · BEIJING · SHANGHAI · HONG KONG · TAIPEI · CHENNAI · TOKYO

Published by

World Scientific Publishing Co. Pte. Ltd.
5 Toh Tuck Link, Singapore 596224
USA office: 27 Warren Street, Suite 401-402, Hackensack, NJ 07601
UK office: 57 Shelton Street, Covent Garden, London WC2H 9HE

Library of Congress Cataloging-in-Publication Data
Names: Xu, Jun, 1970- editor.
Title: Teaching and learning in the digital era : issues and studies /
    editor, Jun Xu, King's Own Institute, Australia.
Description: Singapore ; Hackensack, NJ : World scientific, 2024. |
    Includes bibliographical references and index.
Identifiers: LCCN 2023053684 | ISBN 9789811285615 (hardcover) |
    ISBN 9789811285622 (ebook) | ISBN 9789811285639 (ebook other)
Subjects: LCSH: Education--Effect of technological innovations on. |
    Educational innovations. | Internet in education. | Web-based instruction. |
    Computer-assisted instruction.
Classification: LCC LB1028.3 .T3747 2024 | DDC 371.33/4--dc23/eng/20231212
LC record available at https://lccn.loc.gov/2023053684

British Library Cataloguing-in-Publication Data
A catalogue record for this book is available from the British Library.

Copyright © 2024 by World Scientific Publishing Co. Pte. Ltd.

All rights reserved. This book, or parts thereof, may not be reproduced in any form or by any means, electronic or mechanical, including photocopying, recording or any information storage and retrieval system now known or to be invented, without written permission from the publisher.

For photocopying of material in this volume, please pay a copying fee through the Copyright Clearance Center, Inc., 222 Rosewood Drive, Danvers, MA 01923, USA. In this case permission to photocopy is not required from the publisher.

For any available supplementary material, please visit
https://www.worldscientific.com/worldscibooks/10.1142/13658#t=suppl

Desk Editors: Balasubramanian Shanmugam/Steven Patt

Typeset by Stallion Press
Email: enquiries@stallionpress.com

Printed in Singapore

© 2024 World Scientific Publishing Company
https://doi.org/10.1142/9789811285622_fmatter

Preface

Digital technologies have brought disruptions to the education sector, including new market opportunities, learners being able to assemble their learning paths and learning content, an unlimited supply of content and flexible delivery, new value propositions, large-scale platforms, and reimagined systems. Meanwhile, some tough decisions education organizations have to make are delivery model (e.g., online, hybrid, and face-to-face teaching arrangements), revenue model, targeted student cohorts, growing academic integrity issues arising from ChatGPT and other artificial intelligence applications, teacher shortages, the relevance of education to the practice, return of capital and asset investment, student success, the long-lasting impact of COVID-19, automation/digitization issues, demand for better learning experience, security and privacy concerns, and others. This book entitled *Teaching and Learning in the Digital Era: Issues and Studies*, looks at current status and practices of teaching and learning facilitated/enabled by digital technologies, reviews challenges/issues associated with classroom teaching, online teaching and hybrid-learning, and discusses success factors and future directions of teaching and learning in the digital era. On top of high-level discussion of current status, challenges and issues, emerging trends and technology, and future directions of teaching and learning in the digital era, this book will also provide a number of studies looking at different perspectives of using digital technologies for teaching and learning. This book can be used as a good reference book for education organizations (especially higher education providers) to review their current approaches and practices of technology-assisted/enabled teaching and learning and develop their future plans for teaching and learning in the digital era. This book also can serve as a good reference book for teaching staff or administrators at education institutions, who are looking at updating their professional knowledge & skills.

This book has 14 chapters and is divided into two parts. Part 1 focuses on key issues associated with technology-assisted/enabled teaching and learning and includes seven chapters (Chapters 1–7) and Part 2 presents studies on digital technologies for teaching and learning and consists of seven chapters (Chapters 8–14). Chapter 1, by Jun Xu, discusses the impacts of digital technologies on society and the education sector, reviews e-learning and hybrid learning, looks at learning and training in the organization, highlights the recent development of artificial intelligence (especially ChatGPT) and its impact on education, and comments on the role of the government and teacher in the education in the digital era. Chapter 2, by Sanjay Jha, Meena Jha, and Jun Xu, provides an overview of teaching and learning in the digital era, describes the definition, types, and elements of teaching and learning in the digital era, explains the opportunities, and challenges of teaching and learning, and points out emerging patterns and provides insight into future trajectories how the use of digital technologies while providing the required support to enhance teaching and learning activities. Chapter 3, by Jun Xu, Graeme Salter, and Yuxi Lan, presents the background of ChatGPT, discusses the benefits it can provide to higher education, points out its limitations, concerns, and issues, and looks at strategies and success factors for successful implementation of ChatGPT in the higher education organization. Chapter 4, by Sweta Thakur, Farzaneh Mayabadi, Fariza Sabrina, and Shaleeza Sohail, provides an overview of the emerging trends in online education and elaborates on educational tools and how they can be used to enhance the quality of education. Chapter 5, by Smitha Shivshankar, explores the significance of assessment integrity and security and emphasizes their imperative role in preserving the value of academic qualification and genuine knowledge acquisition. It also sheds light on the strategies and digital tools for addressing the challenges and discusses concerns and issues associated with the digital tools. Chapter 6, by Shima Forughi, delves into the realm of online assessments, shedding light on their advantages, prerequisites, and the critical role of student perspectives. It emphasizes the pivotal influence of student attitudes, motivations, and emotions on the outcomes of online assessments and provides a scope to the online evaluation by looking into assessment types, consideration of academic integrity, alternative ways of the learners' evaluation, and different aspects of online examinations. Chapter 7, by Yuxi Lan, Nora Bhangi, and Jun Xu, starts with a brief illustration of academic integrity and online assessment arrangements, including exams. It then proceeds to explore the factors associated with academic misconduct, followed by a discussion on various measures and digital tools that can be utilized to cope with academic integrity. This chapter also provides examples of current practices for deterring academic misconduct at King's Own Institute (KOI), Australia.

Chapter 8, by Graeme Salter, examines the benefits and challenges of creating engaging lessons in an online learning environment. Suggestions for increasing student engagement online are provided. The importance of gaining attention, demonstrating relevance, and providing state changes during a lesson are highlighted. Chapter 9, by Mubashir Hussain, explores the potential of "Game-Based Learning" (GBL) and gamification as an alternative pedagogy to improve learner's engagement, problem-solving skills and learning skills. It provides insights on GBL and its application in programming education, which enables instructors to make better decisions in their teaching practices for programming courses and improve students' learning experience. Chapter 10, by Behnaz Rezaie Ortakand, discusses predictive models for student engagement and retention issues (e.g., identifying students at risk of attrition during the early phases) and looks at using learning management system as data sources for such models. Chapter 11, by Mehrdad Razmjoo, discusses different machine learning algorithms and dives into the importance of student engagement, the challenges involved, and the utilization of learning analytics in the educational process. The findings highlight the potential of machine learning in identifying at-risk students and optimizing educational outcomes in online learning environments. Chapter 12, by Farzaneh Mayabadi, Sweta Thakur, Shaleeza Sohail, and Fariza Sabrina, sheds light on how big data can be used in curriculum development to ensure that the skills and competencies students learn at educational institutions align with those required in the current and future job market. By exploring three case studies in which big data has been utilized to revise and update curricula in different fields, this chapter suggests that big data allows curriculum designers to make data-driven decisions which leads to a higher rate of employability and satisfaction among students. It also discusses the limitations and challenges of using big data in education. Chapter 13, by Xin Gu, Fareed Ud Din, and Robert M.X. Wu, compiles and examines 51 ICT programs and 1,251 associated ICT courses from 11 universities in China's Shanxi province. This case study discovers that the most sought-after ICT programs primarily center around Information and Computing Science, as well as Computer Science and Technology. Mathematics and Programming-related courses lay the foundation for ICT programs, while Programming is the most frequently offered course in ICT programs at Shanxi Universities. Chapter 14, by Gazi Farid Hossain, Deb Case, and Caitlin Smith, looks at different technology-centric feedback collection and analysis tools for collected survey data. It also suggests some factors for making the students' feedback and survey more successful.

We would like to express our sincere gratitude to the CEO and President of King's Own Institute, Professor Doug Hinchliffe for his great support, and thank Dr Nicky Antonius and Dr Daniel O'Sheedy, for their suggestions and assistance. Finally, we would like to thank World Scientific for the opportunity to work on the book, and thank Editor Steven Patt and his colleagues, at World Scientific, for overseeing the publishing process of the book, for their great assistance, and for giving us such a wonderful publishing experience.

About the Editor

Jun Xu currently works with King's Own Institute, Sydney, Australia, as Vice President (Academic). He earned his Bachelor of Engineering (1992) from China University of Petroleum and received his MBA (1999) and PhD (2003) degrees from Curtin University, Australia. On top of his significant experience of working with Australian and Chinese governments and businesses across various industries, and his good experience of working with major international oil & gas companies in Singapore and China, he also possesses good experience of working with e-business and digital technology start-ups in Australia and China, good experience of higher education management, sound experience of property management & development, and extensive teaching, research, and doctoral research project supervision experience in the areas of information management/knowledge management and e-business/digital enterprise. He has published eight books on e-business, knowledge management, information systems, digital enterprise, and teaching & learning, and he is the Foundation Editor-in-Chief of the journal *The International Technology Management Review*.

© 2024 World Scientific Publishing Company
https://doi.org/10.1142/9789811285622_fmatter

Contents

Preface		v
About the Editor		ix
Part 1	**Issues**	**1**
Chapter 1	Overview of Teaching and Learning in the Digital Era *Jun Xu*	3
Chapter 2	Teaching and Learning in the Digital Era: Opportunities and Challenges *Sanjay Jha, Meena Jha, and Jun Xu*	51
Chapter 3	ChatGPT and Higher Education *Jun Xu, Graeme Salter, and Yuxi Lan*	87
Chapter 4	Online Education: Challenges, Tools, and Emerging Trends *Sweta Thakur, Farzaneh Mayabadi, Fariza Sabrina, and Shaleeza Sohail*	121
Chapter 5	Assessment Integrity and Assessment Security in the Digital Era *Smitha Shivshankar*	137
Chapter 6	Designing Effective Online Assessment *Shima Forughi*	165

Chapter 7	Academic Integrity and Online Teaching and Learning Yuxi Lan, Nora Bhangi, and Jun Xu	193
Part 2	**Studies**	**213**
Chapter 8	Creating Engaging Online Lessons Graeme Salter	215
Chapter 9	Effectiveness of Game-Based Learning for Programming Courses Mubashir Hussain	235
Chapter 10	Monitor and Predict Student Engagement and Retention Using Learning Management System (LMS) Behnaz Rezaie Ortakand	259
Chapter 11	Enhancing Student Engagement by Using Machine Learning Algorithms Mehrdad Razmjoo	279
Chapter 12	Application of Big Data in Curriculum Development Farzaneh Mayabadi, Sweta Thakur, Shaleeza Sohail, and Fariza Sabrina	291
Chapter 13	ICT Programs in China: A Case Study of Shanxi Universities Xin Gu, Fareed Ud Din, and Robert M.X. Wu	303
Chapter 14	Technologies and Student Feedback Collection and Analysis Gazi Farid Hossain, Deb Case, and Caitlin Smith	327

Index   343

Part 1
Issues

© 2024 World Scientific Publishing Company
https://doi.org/10.1142/9789811285622_0001

Chapter 1

Overview of Teaching and Learning in the Digital Era

Jun Xu

King's Own Institute, Australia

Abstract

This chapter discusses the impacts of digital technologies on society and on the education sector, reviews e-learning and hybrid learning, looks at learning and training in the organization, highlights the recent development of artificial intelligence (especially ChatGPT) and its impact on education, and comments on the role of the government and teacher in the education in the digital era.

Keywords: Digital technology, E-learning, Online learning, Remote learning, Hybrid learning, Future skills, Artificial intelligence (AI), ChatGPT.

1. Impacts of Digital Technologies

Digital technologies such as Advanced connectivity (e.g., optical fiber, LPWA network, Wi-Fi 6, 5G/6G Cellular, LEO satellite constellations), Applied artificial intelligence (e.g., computer vision, natural-language processing, deep reinforcement learning, knowledge graphs), Cloud & Edge Computing (e.g., device edge, remote edge, branch edge, enterprise edge, telecom/MEC edge, cloud), Immersive reality technologies (e.g., spatial computing, mixed reality, augmented reality, virtual reality, metaverse), Industrializing machine learning (e.g., tooling optimizing ML workflows, automated data management, structure and collaborative development, controlled production release decisions, automated continuous integration and continuous development (CI/CD) for test and validation of all releases), Next generation software development (e.g., greater participation of citizen developers, automated configuration and monitoring, AI-based pair programmers, fully automated CI/CD pipelines), Quantum technologies (e.g., Quantum computing, Quantum communication, Quantum sensing), Trust architecture and digital identity (e.g., zero-trust architecture, digital identity, privacy engineering, and explainable artificial intelligence), Web 3 (e.g., digital assets and tokens, smart contracts, blockchain), Future of Bio-engineering (e.g., viral-vector gene therapy, mRNA therapy, Cultivated meat, Drop-in, Bio-replacements, Biobetter), Future of clean energy (e.g., Solar photovoltaics, On-and offshore wind generations, nuclear vision, Electrolyzers), Future of mobility (e.g., Radar and cameras, HD maps, Infotainment, Digital twin, Hybrid propulsion, nanomaterials, green primary materials), Future of space technologies (e.g., Laser communication, Edge computing & AI, Nuclear propulsion, In-orbit servicing), and Future of sustainable consumption (e.g., CCUS, Carbon removal, Green construction, Natural capital ad nature, Alternative protein and sustainable agriculture, Circular technologies), have great impacts on the way we do things, the way we live, and the way we teach and learn (Chui *et al.*, 2022b: 5, 34, 41, 46, 74, 95, 111, 140, 153, 160, 180; the author's own knowledge). Among all the technology trends, it can be said that artificial intelligence has the greatest potential, especially in terms of innovation (Chui *et al.*, 2022b, 3, 21).

Some of the most significant shifts for organizations, which could be enabled by rapidly evolving digital technologies discussed in the last paragraph are as follows (Bort, 2023; Simon *et al.*, 2023; the author's own knowledge):

- More resilience and faster speed are required (e.g., through re-organization for faster responses, empowering people, and encouraging and facilitating continuous learning in the organization).
- A hybrid work model balancing in-person and remote working is needed (e.g., having a supporting structure, business processes, and performance management mechanism).

- Artificial intelligence should be used for building better organizations (e.g., improving business processes, creating talent pipelines, hiring and developing AI-savvy leaders, fostering data-driving decision-making, and being actively aware of the limitations, risks, and ethical concerns associated with artificial intelligence).
- New rules of attracting, developing, and retaining talent need to be developed (e.g., providing individuals with tailored value propositions by adopting a multidimensional approach including salary, work-life balance, professional development, and purpose).
- Digital capabilities need to be built up in the organization (e.g., sufficient training, resources, commitment to digitization initiatives, development of required digital skills including digital analytics, software development, customer insights, data science, product development, and digital marketing).
- Organizations need to focus on finding and retaining high performers who can be up to 800% more productive than average performers in the same role (e.g., finding talent for critical roles, marching talent for the highest-value roles, developing and looking after talent and keeping talent in the organization).
- Leaders have to be capable and inspiring (e.g., having the ability to lead and inspire others, having equipped themselves with advanced digital intelligence and other digital skills, and having the skills to influence others and win friends in the digital era).
- Organizations need to make meaningful progress on diversity, equity, and inclusion (e.g., identifying and working on both internal opportunities and external community issues, making diversity, equity, and inclusion part of its strategic goals, investing in people's knowledge and skills of diversity, equity, and inclusion).
- Organizations have to be more serious about people's mental health and well-being issues (e.g., taking a more systematic approach, addressing the root causes, and allocating dedicated resources).
- Better efficiency/productivity and effectiveness needs to be achieved (e.g., deploying resources more effectively, achieving better and faster decision-making, establishing appropriate delegation mechanism and arrangements, actively monitoring technological advancements and applying new technologies to improve its operations, enhance external relations, and develop or sustain competitive advantages).
- Information security and privacy protection measures need to be constantly reviewed and updated (e.g., given the rapid development of

digital technologies, widely available networks, and global adoption of computing equipment (especially mobile devices), more and more data can be collected, stored, and processed. Consequently, how to protect personal information and prevent unethical uses of personal information becomes a paramount issue.

2. Impacts of Digital Technologies on Education

Digital technologies have brought disruptions to the education sector (Moore & Martinotti, 2016; the author's own knowledge), such as:

- New market opportunities (e.g., market opportunities arising from new digital capabilities, remote learning/e-learning opportunities, hybrid/blended learning opportunities, personalized learning opportunities).
- Allowing learners to assemble their own learning pathways and content rather than relying on traditionally bundled degrees (e.g., microcredentials and badges).
- Unlimited supply of content and flexible delivery (e.g., open educational resources, crowdsourcing, virtual delivery, blended delivery, co-working spaces/innovation labs).
- New value propositions (e.g., student-centered approach and tailored learning options, competency-based learning, and outcome-based funding model, global learning platforms, global digital degrees, and global access to learning material facilitated by digital ID).
- Large-scale platforms (e.g., online education platforms integrating learning resources from various sources and having Amazon-type learning portals with Google-type search function, and ChatGPT-type assistance).
- Reimagined systems (e.g., mobile/online courses (such as MOOCs) with a mix of curriculum and project-based learning, experiential/immersive learning with augmented, reality, virtual reality, and mixed reality, classes delivered by human teachers and virtual assistants).

Some particular changes and challenges that education organizations (particularly higher education providers) are facing include (Barber & Mourshed, 2007; Boggs *et al.*, 2021; Brassey *et al.*, 2019; Bryant *et al.*, 2020, 2022; Chen *et al.*, 2019; Diaz-Infante *et al.*, 2022; Dorn *et al.*, 2019;

Ferrari and Phan, 2018; Fuller & Kirkland, 2018; Gallagher, 2023; Hall et al., 2022, 2023; Hancock et al., 2022; Heitz et al., 2020; Khan & Kirland, 2019; LinkedIn Learning, 2023; Microsoft, 2023; Pandit et al., 2012; the author's own knowledge; UNESCO, 2023b; University of Queensland, 2023; Welch, 2023):

- *Deciding learning/delivery models*: The hybrid/blended delivery model, which combines face-to-face and online delivery approaches, arguably would be the suitable model for many education providers.
- *Financial viability issues*: Education providers need to look for multiple avenues for generating revenue (e.g., new courses, extension of existing courses (e.g., adding in new specializations into existing courses), double degrees, micro-credentials, online courses, short vocational courses, adult learning, new student markets and cohorts, better student retention strategies, more targeted outreach, improving efficiencies of current investments (e.g., via innovative teaching delivery), improving internal efficiency via streamlining business processes and digital transformation).
- *Changing student demographics and unstable student enrolment*: More targeted approach and more individualized value propositions as well as diversification in markets and products should be implemented.
- *Increasing academic integrity issues arising from ChatGPT and other artificial intelligence applications and systems*: AI applications such as ChatGPT have made academic cheating easier and detection of academic cheating more challenging. Such challenges have to be dealt with combined forces of humans and technology.
- *Teacher shortages around the world*: The government has to put more investment and resources into training and developing teachers and provide them with good benefits. More social recognition is needed for those human's social engineers. Compared to medical doctors, who are viewed as human's body engineers, the significance of teachers should be more and better publicized by the government and society. On a related note, while there are various issues associated with AI and other digital technologies, we should explore ways that they can assist teachers in teaching students (e.g., facilitating self-learning, personalized learning).
- *Relevance of education (especially higher education) to the real world*: More practice-oriented courses, more practice-based projects,

more industry-based projects, more work-integrated learning projects, and internship programs should be adopted. And more engagement with the industry (e.g., co-designing the courses, internship with industrial partners) should be pursued by education providers as well.
- *Fast-growing operating costs*: Operational efficiencies in areas such as faculty staff/teachers, academic support services, student support services, facilities, and administrative services should be looked at closely, and ways to streamline processes and speed up the decision-making (e.g., adopting data-driven decision-making approach, learning analytics) as well as strategies for more effectively allocating organizational resources (e.g., adopting the value-chain model for value creation in each internal and external activity) should be explored.
- *Pressure on securing research funding*: In many countries, the government is reducing research funding for education providers (especially universities). Education providers need to be innovative in securing research funding (e.g., working more closely with businesses, co-developing and funding research projects with the industry, encouraging entrepreneurship among faculty members, seeking donations, establishing closer relations with alumni, enhancing internal capabilities of commercializing research results).
- *Pressure on return of capital and asset investment*: Education organizations may need to look at the "light company model" (or "the agile company model") if possible (but you need to have sufficient resources for sustainability and future growth, and in different growth stages of the firm, the resource requirements will differ), examine underutilized assets and facilities as well as underperforming courses, and digitize business processes and activities as many as possible.
- *Pressure on student success*: Education organizations need to focus on getting the right people into suitable teaching positions, developing them into effective teachers, working on a system to deliver the best possible teaching to every student, and providing excellent student support.
- *The long-lasting impact of COVID-19*: The remote learning (also e-leaning, online learning, digital learning) adopted during COVID-19 period will stay even after COVID-19. Education providers need to strategically integrate remote learning into the teaching and learning plan and make it more individual/personalized and adaptive.

- *Dealing with automation/digitization issues*: Teachers need to take on reskilling and adopt the learning philosophy of lifelong learning, and they should use technologies to help them with some routine tasks such as quiz grading and attendance marking so they can focus on more value-added tasks such as coaching and one-to-one tutoring. Education providers should think carefully about the possible losses of social connection and human interaction and caring in the process of automation/digitization.
- *Getting the online learning right*: The online education market (in terms of rapidly increasing student number, influx of investing and rising standard of online education quality and assurance) is growing dramatically. Online education providers need to design courses meeting students' needs, integrate degree and no-degree offers, offer students with courses and skills aligning with students' career planning, provide more personalized learning experiences, establish closer partnership with employers, adopting a student-centered approach, engaging students through multiple channels and touch points, investing heavily in marketing and management, and choosing a suitable operation model (e.g., looking at options of having an online program manager for online programs (both in-house and outsourced programs), working with an independent contractor, partnering with large existing providers, in-housing operations with separate entity), and having clear accountability for online learning organization/entity.
- *Demand for better learning experiences*: Education providers need to offer good learning experience (e.g., seamless journey, engaging teaching approach, caring network/support, seamless connections, captivating experiences, real-world skills, and strong community), and learning experiences should be supported by factors such as access to high-quality and relevant content, well-trained teachers, personalized approach, good and frequent evaluation and feedback and good data analytics and benchmarking.
- *Exploring additional education market*: Education organizations need to understand the reasons for additional education and take appropriate actions. Some reasons that people pursue additional education include: career setbacks, important life events, community building, influences from family members or friends, having problems requiring more learning to resolve, seeing promotion and advertisement, not

engaging at work, overlooked for a promotion opportunity, and New Year's resolution.
- *Focusing on access and equity*: Given the economic and digital divide for different regions and countries, education providers have to work on providing computing equipment and educational resources to the students who need them.
- *Competence-based learning vs. traditional classroom learning*: Opportunities for both mastering competence (not time-based) and learning academic knowledge (normally within fixed timeframe) should be provided to students/learners, and it could be done via collaborating with independent learning providers (such as Khan Academy, Udemy). On a related note, the significance of lifelong learning should be highlighted again here since competence-based learning is closely related to lifelong learning (e.g., continually update your competence and skills after you have got formal education from colleges and universities).
- *Different skills needed*: Skills-focused training for higher education students can be greatly facilitated by digital technologies. On the other hand, curriculum-focused teaching is more for younger students that needs intensive human interaction to progress.
- *Important skills thought by teachers vs. Important skills perceived by students*: While teachers believe skills such as literacy, critical thinking, social awareness, communication, self-awareness and collaboration are important, students think skills important to them are such skills as digital skills, creativity, relationship skills, intercultural understanding, ethical understanding, self-management. Another part of this discussion is Teacher-led learning vs. Student-led learning.
- *The impacts of digital technologies on education*: Education organizations need to be well prepared for the impacts (both positive and negative impacts) of digital technologies (especially artificial intelligence) on the education systems. Stanford University's AIRE (Artificial Intelligence, Robotics and Education) is a good example of such initiative (refer to https://aire.stanford.edu/). It is dedicated to "find the best approach to redesigning our education systems to accommodate the coming area of robotics and artificial intelligence" by bringing together knowledge and experiences from various areas such as Design thinking, Robotics, Artificial Intelligence, Neurology and Education.

- *Competition for talent*: Education providers need to make their human resources (HR) function stronger, more agile and smarter (e.g., aligning HR strategy with business strategy, taking a more agile and collaborative HR approach, continually investing in HR staff development and HR technology, working with universities on recruiting and developing talent (such as via work-integrated learning projects, internship programs)). HR department could be called talent department and the head of the HR could be called Chief Talent Officer.
- *The external environment issues*: In many countries, lack of teachers and administrators and lack of funding are serious issues. On top of the local government's efforts, international communities have to lend their helping hands. Technologies and technology firms could play important roles (e.g., supporting e-learning, m-learning, personalized learning).
- *Security and privacy issues*: Education providers need to continuously invest in security and privacy measures to ensure the continuity of teaching and learning and provide a safe learning environment.

3. E-Learning and Hybrid Learning

3.1. *E-Learning*

E-learning (also called Remote Learning or Online Learning) has been widely adopted by both educational and non-educational organizations. For example, it is reported that more than 25% of college students have taken at least one (1) online course, and about 71% of academic leaders believe that online learning could achieve same or similar learning outcomes as the traditional approach (Chen *et al.*, 2019; Xu & Gao, 2021: 110). E-learning could be provided at the traditional schools, colleges, and universities, workplaces (e.g., via corporate universities and training centers, doing on the job-tasks), communities and training and development agencies, online learning portals/platforms (e.g., Coursera, Udacity, Udemy, edX), and it also self-paced (McKinsey, 2017; the author's own knowledge; Xu & Gao, 2021: 110–111).

E-learning offers many benefits (such as convenience, flexibility, self-paced learning, individualized/personalized learning, 24/7 availability, access to much more learning material, more course and unit options, cost-efficiency, capacity of teaching large number of students without the constraint of space limitation, being cheaper and easier to update and store content, access to global expertise, democratization of knowledge, contribution to education equality via providing people in the less developed regions with access to global teaching and learning resources), but it also has a number of challenges and drawbacks (Xu 2014, p. 99).

3.1.1. *Barriers/Challenges/Issues of E-Learning*

Some barriers/challenges/issues of E-learning include (Brasca *et al.*, 2022; Child *et al.*, 2022; Cusumano *et al.*, 2013; Gallagher, 2023; Hall *et al.*, 2023; Keppell, 2023; Maiolo, 2014; McKinsey, 2017; the author's own knowledge; Turban *et al.*, 2012: 243; Xu, 2014: 100–101; Xu & Gao, 2021: 110–112):

- Security and privacy issues (e.g., learners' online safety and privacy issues, security of online testing and assessment, difficulties in ensuring who actually have completed the online tasks).
- Online content, assessment and curriculum development (e.g., digital teaching and learning has different pedagogical perspectives and issues, simply digitizing student materials and using the same traditional teaching approach will not work. In addition, there are challenges associated with digital assessments (including online essays, online quizzes, online group work, forums, online presentations, online exam, online projects, online reflective journal, online self-assessment, e-portfolio, online peer assessment, online tutorials) in the perspectives of assessment validity, reliability, fairness, variability and efficiency).
- Different teaching and support expertise required (e.g., professional development of teaching and admin and other support staff for online teaching and learning is required).
- Lack of common standards for e-learning platforms (e.g., difficulties in integrating different learning platforms).
- Failing to engage with students (e.g., not providing timely and adequate feedback, not providing enough opportunities for team/group work).
- Mobile learning challenges (e.g., limitations arising from the mobile devices and networks).
- Lack of required infrastructure and access equality issues (e.g., required Internet and Wi-Fi access and computing equipment in some countries and regions are not available).

- Lack of internal capabilities to deploy E-learning (e.g., there is a lack of required strategy, leadership, capacity, skills and resources for learning initiatives).
- Perceived difficulties in developing higher-level cognitive skills (e.g., it could be really challenging to develop students' cognitive skills by watching online sessions, doing online activities with human connection and social interaction).
- Issues of intellectual property protection (e.g., difficulties in controlling the transmission of copyrighted works downloaded from the e-learning sites/platforms).
- Believing e-learning has little or no impact on learning and online programs are not motivating enough.
- Getting more distracted when studying online and Lacking the discipline to do online programs, which have significant impact on learning experiences and learning outcomes.
- Believing that online programs don't offer the same extracurricular options and online programs don't offer the opportunity to interact with other students.
- Lack of face-to-face in-person social interaction and campus life.
- Under-estimating the cost of e-learning, especially when the student number is not sufficient to justify the capital investment and high-fixed cost associated with e-learning.
- Over-estimating the achievement of e-learning: e-learning has its limitation and may only be suitable for certain student cohorts (e.g., students who have full-time employment or live far away from the campus), especially in the early stage.
- Overlooking the difficulties of self-study: some people are not capable of doing or are not willing to do self-study.
- Treating content/study material as commodity could lead to a lack of attention to quality and learning experience.
- Having too much emphasis on technology or not fully utilizing available tools: A balanced approach should be adopted.
- Assuming learned knowledge will be applied: Learned knowledge needs to be applied in real-life actions or work-integrated projects, which could be difficult in the digital learning environment.
- Confusing with adoption and diffusion issues: even people have adopted e-learning systems, they may not use them or use them properly. The assumption of once e-learning system is developed, people will use it, is not true.

3.1.2. Success Factors of E-Learning

Some success factors of E-learning include (Brasca *et al.*, 2022; Child *et al.*, 2021; Child *et al.*, 2023; Cusumano *et al.*, 2014; Epignosis LCC, 2014; Gilbert *et al.*, 2018; Hall *et al.*, 2023; Henry *et al.*, 2014; Pandit *et al.*, 2012; the author's own knowledge; Xu, 2014: 99–102):

- Designing online journey carefully.
- Having clear understanding of the needs of the students and pros and cons of the current programs being offered.
- Deciding a clear vision/strategic direction for your online learning.
- Planning your transformation journey properly (e.g., online program structure, structured course maps, online assessment and integrity issues, online course design).
- Addressing key teaching and learning activities (e.g., content, delivery, evaluation and assessment, engagement and learning, and learning outcomes).
- Providing students with seamless journey via developing clear education road map and offering seamless connections and access to student portals and learning resources.
- Allocating sufficient resources and making necessary adjustments to organizational culture and structure to facilitate the implementation of e-learning strategy.
- Providing sufficient training to teachers (including online teaching pedagogy, effective use of digital technologies for teaching, developing high-quality digital content, and hybrid/blended teaching and learning approach).
- Keeping on monitoring students' e-learning experience and making necessary adjustments.
- Having clear expectations and communicate them effectively to students in every possible opportunity.
- Developing quality content and maintaining its currency.
- Adopting technology platforms, which have the interoperability and integration flexibility, and providing students with easy digital experiences via multiple channels and touch points (e.g., through offering omnichannel experience).
- Ensuring learning platforms are both useful and user friendly (e.g., even a e-learning system has many functions, if it is difficult to use, students will not use it).

- Ensuring engaging teaching via providing range of learning formats (e.g., asynchronous classes, asynchronous classes, peer-to-peer learning), captivating delivery and experiences (e.g., updated content, relevant faculty, content in various formats), opportunities of applying learned knowledge to real-world cases/situations, and tailored learning.
- Ensuring that e-learning is designed to help to personalize learning, provide access to resources/instructors, improve ability to learn, make learning more efficient, and make learning more entertaining.
- Putting caring network and strong community (student led or teacher-led) in place to assist students timely and adequately (including academic support, non-academic support, coaching, career support and IT support).
- Providing reliable and responsive support to students (including actively participating online discussions with students and providing feedback to their inquiries in a timely manner).
- Listening to students and seeking their input for improvement (e.g., via direct observations, student surveys).
- Using data analytics for better understanding thus more informed decision making and continuous improvement.
- Providing opportunities and channels for face-to-face interactions (e.g., contact offices, meeting places, service hubs).
- Making both explicit knowledge (e.g., study material and digital content) and tacit knowledge (e.g., professors' expertise) available to students.
- On top of offering online courses to existing markets, using online channels to tap into new segments and domestic and international markets (e.g., domestic and international students) are not able to attend on-campus studies) should be explored (e.g., such approach would improve the operation of online programs an cause less disruptions to existing operations, especially in the early stage).
- Establishing distinctive unit/entity for managing online programs only when necessary.
- Taking into consideration other relevant factors associated with online programs (including scale of growth, customization level, required talent, speed to market, legal constraints and budget and financial constraints).

According to UNESCO (2020b), in certain countries, there are significant issues/challenges in establishing remote learning/e-learning systems:

- *Student perspectives*: For example, in Sub-Saharan Africa, only 11% households have computers and only 18% of households have Internet connections.
- *Teacher and Curriculum perspectives*: For example, in Sub-Saharan Africa, there is a shortage of 17 million qualified primary and secondary school teachers.
- *Technology solution perspectives*: For example, the total size of e-learning in Sub-Saharan Africa is smaller than 2% of the global total.
- *School system perspectives*: most educations in low and middle-income countries are underfunded.

UNESCO (2020b) further points out that remote learning/e-learning strategy should include elements such as assignment and information (e.g., how to communicate new assignment and information), methods for teaching (e.g., how to teach remotely), methods for student practices (e.g., how students can practice remotely), and formative feedback and coaching (e.g., how teachers can provide formative feedback and coach remotely). In addition, in countries and regions with poor educational resources, very often there are challenges in securing some common tools and resources for learning, including paper textbook, physical notes, TV/radio program, recorded videos, adaptive software programs, live video-conference, online platforms, email messages and text messages, and discussion boards.

3.2. *Hybrid Learning*

Hybrid Learning (also called Blended Learning) includes combinations of online and offline learning, synchronous and asynchronous learning, classroom learning and real-life learning, and in-person learning and online learning (or e-learning or remote learning), student-led learning and teacher-led learning, and self-paced learning and instructed learning (Keppell, 2023; the author's own knowledge). The combined teaching and learning approach of the hybrid delivery is very critical to the knowledge-intensive business (e.g., education). The creation and sharing of our tacit knowledge (e.g., the teacher's experience and expertise) and the emotional/caring side of the teaching cannot be done by the technology itself even though it may provide some facilitating roles (e.g., connecting people who need knowledge (such as students) with people have the required knowledge and experience (such as teachers). Hybrid learning approach is a balanced approach, which could deliver benefits of both traditional classroom teaching and the online education. In addition, the results of a federal study in the U.S. suggested blended learning models can producing learning outcomes that are equal to or better than face-to-face or pure online learning (Henry *et al.*, 2014; Xu, 2014: 102).

Hybrid learning could also address the concerns in both remote learning (e.g., difficulties in achieving the same learning outcomes as in person learning, digital divide issues) and in-person learning (e.g., staffing issues, the physical premise requirements), and it can follow a three-stage process: assessing the needs and capabilities and current practices (including guiding principles for learning, students' needs for remote and in-person learning, accessibility and effectiveness of current remote learning outcomes, teacher's ability, availability of physical space, availability and flexibility of support), determining suitable learning model (e.g., looking at such perspectives as distributing capacity evenly or prioritizing certain segments, assessing online learning and in-person learning, and following on support to vulnerable groups in various options and student number projections and required learning resources), and operationalizing hybrid learning method (e.g., reviewing subjects for remote learning and in-person learning, learning activities for remote learning and in-person learning, optimal distribution of hybrid model, teacher allocation model, capability model) (UNESCO, 2020).

Hybrid learning could bring many benefits to educational organizations, especially higher education providers (such as providing students with more choices and more flexibility in dealing with their busy schedule of study, part-time work and personal activities; allowing the teachers to deliver live classes to and interact with students at different locations; improving teaching efficiency and productivity, bettering teaching and learning resources and environments, applying latest technology to teaching and learning, updating teachers' knowledge and skills of using technology for teaching, and enhancing students' learning interest and class participation) (Hall *et al.*, 2023; the author's own knowledge).

Hybrid classroom has become popular in recent years, it typically includes tracking cameras, wireless microphones, interactive white boards, and smart screens. Figures 1 and 2 show the hybrid classroom set-up at King's Own Institute, Australia, and the hybrid classroom equipment include: BenQ Interactive Whiteboards, AVER DL30 Tracking

Figure 1: KOI's Hybrid Classroom 1.
Source: King's Own Institute 2023.

Figure 2: KOI's Hybrid Classroom 2.
Source: King's Own Institute 2023.

Cameras, Smart Screens, Computers and Screens for the Teacher as well as overhead projector and pull down screen. Meanwhile students can join the activities on the BENQ Interactive Whiteboards from their smartphones and mobile devices.

What are the (negative) impacts of digital technologies on humanity and society? Should we care about such impacts (especially when focusing on such impacts could mean sacrificing certain benefits of digital technologies)? It can be said that people have different answers on those questions. One of the impacts is the concern of that we become less human (for example, We are more and more recognized by user names, passwords, mobile phone numbers and represented only by a series of the number of 0 and the number of 1?; Have we lost our ability of thinking, writing and research by over-relying on search engines, spell check and grammar software, and Wikipedia-type applications?; How about the initiatives of hybrid human and technology being pursued? (such as Neuralink's brain implants and mind reading technology researched by Facebook, MIT, and University of California) (Xu 2019: 19; the authors' own knowledge).

Cyberbullying, abusive language, and predation targeting vulnerable people (especially children), online pornography, online cigarettes and drugs sales, and online gambling are having dramatic damages on families and society (Laudon & Traver, 2018: 604). While it is critical for government to establish appropriate regulations (e.g., The Children's Internet Protection Act and Federal & State laws on regulating online cigarettes and drug sales and online gaming) and it is necessary to use technologies (e.g., filtering software) to deal with such issues, it is essential all the stakeholders (e.g., government agencies (including police), parents, children, teachers and schools, communities, technology firms, businesses) to work together to win the battle (Laudon & Traver, 2018: 617; the authors' own knowledge).

Automation, AI and Robotics will have huge impact on employment and job safety in the future (Heltzel, 2017; Manyika, 2017; the authors' own knowledge). It is predicted nearly half of all jobs in the U.S. could be automated by 2050 (Bhalla *et al.*, 2017: 4) even though discussions such as what can be automated, costs and benefits of replacing human, and how new jobs will be created in the process of automation, are still going on (Rotman, 2018). It is fair to say that automation will not only result in job losses, but also lead to creating new jobs (e.g., via increased spending and investment on technology development and deployment) as well as changing existing jobs (e.g., changing occupations, requiring different skills, changing workplace) (Manyika et al., 2018). However, people are really worried about their job security and next generation's employment prospects. On top of the employment concerns, digital technologies (especially AI and robotics) could impose us to such threats as: Privacy and surveillance concerns; Manipulation of behavior (e.g., algorithms developed by collected data could be used to influence certain individuals or groups into believing and doing things based on analyzing the collected data); Bias and opacity concerns (e.g., predictive analytics without due process, accountability, community engagement, and auditing); Uncertainties and difficulties in ensuring effective and accurate communication and interaction between human and robots, autonomous systems concerns (e.g., Who is in control? Who is responsible?); Robotizing humanity and thus destroying human's heart and soul, compassion, creativity, empathy, and stewardship; Responsibilities and rights of robots; and Technological singularity and superintelligence concerns (e.g., AI systems have higher level of intelligence than human, can develop AI systems themselves, and become uncontrollable) (Müller, 2020; Schwab, 2016).

So what should we do? Simply complaining and panicking won't be helpful?! We need to have a thorough understanding of the issues and prepare for the future (Brynjofsson & McAfee, 2012; Dickson, 2017, 2018; Frank et al., 2017; Goodwin, 2018; Heywood et al., 2014: 7; Manyika et al., 2018; Ted, 2018; Trieu, 2016; Xu, 2019: 26; Xu, 2019: 27; the authors' own knowledge):

- Even though machines are getting better, more powerful and smarter, they are still not good at many things requiring intuition, judgment, experience, and insight (e.g., computers can't decide what analyses to carry out and how to interpret the results), can't do negotiation and group dynamics, can't produce good writing, can't frame problems and solve open-ended problems, and can't do persuasion and human interaction and nurturing).
- While repetitive (e.g., tele-sales, customer support), routine (e.g., truck driver, security guards), or optimizing (radiologist and reporter) types of job will be gradually replaced by machines, some jobs that are complex and creative and need human compassion, intuition, and judgment should be still in demand in the future (e.g., social workers, scientists, artists, economists, professors, senior executives).

- Even though some jobs (e.g., very labor-intensive and dangerous jobs, jobs requiring very low human compassion, intuition and judgment) will be replaced by machines, human can coexist with AI and other advanced technologies, and can work together (e.g., AI can be a useful tool for human, AI can assist human to become more creative, and AI can partner with human).
- While it is essential to acknowledge and accept that the robots are here already not coming, it is also true that people still need to have face-to-face contact and social (physical) interactions, which can't be digitized or automated or done by robots.
- Human has gone through three industry revolutions (e.g., steam turbine representing first industry revolution, electricity symbolizing second industry revolution, and personal computer reflecting third industry revolution), each time human faced the same issues of the impacts of the new machines on human conditions and opportunities, and each time human survived and found new uses for labor. We are now in the period of 4th industry revolution (arguably typified by 5G and AI), based our experiences of past three industry revolutions, we should be confident that we (human) can grow together with new technologies (e.g., AI) and work with them to create better tomorrow for humankind.
- Maybe AI (artificial intelligence) should be called Augmented Intelligence (term coined by former IBM CEO Ginni Romett), which views technological intelligence is to complement human intelligence not to replace human intelligence, focuses on the partnership between technology and human, and looks at using technology to make human faster and smarter at what they do and building better machines to enable human to achieve higher performance.
- Ethics and social impacts should be educated and scrutinized closely all the time and should be on the mind of all the stakeholders and should be part of the culture (i.e., the way we do things).
- We should pay more attention to responsible computing, including developing and deploying systems, applications and networks responsibly, dealing with data responsibly, ensuring ethical and safe use of AI and other computing technologies, sharing best practices of responsibly using and deploying AI and other computing technologies, and keeping on innovating the way of responsibly using and deploying AI and other computing technologies.

- While certain advanced technologies (such as Neuralink's brain implants) could have medical benefits, the associated ethical concerns should be examined closely at the same time. Can we argue that the natural human body and the natural systems in the human body should not be interfered and changed by external stuff (such as computer chips)? Having said that, we have already put such things as Artificial Heart and Artificial Ear into our body to replace or enhance human organs.

4. Learning/Training in the Organization

In 2016 organizations spent $359 billion on training, meanwhile the majority of training is not effective and have flaws in purpose, timing and content of training (Glaveski, 2019). It is also reported that:

- 90% of corporations adopt e-learning (Edgepoint learning cited in RWS, 2022).
- 67% of organizations embark on mobile learning (eLearning industry cited in RWS, 2022).
- 72% of organizations suggest that e-learning give them competitive advantages (Certifyme.net cited in RWS, 2022).
- The corporate e-learning is set to reach $50 billion by 2026 (TalentLMS, 2023).
- E-learning could increase retention rates by up to 60% and link to higher revenue and faster growth for 42% US organizations (TalentLMS, 2023).

According to a survey done by McKinsey (reported in Glaveski, 2019): 75% of surveyed managers are not happy with the training in the organization, 70% of employees report that they don't have the required skills for the job, 88% of employees are not able to apply their new skills they gained via training in the organization, and 75% of survey respondents believe that the training in the organization had impact on their performance. Meanwhile a study conducted in 2021 by LinkedIn (reported in Brainier, 2023) unveiled that 62% of participating CEOs viewed upskilling as a priority for the organization and investing in upskilling and reskilling the global workforce will grow GPD by 30% by 2030.

Accenture (cited in Das *et al.*, 2023) suggests that 94% of workers would stay with their firms longer if their firms invested in their career development. Learning and Training could be provided internally by the organization itself, alternatively organizations could use external training providers, such as: Afya Educational, Eruditue, Unacademy, Udemy, BYJUS, BetterUp, MasterClass, 360Learing, Go1, upGrad, Degreed, Guild and CoachHub (Sanghvi & Westhoff, 2022).

Some suggestions for effectively learning/training in the organization include (360Learning, 2023; Brainier, 2023; Das *et al.*, 2023; Glaveski, 2019; Wentworth, 2023):

- Aligning learning with learner's performance and business objectives.
- Making learning relevant to people's needs and embarking on a learner-centred approach.
- Adopting lean learning in the organization (e.g., focusing on core knowledge first) and offering short-bite sized learning and micro courses.
- Applying learning to real-world issues quickly.
- Improving training based on the feedback.
- Repeating the cycle of learning, applying and receiving feedback and improving.
- Encouraging peer-learning/collaborative learning.
- Establishing mentoring relationships.
- Emphasizing and promoting internal experts to keep them and their knowledge.
- Empowering people to learn.
- Offering ongoing support.
- Creating conducive learning environments (e.g., organizing lunch events for knowledge sharing and encouraging internal collaboration).
- Encouraging and facilitating both formal and informal learning.
- Concentration on learning outcomes (rather than credits and number of people completing the training.
- Setting realistic training expectations.
- Using learning analytics to analyze people's learning patterns and assess the impact of training.

5. Future Skills, Future Trends, and Opportunities

5.1. *Opportunities in the Teaching and Learning Areas*

For educational organizations (e.g., schools, colleges and universities), opportunities could be found in teaching and learning areas (their main activities) and supporting areas of teaching and learning. Table 1 presents opportunities in the teaching and learning areas and the roles of digital technologies in addressing identified opportunities.

5.2. *Opportunities in the Supporting Areas of Teaching and Learning*

Table 2 shows opportunities in the supporting areas of teaching and learning and the roles of digital technologies.

Table 1: Future trends and opportunities in the teaching and learning areas.

Business Process	Trends and Opportunities	Technologies for Addressing the Identified Trends/Opportunities
Teaching and Learning Activities	• Enhancing Classroom Learning Experiences	• Tools for Classroom interactions (e.g., polls, chats, breakout rooms) and systems for Classroom exercises (e.g., learning games, badges, rewards) could enhance classroom learning experiences.
	• Personalized Learning	• Applications/systems such as Applications/systems for assessment and factor checking (e.g., ChatGPT, Grammarly, Microsoft Word Spelling and Grammar Checker, Turnitin) could support personalized learning. • Intelligent Tutoring Systems that provide immediate and customized instruction feedback to learners according to their characteristics and needs (typically based on the assessment based on their responses to assigned tasks and questions), very often without requiring intervention from a human teacher (e.g., Algebra Tutor, Cognitive Tutor, SQL Tutor, ITSS, Dragon 2, PCAR, Mouse Work, Living Letters, SARA, Nanotutors, DME, ALEKS, ASSISTments, CTAT, HINTS, SKOPE-IT, My Science Tutor, GraphicGame Rime) could also assist personalized learning.

Table 1: (*Continued*)

Business Process	Trends and Opportunities	Technologies for Addressing the Identified Trends/Opportunities
	• Adaptive Learning	• Adaptive Learning Systems, which automatically adapts teaching process (i.e., delivering customized resources and learning activities) and can arguably be viewed as a type of Intelligent Tutoring Systems, include applications such as ELAN, Reading Plus, Dutch Education System, FB-TS, Adaptive Mobile Learning Systems, Personalized Adaptive Learning Dashboard, AL, Adaptemy, EdApp, Cogbooks, Knewton, Realizeit, Pearson Interactive Labs, Adaptive Learning, Design Digitally, Impelsys Scholar ALS.
	• Self-Learning	• Virtual Classroom (e.g., digital avatars, engaging interfaces, virtual reality, augmented reality and mixed reality tools, gamified learning systems), One-to-one online tutorial between the teacher and the student, and Learning management systems serving as a gateway or central hub for learning (e.g., Blackboard, Canvas, Moodle), could assist self-paced learning. • Self-paced technology-assisted learning (either synchronous or asynchronous) (e.g., attending online learning activities and reviewed online learning materials (including online content, recordings, videos, discussion forums, learning communities, collaborative platforms and classes) and Technologies for self-evaluation (e.g., Turnitin, Speedgrader, GradeScope) could facilitate self-paced learning as well.
	• Active Learning	• Active learning could be enabled by tools such as In-class Polling Systems, Google Slide Decks, Zoom Breakout Rooms, Classroom Response Systems; Group Decision Support Applications.
	• Peer Learning/ Collaborative Learning	• Peer learning/Collaborative learning could be facilitated by technologies such as social media platforms, video conferencing tools, and virtual collaboration and learning management systems.

(*Continued*)

Table 1: (*Continued*)

Business Process	Trends and Opportunities	Technologies for Addressing the Identified Trends/Opportunities
		• Collaborative learning could be supported by technologies such as Wikis, Smart Panels, Concept Mapping, Real-time Collaborative Editing tools (such as Google Doc, Google Shared Drive), Virtual Whiteboards, Online meeting/conferencing tools (such as Zoom, Microsoft Team, Google Meet), Instant Messaging, Project Management Tools, Discussion Boards/Forums, Blogs, Emails, Social Media, Online Communities.
	• Visualized Learning	• Information visualization tools (e.g., Geographic information systems, Gapminder.com, JMOL, Google Earth) could help student understand and present complex data.
	• Game-based Learning/ Gamification	• Gaming tools and platforms (e.g., Duolingo, Kahoot, Goold Read-Along App, Quizlet) could assist game-based learning.
	• Immersive Learning/ Situation Learning/ Scenario Learning	• Virtual reality (VR), Augmented reality (AR), Mixed reality, Spatial computing, Metaverse-based content learning experience platforms, gamification and scenario-based learning, story-based learning, and branch simulations for developing immersive learning environments, could enable immersive, situational, and scenario learning.
	• Mobile Learning	• Mobile learning platforms (e.g., Mobile version of Learning Management Systems; Mobile apps) could enable mobile learning.
	• Hybrid Learning	• Classroom technologies for Hybrid Class (e.g., Tracking cameras, Wireless microphones, Smart Panels, Online Video Conferencing Tools such as Zoom).
	• Online Learning	• Online learning (or e-learning) has been and will be supported by various technologies (e.g., High speed Internet, Wi-Fi, Learning Management Systems, Online learning portals, Video Conferencing tools, Online video sites).

Table 1: (*Continued*)

Business Process	Trends and Opportunities	Technologies for Addressing the Identified Trends/Opportunities
	• Open Learning	• Open educational resources (e.g., Open Source Software, Open Access, Open Data and Crowdsourcing Platforms) could support open learning.
	• Online Academic Integrity	• Tools such as Zoom, Webcams, Moodle Proctoring, Canvas's Respondus Lockdown Browser and Monitor, could assist in ensuring online academic integrity.
	• Remote Learning continuing after COVID-19 (Remote learning will stay after COVID-19)	• Remote learning facilitating tools (e.g., Video conferencing systems such as Zoom, Google Meet, Microsoft Team) could support remote learning/e-learning.
	• Experiential Learning	• Tools such as Simulations, AR/VR and Gaming for hands-on experience could support experiential learning.
	• Lifelong Learning	• Self-learning or teaching assistant platforms (such as Khan Academy, Udemy, Coursera, Edx, Udacity., MOCC) and open source platforms (e.g., Open edX, Sakai) could assist students/learners' lifelong learning and competence-based learning. Virtual assistant could assist in answering routine questions while machine learning and predictive modeling could assist in marking.
	• Competence-based Learning	• Self-learning or teaching assistant platforms (such as Khan Academy, Udemy, Coursera, Edx, Udacity., MOCC) and open source platforms (e.g., Open edX, Sakai) could assist lifelong learning and competence-based learning. Virtual assistant could assist in answering routine questions and follow-ups while machine learning and predictive modelling could assist in marking.

(*Continued*)

Table 1: (*Continued*)

Business Process	Trends and Opportunities	Technologies for Addressing the Identified Trends/Opportunities
	• Micro-Learning	• Microlearning caters learners' specific needs and interests and allows them to choose their own learning content and format, and it is a type of personalised learning. It can be delivered via learning management systems, mobile apps and social media platforms.
	• Video Learning	• Video learning could be facilitated by videos and interactive videos.
	• Informal Learning	• Tools such as short message services (SMS) and Social media chats could facilitate informal and social learning.
	• Social Learning	• Tools such as SMS and Social media chats could facilitate informal and social learning.
	• Metaverse Learning	• Virtual universe (the Metaverse) enabled by technologies such as 5G, VR, AR, and 3D could provide learners with more advanced level immersive and interactive learning.
	• Decentralized Learning (Learning anytime and anywhere and moving around tools seamlessly)	• Technologies such as Web3 could provide decentralized learning to learners, which will be more personalized, more interactive and more immersive.
	• Micro-Learning	• Tools (such as text, images, videos, audios, tests and quizzes, and games) could facilitate micro-learning (bite-sized learning (normally 3–5 minutes learning)).
	• Nudge Learning	• Nudge Learning could be facilitated by personalized messages and task-oriented nudges (e.g., auto-reminders and push notifications).

Table 1: (*Continued*)

Business Process	Trends and Opportunities	Technologies for Addressing the Identified Trends/Opportunities
Evaluation of Teaching and Learning	• Real-time Student Feedback • Learning (Analytics for better understanding students' needs and learning performance and thus enhancing teaching quality)	• Tools such as Real-time survey tools, Real-time applications for capturing and analyzing facial expressions of students, could support collecting students' feedback. • Tools for analyzing learning trends and behavior include: Visual data mining, Tree learning methods, Text mining, Support vector machines, Smooth inverse frequency algorithm, Sequential pattern mining, Recurrent neural networks, Probabilistic learning methods, Parallel practice swarm optimization, Outliner detection, Neural networks, Generic algorithm, Deep Q-learning algorithm, Native bayes algorithm, Fizzy logic, K-nearest neighbor, Differential sequence mining, Decision trees, Correlation mining, Content based filtering techniques, Collaborative filtering techniques, Clustering, Classifications, Bayesian networks, Bayesian knowledge tracing, Association rules mining, Ant colony optimization, Data visualization, Maximum likelihood analysis, Semantic similarity analysis, and Natural learning process as well as tools for presenting results of learning analytics including Learning analytics dashboard for advisers, Learning dashboard for insights and support, SmartKlass, Acrobatiq, Signals and Klassdata.

Sources: 360Learning (2023); Baig *et al.* (2023); Brasca *et al.* (2022); Brussels *et al.* (2017); Bujan (2021); Chui *et al.* (2022c); Chui *et al.* (2022b); CMU (2023a, 2023b: 46); Das (2023); Das *et al.* (2023); Deveau *et al.* (2023); Hall *et al.* (2023); Hancock *et al.* (2022); Hancock *et al.* (2023); Harbinger Group (2023); Hatami *et al.* (2023); Hyler (2006); Kabudi *et al.* (2021); Keppell (2023); Khan and Kirland (2019); Laverdiere *et al.* (2023); McKinsey (2017); McKinsey Explainers (2023); Microsoft (2020); Monash University (2023); Mougiakou *et al.* (2023); Moore and Martinotti (2016); Pandit *et al.* (2012); Pappas (2020: 29–32); Pappas (2023: 20–23); Pappas (2023b); Polito and Temperini (2021); Sanghvi and Westhoff, (2022); Small (2022); Spice (2020); Tauscher and Kietzmann (2017); the author's own knowledge); Torbet, (2022); UNESCO (2019); UNESCO (n.d.); Wang *et al.* (2022: Wikipedia (2023a, 2023b, 2023c); Xu (2019: 103–104); Xu and Gao (2021: 110–112).

Table 2: Future trends and opportunities in the supporting areas.

Business Process	Trends and Opportunities	Technologies for Addressing the Identified Trends/Opportunities
Student Recruitment	• Developing Marketing Materials • Dealing with Inquiries and Provide 24/7 Personalized Services • Promoting products • Analyzing Collected Information and Providing Forecasting	• AI tools (such as ChatGPT) could assist in developing the content of marketing documents. • AI tools (such as Chatbots, Virtual Assistants, Intelligent Agent, Generative AI applications for generating personalized emails/messages) could answer questions in real-time and provide 24/7 personalized customer services. • Applications (such as Collaborative filters recommendation systems) could make personal recommendations to customers. • Applications (such as Google Analytics, Dynamic audience targeting and segmentation tools, Predictive models) could help analyze the online traffic and make forecasts.
IT Support/ Services	• Integrating artificial intelligence (AI) into technical infrastructure • Integrating learners' own devices into learning platforms	• Integrating generative AI model at key customer touchpoints to facilitate a tailored customer journey (e.g., customer>>Customer facing interaction applications>>Generative AI model>>Backend applications>>Data source>>Infrastructure and Compute). • Bring your own devices (BYOD has been becoming the norm. Learners typically have multiple devices (e.g., smart phone, laptop, game console, i-pad, i-watch), their devices should be allowed to integrate into the learning provider's networks and access the learning content seamlessly.
Teaching Staff and Professional Staff Recruitment and Other HR Matters	• AI tools for identifying suitable candidates • Online portals for HR related matters	• AI-enabled software could assist in matching candidates with job descriptions. • Online portals could provide many self-services of HR matters (e.g., leave application, travel requests, travel expense reconciliation, training and development activities).

Table 2: (*Continued*)

Business Process	Trends and Opportunities	Technologies for Addressing the Identified Trends/Opportunities
	• AI tools for writing job requirements and providing services to candidates.	• AI tools for developing job requirements and position descriptions. • AI tools for providing personalized services to candidates.
Student Experience, Services and Information Management	• Platforms and Systems for centrally managing student information • Connectivity and Community Building • Student progress monitoring and at-risk alerts	• Cloud-based ERP systems (e.g., TechOne and SAP) could help manage student information. • AI enabled student management system could help monitor student learning activities. • Virtual collaboration and social media tools can assist in connectivity and community building. • Student management systems, learning management systems and AI applications could help track the student's progress.
Business Strategy	• Using digital technology to facilitate learners' lifelong learning journey • Partnership development • Working on factors shaping future digital education	• Best of breed of formal and informal digital content could support lifelong learning. • Digital learning credentials, digital identification, and talent analytics across systems could support end to end (E2E) personalized lifelong learning. • Extranet/Portals/Hubs for partnerships between e-learning platforms and corporations, training and development agencies, traditional educational institutions, are emerging. Another trend is recruitment and human resources service firms are entering the e-learning arena. For example, the leading recruitment site in Australia and New Zealand Seek.com and offers online courses (in areas of Business, Information Technology, Healthcare, Logistics and Transport) via its Seeklearning site and has partnership with universities and industry collaborators. Recruitment firms such as

(*Continued*)

Table 2: (*Continued*)

Business Process	Trends and Opportunities	Technologies for Addressing the Identified Trends/Opportunities
		Seek could have more updated and comprehensive understanding of the job market, required skills, and business expectations than traditional training providers (e.g., universities and colleges). • Leveraging opportunities from factors shaping future digital education, including Common accreditation for digital curriculum and credentials, Transparency around outcomes, Data privacy regulations and IP rights, Building and strengthening digital capabilities at all levels, Integration of real-world application of skills, Investing in building communities and networks, and Efficient setup and deployment of secure IT infrastructure and devices.
Governance and Organization	• Creating learning experiences and resources	• Dedicated platforms and open ecosystems as well as outcome-based/skills-based educational approach with predictive analytics and feedback systems could assist in developing governance and managing organization for creating learning resources and environments.
Leadership, Talent and Culture	• Focusing on internal capabilities and needs	• Building centres of excellence, sharing capabilities, internal virtual corporate universities/training centres, and digital talent management tools could facilitate efforts of developing internal capabilities of leadership, talent and culture.
Technology and Operations	• Concentrating on technological infrastructure and standards deployment	• Adoption of scalable cloud solutions with open API (application programming interface) and LTI (learning tools interoperability) standards and integration of platforms and systems based on common standards could assist in technology infrastructure and standards.

Sources: Refer to Table 1.

5.3. Opportunities Arising from Future Skills and Future Trends

Hall *et al.* (2023) report that the impact of automation and digitization on the workforce will be seen at least next 10–15 years, and almost 50% of all work activities could be potentially automated, and 1 in 16 workers might have to change occupations by 2030. Manyika *et al.* (2017) further suggest that by 2030 75 million to 375 million workers (i.e., 3%–14% of the global work force) will need to change occupation and upgrade skills due to automation.

According to a recent survey conducted by Sweetrush (reported in Soto *et al.* 2023: 10), some identified top skills in demand in the organization are (in the order): Agility and adaptability, Analytics and reporting, Collaboration, Diversity, equity, inclusion, and belongings, Coaching mindset, Emotional intelligence, Leadership, Strategic thinking, Critical thinking, and Innovation. In the same survey, some top learning challenges in the organizations are: Future-proofing the organization to address skill gaps, Establishing a culture of learning, Providing engaging learning experiences, Elevating the strategic position of learning and development, Developing learning programs in an uncertain economic environment, Keeping up with the needs of the business, Aligning learning needs with business objectives, Offering people with learning and growth opportunities, Using data for learning improvement, and Properly designing learning delivery models (e.g., remote learning/e-learning and hybrid/blended learning) (Soto *et al.*, 2023: 26). To be successful with their learning and development, organizations need to: embrace technology, have a culture of continuous learning, measure the outcomes, and make learning a strategic priority (Soto *et al.*, 2023: 30–31).

Craig (2021) argues that digital platforms skills (e.g., skills required for SaaS (software as a service) platforms) and other demanded digital transformation skills have not been addressed by universities. Meanwhile According to LinkedIn Learning (2023), Some highly demanded skills by companies are (in the order): Management, Communication, Customer Service, Leadership, Sales, Project Management, Research, Analytical Skills, Marketing, and Teamwork. Table 3 presents some highly demanded skills by business function.

Bughin *et al.* (2016) suggest that if firms adopted currently available technology for their digitization initiatives, approximately 70% of the activities of some 20% of all occupations could be automated. They further point out that the following future changes in the occupation:

Table 3: Highly demanded skills by business function.

Business Function	Highly Demanded Skills (in the Order)
Business	Management, Communication, Customer service, Leadership, Sales, Marketing, Project Management, Finance, Analytics skills, and Teamwork.
Finance/ Accounting	Management, Analytical skills, Customer Service, Communication, Leadership, Financial Analysis, Sales, Teamwork, Research, and Financial Planning.
Engineering	JavaScript, Java, SQL, Python programming language, Cascading style sheets, HTML, Management, Cloud Computing, Git, and C++.
Information Technology	Management, SQL, Microsoft Office, Project management, Analytics skills, Communication, Customer service, Leadership, Cloud computing, and Python programming language.
Marketing	Social media, Management, Digital marketing, Communication, Strategy, Marketing strategy, Leadership, Project management, Advertising, and Customer service.
Project and Program Management	Management, Leadership, Communication, Engineering, Analytical skills, Customer service, Strategy, Team leadership, Marketing, and Research.
Sales	Customer service, Management, Communication, Marketing, Leadership, Account management, Sales management, Microsoft Office, Business development, and Business.

Source: LinkedIn Learning 2023.

- Unbundling and rebundling the jobs/tasks enabled by digital technologies.
- Shifting to project-based work (rather than function-based) supported by digital technology-enabled workflows.
- Changing from salaried job to independent work that gives people great autonomy and control over their time and it is made possible by the Internet and digital tools.
- Focusing more on skills (including both technical and soft skills) than formal educational credentials and degrees (such change could be facilitated by digital tools such as online work platforms, online rating systems).

- Using online communities more than other employee associations (e.g., unions) to gain peer support and present employees' joint forces directly to the firm and the government.
- Instead of using digitization and automation to replace human labor, firms need to invest in human labor to equip them with both digital literacy/skills (e.g., literacy/skills for cloud computing, data analytics) and business skills otherwise the collected large volume data and the manufactured large number of robots will not achieve their intended effects.
- Changing employment from companies to platforms and ecosystems (e.g., freelancer Youtubers and people making a living on social media platforms).

On a related note, 93% of organizations are worried about employee retention, and many organizations believe that providing learning opportunities is the most effective way to improve retention (Soto *et al.* 2023: 28). In other words, if organizations could provide people with training for the demanded skills discussed in the previous sections, then people will be more likely to stay and make greater contribution. The digital technologies and applications discussed in the beginning of this chapter and in the Sections 5.1 and 5.2 of this chapter could definitely enable or facilitate learning and training activities pursued by organizations.

6. Focusing on Artificial Intelligence (AI)

It is forecasted that the economic value from AI (including both generative AI and non-generative AI) is $13.6–22.1 trillion (i.e., $11–17 trillion for non-generative AI and $2.6–4.4 trillion for generative AI) (reported in Chui *et al.*, 2022b: 23; Chui *et al.*, 2023). The differences between generative AI (e.g., ChatGTP, Virtual Assistants, Virtual Experts, Virtual Collaborators, Automatic Content and Document Creation Applications) and non-generative (traditional) AI are: the former could generate similar data based on training data and generate content/responses based on users' prompts while the latter has been typically used for analysis, predication and pattern identification enabled by technologies such as advanced analytics, traditional machine learning and deep learning.

Some widely used AI capabilities in the organization include: Robotic process automation, Computer vision, Natural-language text understanding, Virtual agents or conversational interfaces, Deep learning, Knowledge graphs, Recommender systems, Digital twins, Natural-language speech understanding, Physical robotics, Reinforcement learning, Facial recognition, Natural-language generation, Transfer learning, Generative adversarial networks, and Transformers. Meanwhile AI capabilities have been used for functional activities such as: Service operations optimization, Creation of new AI-based products, Customer service analytics, Customer segmentation, New AI-based enhancement of products, Customer acquisition and lead generation, Contact-center automation, Product feature optimization, Risk modeling and analytics, and Predictive service and intervention (Chui *et al.*, 2022). Meanwhile some AI-related positions in the organization include: Software engineers, Data engineers, AI data scientists, Machine learning engineers, AO product owners/managers, Design specialists, Data visualization specialists, and Translators (Chui *et al.*, 2022).

The adoption of AI around the world has increased rapidly due to factors such as faster global expansion (e.g., 56% of participants of a recent McKinsey global survey are embarking on AI), easier and more affordable AI implementation (e.g., 94.4% improvement in training speed for AI training models since 2018), fast-growing innovation (e.g., compound annual growth rate of filed patents for the period of 2015–2021 is 76.9%), and significant investment growth (e.g., private investment in AI-related companies increased 100% to $93.5 billion for the period of 2020 to 2021) (Chui *et al.*, 2022b: 22). On the other hand, adoption of AI could be a challenging task. For example, in a recent McKinsey global survey, 72% of participating organizations have not successfully adopted or scaled their AI initiatives, and some reported reasons are: difficulties in transition from pilots to products, model failure in production, stalling team productivity and limitations in protection against potential risks from unknown variables (Chui *et al.*, 2022b: 61). Forth *et al.* (2023) indicate that implementation challenges and data sensitivity issues are key AI adoption barriers, and they suggest a number of success factors, including aligning AI strategy with organizational strategy and goals, leaders' commitment, access to high caliber talent, agile governance, measuring and monitoring outcomes, and developing business-led modular technology and data platforms. Pappas (2023b) further point out that factors such as insufficient or low-quality data, outdated infrastructure, issues of integrating with existing issues, lack of AI talent, overestimating the capabilities of AI system, cost concerns, discrepancies in AI availability in different places, and legal and ethical concerns surrounding AI (e.g., recent iTutor

Group case in the U.S. (Wiessner, 2023)), could make AI adoption more difficult. He also suggests that when organizations are embarking on AI, they should:

- Conducting thorough research.
- Clearly defining your problems and goals.
- Putting together a good AI team and training the team properly.
- Effectively evaluating your tools.
- Starting small.
- Preparing your organization for AI.
- Having good understanding of your data.
- Properly training your AI models with good-quality data.
- Determining suitable use cases.
- Measuring and monitoring the results.

Chui *et al.* (2022) suggest successful AI implementation could be looked at the following four perspectives:

- Strategy (e.g., Clear road map, Senior management's support, Clearly defined AI vision and strategy, Alignment between AI strategy and business strategy, Creditable AI leaders, Well-defined KPIs to measure AI impacts, Clear frameworks for AI governance).
- Data (e.g., Integration of data from various sources into AI models, Process of preparing data for AI models).
- Models, tools and technologies (e.g., Models for small data, Refreshing AI models regularly, Development of modular components, Automating the full cycle for AI model development).
- Talent and ways of working (e.g., life cycle approach to developing and deploying AI models, integration of AI technologies with business processes, AI working teams, well-defined capability-building programs, Training of non-technical employees to use AI, AI development teams following standards and protocols).

Artificial intelligence (AI) applications (include ChatGPT-type AI applications) could only be good if they have been trained properly with good data and AI engines (software/algorithm developed by human experts), and even "the most advanced AI models can make significant mistakes or fabricate information altogether" (Huddleston Jr., 2023). It also can be argued that even though AI could be capable of processing quality content, the original content needs to be developed from human expertise (Bernhardt, 2023). Chatbots of large language models (e.g., ChatGPT) cannot replace the teacher's expertise. In addition, AI and any other digital technologies have no feeling and cannot check the students' well-being (an important role of the teacher), students need to speak to their teachers and peers to have interactions and experience eknowledge (especially tacit knowledge) creation and sharing (Xu, 2023). In addition, AI applications (such as ChatGPT) could bring a number of challenges/ issues to teaching and learning, including the loss of students' independent thinking abilities and curiosity, the copyright and plagiarism issues, students' increasing laziness and unwillingness to spend time on learning, and the consequences of misusing or mishandling data (Chin, 2023; Gordon, 2023); however we need to embrace new technologies (like ChatGPT) and use them to help students enhance their skills, knowledge and critical thinking (e.g., students can be asked to critique content generated by ChatGPT) (Goddon, 2023).

For educational organizations, academic integrity issues associated with the uses of AI applications (especially ChatGPT) are of significance. Many educational organizations are still developing their policies for responding to ChatGPT and other AI applications. Academic integrity solutions provider Turnitin has recently added AI detector for content generated by AI into their products/services, for reasons such as a new product/service and the difficulty in identifying the content generated by AI, its performance has not always been reliable and consistent (Fowler, 2023), The teacher's intelligence and experiences definitely play important roles in identifying content generated by AI. Meanwhile measures such as education, clear guidelines on using AI, more real-world/practice-focused assessment items, work-integrated learning projects, more in-class face-to-face tasks and exams, and more personalized assignments and projects as well as requirements of asking students to demonstrate the process and evidence of research and assignment writing, designing tasks connecting course content, class discussion and real-life experience and synthesizing information from various sources, would be effective in dealing with AI-enabled academic misconducts (Cotton et al., 2023; Craig, 2021; Gecker and The Associated Press, 2023; the author's own knowledge, University of Washington, 2023). And assignments could be also designed in the formats of presentations, videos, journaling, podcasts, portfolios, group projects, interviews, and role-playing (University of Illinois Urbana-Champaign, 2023).

Organizations (both educational and non-educational) need to have clear understanding of the risks associated with AI and have measures to deal with such risk. Some AI risks are: Privacy issues (e.g., how customers' data are managed?), Security issues (e.g., are security standards for model selection and training appropriate and updated?), Fairness concerns (e.g., bias in data selection and in the model), Transparency and explainability (e.g., the lack of clear explanation of how the data are selected and how the model is developed), Safety and performance (e.g., what are the safety and performance consequences if the AI models are not properly implemented and tested?), and Third-party risks (e.g., what are the risks of using external providers for data collection, model selection or deployment environments?). Such risks could be addressed by some common approaches, including standard practices and proper documentation and independent reviews (Buehler *et al.*, 2021).

7. The Role of the Government in the Digital Era

According to a recent survey of 18,000 people in 15 countries done by McKinsey (reported in Dondi *et al.*, 2021), some demanded citizens skills for future work include:

- *Cognitive*: critical thinking, planning, communication, and mental flexibility.
- *Interpersonal*: mobilizing systems, developing relationships, and teamwork effectiveness.
- *Self-leadership*: self-awareness and self-management, entrepreneurship, and goals achievement.
- *Digital*: digital fluency and citizenship, software use and development, and understanding digital systems.

To help citizens to prepare for skills required for future work, the government could take initiatives in reforming education systems (e.g., revising curriculum to focus on future skills, funding research focusing on future skills), making changes to adult learning system (e.g., using technology to facilitate adult learning and support lifelong learning, establishing skill-based certification system, and funding for supporting future skills learning), and making lifelong learning affordable (e.g., using technological innovations to deliver universal, high-quality, and affordable education to all citizens (from childhood to retirement). In addition, government should have clear guidelines on using digital technologies for various perspectives of teaching and learning, and it should also work with non-governmental organizations, technology firms, businesses, relevant industry associations and others on help reinventing the education systems (Madgavkar & Sankhe, 2015).

The e-learning (remote learning) and hybrid learning (blended learning) will continuously stay in foreseeable future. Some considerations for effective remote and hybrid learning include (Dorn *et al.*, 2020):

- Looking after different needs of respective student cohorts (e.g., vulnerable students at risk, transition students (such as transiting from junior school to high school), general students, students whose parents do not support an in-person return to school, students having personal-health risks, different grades of students, students who cannot attend class physically, cannot access required physical teaching facilities).
- Considering different levels of digital maturity of schools (e.g., from no-tech maturity (paper-based) to low maturity to medium maturity to high maturity (high level of virtual learning systems).
- Designing appropriate systems for e-learning and hybrid learning (e.g., having synchronous and asynchronous digital learning for hybrid learning; including flipped classroom into traditional in-person learning).
- Working on relationships (e.g., teachers feeling safe and equipped to teach, parents being part of the team, students feeling safe and equipped to learn).

Significant events like COVID-19 have made governments around world to rethink their education systems. The governments could look at factors closely linked to student success, including Instruction (e.g., focusing on core skills and instruction, adopting technology for enhancing teaching and learning and allowing teachers to focus on high-value tasks requiring their expertise and relationship building, preparing students for future work, providing required support to students whether they are doing studies via remote/online, hybrid/blended or fully in-person modes), Teachers and school leaders (e.g., achieving or maintaining high quality teaching and learning by recruiting and developing top talent to become effective teachers, more investment and thinking for teacher preparation and development to prepare for the mixed delivery modes of remote/online, hybrid/blended and fully in-person), Education systems and structures (e.g., using data for better performance management, having school structures to support student holistically, revising school calendar to suit different delivery modes, researching and pilot-testing different structures), and Social and economic influences (e.g., implementing fit-to-context performance by working on the balanced approach, combining central control for building basic infrastructure with decentralized innovation, peer-led learning and collaborative planning, and allocating sufficient resources for large scale personalized support) (Bryant et al., 2020). In addition, the government should hold technology providers accountable (e.g., via developing required regulations and promptly working on preventing the misuse of new technology) (Wilichowski & Cobo, 2023).

UNESCO (2023) suggests that the government should play significant roles on Artificial Intelligence (AI) and Education:

- Having a system-wide vision and making decisions on strategic priorities.
- Establishing guiding principles for AI and education policies.
- Developing interdisciplinary planning and inter-sectoral governance.
- Putting policies and regulations in place for equitable, inclusive, and ethical use of AI.
- Designing master plans for using AI in education management, teaching, learning, and assessment.
- Testing AI thoroughly and building an evidence base.
- Fostering AI innovations for education.

8. The Role of Teacher in the Digital Era

While technologies could provide great assistance in teaching, the critical role of the teacher will be further enhanced rather than diminishing (Microsoft, 2020). It could be argued that "while great use of technology in education may be inevitable, technology will never replace a great teacher. In fact, a single teacher can change a student's trajectory" (Bryant et al., 2020). Digital technologies present us with great opportunities to make teachers more effective and empower them (Madgavkar & Sankhe, 2015).

In the digital era, while there is no doubt that we must actively integrate digital literacy/skills into our teaching curriculum design, but it is not replacing our traditional curriculum but complementing it (Bryant et al., 2020). Students learn best from teachers, and their interactions with their teachers and the knowledge exchange between teachers and students have huge impact on their learning outcomes (Chen et al., 2022; Xu, 2023). While digital technologies (such as 5G. VR/AR, Web3, ML, DL & AI, and Big Data & Data Analytics) are having impact on education(e.g., enhancing connectivity, supporting self-paced learning and informing learning process), learners appreciate value-added services (e.g., personalized mentoring, getting human's caring and emotional intelligence, interview preparation, and support in securing a job) provided by human instructors/teachers more than technology and content (Hall et al., 2022; Pappas, 2023b; Sanghvi & Westhoff, 2022). In addition, self-paced learning, which could be significantly enabled by digital technologies, is only suitable for a small minority, most learners still need the teachers' guidance/teaching (Craig, 2021). Furthermore, as mentioned previously there have been global shortages of teachers (UNESCO, 2023b; Welch, 2023), while digital tools could assist in teaching and learning, but the virtual teaching assistants will not replace human teachers.

References

360Learning (2023). *Hijack Your Learning KPI with Science: 3 Theories Explaining Why Most eLearning Fails*. 360Learning, pp. 1–31.

Baig, A., Blumberg, S. Li, E., Merrill, D., Pradhan, A, Sinha, M., Sukharevsky, A. & Xu. S. (2023). *Technology's Generational Moment with Generative AI: A CIO and CTO Guide*. Brisbane: McKinsey Digital, pp. 1–12.

Barber, M. & Mourshed, M. (2007). *How the World's Best Performing School Systems Come Out on Top*. Brisbane: McKinsey & Company, pp. 1–49.

Bernhardt, M. (2023). *AI's Increasingly Important Role in L&D*. Learning Guild 2023, pp. 1–62.

Boggs, H., Forero-Hernandez, P., Laboissiere, M. & Neher, K. (2021). *Scaling Online Education: Five Lessons for Colleges*. Brisbane: McKinsey & Company, pp. 1–7.

Bort, J. (2023). I am an AI software engineer and I predict that most AI startups being funded today will die. *Business Insider*, July 15, 2023. Accessed on July 16, 2023. Available at https://www.businessinsider.in/tech/news/im-an-ai-software-engineer-and-i-predict-that-most-ai-startups-being-funded-today-will-die/articleshow/101767316.cms#:~:text=today%20will%20die-,I'm%20an%20AI%20software%20engineer%20and%20I%20predict%20that,being%20funded%20today%20will%20die&text=An%20AI%20engineer%20says%20most,when%20they're%20mostly%20hype.

Brasca, C., Krishnan, C., Marya, V., Owen, K., Sirois, J. & Ziade, S. (2022). *How Technology Is Shaping Learning in Higher Education: Education Practice.* Brisbane: McKinsey & Company, pp. 1–10.

Brassey, J., Christensen, L. & Dam, N.V. (2019). *The Essential Components of a Successful L&D Strategy.* Brisbane: McKinsey & Company, pp. 1–8.

Brainier (2023). *A Holistic Approach to Upskilling Employees.* Minneapolis: Brainier, pp. 1–11.

Bryant, J., Dorn, E., Hall, S. & Panier, F. (2020). *Reimagining a More Equitable and Resilient K-12 Education System.* Brisbane: McKinsey & Company, pp. 1–6.

Bryant, J., Child, F., Espinosa, J., Dorn, E. Hall, S., Schmautzer, D., Kola-Oyeneyin, T., Lim, C., Panier, F., Sarakatsannis, J., Ungur, S. & Wood, B. (2022). *How COVID-19 Caused a Global Learning Crisis.* Brisbane: McKinsey & Company, pp. 1–21.

Brussels, J.B., Paris, E.H., Ramaswamy, S., Chui, M., Sahlsgrom, P., Henke, N. & Trench, M. (2017). Artificial intelligence: The next digital frontier. Discussion Paper, McKinsey Global Institute, pp. 1–75.

Buehler, K., Dooley, R., Grennan, L. & Singla, A. (2021). *Getting to Know and Manage Your Biggest AI Risks.* Brisbane: McKinsey Analytics, pp. 1–6.

Bughin, J., Lund, S. & Remes, J. (2016). *Rethinking Work in the Digital Age.* Brisbane: McKinsey Quarterly, pp. 1–6.

Bujan, M. (2021). Gamification for learning: Strategies and examples. eLearning Industry. 15 November 2021. Accessed on May 18, 2023. Available at https://elearningindustry.com/gamification-for-learning-strategies-and-examples#:~:text=Duolingo%20is%20an%20education%20platform,motivated%20in%20the%20learning%20process.

Chen, L.K., Brasca, C., Honnacki, M. & Krishnan, C. (2019). *Transformation 101: How Universities Can Overcome Financial Headwinds to Focus on Their Mission.* Brisbane: McKinsey & Company, pp. 1–8.

Child, F., Frank, M., Lef, M. & Sarakasannis, J. (2021). Setting a new bar for online higher education. *Public & Social Sector Practice*, October pp. 1–7.

Child, F., Marcus, F., Law, J. & Sarakasannis, J. (2023). What do higher education students want from online learning. *Education Practice*, June pp. 1–9.

Chin, L.K. (2023). A New Buzz in Teaching and Learning: ChatGPT. eLearning Industry. 5 February 2023. Accessed on May 15, 2023. Available at https://elearningindustry.com/a-new-buzz-in-teaching-and-learning-chatgpt.

Chui, M., Roberts, R. & Yee, L. (2022a). *Generative AI Is Here: How Tools Like ChatGPT Could Change Your Business.* Brisbane: Quantum Black, AI by McKinsey, pp. 1–5.

Chui, M., Roberts, R. & Yee, L. (2022b). *McKinsey Technology Trends Outlook 2022 Report.* Brisbane: McKinsey & Company, pp. 1–183.

Chui, M., Hall, B., Mayhew, H., Singla, A. & Sukharevsky, A. (2022c). The State of AI in 2022 — And a Half Decade in Review. *Quantum Black*, December, pp. 1–20.

Chui, M., Hazan, E., Roberts, R., Singla, A., Smaje, K., Sukharevsky, A., Yee, L. & Zemmel, R. (2023). *The Economic Potential of Generative AI: The Next Productivity Frontier*. Brisbane: McKinsey & Company, pp. 1–65.

CMU (Carnegie Mellon University) (2023a). Technology for education. Eberly Center, Carnegie Mellon University. Accessed on August 2, 2023. Available at https://www.cmu.edu/teaching/technology/index.html.

CMU (Carnegie Mellon University) (2023b). Remote teaching and learning, Eberly Center, Carnegie Mellon University. Accessed on August 2, 2023. Available at https://www.cmu.edu/teaching/online/.

Cotton, D.R., Cotton, P.A. & Reubin Shipway, J. (2023). *Chatting and Cheating: Ensuring Academic Integrity in the Era of ChatGPT*. Innovations in Education and Teaching International, 13 May 2023, pp. 1–12.

Craig, R. (2021). How Higher Ed Can Prepare Students for Today's Digital Jobs. *Harvard Business Review*, 24 November 2021. Accessed on January 20, 2023. Available at https://hbr.org/2021/11/how-higher-ed-can-prepare-students-for-todays-digital-jobs.

Cusumano, M., Page, G., Sahai, E. & Zarate, A. (2013). MOOCs: Contexts and Consequences. Working Paper, The MIT Center for Digital Business, pp. 1–17.

Das, A. (2023). *Imagine Experience Connect: Driving Value through Immersive Learning*. EI, pp. 1–48.

Das, A., Bhadur, S. & D'Souza, T. (2023). *2023 Learning Trends for the Connected Workplace*. EI, pp. 1–69.

Deveau, R., Griffin, S.J. & Reis, S. (2023). *AI-Powered Marketing and Sales Reach New Heights with Generative AI: Growth Marketing & Sales Practices*. Brisbane: McKinsey & Company, pp. 1–10.

Diaz-Infante, N., Lazer, M., Ram, S. & Ray, A. (2022). *Demand for Online Education is Growing. are Providers Ready? Education Practice*. Brisbane: McKinsey & Company, p. 1012.

Dondi, M., Klier, J., Panier, F. & Schubert, J. (2021). *Defining the Skills Citizen Will Need in the Future World of Work. Public & Social Sector Practice*. Brisbane: McKinsey & Company, pp. 1–19.

Dorn, E., Hancock, B., Sarakatsannis, J. & Virtleg, E. (2019). *COVID-19 and Student Learning in the United States: The Hurt Could Last a Lifetime. Public Sector Practice*. Brisbane: McKinsey & Company, pp. 1–9.

Dorn, E., Probst, N., Sarakatsannis, J. & Panier, F. (2020). *Back to School: Lessons for Effective Remote and Hybrid Learning. Public & Social Sector Practice*. Brisbane: McKinsey & Company, pp. 1–10.

Epignosis LCC (2014). *E-Learning: Concepts, Trends, Applications*, Version 1.1, January 2014.

Ferrari, B.T. & Phan, P.H. (2018). *Universities and the Conglomerate Challenge*. Brisbane: McKinsey Quarterly, pp. 1–3.

Forth, P., Schniering, M., Arcuri, A. & Lovelock, J. (2023). Accelerating Australia's AI Adoption. Boston Consulting Group. 11 May 2023. Accessed on June 18, 2023. Available at https://www.bcg.com/publications/2023/accelerating-australia-ai-adoption.

Fowler, G.A. (2023). We Tested a New ChatGPT Detector for Teachers. It Flagged an Innocent Student. *The Washington Post*, 3 April 2023. Accessed on June 15, 2023. Available at https://www.washingtonpost.com/technology/2023/04/01/chatgpt-cheating-detection-turnitin/.

Fuller. J. & Kirkland, R. (2018). *How Google.org Is Helping Workers Prepare for a Digital Skill Shift*. Brisbane: McKinsey & Company, pp. 1–3.

Gallagher, S. (2023). Investing in talent with work-integrated learning. *Forbes*, August 28, 2023. Accessed on August 29, 2023. Available at https://www.forbes.com/sites/stand-together/2023/08/28/investing-in-talent-with-work-integrated-learning/?sh=5340c3cc782f.

Gecker, J. & The Associated Press (2023). College professor are in 'full-on crisis mode' as they catch one "ChatGPT plagiarist" after another. Fortune, August 11, 2023. Accessed on August 14, 2023. Available at https://fortune.com/2023/08/10/chatpgt-cheating-plagarism-college-professors-full-on-crisis-mode/.

Gilbert, C. G., Crow, A.M. & Anderson, D. (2018). Design thinking for higher education. Stanford Social Innovation Review, Winter 2018. Accessed on 20 January 2023. Available at https://ssir.org/articles/entry/design_thinking_for_higher_education#.

Glaveski, S. (2019). Where companies go wrong with learning and development. *Harvard Business Review*, October 2, 1–8.

Gordon, C. (2023). How are educators reacting to ChatGPT? *Forbes*, April 30, 2023. Accessed on 15 May 2023. Available at https://www.forbes.com/sites/cindygordon/2023/04/30/how-are-educators-reacting-to-chat-gpt/?sh=586815d22f1c.

Hall, S., Schmautzer, D., Tmiri, S. & Tschupp, R. (2022). *Reimagining Higher Education in MENAP. Education Practices*. Brisbane: McKinsey & Company, pp. 1–8.

Hall, S., Schmautzer, D., Tmiri, S., Ibrahim, H., Emma, D. & Sarfraz, S. (2023). *The Skills Revolution and the Future of Learning and Earning*. World Government Summit 2023, pp. 1–49.

Hancock, B., Laboissiere, M., Moore, D. & Rounsaville, T. (2022). *Transforming HR to Better Support Higher Education Institutions. Education Practice*. Brisbane: McKinsey & Company, pp. 1–31.

Hancock, B., Schaninger, B., Yee, L. & Rahilly, L. (2023). *Creative AI and the Future of HR. People & Organizational Performance Practice*. Brisbane: McKinsey & Company, pp. 1–7.

Harbinger Group (2023). *Top eLearning Trends to Watch out for in 2023: The eLearning Growth Book*. Redmond: Harbinger group, pp. 1–37.

Hatami, H., Maor, D. & Simon, P. (2023). *All Change: The New Era of Perpetual Organizational Upheaval. People & Organizational Performance Practice*. Brisbane: McKinsey & Company, pp. 1–6.

Heitz, C., Laboissuiere, M., Sanghvi, S. & Sarakatsannis, J. (2020). *Getting the Next Phase of Remote Learning Right in Higher Education. Public Sector Practice*. Brisbane: McKinsey & Company, pp. 1–5.

Henry, T., Pagano, E., Puckett, J. & Wilson, J. (2014). Five trends to watch in higher education. BGG Perspective, April 10, 2014.

Huddleston Jr. (2023). Bill Gates watched ChatGPT ace an AI bio exam and went into 'a state of shock: 'Let's see where we can put it to good use. Next Gen Investing, CNBN, 11 August 2023. Accessed on August 14, 2023. Available at https://www.cnbc.com/2023/08/11/bill-gates-went-in-a-state-of-shock-after-chatgpt-aced-ap-bio-exam.html#:~:text=On%20Thursday%2C%20 Gates%20opened%20up,Khan%20Academy%20CEO%20Sal%20Khan.

Hylen, J. (2006). Open educational resources: Opportunities and challenges. OECD's Center for Educational Research and Innovation, January 2006.

Kabudi, T., Pappas, I. & Olsen, D.H. (2021). AI-enabled adaptive learning systems: A systematic mapping of the literature. *Computers and Education: Artificial Intelligence*, 2, 1–12.

Keppell, M. (2023). Opportunities and challenges of digital assessment, pp. 1–49.

Khan, S. & Kirland, R. (2019). *Beyond the Industry Revolution Education Model: Sal Khan on Training and Skill on the 21st Century*. Brisbane: McKinsey & Company.

King's Own Institute (2023). Hybrid classroom. King's Own Institute, Sydney, Australia, 15 August 2023.

Laverdiere, R., Henry, T., Parro, M., Allan, B. & Alexander, S. (2023). Five ways higher education can leverage generative AI. Boston Consulting Group, July 27, 2023. Accessed on August 9, 2023. Available at https://www.bcg.com/publications/2023/five-ways-education-can-leverage-gen-ai.

LinkedIn Learning (2023). *Building the Agile Future. Workplace Learning Report*. California: LinkedIn, pp. 1–50.

McKinsey (2017). *Learning Innovation in the Digital Age*. Brisbane: McKinsey Quarterly, pp. 1–7.

McKinsey Explainer (2023). *What Is the Future of Work*. Brisbane: McKinsey & Company, pp. 1–5.

Madgavkar, A. & Sankhe, S. (2015). Empowering teachers and trainers through technology. *LiveMint.* January 2, 2015. Available at https://www.mckinsey.com/mgi/overview/in-the-news/empowering-teachers-and-trainers-through-technology (Accessed on 2 August 2023).

Maiolo, A. (2014). Online study debate rages. Campusreview.com.au, March 31, 2014. Accessed on April 20, 2014. Available at http://www.campusreview.com.au/2014/03/online-study-debate-rages/.

Mougiakou, S., Vinatsella, D., Sampson, D., Papamitsiou, Z., Giannakos, M. & Ifenthaler, D. (2023). *Educational Data Analysis for Teachers and School Leaders, Advances in Analytics for Learning and Teaching.* Berlin: Springer.

Manyika, J., Lund, S., Chui, M., Bughin, J., Woetzel, J., Batra, P., Ko, R. & Sanghvi, S. (2017). *Jobs Lost, Jobs Gained: Workforce Transitions in a Time of Automation.* Brisbane: McKinsey Global Institute, pp. 1–75.

Microsoft (2020). *The Class of 2030 and Life-Ready Learning: The Technology Imperative.* Washington: Microsoft, pp. 1–29.

Monash University (2023). Using artificial intelligence-student academic success. Available at https://www.monash.edu/student-academic-success/build-digital-capabilities/create-online/using-artificial-intelligence.

Moore, J.P.A. & Martinotti, S. (2016). Enabling seamless lifelong learning journey — the next frontier of digital education. *McKinsey Digital,* pp. 1–5.

Pandit, V., Lebraud, J.C. & Seetharaman, R. (2012). Transforming learning through mEducation. *McKinsey & GSMA Report,* pp. 1–34.

Pappas, C. (2020). *Gen Z Training: How to Create Exceptional Personalized Learning Experiences for the Next Generation Employees.* E-learning industry.

Pappas, C. (2023). *Ten Essential DEI Guide: How to Promote Inclusive through Online Training.* E-Learning Industry, pp. 1–30.

Pappas, C. (2023b). *The Ultimate AI in eLearning Guide.* E-Learning Industry, pp. 1–31.

Pertz, K. (2014). *Low Completion Rates for MOOCs.* IEEE Roundup.

Polito, G. & Temperini, M. (2021). A gamified web-based system for computer programming learning. *Computers and Education: Artificial Intelligence,* 2, 1–13.

RWS (2022). *Creating Better Global eLearning Experiences.* RWS, pp. 1–15.

Sanghvi, S. & Westhoff, M. (2022). Five trends to watch in the edtech industry. *Education Practice,* pp. 1–5.

Simon, P. Maor, D., Guggenberger, P., Park, M., Luo, M., Klingler, D., D'Auria, G., Weddle, B., Smet, A.D., Fletcher, B., Thaker, S. & Lodovico, A.D. (2023). *The State of Organizations.* Brisbane: McKinsey Company, pp. 1–85.

Small, G. (2022). 10 Adaptive learning platforms. Accessed on June 28, 2023. Available at https://www.edapp.com/blog/adaptive-learning-platforms/

Soto, A., Hedstorm, A., Hodson, A., Schwartzberg, A., Dygert, C., Johnson, D., Silver, D., Klosson, E., Dale, E., Eisenstein, G., Kendirick, G., Harb, H., Jackson, J., Lozano, J.C., Redondo, J., Brilliantes, K., Powell, O., Salazar, R. & Vojnovski, T. (2023). L&D and learner experience: 2023 trends report: How L &D is elevating human potential in a time of rapid change, pp. 1–65.

Spice, B. (2020). New AI enables teachers to rapidly develop intelligent tutoring systems. Carnegie Mellon University, May 6, 2020. Accessed on 20 July 2023. Available at https://www.cmu.edu/news/stories/archives/2020/may/intelligent-tutors.html#:~:text=Using%20a%20new%20method%20that,computer%20if%20it%20responds%20incorrectly.

TalentLMS (2023). How to elevate your training with a content library, pp. 1–28.

Tauscher, K. & Kietzmann, J. (2017). Learning from failures in the sharing economy. *MIS Quarterly Executive*, 16(4), 253–264.

Torbet, A. (2022). Adaptive learning in practice. eLearning Industry, December 9, 2022. Accessed on May 20, 2023. Available at https://elearningindustry.com/adaptive-learning-in-practice.

Turban, E., King, D. Liang, T.P. & Turban, D. (2012). *Electronic Commerce: A Managerial and Social Networks Perspective*, Global Edition, 7th edn. London: Pearson Education.

UNESCO (n.d.). OER in action. Accessed on July 20, 2023. Available at https://www.unesco.org/en/open-educational-resources/oer-action.

UNESCO (2019). Recommendation on open educational resources (OER). Available at https://www.unesco.org/en/legal-affairs/recommendation-open-educational-resources-oer.

UNESCO (2020). COVID-19 response-hybrid learning, July 2020, pp. 1–62.

UNESCO (2020b). COVID-19 response-remote learning strategy, July 2020, pp. 1–92.

UNESCO (2023a). ChatGPT and artificial intelligence in higher education, pp. 1–14.

UNESCO (2023b). World teachers' day: UNESCO sounds the alarm on the global teacher shortages crisis. Available at https://www.unesco.org/en/articles/world-teachers-day-unesco-sounds-alarm-global-teacher-shortage-crisis#:~:text=New%20UNESCO%20figures%20unveiled%20for,set%20by%20the%202030%20Agenda.

University of Illinois Urbana-Champaign (2023). ChatGPT: Artificial intelligence implications in teaching and learning. Center for Innovation on Teaching & Learning, Center for Innovation in Teaching & Learning. Accessed on July 10, 2023. Available at https://citl.illinois.edu/citl-101/instructional-spaces-technologies/teaching-with-technology/chatgpt.

University of Queensland (2022). *Final Report: Modes of Delivery in Higher Education*. Queensland: Institute for Social Science Research & Institute for Teaching and Learning Innovation, pp. 1–57.

University of Washington (2023). ChatGPT and other AI-based tools. Center for Teaching and Learning. Assessed on March 10, 2023. Available at https://teaching.washington.edu/course-design/chatgpt/.

Wang, H., Tlili, A., Huang, R., Cai, Z., Li, M., Cheng, Z., Yang, D., Li, M. & Zhu, X. (2022). Examining the applications of intelligent tutoring systems in real educational contexts: A systematic literature review from the social experiment perspective. *Education and Information Technologies*, 28, 9113–9148.

Welch, A. (2023). Teacher shortages are a global problem — Prioritising Australian visas won't solve ours. *The* Conversation, August 31, 2022. Available at https://theconversation.com/teacher-shortages-are-a-global-problem-prioritising-australian-visas-wont-solve-ours-189468.

Wentworth, D. (2023). Lead the change: Leveraging technology to meet learning's biggest challenges. *White Paper*, Schoox, pp. 1–17.

Wiessner, D. (2023). Tutoring firms settles US agency's first bias lawsuit involving AI software. Reuters, 11 August 2023. Assessed on August 14, 2023. Available at https://www.reuters.com/legal/tutoring-firm-settles-us-agencys-first-bias-lawsuit-involving-ai-software-2023-08-10/#:~:text=Tutoring%20firm%20settles%20US%20agency's%20first%20bias%20lawsuit%20involving%20AI%20software,-By%20Daniel%20Wiessner&text=Aug%2010%20(Reuters)%20%2D%20A,weed%20out%20older%20job%20applicants.

Wilichowski, T. & Cobo, C. (2023). How to use ChatGPT to support teaches: The good, the bad, and the ugly. World Bank, 2 May 2023. Accessed on June 10, 2023. Available at https://blogs.worldbank.org/education/how-use-chatgpt-support-teachers-good-bad-and-ugly.

Wikipedia (2023a). Intelligent tutoring systems, July 22, 2023. Accessed on July 23, 2023. Available at https://en.wikipedia.org/wiki/Intelligent_tutoring_system#:~:text=The%20Domain%20model,The%20User%20interface%20model.

Wikipedia (2023b). Adaptive learning, July 21, 2023. Accessed on July 23, 2023. Available at https://en.wikipedia.org/wiki/Adaptive_learning.

Wikipedia (2023c). Open educational resources, July 24, 2023. Accessed on July 25, 2023. Available at https://en.wikipedia.org/wiki/Open_educational_resources.

Xu, J. (2014). *Managing Digital Enterprise: Ten Essential Topics*. Berlin: Springer & Atlantis Press.

Xu, J. (2019*). Essential Topics of Managing Information Systems*. Singapore: World Scientific.

Xu, J. (2023). *Presentation Slides for KOI New Students Orientation.* Sydney: King's Own Institute, Sydney.

Xu, J. & Gao. X. (2021). E-services, Digital platforms & ecosystems and mobile business. In J. Xu, & X. Gao (eds.), *E-Business in the 21st Century: Essential Topics & Studies.* Singapore: World Scientific. pp. 107–124.

© 2024 World Scientific Publishing Company
https://doi.org/10.1142/9789811285622_0002

Chapter 2

Teaching and Learning in the Digital Era: Opportunities and Challenges

Sanjay Jha*, Meena Jha†, and Jun Xu*

*King's Own Institute, Australia
†Central Queensland University, Australia

Abstract

Teaching and learning in the digital era refers to the use of digital technologies to support and enhance teaching and learning activities. Advancement in digital technologies has revolutionized the way teaching and learning are conducted, making education more accessible, interactive, and personalized. Digitalization of higher education systems has been considered a powerful means to promote student learning. Digital technologies can positively affect student learning in higher education and it becomes effective when teachers use it to promote student involvement in constructive and interactive as opposed to passive and traditional learning methods (Wekerle et al., 2022). Embracing technology in education is crucial for keeping up with the rapidly evolving world and preparing students for the future. This chapter provides an overview of teaching and learning in the digital era, describes the definition, types, and elements of teaching and learning in the digital era, explains the opportunities, and challenges of teaching and learning, and points out emerging patterns and provides insight into future trajectories how the use of digital technologies while providing the required support to enhance teaching and learning activities.

Keywords: Teaching and learning, Online education platforms, Personalized learning, Open educational resources, Learning analytics, Digital citizenship.

1. Introduction

The integration of technology into daily life has had a significant impact on routine daily tasks. Seamless incorporation of technology into daily activities, including reading online, buying, and locating destination locations using Global Positioning System (GPS) (Smith et al., 2016). Since technology has become more widely available over the past 15 years, there has been a significant increase in using desktops, laptops, and mobile devices to access information (Cheung, 2022; Ng et al., 2017; Poushter, 2016). People will use 5G more frequently once fully deployed, and more will realize its advantages, These technologies are already emerging in the market, alongside the anticipated sixth-generation broadband cellular network technologies that are currently in the phase of research and development (Oinas-Kukkonen et al., 2021). What the 6G constitutes is yet to be determined, but it serves as a mental model of what lies ahead in the roadmap to 2030 (Matinmikko-Blue et al., 2021).

Article 26 of the Universal Declaration of Human Rights underscores the significance of quality education access. This article asserts education as a fundamental human right, enabling individuals to enhance their lives, realize their potential with dignity, and attain autonomy through knowledge and skills (United Nations, 1948). With the rise of digital technologies, education has shifted towards a more digitalized approach, where traditional classroom settings are supplemented or even replaced by digital tools and resources. There are several technology-based teaching and learning support to increase student engagement, such as online forums, gamification, audios, videos, personalized activities, flipped classrooms, Google classrooms, online quizzes, student response systems, and technology-based assessments. The integration of new practices to improve the outcome of higher education has always been there, and universities are using digital technologies such as videos, audios, and teleconferencing to augment traditional instructional delivery methods (Kaware & Sain, 2015).

Digital technologies have significantly impacted teaching and learning in many ways (Barton & Dexter, 2020; Chiu, 2020; Tondeur *et al.*, 2020) and have made accessing information and resources easier for students and teachers offering equal learning opportunities for all, and promoting lifelong learning (UNESCO, 2014, 2021). With the Internet, students can access a wide range of information, research papers, and educational materials which was not possible earlier. This has expanded the possibilities for learning and teaching, allowing students to learn at their own pace and convenience, however, according to a study (Okoye *et al.*, 2023), obstacles like inadequate training and resources, lack of internet connection, and inadequate infrastructure all significantly impact the adoption of digital technologies in education in many parts of the world.

The volume of data generated by digital tools and their computational capacity has increased significantly along with the development of these products and their greater connectedness. The adoption of digital technology has enabled personalized learning, where students can receive tailored instruction and feedback based on their needs and learning preferences (van der Vorst & Jelicic, 2019). With adaptive learning software, for example, students can receive immediate feedback and support, and the software can adjust the difficulty level of the material based on their progress (Castañeda & Selwyn, 2018; Jha *et al.*, 2019). In order to create effective adaptive learning environments, it is crucial to teach students how to learn. This can be done by adapting instructional methodologies and designs to accommodate the interests, expectations, and skills of varied learners (Biten, 2017).

Digital technology has made it easier for students to collaborate and communicate with each other and teachers. With tools like online discussion forums, collaborative documents, and video conferencing, students can work together on projects, receive feedback from peers and teachers, and participate in class discussions, even if they are not physically present in the same location. Digital technology has become an essential part of modern life, and digital literacy has become an essential skill for students to develop. By using digital technology in the classroom, students can reform their literacy in digital skills, such as searching for and evaluating information, using digital tools for communication and collaboration, and understanding how to protect one's privacy and security online.

Digital technology has made learning more flexible and convenient. With online learning platforms, for example, students have the flexibility to retrieve course materials and fulfill assignments according to their preferred schedule and convenience. This is particularly useful for students with other commitments, such as work or family responsibilities.

Digital technology can address cognitive load in several ways for learners and can help learners navigate and organize information more effectively. For example, e-books and online articles can provide hyperlinks and search functions that allow learners to quickly find and access relevant information. Similarly, learning management systems (LMS) can organize course materials and assignments logically and intuitively, reducing cognitive load and promoting efficient learning.

It is often taken for granted that using technology (Kirkwood & Price, 2014) will enhance learning leading to student engagement (Gillett-Swan, 2017). Orlando and Attard (2015) stated that "teaching with technology is not a one-size-fits-all approach as it depends on the types of technology in use at the time and also the curriculum content being taught" (p. 119). Progress in digital technologies for education, such as smartboards, gamification, mobile devices, dynamic visualizations tablets, laptops, simulations, virtual laboratories, Large Language Models (Generative AI), mobile apps, and innovative digital learning experiences, these changes in education are reshaping the landscape and creating fresh opportunities for measuring, developing theories and designing teaching strategies. These strategies can aid in maintaining student engagement with their learning tasks.

Student engagement and learning are closely connected and critical to achieving required educational outcomes. When students actively engage in the learning process, they are more likely to develop a deeper understanding of the subject matter, retain information, and apply their knowledge in real-world scenarios.

2. Definition, Types, and Elements of Digital Technology Used in Higher Education

Digital technologies in higher education are defined as the technologies that are used to support teaching and learning such as laptops, tablets, mobile phones, online resources, digital tools, systems devices, and digital learning resources (Vuorikari *et al.*, 2016). Digital technology facilitates blended, online, and mobile learning and is referred to as Digital Educational Technology. Digital technologies also denote a wide range of technologies, tools, services, and applications using various types of hardware and software (Rice, 2003). Digital technology used in education is educational technology. Educational technology also referred to as EdTech is the use of technology in different educational settings to enhance learning to improve educational outcomes. Association for Technology and Educational Communications has defined educational technology as "the study and ethical practice of facilitating learning and improving performance by creating, using and managing appropriate technological processes and resources" (Januszewski & Molenda, 2007). Education is moving toward an active involvement of students instead of a passive traditional style of teaching. Digital technology supports student-centered learning environments (SCLEs) (Moeller & Reitzes, 2011) to provide complimentary activities that enable individuals to address unique learning interests and needs (Hannafin & Land, 2000). Digital technology in higher education is a broad spectrum of devices, applications, and resources that support learning and teaching, aiming to create more student-centric, interactive, personalized, and efficient educational experiences while reducing the cognitive load for both students and educators.

Digital technologies have the potential to disrupt traditional teaching and learning activities, while also complementing and enhancing existing educational practices. Social media such as Instagram, Facebook, YouTube, and others have impacted the way students learn as they provide free access to information. Having access to different devices, such as Google Chromebooks, MacBooks, Windows laptops, iPads, and Android tablets, provides students with a diverse set of tools for learning and accessing educational content Table 1 lists some of the digital educational technologies that are used for higher education.

Digital technology creates an instant learning environment, expedites assessments, and fosters heightened engagement, as opposed to traditional classroom instructions as it enables access to educational content and resources at any time and from virtually anywhere with an Internet connection. This flexibility allows learners to engage with learning materials at their own pace, accommodating different learning styles and schedules. Digital technology provides access to a wide range of resources, including videos, articles, online courses, and more. This diversity can enhance the depth and breadth of learning experiences beyond what traditional textbooks and lectures might offer.

Table 1: Digital technology types used in higher education.

Digital Technologies	Brief Explanation
Podcasting	Podcasting, a method of spreading audio information is a popular medium for distributing audio/video content. Podcasting relies on Really Simple Syndication (RSS) feeds to distribute audio and video files to subscribed participants.
Gamification	Gamification involves incorporating elements from games, along with their design principles and immersive experiences, into non-game settings. This approach aims to captivate and inspire individuals, fostering engagement and motivation. to achieve specific goals. It involves incorporating elements commonly found in games, such as points, rewards, badges, challenges, and competition, into various activities to make them more enjoyable and engaging. Gamification aims to increase collaboration, sharing and interaction engagement.
Interactive Whiteboards (IWB)	An IWB is an electronically operated screen-based board for presentations, teaching, and group discussions. Interactive Whiteboards allow users to share real-time information and record conversation digitally.
Learning Management Systems (LMS)	LMS is a software application for delivering, managing, and tracking educational courses. LMS may include features such as virtual classrooms, video conferencing, and social learning tools.
Online Collaboration Spaces	Online collaboration spaces are virtual environments used for an individual and teams to work together for project management, video conferencing, file sharing, messaging, and many calendar-based reminders. It provides a powerful platform for remote teams to collaborate and work efficiently and effectively, irrespective of time and place.
The Cloud	The Cloud offers third-party assistance which includes Platform as a Service (PaaS), Software as a Service (SaaS), and Information as a Service (IaaS) and, most famous, for storage purposes. The Cloud offers virtually unlimited storage capacity, allowing educational institutions to store and manage vast amounts of data, including educational content, research materials, and student records. Cloud storage facilitates convenient data retrieval from any Internet-connected device, thereby encouraging adaptable and mobile learning experiences.

Table 1: (*Continued*)

Digital Technologies	Brief Explanation
Virtual Reality (VR)	VR is a computer-generated environment that allows users to experience as if they were physically present. This technology has many potential applications in teaching and learning and is already used in various educational settings. VR has emerged as a powerful educational tool that enhances learning experiences by providing immersive, interactive, and engaging environments.
Augmented Reality (AR)	AR combines the natural world and computer-generated content with an interactive experience. AR enables interactive and hands-on learning experiences by overlaying digital content onto physical objects or learning materials. Students can interact with virtual elements, explore concepts in 3D, and manipulate content in real-time.
Internet Of Things (IoT)	The Internet of Things (IoT) uses a network of physical devices works with sensors and software, and share data among itself and with other systems through the Internet. It is helpful in smart classrooms, personalized learning, smart campuses and remote learning.
Spatial Computing	Spatial computing, also known as spatial computing, is a technological concept that focuses on integrating the virtual world with the physical world in real-time. It involves the use of technologies like Virtual Reality (VR), Augmented Reality (AR), Mixed Reality (MR), and 3D mapping to immersive experiences and create interactive that respond to users' spatial context and movements. In education, spatial computing holds significant potential to revolutionize the learning process and enhance students' understanding of complex concepts.

Sources: Wekerle *et al.* (2022); Hasselbring and Glaser (2000); Ng *et al.* (2017); Tang *et al.* (2022; the authors' own knowledge).

3. Student Engagement and Learning Through Digital Educational Technology

Digital technology in higher education has been known to enhance student experiences in different aspects. It plays an essential role in student engagement by exploring new academic content. It has transformed how students interact with learning materials, engage with course content, and collaborate with peers and instructors. By using digital technology to engage students in the classroom, educators may be able to foster a sense of belonging, accessibility, support, motivation, enthusiasm to learn, and help students be lifelong learners (Bond & Bedenlier, 2019). Digital technology supports learning in students with diverse learning needs, including at-risk and special education students. Students with diverse needs cannot become a part of a traditional classroom setting. For these students, digital technologies can play an especially important role. The creation of sophisticated digital educational tools has helped the two million students with more severe disabilities to overcome a variety of restrictions that prevent classroom participation from speech and hearing impairments to blindness and severe physical disabilities (Hasselbring & Glaser, 2000). There are various assistive technologies available for students with disabilities or learning challenges. For example, screen readers for visually impaired students, speech-to-text software for those with writing difficulties, and alternative input devices for students with motor skill impairments.

In Australia, the first IWB was bought in June 2005 by La Trobe University Bendigo Faculty of Education. At this time, a session with the workers to expose them to IWBs was conducted. This program concentrated on the pedagogy of IWB use in the classroom and offered hands-on training. All first-year pre-service teachers taking the "ICT for Education" course could access the board at this location (Campbell & Kent, 2010).

Listening to an enthusiastic podcast compared to neutral podcast has shown to improve motivation in learners. König (2021) conducted a research on two versions of educational podcasts, i.e., neutral and enthusiastic. The enthusiastic version of podcasts used in educational institutions to impart education in a new interactive way to improve the teaching and learning methods had better recognition than neutral podcasts. A digital enthusiastic presentation of instructional content can have a transformative impact on the learning process. Digital presentations allow for the integration of captivating visuals such as images, videos, animations, and infographics. These visuals not only enhance understanding but also stimulate curiosity and interest among learners (Shabiralyani *et al.*, 2015; Tang *et al.*, 2022).

The education sector has revealed the benefits of gamification in education, including a higher level of engagement, improved retention, and connecting learning to the real world. According to Nadi-Ravandi and

Batooli (2022), gamification can be used to provide instant feedback and reinforcement and get students hooked on learning. Incorporating game-like elements in the presentation, such as badges, points, and rewards for completing certain tasks, can turn the learning process into a fun and challenging experience. Nonetheless, a distinction exists between gamification and Game-Based Learning (GBL). Gamification involves transforming the learning journey into a game-like experience, whereas GBL employs an actual game as an integral aspect of learning. Educational games amalgamate elements of entertainment with educational principles to heighten student motivation and engagement. GBL motivates students to engage with learning through play, infusing enjoyment into the educational journey. This approach has demonstrated a favorable impact on cognitive development, as evidenced by Lin *et al.* (2014), by addressing the issues faced by learning resources that are dry and have technical and boring subject matter that is really difficult to understand. The concept is used where students have difficult assessments, complex understanding processes, and have difficulties in the learning process and are de-motivated (Andreas & Ebner, 2007; Ke, 2008). The motivational psychology involved in GBL allows students to engage with educational materials in a playful and dynamic way (Al-Azawi *et al.*, 2016).

There are four types of interactions that can enhance students' engagement using educational technology. It is learners to teachers; learners to learning resources; learners to learners; and teacher to learning resources interactions (Jha *et al.*, 2022). Society has been revolutionized by digital technologies, yet the evolution of assessment design might not have matched this digital progress. Educational technologies often replicate existing academic methods, and even though new implementations like GBAs have emerged, the core principles of assessment design seem to endure. (Jha *et al.*, 2023). Through gamification, a mindset can be created among students that encourages them to try new things and not to be afraid of failing as in traditional form of learning, and enables students to engage in enjoyable experiences for the purpose of learning (Al-Azawi *et al.*, 2016), focusing on pedagogy, domain experts, feedback, learning mechanics, and game design to design game-based assessments to achieve learning objectives (Makhija *et al.*, 2023).

According to (Iqbal *et al.*, 2022) reading books is highly theoretical, but firms that make instructional virtual reality software, like Mondly, can offer an immersive language-learning experience without requiring you to fly abroad. Language learning can be more effective and likely to stick if you genuinely interact with real people in Mondly's Virtual Reality realms. VR has given a campus concept in the space, a sense of space for students, and teaching materials beyond 2D images and videos. Incorporating VR technology into educational settings has provided a new dimension to the way students interact with learning environments. Through the power of VR, students are also able to explore campus grounds, lecture halls, and other spaces as if they were physically present. This technology goes beyond mere visuals, enabling users to feel a sense of presence and engagement that was previously unattainable through static media (Atif et al., 2021).

The use of spatial computing in education can produce immersive learning environments. For instance, rather than reading about historical locations or scientific phenomena in a textbook, students might encounter them in a more engaging way using VR or AR (Heo et al., 2021). Educational technology across all disciplines has been deployed extensively to meet the evolving needs of the higher education industries transitioning from traditional classrooms to online education. Higher levels of technological integration into curriculum design and delivery are becoming increasingly desirable and expected from institutions. Educational technologies create opportunities for designing and providing learning resources. VR has proven to be a valuable tool in assessment design (Hamilton et al., 2021). VR's immersive capabilities allow educators to create unique and authentic assessment environments that closely mimic real-world scenarios (Chang et al., 2023; Jha et al., 2020). While the research on educational technology is expanding, systematic research on how well this new technology affects student involvement is still lacking (Jha et al., 2022). All educators need to pay attention to the problem of adopting educational technology in their curricula and methods of instruction to engage students.

Teachers and students are now using social media to aid teaching and learning. EDMODO was one of the most popular social networking sites for learning. In a mixed learning strategy, Balkesir University in Turkey has utilized EDMODO (Dewi, 2014). Edmodo served as an educational technology platform catering to K-12 schools and educators. It facilitated content sharing, quiz, and assignment distribution, as well as communication management among teachers, students, colleagues, and parents. Regrettably, it ceased operations on 22 September 2022, according to Mollenkamp (2022).

Student engagement spans various technologies, including social media, video, and collaborative learning tools, which are often layered atop the LMS. LMSs play a significant role in higher education, aiding teaching and learning, as noted by Beer et al. (2010) and Cabero-Almenara et al. (2019). An LMS is a digital platform that helps educators manage and deliver educational content, track student progress, facilitate communication, and assess learning outcomes. It serves as a foundational tool in the modern educational environment.

Student retention and engagement are essential for the success of any educational program. Digital technology may not directly contribute to student engagement and retention, but it can undoubtedly assist these outcomes (Haleem et al., 2022). Educational technology should not be utilized to replace student participation but rather as a complement to it. Integrating social media platforms into the educational process can foster engagement and interaction among students and instructors. Features such as discussion forums, groups, and chat functionalities within the LMS can mimic social media interactions and encourage collaborative learning. Social media integration can also provide opportunities for informal communication, sharing of resources, and peer-to-peer support.

Video content has become a powerful tool for delivering lectures, tutorials, and other educational materials. Video platforms integrated into the LMS can provide flexibility for both synchronous and asynchronous learning. Recorded lectures, tutorial videos, and demonstrations can enhance the learning experience by catering to different learning styles. Additionally, interactive elements like quizzes and discussions can be incorporated into video content to keep students engaged.

4. Online Education Platforms

Online education platforms are digital platforms in higher education that provide learning materials and materials required to conduct courses and provide students remote access to the required content online. Technologies play a vital role in using the present internet technology. According to Chen et al. (2020), "The rapid popularization of the 'Internet+' has brought new vitality and technical support to online education".

Online education platforms make learning accessible to a wider audience by eliminating geographical barriers. Students from different parts of the world can access courses and materials from the comfort of their own homes, at their own pace, and according to their schedules. Essential terms to define online education platforms are accessibility, variety of courses, interactive learning resources, certification, and credential recognizing, which includes collaboration and communication with cost-effectiveness.

According to Wills (2007), sharing information and experience can persuade students to use online learning platforms, engage in role-playing online, and boost their learning outcomes by combining online study with offline engagement. Considering every country's national circumstance and culture are unique, countries should not duplicate the online education systems used by other nations, but instead, they should get inspiration from their inventive solutions. According to Xie et al. (2016), incentives are major influencing elements that may increase learners' motivation to learn, and incentive programs should be oriented toward cognitive goals to increase learners' motivation to learn in an online education platform.

Massive Open Online Courses (MOOCs) are considered online education platforms offering access to courses and educational materials involving many participants. MOOCs gained popularity in the early 2010s and have since become an integral part of the online learning platform. Popular education platforms include Coursera, Udemy, edX, etc., with unique features, course offerings, and different pricing models. The following key points about MOOCs define their landscape. MOOCs, or Massive Open Online Courses, are online learning platforms tailored for extensive participation, accessible globally to individuals with Internet connectivity. They are open to all, without prerequisites, and provide comprehensive course experiences entirely online at no cost, as defined by Jansen et al. (2015) because they make use of e-learning platforms. The terms "massive" and "open" in this context alluded to the lack of enrolment limits, which allows many students to enroll, "online" refers to studying online, while the terms "online" and online learning" related to learning through the Internet, respectively (Liu et al., 2021). MOOCs have rapidly spread throughout the world during the past 10 years. In certain countries, MOOCs are integrated into their formal degree programs (Huang, 2022).

MOOCs are designed to access a large number of learners by keeping open access, scalability, and diverse course offerings, which include flexible learning. MOOCs employ various multimedia tools and resources to enhance the learning experience, so flexible learning employs different interactive learning resources. MOOCs create virtual learning communities where learners from different backgrounds and locations can interact, collaborate, and learn from each other, also termed Global learning communities. Many MOOCs offer certificates of completion or even accredited certificates for a fee (Irwanto et al., 2023). Mainly it collaborates with institutions to offer courses taught by renowned professors and subject matter experts. This collaboration enhances the quality and credibility of the courses, providing learners with access to high-quality educational content.

MOOCs gained popularity during the COVID-19 outbreak, as all around the world students wanted to advance their knowledge and abilities sitting from the comfort of their home. MOOCs have changed traditional educational methods and more predominantly during the COVID-19 epidemic. This transition from traditional classroom settings to MOOCs is a type of emergency response to the epidemic; students and teachers eventually changed their teaching style. MOOCs are "the next evolution of networked learning" (Johnson et al., 2013). It was visualized as a platform to increase higher education access. MOOCs have been said to impact online education and have shown great potential to provide free and open courses to large numbers of students from anywhere without requiring prerequisites for participation (Downes, 2010; Sezgin, 2021). In addition, MOOCs provide learning flexibility in time and place, allow a variety of assignments in one course, permit diverse assignments within a single course, and offer learning flexibility in terms of time and location (Zhu et al., 2020).

LMS is a very widely used online education platform and has a significant role in the digital era and is very popular in educational institutions, corporate settings, and those organizations that require online learning. The LMS Moodle (Modular Object-Oriented Dynamic Learning Environment) invented first by Martin Daugiamas in August 2002 with Moodle version 1.0 (Haskari, 2012). Moodle has evolved since then and now is a form of e-Learning that involves the use of digital technological tools helping learners to study anytime and anywhere, hence extending the classroom to the web. Moodle is designed to support student activities in online teaching and learning (Haskari, 2012).

LMSs help administrators organize courses, modules, and lessons to manage course content. User management is another important aspect for students, instructors, and administrators to do user registration, enrolment, and manage user accounts. A vital role of LMS is to maintain communication and collaboration, which includes discussion forums, chat features, and messaging systems. It helps in assessment and grading by offering assessment tools for quizzes, exams, and assignments. LMS can track learner progress and provide analytics and reporting features. Through visual dashboards and reports, instructors, and administrators can monitor learner engagement, completion rates, and performance (Simanullang & Rajagukguk 2020). They are designed to access course materials through smartphones or tablets. It allows integration with other software systems, such as student information systems, video conferencing platforms, and learning analytics tools. Customization of the user interface, branding, and course design is also an integrated part of LMS. A few popular LMS apart from Moodle are Canvas, Blackboard, Google Classroom, and Schoology.

Moodle-based online LMS was created during COVID-19 pandemic. The guiding principles of this platform are compatible with Moodle's design, which focuses on providing interactive teaching methods. The social construction hypothesis (Nash & Rice, 2018) contends that interaction with learning materials, creating new learning materials for others, and discussing with peers about a subject are all beneficial aspects of learning. According to recent studies, LMS based on Moodle can offer interactive web-based learning that mimics traditional learning (Coman *et al.*, 2020). Students get introduced to different learning resources with various online activities, group discussions, and hands-on projects. It provides a flexible model that engages with face-to-face interactions with teachers and peers for support, guidance, and assessments online monitoring.

LMS has played a crucial role in enabling and facilitating blended learning, which combines traditional in-person instruction with online learning activities. Blended learning aims to leverage the benefits of both face-to-face interaction and online resources to create a more flexible and personalized learning experience. Albeit, Flipped classroom is an e-learning approach within blended learning that emphasizes the use of digital educational technology to enhance the learning experiences of learners in which traditional in-class instruction and homework assignments are reversed.

Blended learning has increased to be commonly used in education, where there is a need to mix online educational resources and possibilities for online engagement using technological tools, also known as technology-mediated instruction or mixed-mode instructions. Blended learning resources can include pre-recorded lectures, interactive simulations, online discussions, and assessments, and LMS plays a crucial digital platform to host these resources.

Blended learning offers flexibility in terms of time and place. Students can engage with online materials at their own pace, allowing for personalized learning experiences giving rise to a new traditional model for teaching (Ross and Gauge 2006). And Norberg *et al.* (2011) called blended learning a "new normal for course delivery". Blended learning has been found to be successful in many educational settings when implemented effectively (Tong *et al.*, 2022). The goal of blended learning is to optimize learning outcomes by combining the strengths of face-to-face interactions (such as instructor guidance and peer collaboration) with the advantages of online resources (such as self-paced learning and access to diverse content) (Kintu *et al.*, 2017; Vallée *et al.*, 2020). Blended learning is used to deliver content outside of class, freeing up in-person class time for interactive activities.

As higher education institutions are recovering from the impacts of COVID-19, the pandemic has provided many opportunities to utilize digital technologies within the higher education system. The most obvious of which is a wholesale move to online learning and teaching. This could become possible just because of digital technologies used in higher education. Online learning and teaching, now adopted by higher education institutions globally, including Australia, offer numerous benefits. These include the flexibility for students to learn from any location and at their preferred times, whether synchronously or asynchronously, as highlighted by Singh and Thurman (2019).

5. Academic Integrity in the Age of Digital Era

Maintaining academic integrity is crucial in the digital era, as technology has made it easier for students to access and share information with each other. Academic integrity is a critical aspect of the academic community, and it is essential that students, researchers, and educators uphold ethical standards in their work. Academic integrity is the basis of ethical academic practice. According to the Australian Tertiary Education Quality and Standards Agency (TEQSA) — "Academic integrity is the expectation that teachers, students, researchers and all members of the academic community act with honesty, trust, fairness, respect and responsibility". According to Universities Australia (2017), the university is responsible for increasing academic integrity across Australia and endorses the definition provided by TEQSA. According to Harvard University, "Academic integrity is truthful and responsible representation of yourself and your work by taking credit only for your own ideas and creations and giving credit to the work and ideas of other people".

An essential value supported by educational institutions throughout the world is academic integrity. There are various universal concepts and norms that regulate academic integrity, including originality and respect for intellectual property, to mention a few. While exact rules and regulations may differ across nations and higher education institutions, they all generally apply to academic integrity. The work that the students turn in must be original and reflect their own thoughts, investigation, and analysis. Academic misconduct includes presenting someone else's work as one's own, including utilizing ghostwriters, submitting essays that were purchased, collusion, plagiarism, falsification, and cheating. These sorts of academic misconduct are referred to as "human reliant academic misconduct" since they center on interactions between individuals.

The implementation of effective strategies to promote academic integrity has been a longstanding topic in higher education. Nevertheless, there is a prevalent perception that ethical lapses are on the rise due to the increased shift of higher education to online platforms, as indicated by Jha *et al.* (2021). Additional opportunities for "e-cheating" have emerged as a result of the integration of digital educational technology into the classroom and the popularity of online courses (King & Case, 2014).

Students engage in academic misconduct because of several reasons such as pressure to perform, time management issues, procrastination, lack of understanding of the implications, struggling with a particular subject, expectations around education, highly competitive academic environment, fear of failure, and lack of interest (Mathrani *et al.*, 2021; Schwartz *et al.*, 2013; Tolman, 2017; Watson & Sottile, 2010). There is a general perception that cheating happens more frequently in online classes than in-person classes, especially for exams and other high-stakes assignments. Approximately 42%–74% of students think it is simpler to cheat in an online class (Watson & Sottile, 2010).

Digital technology has both facilitated and complicated the issue of academic misconduct. Generative-AI has made contents easily available for students to copy without much human involvement, which raises another concern about potential misuse and increased opportunities for academic misconduct, such as AI-copying and AI-plagiarism. The rise of Generative-AI has introduced new challenges and considerations in the realm of academic misconduct by introducing the academic world to the AI-Generated plagiarism; AI-Based cheating; AI-Generated fake content; and AI-Powered ghost-writing.

While digital technology has brought numerous benefits to education, it has also introduced new avenues for cheating, plagiarism, and other forms of academic dishonesty. Here we can briefly describe the facilitators of academic misconduct that are enabled in the age of digital era.

- *Easy Access to Information*: Digital technology has made it incredibly easy for students to access a wide range of information online. While this can be beneficial for research, it also makes it easier for students to copy and paste content without proper attribution.
- *Plagiarism Detection Tools*: Paradoxically, the same technology that enables plagiarism can also be used to detect it. Plagiarism detection software can identify instances of copied content in assignments and essays such as Turnitin. Despite its capabilities, Turnitin currently has limitations in accurately detecting content that has been fully generated using AI.
- *Online Paper Mills*: Websites offering pre-written essays or papers for sale have become more prevalent, providing students with the opportunity to submit someone else's work as their own.
- *Sharing Answers*: Students can use instant messaging, social media, or collaborative platforms to share answers during exams or assignments.
- *Remote Learning Challenges*: During remote learning, students may be tempted to use unauthorized resources during online assessments, as it's more difficult for educators to monitor their behavior.

To address the issues and to promote academic integrity, educators and institutions can take proactive steps, such as: clearly communicating expectations regarding academic honesty and misconduct; providing education about plagiarism, citing sources, and proper research techniques; designing assignments that encourage critical thinking and originality; offering support services for time management, study skills, and academic writing; implementing assessment methods that make cheating and plagiarism more difficult; fostering a positive learning environment that emphasizes learning over grades; implementing deterrents, such as honor codes or integrity pledges; providing resources for reporting and addressing instances of academic misconduct.

6. Personalized Learning

Digital technology has equipped education providers with the ability to provide personalized products and services (i.e., tailored products and services) for each individual consumer (e.g., learner in the educational context), which could be very expensive or nearly impossible in the offline world (Xu, 2014: 79). More specially, personalized learning can be viewed as "a teaching technique that aims to help educator, tutors, and instructors identify the unique needs, interests, and abilities of a learner and create a customized learning path to accommodate them" (Pappas, 2020: 5), and it is supported, optimized and scaled by technology (Microsoft, 2022: 5).

Some applications/systems supporting personalized learning include (Kabudi *et al.*, 2021; Microsoft, 2020; Pappas, 2020: 29–32; Polito & Temperini, 2021; Small, 2022; Spice, 2020; the authors' own knowledge; Torbet, 2022; Wang *et al.*, 2022: Wikipedia, 2023a, 2023b):

- Applications/systems for assessment and factor checking (e.g., Non-generative Applications (such ChatGPT, Grammarly, Microsoft Word Spelling, and Grammar Checker).
- Intelligent Tutoring Systems that provide immediate and customized instruction feedback to learners according to their characteristics and needs (typically based on the assessment based on their responses to assigned tasks and questions), very often without requiring intervention from a human teacher (e.g., Algebra Tutor, Cognitive Tutor, SQL Tutor, ITSS, Dragon 2, PCAR, Mouse Work, Living Letters, SARA, Nanotutors, DME, ALEKS, ASSISTments, CTAT, HINTS, SKOPE-IT, My Science Tutor, GraphicGame Rime).
- Adaptive Learning Systems that automatically adapt teaching process (i.e., delivering customized resources and learning activities) and can arguably be viewed as a type of Intelligent Tutoring Systems (e.g., ELAN, Reading Plus, Dutch Education System, FB-TS, Adaptive Mobile Learning Systems, Personalized Adaptive Learning Dashboard, AL, Adaptemy, EdApp, Cogbooks, Knewton, Realizeit, Pearson Interactive Labs, Adaptive Learning, Design Digitally, Impelsys Scholar ALS).

- Virtual Classroom (e.g., digital avatars, virtual reality, augmented reality and mixed reality tools, gamified learning systems).
- One-to-one online tutorial between the teacher and the student.
- Self-paced technology-assisted learning (either synchronous or asynchronous) by attending online learning activities and reviewing online learning materials (e.g., online content, recordings, videos, discussion forums, learning communities, collaborative platforms, and classes).

Some challenges of personalized learning are (Alexander, 2021; Briggs, 2014; Bryant *et al.*, 2020; Microsoft, 2020: 15–19; Molenaar, 2021; Mousrshed *et al.*, 2017; Pappas, 2020: 9–12; Rawson *et al.*, 2016; the authors' own knowledge; Wikipedia, 2023a; Young Entrepreneur Council, 2023):

- Defining personalized learning (e.g., What does personalized learning mean for your organization? What is your organization trying to achieve in personalized learning? How do we align personalized learning with learning goals and organization goals?)
- People's acceptance (e.g., How do we encourage the teachers to adopt personalized learning (especially it could mean extra effort)? How do we deal with the resistance from students (especially for students from certain cultural backgrounds who are not willing to ask questions directly to the teacher)?).
- Required technology (e.g., Has the organization put the required technological infrastructure (e.g., sufficient network capacity in terms of being fast, resilient, and reliable) and human resources in place? Have personalized learning systems properly developed and implemented? Have the security and privacy issues associated with personalized learning systems/applications been thoroughly thought and tested? Have our teachers and students been equipped with the right devices (including tablets, smartphones, laptops, which provide them with connectivity and mobility)?).
- Organization's readiness/adjustment for personalized learning (e.g., How about supporting organizational structure and culture? How about required training and development for staff in terms of pedagogical and technical perspectives? How about required top management support? How about the establishment of communities of practice for engaging human contribution? Have appropriate policies and adequate resources been materialized? How do we identify

learner champion and instructor champion of personalized learning? and promote them?)
- The human involvement/element (e.g., even though the recent development of personalized learning systems has attempted to simulate natural conversations of human beings, the challenge is an easy one to deal with, especially the social-emotional sides of human interaction. How about teaching computers how to teach? Will the hybrid/blended learning approach be better? Will the technology-assisted approach of blending teacher-directed and student inquiry be better? How do we specify the role of teachers and technology?).
- Measuring and Communicating (e.g., How do we evaluate the effectiveness of personalized learning applications/systems? Has the organization developed strategies/approaches for measuring the efficiency and effectiveness of personalized learning? Have we developed strong big data & data analytics capabilities? How about strategies/approaches for promoting gained/realized benefits? How about strategies/approaches to respond to people's question of "What is in for me" associated with adopting new things/practices?).

7. Open Educational Resources (OER)

Open educational resources (OER) are part of open solutions, which also include Open Source Software, Open Access, Open Data and Crowdsourcing Platforms (UNESCO, n.d.), and they can be viewed as "learning, teaching and research materials in any format and medium that reside in the public domain or are under copyright that have been released under an open license, that permit no-cost access, re-use, re-purpose, adaption and redistribution educational materials" (UNESCO, 2019). OER include full courses, course materials, modules, learning objects, collections and journals, teaching and learning tools (e.g., software for teaching and learning activities and content development, LMS), open textbooks, openly licensed videos, tests, software, openly published materials, online learning communities and other materials, tools, and software and resources which can facilitate open access to the required knowledge (Hylen, 2006; Wikipedia, 2023c).

OER present teachers and learners with more options and more resources, make significant contributions to achieve educational equity on the global scale, improve the standard of the whole education sector (e.g., via learning from each other), greatly enhance teaching and learning processes and activities, achieve better education quality, reduce the costs for education providers and students, encourage and facilitate knowledge sharing, and foster teaching and learning innovations. Meanwhile some concerns associated with OER include quality assurance issues, copyright and copyright awareness-related matters, technology problems caused by digital divide, available languages of OER, different attitude toward sharing learning resources for free with others (including competitors), and different practices and policies of OER as well as OER awareness at different education organizations (Hylen, 2006; Wikipedia, 2023c).

Factors such as digital technologies, international cooperation, and collaboration among all stakeholders, capacity of stakeholders to create, use, and manage OER, supportive policy, initiatives of education organizations, sustainable OER models, play important roles in the success of OER initiative, providing effective, equitable and inclusive access to OER and managing the use and sharing of OER in the long run (UNESCO, 2019).

8. Data Analytics and Learning Analytics

The combination of hyper-connectivity, large volume data, and powerful analytics, has enhanced organizational ability to understand their customers and the competition, and innovate (Xu & Gao, 2021). Data can manifest in diverse formats, spanning video, image, audio, and text/numeric data. It encompasses a range of types, incorporating conventional enterprise data (like customer and transaction details), machine-generated/sensor data (such as call records, weblogs, and inputs from smart devices), as well as social data (including content from blogs and micro-blogging platforms like Twitter) and social networks (Dijcks, 2012; Xu, 2019: 75; Xu & Quaddus, 2013: 73–75). Analyzing large volumes of data (i.e., Big Data) could create value for organizations in various perspectives: (1) providing transparency and improving efficiency via much easier access to more data across the organization; (2) bettering productivity and organizational performance through quicker, deeper and more accurate discovery, prediction and analysis; (3) achieving better segmentation with more tailored customization actions; (4) having better (automation) support in decision making; (5) improving existing products and services and developing new ones through enhanced understanding customers' needs and stronger capabilities in identifying opportunities for new products and services; (6) developing data-driven competitive advantages, and (7) giving organizations big insights on their operations and customers (Alexander, 2021; Manyika *et al.*, 2011: 5–6; Xu, 2019: 103–104).

The application of Big Data and Data Analytics in the educational context can be viewed as Learning Analytics, which focuses on using data (via collecting, processing and analyzing the collected data) to develop holistic understanding of dynamic information of learners, learning environments, teaching and learning practices, and trends and thus improves processes and systems in education (via such approaches as real-time modeling, prediction, optimization and decision-making) (Baker *et al.*, 2021; Ifenthaler, 2021; Jha *et al.*, 2019).

Learning analytics could have profound impact on students learning and education organizations: Ensuring resources are targeted at the highest impact opportunities; Improving better decision making; Fostering innovation; Facilitating personalized learning; Creating shared understanding of the education organization's successes and challenges; Gaining better reputation/ranking; Optimizing internal operations; Reducing marketing and sales costs; Improving teaching processes and practices, Realizing better understanding of students and their needs; Empowering teachers; Being in a better position to look after students' wellbeing; Improving student enrollment, retention and experience; Being able to more effectively and quickly identify at-risk students and thus apply intervention strategies; Improving students' learning outcomes and success rates; Better monitoring and engaging students; Designing better courses (Analytics Insight, 2022; Brasca *et al.*, 2022; Businesswire, 2022; Krawitz *et al.*, 2018; Rieznikova, 2022; Vijay, 2023). Meanwhile it is reported that the worldwide learning analytics in the education industry could reach $47.8 billion by 2027 (Businesswire, 2022).

In spite of the potential benefits of learning analytics, it is suggested that learning analytics has not been widely adopted among education organizations (Ifenthaler, 2021). Some tools for analyzing learning trends and behavior include: Visual data mining, Tree learning methods, Text mining, Support vector machines, Smooth inverse frequency algorithm, Sequential pattern mining, Recurrent neural networks, Probabilistic learning methods, Parallel practice swarm optimization, Outliner detection, Neural networks, Generic algorithm, Deep Q-learning algorithm, Native bayes algorithm, Fizzy logic, K-nearest neighbor, Differential sequence mining, Decision trees, Correlation mining, Content based filtering techniques, Collaborative filtering techniques, Clustering, Classifications, Bayesian networks, Bayesian knowledge tracing, Association rules mining, Ant colony optimization, Data visualization, Maximum likelihood analysis, Semantic similarity analysis, and Natural learning process as well as tools for presenting results of learning analytics including Learning analytics dashboard for advisers, Learning dashboard for insights and support, SmartKlass, Acrobatiq, Signals and Klassdata (Kabudi *et al.*, 2021; Mougiakou *et al.*, 2023).

Some factors need to be considered when education providers embark on learning analytics could be (Bienkowski *et al.*, 2012; Ifenthaler, 2021; Krawitz *et al.*, 2018; Mougiakou *et al.*, 2023; Southern, 2023; the authors' own knowledge; Xu, 2019: 103–104; Xu & Gao, 2021a; Xu & Gao, 2021):

- What do we want to achieve via educational data analytics?
- What learning processes and systems will learning analytics support? Do the recommendations and decision-making from learning analytics have an appropriate pedagogical foundation? Are we ready for data-guided learning?
- What kind of decision-making and to what extent of decision-making will be influenced by learning analytics?
- What kind of data and volume of data are required for meaningful data analytics? How do we source the required data? What is the reasonable amount of data? How do we integrate data coming from different sources and in different formats? Is our data storage safe?
- Have we developed our internal learning analytics capabilities? Do we have dedicated learning analysts?
- Do our people support the adoption of learning analytics? How about senior management? Have we developed a data-driven decision-making culture? How about data-sharing culture?
- Have we thought about ethical issues such as: Privacy; Informed consent/permission to collect and use the data; De-identification; Over-monitoring and surveillance; Excessive data collection; Over-profiling; Data quality (i.e., data accuracy, data completeness, data consistency, data freshness and data relevancy); Data sharing with third parties; Data use transparency, and Ownership of the data.
- Have we developed an information security policy and have embedded practices to safeguard our learning data? Have we been treating data legal issues seriously?

- Do we have clearly defined learning analytics roles? Do we have an effective talent management strategy for recruiting, developing, and retaining our learning analytics talent?
- Have we thought about the impact of learning analytics on external reporting and compliance? Do we have strategies to realize the impact of learning analytics and implement associated changes to the organization (e.g., in the perspectives of policies, processes, and practices)?
- Remembering that "human beings are decision-makers not the machine and the big data, they are there to support us to make better decision". Learning analytics techniques and technologies alone cannot solve learning issues and leverage identified learning opportunities and they cannot replace human data analyst and decision-makers. The solutions come from the combination of learning analytics techniques and technologies, quality data, business acumen, and knowledge and skills of data analysts and decision-makers, and others.

9. Digital Citizenship and Online Safety

While accessing digital resources and communicating and collaborating virtually is integral part of teaching and learning in the digital era, it is important that educators and students understand the meaning and perspectives of digital citizenship (e.g., how to deal with technology and humanity issues in a thoughtful and empathetic manner, know how to use technology appropriately, how to interact with others properly online, how to respect each other in the digital environments, and how to protect themselves from potential dangers & frauds in the virtual world) (USIDHR, 2022).

Some principles/suggestions of digital citizenship are (Asia Education Foundation, 2023; Davis, 2014; Fran, 2021; eSafety Australia, 2023; Raisingchildren, 2023; Wikipedia, 2023d).

- Respecting each other when you are online.
- Communicating effectively (especially when we don't see each other physically).
- Knowing how to work collaboratively online.
- Doing your part: The educators need to create a safe online environment for students with the right policies, supportive staff, processes and communities, and appropriate management of technology; on the other hand, the students have to behave lawfully online, manage their

own online activities, and look after their online reputation and online safety issues and other risks associated with their online activities.
- Taking into consideration individual, social, cultural, and global perspectives
- Educating/learning about appropriate use of digital technologies and behavior in the digital world (e.g., knowledge of digital footprint, digital literacy, information literacy, copyright issues, children online issues, online fraud, misinformation and disinformation, cyberbullying, cyberstalking, cyber security, online trolling, fake accounts and impersonation, online hate, doxing and swatting, inappropriate content, online incident reporting and resolution, freedom of speech, digital well-being).
- Understanding the importance of online protection and knowing how to protect your online reputation, safety, security, and privacy.
- Addressing the digital skills gap, which could happen even in the same education organization.

10. Summary

This chapter provides an overview of the educational landscape in the age of digital technology. The chapter explores the ways in which technology has transformed the methods of learning and teaching. It delves into the opportunities and challenges that arise as traditional educational practices intersect with digital innovations. The impact of digital tools on student engagement, personalized learning, collaborative environments, and the role of educators as facilitators of knowledge rather than just sources of information has been explored. This chapter also discusses the importance of online learning and maintaining academic integrity in navigating the vast amount of information available online. Overall, this chapter offers insights into the evolving dynamics of education and the need for educators to adapt their strategies to effectively leverage digital resources for enhanced learning outcomes.

References

Al-Azawi, R., Al-Faliti, F. & Al-Blushi, M. (2016). Educational gamification vs. game based learning: Comparative study. *International Journal of Innovation, Management and Technology*, 7(4), 131–136.

Alexander, S. (2021). Adaptive learning: How technology is breaking down barriers in education. *Forbes Technology Council*. Accessed on March 3, 2023. Available at https://www.forbes.com/sites/forbestechcouncil/2021/05/21/adaptive-learning-how-technology-is-breaking-down-barriers-in-education/?sh=25983dac126f.

Analytics Insight (2022). Data analytics at the fore-front powering learning and education. *Industry Trends*. Accessed on March 3, 2023. Available at https://www.analyticsinsight.net/data-analytics-at-the-fore-front-powering-learning-and-education/.

Andreas, H., and Ebner, M. (2007). Successful implementation of user-centered game-based learning in higher education: An example from civil engineering. *Computers and Education*, 49(3), 873–890.

Asia Education Foundation (2023). Digital citizenship. Accessed on June 21, 2023. Available at https://www.asiaeducation.edu.au/professional-learning/pathways-and-toolkits/global-collaboration/digital-citizenship.

Atif, A., Jha, M., Richards, D. & Bilgin, A.A. (2021). *Intelligent Systems and Learning Data Analytics in Online Education*. S. Caballé, S. N. Demetriadis, E. Gómez-Sánchez, P.M. Papadopoulos and A. Weinberger (eds.). Academic Press. https://www.sciencedirect.com/science/article/pii/B9780128234105000139.

Baker, R.S., Gasevic, D. and Karumbaiah, S. (2021). Four paradigms in learning analytics: Why paradigm convergence matters. *Computers and Education: Artificial Intelligence*, 2, 1–9.

Barton, E.A. & Dexter, S. (2020). Sources of teachers' self-efficacy for technology integration from formal, informal, and independent professional learning. *Educational Technology Research and Development*, 68, 89–108.

Beer, C., Clark, K. & Jones, D. (2010). Indicators of engagement. Paper presented at the curriculum, technology transformation for an unknown future. *Proceedings Ascilite*, Sydney.

Bienkowski, M., Feng, M. & Means, B. (2012). Enhancing teaching and learning through educational data mining and learning analytics: An issue brief. US Department of Education.

Biten, S.Y. (2017). Adaptive learning technologies to personalize learning environment. In *Society for Information Technology & Teacher Education International Conference*. Association for the Advancement of Computing in Education (AACE), pp. 1886–1893. https://www.learntechlib.org/primary/p/177478/.

Bond, M. & Bedenlier, S. (2019). Facilitating student engagement through educational technology: Towards a conceptual framework. *Journal of Interactive Media in Education*, 1(1), 1–14.

Brasca, C., Kaithwal, N., Kirshnan, C., Lam, M., Law, J. & Marya, V. (2022). *Using Machine Learning to Improve Student Success in Higher Education. Public & Social Sector Practice*. Brisbane: McKinsey & Company.

Briggs, S. (2014). Intelligent tutoring systems — Can they work for you. InformED, March 29, 2014. Accessed on May 18, 2023. Available at https://www.opencolleges.edu.au/informed/other/intelligent-tutoring-systems/#:~:text=Unlike%20other%20computer%2Daided%20forms,align%20with%20students'%20learning%20needs.

Bryant, J., Heitz, C., Sanghvi, S. & Wagle, D. (2020). *How Artificial Intelligence Will Impact K-12 Teachers. Public Sector of Practices & Social Sector Practice.* Brisbane: McKinsey & Company.

Businesswire (2022). The worldwide big data analytics in education industry is expected to reach $47.8 billion by 2027. *Businesswire*, March 29, 2022. Accessed on May 15, 2023. Available at https://www.businesswire.com/news/home/20220329005684/en/The-Worldwide-Big-Data-Analytics-in-Education-Industry-is-Expected-to-Reach-47.8-Billion-by-2027---ResearchAndMarkets.com.

Cabero-Almenara, J., Arancibia, M. & del Prete, A. (2019). Technical and didactic knowledge of the Moodle LMS in higher education. Beyond functional use. *Journal of New Approaches in Educational Research (NAER Journal)*, 8(1), 25–33.

Campbell, C. & Kent, P. (2010). Using interactive whiteboards in pre-service teacher education: Examples from two Australian universities. *Australasian Journal of Educational Technology*, 26(4), 447–463.

Castañeda, L. & Selwyn, N. (2018). More than tools? Making sense of the ongoing digitizations of higher education. *International Journal of Educational Technology in Higher Education*, 15(1), 1–10.

Chang, C.Y., Kuo, H.C. & Du, Z. (2023). The role of digital literacy in augmented, virtual, and mixed reality in popular science education: A review study and an educational framework development. *Virtual Reality*, 27(3), 1–19.

Chen, X., Xia, E. & Jia, W. (2020). Utilisation status and user satisfaction of online education platforms. *International Journal of Emerging Technologies in Learning (iJET)*, 15(19), 154–170.

Cheung, M.C., Lai, J.S.K. & Yip, J. (2022). Influences of smartphone and computer use on health-related quality of life of early adolescents. *International Journal of Environmental Research and Public Health*, 19(4), 2100.

Chiu, M.-S. (2020). Exploring models for increasing the effects of school information and communication technology use on learning outcomes through outside-school use and socioeconomic status mediation. *The Ecological Techno-Process. Educational Technology Research and Development*, 68, 413–436.

Coman, C., Țîru, L.G., Meseșan-Schmitz, L., Stanciu, C. & Bularca, M.C. (2020). Online teaching and learning in higher education during the coronavirus pandemic. *Students' Perspective. Sustainability (Switzerland)*, 12(24), 1–22.

Davis, V. (2014). What your students really need to know about digital citizenship. George Lucas Educational Foundation, October 24, 2014. Accessed on March 12, 2023. Available at https://www.edutopia.org/blog/digital-citizenship-need-to-know-vicki-davis.

Dijcks, J.P. (2012). Big data for the enterprise. An Oracle White Paper, January 2012, Oracle Corporation, USA. eSafety Australia 2023, eSafety Education. Accessed on July 25, 2023. Available at https://www.esafety.gov.au/educators.

Dewi, F. (2014). Edmodo: A social learning platform for blended learning class in higher education. *Research in Education Technology: Pedagogy and Technology Journal.* SEAMEO-SEAMOLEC, XI/No.2/2014.

Downes, S. (2010). Places to go: Connectivism & connective knowledge. *Innovate: Journal of Online Education*, 5(1), 1–6.

Fran, F. (2021). What is digital citizenship: A guide for teachers. *Future Learn*, September 3. Accessed on February 26, 2023. Available at https://www.futurelearn.com/info/blog/what-is-digital-citizenship-teacher-guide.

Haleem, A., Javaid, M., Qadri, M.A. & Suman, R. (2022). Understanding the role of digital technologies in education: A review. *Sustainable Operations and Computers*, 3, 275–285.

Hamilton, D., McKechnie, J., Edgerton, E. *et al.* (2021). Immersive virtual reality as a pedagogical tool in education: A systematic literature review of quantitative learning outcomes and experimental design. *Journal of Computers in Education*, 8, 1–32.

Hannfin, M.J. & Land, S.M. (2000). Technology and student-centered learning in higher education: Issues and practices, *Journal of Computing in Higher Education Fall*, 12(1), 3–30.

Haskari, F.A. (2012). *Modules for Using Moodle (Modular Object-Oriented Dynamic Learning Environment).* Palembang: Sriwijaya University.

Hasselbring, T.S. & Glaser, C.H.W. (2000). Use of computer technology to help students with special needs. *The Future of Children*, 10(2), 102–122.

Heo, B., Yun, S., Han, D., Chun, S., Choe, J. & Oh, S.J. (2021). Rethinking spatial dimensions of vision transformers. In *Proceedings of the IEEE/CVF International Conference on Computer Vision*, pp. 11936–11945.

Huang, O.H.L. (2022). Integrating MOOCs in formal education: To unveil EFL university students' self-learning in terms of English proficiency and intercultural communicative competence. *International Education Studies*, 15(3), 2022.

Hylen, J. (2006). Open educational resources: Opportunities and challenges. OECD's Center for Educational Research and Innovation, January 2006.

Ifenthaler, D. (2021). Learning analytics for school and system management, OECD Digital Education Outlook 2021. Accessed on May 20, 2023. Available at https://www.oecd-ilibrary.org/education/oecd-digital-education-outlook-2021_d535b828-en.

Oinas-Kukkonen, H., Karppinen, P. & Kekkonen, M. (2021). 5G and 6G broadband cellular network technologies as enablers of new avenues for behavioral influence with examples from reduced rural–urban digital divide. *Urban Science*, 5, 60.

Iqbal, M.Z., Mangina, E. & Campbell, A.G. (2022). Current challenges and future research directions in augmented reality for education. *Multimodal Technologies and Interaction*, 6(9), 75.

Irwanto, I., Wahyudiati, D., Saputro, A.D. & Lukman, I.R. (2023). Massive open online courses (MOOCs) in higher education: A bibliometric analysis (2012–2022). *International Journal of Information and Education Technology*, 13(2), 223–231.

Jansen, D. & Schuwer, R. (2015). Institutional MOOC strategies in Europe: Status report based on a mapping survey conducted in October–December 2014. EADTU. Available at https://www.surfspace.nl/media/bijlagen/artikel-1763-22974efd1d43f52aa98e0ba04f14c9f3.pdf.

Januszewski, A. & Molenda, M. (2017). *Educational Technology: A Definition with Commentary, Sponsored by the Definitions and Terminology Committee Association for Educational Communications and Technology*. Abingdon: Routledge.

Jha, M., Jha, S., Thakur, S. & Xu, J. (2022). Student engagement and learning through digital educational technology. In *2022 IEEE Asia-Pacific Conference on Computer Science and Data Engineering (CSDE), Gold Coast, Australia*, pp. 1–6.

Jha, M., Makhija, A., Richards, D. & Bilgin, A. (2023). Work-in-progress — Game-based assessments for programming. *Immersive Learning Research — Academic*, 1(1), 44–50.

Jha, M., Howah, K., Wibowo, S., Cowling, M., Soon, L. & Jha, S. (2020). Designing a virtual reality simulation to teach elements of network routing. In *2020 6th International Conference of the Immersive Learning Research Network (iLRN)*, San Luis Obispo, CA, pp. 279–282.

Jha, M., Jha, S., Cowling, M., Clark, D. & Picton, J. (2019). A proposal for enhancing students' evaluations through an adaptive and progressive digital feedback system. 2019: *ASCILITE 2019 Conference Proceedings: Personalised Learning. Diverse Goals. One Heart*, pp. 458–463.

Jha, M., Jha, S. & O'Brien, L. (2019). Re-engineering higher education teaching and learning business processes for big data analytics. In Abramowicz, W. & Corchuelo, R. (eds.), *Business Information Systems. BIS 2019. Lecture Notes in Business Information Processing*, 354. Springer, Cham.

Johnson, L., Adams Becker, S., Cummins, M., Freeman, A., Ifenthaler, D. & Vardaxis, N. (2013). Technology outlook for Australian tertiary education 2013–2018: An NMC horizon project regional analysis. *The New Media*

Consortium, 2013. Accessed on August 22, 2023) https://files.eric.ed.gov/fulltext/ED559378.pdf.

Kabudi, T., Pappas, I. & Olsen, D. H. (2021). AI-enabled adaptive learning systems: A systematic mapping of the literature. *Computers and Education: Artificial Intelligence*, 2, 1–12.

Krawitz, M., Law, J. & Litman, S. (2018). How higher-education institutions can transform themselves using advanced analytics, Public & Social Sector, August 2018, *McKinsey & Company*.

Kaware, S.S. & Sain, S.K. (2015). ICT Application in education: An overview. *International Journal of Multidisciplinary Approach & Studies*, 2(1), 25–32.

Ke, F. (2008). Alternative goal structures for computer game-based learning. *International Journal of Computer-Supported Collaborative Learning*, 3, 429–445.

King, D.L. & Case, C.J. (2014). E-cheating: Incidence and trends among college students. *Issues Information System*, 15(I), 20–27.

Kintu, M.J., Zhu, C. & Kagambe, E. (2017). Blended learning effectiveness: The relationship between student characteristics, design features and outcomes. *International Journal of Educational Technology in Higher Education*, 14, 7.

König, L. (2021). Podcasts in higher education: Teacher enthusiasm increases students' excitement, interest, enjoyment, and learning motivation. *Educational Studies*, 47(5), 627–630.

Lin, W.C., Ho, J.Y. Lai, C.H. & Jong, B.S. (2014). Mobile gamebased learning to inspire students learning motivation. In *Proceedings of 2014 International Conference on Information Science, Electronics and Electrical Engineering, ISEEE 2014*, 2, 810–813.

Liu, C., Zou, D., Chen, X., Xie, H. & Chan, W.H. (2021). A bibliometric review on latent topics and trends of the empirical MOOC literature (2008–2019). *Asia Pacific Education Review*, 22(3), 515–534.

Makhija, A., Jha, M., Richards, D. & Bilgin, A. (2023). Using feedback to support learning statistics in higher education within a game-based learning environment. *Immersive Learning Research — Academic*, 1(1), 123–129.

Mathrani, A., Han, B., Mathrani, S. & Jha M. (2021). Interpreting academic integrity transgressions among learning communities. *International Journal of Educational Integrity*, 17(1), 5.

Matinmikko-Blue, M., Aalto, S., Asghar, M.I., Berndt, H., Chen, Y., Dixit, S., Jurva, R., Karppinen, P., Kekkonen, M. & Kinnula, M. (eds.) (2023). White Paper on 6G drivers and the UN SDGs; 6G research visions, No. 2. University of Oulu, Oulu, Finland, 2020. Accessed on August 12, 2023. Available online http://urn.fi/urn:isbn:9789526226699.

Moeller, B. & Reitzes, T. (2011). Integrating technology with student-centered learning. Education Development Center, Inc. (EDC). Quincy, MA: Nellie Mae Education Foundation.

Mollenkamp, D. (2022). Popular K-12 tool edmodo shuts down. *Edsurge News*. Accessed on August 23, 2023. Available at https://www.edsurge.com/news/2022-08-16-popular-k-12-tool-edmodo-shuts-down.

Moore, J.C. (2005). A synthesis of Sloan-C effective practices. *Journal of Asynchronous Learning Networks*, 9(3), 5–73.

Mougiakou, S., Vinatsella, D., Sampson, D., Papamitsiou, Z., Giannakos, M. & Ifenthaler, D. (2023). *Educational Data Analysis for Teachers and School Leaders, Advances in Analytics for Learning and Teaching*. Berlin: Springer.

Mousrshed, M., Krawitz, M. & Dorn, E. (2017). *How to Improve Student Educational Outcomes: New Insights From Data Analytics*. Brisbane: McKinsey& Company.

Microsoft (2020). *The Class of 2030 and Life Ready Learning: The Technology Imperative*. Redmond: Microsoft.

Molenaar, I. (2021). Personalized learning: Towards hybrid human-AI learning technologies. OECD Digital Education Outlook 2021. Accessed on April 15, 2023. Available at https://www.oecd-ilibrary.org/education/oecd-digital-education-outlook-2021_2cc25e37-en.

Moreno-Ger, P., Burgos, D., Martínez-Ortiz, I., Sierra, J.L. & Fer-nández-Manjón, B. (2008). Educational game design for online education. *Computers in Human Behaviour*, 24(6), 2530–2540.

Makruf, I., Rifa'i, A.A. & Triana, Y. (2022). Moodle-based online learning management in higher education. *International Journal of Instruction*, 15(1), 135–152.

Nadi-Ravandi, S. & Batooli, Z. (2022). Gamification in education: A scientometric, content and co-occurrence analysis of systematic review and meta-analysis articles. *Education and Information Technologies*, 27(7), 10207–10238.

Nash, S. S. & Rice, W. (2018). *Moodle 3 E-Learning Course Development*, 4th edn. Birmingham: Packt Publishing.

Ng, S.F., Hassan, N.S.I.C., Mohammad Nor, H. & Abdul Malek, N.A. (2017). The relationship between smartphone use and academic performance: A case of students in a Malyasian Tertiary Institution. *Malaysian Online Journal of Educational Technology*, 5(4), 58–70.

Norberg, A. (2017). From blended learning to learning onlife: ICTs, time and access in higher education. Doctoral dissertation, Umeå University.

Okoye, K., Hussein, H., Arrona-Palacios, A. et al. (2023). Impact of digital technologies upon teaching and learning in higher education in Latin America: An outlook on the reach, barriers, and bottlenecks. *Education and Information Technologies*, 28, 2291–2360.

Poushter, J. (2016). *Smartphone Ownership and Internet Usage Continues to Climb in Emerging Economies*. Washington, DC: Pew Research Center. Available at http://www.pewglobal.org/2016/02/22/smartphone-ownership-andinternet-usage-continues-to-climb-in-emerging-economies/.

Pappas, C. (2020) *Gen Z Training: How to Create Exceptional Personalized Learning Experiences for the Next Generation Employees*. E-Learning Industry.

Polito, G. & Temperini, M. (2021). A gamified web-based system for computer programming learning. *Computers and Education: Artificial Intelligence*, 2, 1–13.

Ross, B. & Gage, K. (2006). Global perspectives on blended learning: Insight from WebCT and our customers in higher education. In Bonk, C.J. and Graham, C.R. (eds.), *Handbook of Blended Learning: Global Perspectives, Local Designs*. San Francisco, CA: Pfeiffer, pp. 155–168.

Rice, M. (2003). Information and communication technologies and the global digital divide: Technology transfer, development, and least developing countries. *Comparative Technology Transfer and Society*, 1(1), 72–88.

Raisingchildern (2023). Digital citizenship: Teens being responsible, June 2, 2023. Accessed on July 3, 2023. Available at https://raisingchildren.net.au/pre-teens/entertainment-technology/digital-life/digital-citizenship.

Rawson, G. Sarakatsannis, J. & Scott, D. (2016). *How to Scale Personalized Learning, Social Sector*. Brisbane: McKinsey & Company.

Rieznikova, A. (2022). Is data analytics and data analytic trends important in reshaping the EdTech industry. eLearning Industry, March 19, 2022. Accessed on April 20, 2023. Available at https://elearningindustry.com/is-data-analytics-and-data-analytic-trends-important-reshaping-edtech-industry#:~:text=Data%20analytics%20can%20also%20help,and%20how%20to%20market%20them.

Sezgin, S. & Sevim Cirak, N. (2021). The role of MOOCs in engineering education: An exploratory systematic review of peer-reviewed literature. *Computer Applications in Engineering Education*, 29(4), 950–968.

Shabiralyani, G., Hasan, K.S., Hamad, N. & Iqbal, N. (2015). Impact of visual aids in enhancing the learning process case research: District Dera Ghazi Khan. *Journal of Education and Practice*, 6(19), 226–233.

Simanullang, N.H.S. & Rajagukguk, J. (2020). Learning management system (LMS) based on Moodle to improve students learning activity. *Journal of Physics: Conference Series*, 1462, 012067.

Singh, V. & Thurman, A. (2019). How many ways can we define online learning? A systematic literature review of definitions of online learning (1988–2018). *American Journal of Distance Education*, 33(4), 289–306.

Smith, A. & Anderson, M. (2016). *Online Shopping and E-Commerce*. Washington, DC: Pew Research Center. Available at http://www.pewinternet.org/2016/12/19/online-shopping-and-e-commerce/.

Small, G. (2022). 10 adaptive learning platforms. Accessed on June 28, 2023. Available at https://www.edapp.com/blog/adaptive-learning-platforms/.

Southern, B. (2023). I have worked as a data analyst at companies like amazon for 20 years. using ChatGPT for data analytics is a risky move — AI can't do the work we do. *Yahoo Finance*, June 20, 2023. Accessed on July 24, 2023. Available at https://finance.yahoo.com/news/ive-worked-data-analyst-companies-090001056.html?guce_referrer=aHR0cHM6Ly93d3cuZ29vZ2xlLmNvbS8&guce_referrer_sig=AQAAAH4Qp3ogLG7tJ2gPL9wqP7Oj67-_M1SveU_9a31C7vT2nUid8XmVj9p8tVft2DFsAHfOCKh4bBMoe1XPBamSebLiUcrg6CXSkpTi48kFQtnkK-aiSXo1R3hffevoctmC4S5do5ZcBAehB-ftb_NvLVQLnTa5nJu5mwPWxLPJ1Cia.

Spice, B. (2020). New AI enables teachers to rapidly develop intelligent tutoring systems. Carnegie Mellon University, May 6, 2020. Accessed on July 20, 2023. Available at https://www.cmu.edu/news/stories/archives/2020/may/intelligent-tutors.html#:~:text=Using%20a%20new%20method%20that,computer%20if%20it%20responds%20incorrectly.

TEQSA (2023). What is academic integrity. Accessed on August 24, 2023. Available at https://www.teqsa.gov.au/students/understanding-academic-integrity/what-academic-integrity.

Tolman, S. (2017). Academic dishonesty in online courses: Considerations for graduate preparatory programs in higher education. *College Student Jobs*, 51, 579–584.

Tong, D.H., Uyen, B.H. & Ngan, L.K. (2022). The effectiveness of blended learning on students' academic achievement, self-study skills and learning attitudes: A quasi-experiment study in teaching the conventions for coordinates in the plane. *Science Direct, Heylion*, 8(12), 1–15.

Universities Australia (2017). Academic integrity best practice principles. Available at https://www.universitiesaustralia.edu.au/wp-content/uploads/2019/06/UA-Academic-Integrity-BestPractice-Principles.pdf.

Vuorikari, R., Punie, Y., Gomez, S., Van Den Brande, G., et al. (2016). *DigComp 2.0: The Digital Competence Framework for Citizens*. Update phase 1: The conceptual reference model. Technical report, JRC-Seville site.

Watson, G., and & Sottile, J. (2010). Cheating in the digital age: Do students cheat more in online courses? *Online J. Distance Learn. Adm.* 13 (1). Available at: http://www.westga.edu/~distance/ojdla/spring131/watson131.html.

Wekerle, C., *et al.* (2022). Using digital technology to promote higher education learning: The importance of different learning activities and their relations to learning outcomes. *Journal of Research on Technology in Education*, 54(1), 1–17.

Tang, C., Mao, S., Naumann, S.E. & Xing, Z. (2022). Improving student creativity through digital technology products: A literature review. *Thinking Skills and Creativity*, 44, 101032.

Tondeur, J., Scherer, R., Siddiq, F. & Baran, E. (2020). Enhancing pre-service teachers' technological pedagogical content knowledge (TPACK): A mixed-method study. *Educational Technology Research and Development*, 68, 319–343.

Torbet, A. (2022). Adaptive Learning in Practice, eLearning Industry, December 9, 2022. Accessed on May 20, 2023. Available at https://elearningindustry.com/adaptive-learning-in-practice.

UNESCO (2014). Global Citizenship Education: Preparing Learners for the Challenges of the 21st century. UNESCO Digital Library. Accessed on July 24, 2023. Available at https://unesdoc.unesco.org/ark:/48223/pf0000227729.

UNESCO (2021). Global education coalition. Accessed 18 July 2023. Available at https://en.unesco.org/covid19/educationresponse/globalcoalition.

United Nations (1948). Statement on human rights. UNESCO and OER In Action 25 July 2023. Available at https://www.unesco.org/en/open-educational-resources/oer-action.

UNESCO (2019). Recommendation on open educational resources (OER). Accessed on July 20, 2023. Available at https://www.unesco.org/en/legal-affairs/recommendation-open-educational-resources-oer.

USIDHR (2022). What is digital citizenship and why is important? USIDHR, May 26, 2022. Accessed on June 18, 2023. Available at https://usidhr.org/what-is-digital-citizenship-and-why-is-it-important/.

Vallée, A., Blacher, J., Cariou, A. & Sorbets, E. (2020). Blended learning compared to traditional learning in medical education: Systematic review and meta-analysis. *Journal of Medical Internet Research, 22*(8), e16504.

van der Vorst, T. & Jelicic, N. (2019). Artificial intelligence in education: Can AI bring the full potential of personalized learning to education? *30th European Conference of the International Telecommunications Society (ITS): "Towards a Connected and Automated Society"*, Helsinki, Finland, 16–19 June, 2019.

Vijay, N. (2023). Unlocking new possibilities with data analytics in the education sector. *Times of India*, February 25. Accessed on March 10, 2023. Available at: https://timesofindia.indiatimes.com/blogs/voices/unlocking-new-possibilities-with-data-analytics-in-the-education-sector/.

Wills, S., Devonshire, E., Leigh, E., Rosser, E., Shepherd, J. & Vincent, A. (2007). Encouraging role-based online learning environments. Accessed on August 22, 2023. Available at https://ro.uow.edu.au/asdpapers/67/

Wang, H., Tlili, A., Huang, R., Cai, Z., Li, M., Cheng, Z., Yang, D., Li, M. & Zhu, X. (2022). Examining the applications of intelligent tutoring systems in real educational contexts: A systematic literature review from the social experiment perspective. *Education and Information Technologies, 28*, 9113–9148.

Wikipedia (2023a). Intelligent tutoring systems, 22 July 2023. Accessed on July 23, 2023. Available at https://en.wikipedia.org/wiki/Intelligent_tutoring_system#:~:text=The%20Domain%20model,The%20User%20interface%20model.

Wikipedia (2023b). Adaptive learning, 21 July 2023. Accessed on July 23, 2023. Available at https://en.wikipedia.org/wiki/Adaptive_learning.

Wikipedia (2023c). Open educational resources, 24 July 2023. Accessed on July 25, 2023. Available at https://en.wikipedia.org/wiki/Open_educational_resources.

Wikipedia (2023d). Digital citizen, July 7, 2023. Accessed on July 18, 2023. Available at https://en.wikipedia.org/wiki/Open_educational_resources.

Xie, H., Lui, J.C.S. & Towsley, D. (2016). Design and analysis of incentive and reputation mechanisms for online crowdsourcing systems. *ACM Journals*, 1(3): 1–27.

Xu, J. & Quaddus, M. (2013). *Managing Information Systems: Ten Essential Topics*. Berlin: Springer & Atlantis Press.

Xu, J. (2014). *Managing Digital Enterprise: Ten Essential Topics*. Berlin: Springer & Atlantis Press.

Xu, J. (2019). *Essential Topics of Managing Information Systems*. Singapore: World Scientific.

Xu, J. & Gao. X. (2021). E-business enabling technologies and building capacities. In Xu, J. & X. Gao (eds.), *E-Business in the 21st Century: Essential Topics & Studies*. Singapore: World Scientific, pp. 29–62.

Young Entrepreneur Council (2023). How to develop a personalized learning strategy for your workforce. Forbes, February 8, 2023. Accessed on March 20, 2023. Available at https://www.forbes.com/sites/theyec/2023/02/08/how-to-develop-a-personalized-learning-strategy-for-your-workforce/?sh=3e3469253871.

Zhu, M., Sari, A.R. & Lee, M.M. (2020). A comprehensive systematic review of MOOC research: Research techniques, topics, and trends from 2009 to 2019. *Educational Technology Research and Development*, 68, 1685–1710.

Chapter 3

ChatGPT and Higher Education

Jun Xu, Graeme Salter, and Yuxi Lan

King's Own Institute, Australia

Abstract

This chapter presents the background of ChatGPT, discusses the benefits it can provide to higher education, points out its limitations and concerns and issues, and looks at strategies and success factors for the successful implementation of ChatGPT in the higher education organizations.

Keywords: ChatGPT, Higher education, Benefits, Limitations, Implementation, Success factors.

1. Introduction

ChatGPT (GPT stands for Generative Pre-trained Transformer) is an AI system developed by OpenAI and is built on a large language model (also called large-scale language model) (with 175 billion parameters or more), which is a type of generative AI system and can generate responses/content to questions in text (Hulick, 2023; OpenAI, 2023; Rouse, 2023). It is trained with huge amounts of data in various formats (e.g., texts and images, structure data and unstructured data, labeled data and unlabeled data) from various sources (e.g., information on the Internet; published information in the public domains; digitized books and academic journals; information made available for use by researchers and governments;

ChatGPT users' feedback and their use history and patterns) via AI models (e.g., machine learning, unsupervised learning, semi-supervised learning, supervised learning, deep learning, reinforcement learning) (Chui et al., 2022; Rouse, 2023; the authors' own knowledge). It basically goes through a process of firstly unsupervised learning by AI systems >> improving based on human feedback or intervention >> AI systems learning again >> improving again based on human feedback or intervention >> and so on, and high-quality feedback is critical to the process. The current free version of ChatGPT is ChatGPT 3.5 (version 3.5), and ChatGPT-4 (version 4.0) is available for fees (i.e., $20 per month) or for free via Microsoft Bing Chat. It is suggested that ChatGPT-4 could be smarter and more accurate and able to handle longer prompts, it could offer great reliability, faster access to new versions of tools, and it could also take both text and image inputs (Kunerth, 2023; Liu, 2023; UNSECO, 2023; Vaughan-Nicolas, 2023). Some competitors of ChatGPT could include Google's Bard, Facebook's Blender, and Baidu's ERNIE Bot.

Some people question whether we should use AI applications/systems (including ChatGPT) in the first place and suggest that we could stop ChatGPT just like we did to genetic cloning (Serrels, 2023), in addition, technology entrepreneurs and leaders like Elon Musk, Steve Wozniak, and others signed an open letter calling for a 6-month pause on AI development (Kahn, 2023). However, we should not avoid or ban ChatGPT (and other generative AI applications), we need to embrace new technology. Blocking ChatGPT will not stop students from accessing ChatGPT on other networks/computers since there are many other AI generators and they will continue to increase (impossible to block them all); the question is not about whether we should use it or not, but rather how to use it safely, effectively, and appropriately (Kirk, 2023; the authors' own knowledge).

2. Benefits

ChatGPT could assist higher education providers in many perspectives. Table 1 presents some ChatGPT's benefits to higher education, such benefits are discussed from the following perspectives: Streamlined and Personalized Teaching and Learning, Enhancing Classroom Teaching, Augmenting teachers' Ability and Allowing them to focus on

Table 1: ChatGPT benefits to higher education.

Benefits	Comments/Notes
Streamlined and Personalized Teaching and Learning	ChatGPT could provide assistance in areas such as course plan preparation, quiz question development, ideas for assessment items, marking rubric development, development of personalized learning content, instant feedback for writing, individualized content and responses, explanation of complex issues, research development, critique and evaluation of presented information. Appendix 1 presents some sample curriculum and teaching resources generated using ChatGPT 3.5.
Enhancing Classroom Teaching	ChatGPT could be powerful classroom teaching aids, make teaching more interesting and interactive (e.g., via facilitating role-playing and debating about content generated by ChatGPT).
Augmenting teachers' Ability and Allowing them to focus on Value-Added Services/Areas	Teachers could spend more time on value-added services (e.g., personalized mentoring, getting human's caring and emotional intelligence) while ChatGPT could assist in other areas (e.g., course planner, content development, grading).
Providing students with Support Given the Current Teachers' Shortages Around the World	ChatGPT could provide assistance to students where there are not enough teachers around.
A Reminder of Continuous Improvement	ChatGPT is a reminder that we cannot keep on doing the old thing again and again. For example, if the assessments are making cheating easy (via ChatGPT and other AI applications and systems), then we need to redesign the assessments and put proper design processes and mechanisms in place (A good example is Flinders University's process for designing assessment for artificial intelligence and academic integrity).
Allowing More Focus on Teaching and Learning	ChatGPT could help us change a system focusing on marking/grading and spending not enough time on teaching and learning.

(*Continued*)

Table 1: (*Continued*)

Benefits	Comments/Notes
Making Us to Review Our Education Systems	New digital technologies such as ChatGPT could lead us to think questions such as: What are the roles of students? What are the roles of teachers? What are the roles of technology? What are the roles of curriculum? What are the roles of assessment? What are the roles of the government? and so on.
Developing Students' Research Skills	Digital tools such as Google's Search Engine, Wikipedia, and ChatGPT could allow students to access huge amounts of information and provide assistance in areas such as research design (e.g., generating ideas and suggesting data sources), data collection (e.g., searching the databases and translating materials in other languages), data analysis, (e.g., coding data, suggesting topics/themes for analysis) and writing up (e.g., improving writing, translating writing); but the key questions are how to do search effectively, how to ask right questions, what keywords and prompts to use, and what to make the results of searches and inquiries.
Developing Students' Future Employability	Being able to use digital tools such as ChatGPT effectively is part of the demanded future skills and will prepare students for future employment. We cannot use the old tools to deal with the future.
Providing Better Support to Students	ChatGPT could provide support to students who have language barriers or cannot access adequate learning resources, and ChatGPT also could act as a personal tutor, study buddy, co-designer, motivator, and dynamic assessor for students.

Sources: Abecina, 2023; Arasa, 2023; Confino, 2023; Entrepreneur Staff, 2023; Flinders University, 2023; Hall *et al.*, 2022; Heaven, 2023; Hulick, 2023; Javaid *et al.*, 2023; Liu *et al.*, 2023; Monash University, 2023; NSW, Department of Education, 2023; OpenAI, 2023; Pappas, 2023b; Rim, 2023; Sanghvi & Westhoff, 2022; Smith, 2023; Rose, 2023; Serrels, 2023; the authors' own knowledge; UNESCO, 2023; UNESCO, 2023b; University of Waterloo, 2023; Wilichowski & Cobo, 2023.

Value-Added Services/Areas, A Reminder of Continuous Improvement, Allowing More Focus on Teaching and Learning, Making Us to Review Our Education Systems, Developing Students' Research Skills, Developing Students' Future Employability, and Providing Better Support to Students.

3. Limitations and Concerns and Issues

Like any other new technologies and digital tools, ChatGPT does have certain limitations and causes some concerns and issues. Table 2 discusses some of them, including Academic Integrity Issues, Ethical Concerns, Privacy Concerns, Security Issues, Transparency & Explain-ability,

Table 2: ChatGPT limitations, concerns and issues related to higher education.

Limitations and Concerns	Comments/Notes
Academic Integrity Issues	Currently, there are no reliable tools to detect AI-generated content (including Turnitin's AI detector, OpenAI's AI detector). The identification and confirmation of AI-generated content probably need more input from teachers than AI detection tools (e.g., taking a holistic approach and looking at different perspectives). Education is critical, students have to be educated about what is expected, what is allowed (or not allowed), and the potential consequences of using AI-generated content without proper permission and acknowledgment. Similarly teaching staff needs to have a good understanding of AI as well. On a related note, in many cases, the references produced by ChatGPT are not correct.
Ethical Concerns	As with many new technologies (if not every new technology), ChatGPT does present ethical challenges. Students may not have required ethical understanding when dealing with information from various (unknown) sources provided by ChatGPT. Furthermore, it is reported that ChatGPT is not governed by ethical principles and cannot tell what is right and what is wrong.
Privacy Concerns	It is not certain how ChatGPT manages the collected user data. Meanwhile, its privacy policy states its collected data can be shared with third parties. In addition, even after the account is deleted, the user's data in the system could still be kept. Furthermore, it could be argued that whether there is a legal basis for ChatGPT to collect and store personal data as its training data.

(Continued)

Table 2: (*Continued*)

Limitations and Concerns	Comments/Notes
Security Issues	It is not clear whether ChatGPT's security standards for model selection and training are appropriate and updated. It is also difficult to predict the consequences of misusing or mishandling data by ChatGPT.
Transparency & Explain-ability	There is a lack of clear explanation of how the data are selected and how the model is developed by ChatGPT.
Accuracy	While ChatGPT could provide reasonable even amazing responses, they cannot be relied on to be accurate consistently (for reasons such as currency, completeness, complexity, depth, and accuracy of the training data; effective filters for catching inappropriate content). On a related note, the training data for ChatGPT was cut off in September 2021, to be more accurate and updated, ChatGPT needs more updated data from the real world. It could become more challenging for ChatGPT to get data on the Internet and from public domains if content owners/providers refuse to provide access to ChatGPT's web crawlers (e.g., the recent block by The New York Times). Meanwhile, the users of ChatGPT have to be aware that it is their responsibility to verify the responses/information generated by ChatGPT.
Intellectual Property Issues	It is difficult to tell whether ChatGPT has plagiarized a source based on training data or whether ChatGPT has obtained permission to use the copyrighted material.
Safety and Performance	It is hard to predict the safety and performance consequences if the AI models are not properly implemented and tested.
Harmful and Biased Content	OpenAI acknowledges that its model is "generally skewed towards content that reflects Western perspectives and people". Its biases also could come from unintended biases in the collected data, in data selection and in the model. Even though OpenAI has constantly reviewed user feedback and used human to eliminate bias in the training data, given the massive amount of data involved, it is really a challenging task.

Table 2: (*Continued*)

Limitations and Concerns	Comments/Notes
Assessment Issues	The users of ChatGPT have to acknowledge the use of it. On the other hand, it is not appropriate to make decisions about a student's assessment tasks based on the information generated by ChatGPT, which is subject to biases and inaccuracies.
Overreliance on ChatGPT and Loss of Independent Thinking Abilities and Curiosity	Students could simply accept the answers generated by ChatGPT without understanding, thinking, asking questions, checking, and verifying. In addition, students could increasingly develop laziness and are not willing to spend time on studying, put in required work, and go through the required learning journey (i.e., they are willing to take shortcuts).
Equity and Access	Given the current economic and digital divides, students in less-developed countries and regions could be disadvantaged and have no equitable access to ChatGPT and other AI applications, which in turn has a negative impact on their future employment opportunities, which demand skills of using digital tools like ChatGPT. Such things also could happen in some countries and regions due to government regulations, censorship, and other restrictions.
Third-Party Risks	Clear understanding of risks of ChatGPT's using external providers for data collection, model selection or deployment environments needs to be established.
Lack of Common Sense, Social Connection and Human's Caring	ChatGPT does not have human-level common sense and social connection, and it also does not have caring to its users (e.g., the welfare checking on students done by their teachers).
Limited Knowledge	Its training data was cut off in September 2021. Also in many cases, after a few attempts of similar prompts, ChatGPT will provide (almost) identical answers. Consequently, ChatGPT could not be a substitute for our knowledge and understanding, it could be a tool that complements and augments our knowledge and understanding.

(*Continued*)

Table 2: (*Continued*)

Limitations and Concerns	Comments/Notes
Lack of Critical Thinking Ability	ChatGPT could be really good at summarizing information, but not so in analyzing the information from a holistic approach.
Commercialization Concerns	ChatGPT-4 charges a subscription fee ($20 per month). OpenAI is a private firm, if it focuses on making a profit in the future, then collecting and using the data for commercial purposes could be a big issue.
Disrupting Learning Experiences	The use of ChatGPT may disrupt the teacher's teaching plan and teaching process and the student's learning journey/experiences as students may view or take ChatGPT as a shortcut.

Sources: Buehler *et al.*, 2021; Chin, 2023; Chui and Marr, 2023; Davis, 2023; Davis and Peters, 2023; Entrepreneur Staff, 2023; Gordon, 2023; Fowler, 2023; Heaven, 2023; Hulick, 2023; Roberts and Yee, 2022; OpenAI, 2023, Rouse, 2023; Northern Illinois University, 2023; NSW Department of Education, 2023; Rose, 2023; Serrels, 2023; Tech Business News, 2023; the authors' knowledge; UNESCO, 2023; University of Rhode Island, 2023; Woodland, 2023.

Accuracy, Intellectual Property Issues, Safety and Performance, Harmful and Biased Content, Assessment Issues., Overreliance on ChatGPT and Loss of Independent Thinking Abilities and Curiosity, Equity and Access, Third-Party Risks, Lack of Common Sense, Social Connection and Human's Caring, Limited Knowledge, Lack of Critical Thinking Ability, Commercialization Concerns, and Disrupting Learning Experiences.

4. Implementation Strategies/Success Factors

To be successful with ChatGPT implementation, higher education providers need to develop sound strategies and pay attention to a number of success factors, including Developing Institution-wide Policies on ChatGPT and other AI Systems/Applications, Using ChatGPT but not Trusting It, Connecting the Use of ChatGPT with Learning Outcomes, Establishment of A Cross-Functional Team, Putting both Human and Technology in the Center of Teaching and Learning, Raising Awareness and Providing Education & Training to both Teachers and Students, Seeking External Support, Having Faith in the Future, Using Digital Watermark, Communicating Effectively, Reviewing Curriculum and

Teaching Practices & Arrangements, Redesigning Curriculum and Teaching Practices & Arrangements, Including ChatGPT in the Teaching, Safeguarding Personal Information, Establishing the Process Flow Defining Circumstances Where ChatGPT is Safe to Use, Setting Up Peer Support and Mentoring, Conducting AI Audit Regularly, and Allocating Sufficient Resources and Providing Additional Support. Table 3 presents a discussion of strategies and success factors required for the successful implementation of ChatGPT in higher education organizations.

Table 3: ChatGPT implementation strategies/success factors for higher education providers.

Strategies/Success Factors	Comments/Notes
Developing Institution-wide Policies on ChatGPT and other AI Systems/ Applications	The impacts of ChatGPT and the institutions' responses should be reflected in the higher education provider's policies and procedures (e.g., Business Plans, Academic Integrity Policies and Procedures, Curriculum Review and Assessment Design Policies and Procedures; Privacy and Security Policies; Relevant Management Policies). Such policies and procedures should be re-visited and updated regularly, given the fast pace of AI technology advancement.
Using ChatGPT but not Trusting It	Students and Teachers should be encouraged to use ChatGPT for enhancing learning and teaching but they should not trust it as a result of the issues & concerns associated with it.
Connecting the Use of ChatGPT with Learning Outcomes	Connecting the use of ChatGPT with course learning outcomes and subject learning outcomes will help students understand how ChatGPT could support their learning and provide clear expectations for them.
Establishment of A Cross-Functional Team	A cross-department team needs to be established, including Senior Academic Leaders, Academic Integrity Officers, Learning Designers, Course Leaders, Teacher Representatives, Student Representatives, Library, and Learning Resources Specialists.
Putting both Human and Technology in the Center of Teaching and Learning	Human plus technology is the future of teaching and learning, we have to embrace this direction and prepare ourselves for it.

(Continued)

Table 3: (*Continued*)

Strategies/Success Factors	Comments/Notes
Raising Awareness and Providing Education and Training to both Teachers and Students	Both teachers and students need to be aware and have an understanding of the potential positive and negative impacts of ChatGPT and other new digital technologies. Training on how to use it safely, effectively, and appropriately for both teachers and students needs to be provided. And the institution needs to constantly remind its students of the purposes of learning and the importance of equipping them with skills without resorting or cheating or any other sorts of shortcuts. In addition, students and teachers need to understand that ChatGPT is only one of the many tools that can assist our teaching and learning.
Seeking External Support	The higher education organizations would need support from the government in the form of regulation, training, and financial support to leverage the advantages and opportunities of new technology (such as ChatGPT). Meanwhile, higher education providers need to work closely with their external partners to facilitate open communication and collaboration on adopting ChatGPT in higher education.
Having Faith in the Future	We have progressed through four industrial revolutions and have survived many new things (e.g., calculator, search engine, Wikipedia, third-party assessment services). It is logical and confident for us to say that we will be fine with ChatGPT and any other new digital tools.
Using Digital Watermark	Measures such as digital watermarks being developed by OpenAI could assist in deterring academic misconduct.
Communicating Effectively	Clearly spelling out the expectations of using ChatGPT (e.g., whether it is allowed and not allowed?) and providing clear guidelines on using ChatGPT (and AI applications) (e.g., how to use the information generated by ChatGPT, how to cite in the text, and how to include in the reference list).

Table 3: (*Continued*)

Strategies/Success Factors	Comments/Notes
Reviewing Curriculum and Teaching Practices and Arrangements	Higher education providers/institutions need to work on curriculum design and teaching practice and arrangements (e.g., reviewing and revising course learning course outcomes, subject learning outcomes, teaching content, assessment tasks, in-class activities, delivery modes, research methods, referencing practices, academic integrity considerations, teaching evaluation, subject and course development by taking into consideration opportunities, limitations, and risks of AI) and incorporate content such as AI literacy, AI ethics, and Core AI competency and skills. Assignments could be also designed in the formats of presentations, videos, journaling, podcasts, portfolios, group projects, interviews, and role-playing.
Redesigning Curriculum and Teaching Practices and Arrangements	Real world and practice (especially recent news or development or personal experiences) focused on assessment items, work-integrated learning projects, evidence-based projects, in-class face-to-face tasks, and invigilated exams or oral exams, interactive activities (e.g., oral presentation, visual mapping, role-playing), personalized assignments and projects as well as requirements of asking students to demonstrate the process and evidence of research and assignment writing and connecting course content, class discussion, and real-life experience and synthesizing information from various sources, would be effective in dealing with AI-enabled academic misconducts. On a related note, will open book and open exams be appealing to you?
Including ChatGPT in the Teaching	ChatGPT should be taught as part of the curriculum (e.g., including in the teaching content of first-year common units, in the assessment design, in the class activities; allowing students to use ChatGPT for ideas or discussion/critique; and always asking them to check and verify information generated by ChatGPT and trace back to the original sources).

(*Continued*)

Table 3: (*Continued*)

Strategies/Success Factors	Comments/Notes
Safeguarding Personal Information	Making sure personal information is managed properly, and measures of deidentification of personal information are in place to protect users' privacy and comply with relevant regulations.
Establishing the Process Flow Defining Circumstances Where ChatGPT is Safe to Use	As part of laying out clear expectations for using ChatGPT, a process flow defining circumstances where ChatGPT is safe to use should be developed.
Setting Up Peer Support and Mentoring	Peer support and supporting communities would greatly facilitate better learning and knowledge sharing by using ChatGPT.
Conducting AI Audit Regularly	An AI audit would help higher education organizations understand the current AI situations, make decisions on AI tools and approaches, and monitor AI performance and equity.
Allocating Sufficient Resources and Providing Additional Support	Access to ChatGPT (and other AI applications) should be provided to academic staff and students by higher education providers. Additional academic and student service support should be put in place to support students' learning and use of ChatGPT (and other AI applications), and similarly additional professional development should be provided to academic and professional staff to facilitate their learning and use of ChatGPT (and other AI applications).

Sources: Abecina (2023); Abramson (2023); Arasa (2023); Australian Academic Integrity Network (2023); Australian National University (2023); Cotton *et al.* (2023); Chui *et al.* (2022); Craig (2021); Entrepreneur Staff (2023); Fowler (2023); Gallagher (2023); Gleason (2022); Gecker and The Associated Press (2023); Heaven (2023); Hulick (2023); Monash University (2023); NSW Department of Education (2023); OpenAI (2023); Sadler (2023); Serrels (2023); Smith (2023); Tech Business News (2023); TEQSA (2023); the authors' own knowledge); UNESCO (2023); University of Washington (2023); University of Illinois Urbana-Champaign (2023); University of Waterloo (2023); Webster (2023); Wilichowski and Cobo (2023); Woodland (2023).

5. Focusing on Detecting Content Generated by ChatGPT and Other AI Tools

Most, if not all, higher education institutions are concerned about the use of ChatGPT and other Artificial Intelligence (AI) tools by their students.

In order to demonstrate the reasons for this concern, the following introduction was generated by ChatGPT 3.5 to the query — "Why are higher education institutions concerned about the use of ChatGPT by their students?"

The following responses were produced by ChatGPT 3.5:

"Higher education institutions may be concerned about the use of ChatGPT by their students for several reasons, including:

Cheating: One of the main concerns is that students may use ChatGPT or similar AI technology to cheat on exams or assignments. For example, a student could use a chatbot to generate answers to exam questions or to complete homework assignments without truly understanding the material.

Lack of critical thinking: By relying on ChatGPT to provide answers to their questions, students may not be developing their own critical thinking and problem-solving skills.

Misinformation: Another concern is that ChatGPT and other AI technology may not always provide accurate or reliable information, especially when it comes to complex or specialized topics. If students rely on chatbots for answers to their questions, they may be exposed to misinformation or incorrect information that could harm their education and future careers.

Reduced human interaction: The use of ChatGPT may also reduce the amount of human interaction and connection that students have with their professors, advisors, and peers, which can be an important part of the higher education experience.

It's important for higher education institutions to be aware of these concerns and to educate their students about the limitations and potential risks of using AI technology, while also exploring ways to use it in a responsible and effective way that supports, rather than replaces, human interaction and critical thinking."

The above is the exact wording provided by ChatGPT. While this was detected as AI generated by one checker (AICheatCheck), another checker (GPTZero) wasn't so sure (refer to Appendix 2). Many people are using the AI output as a draft which they adapt in their own voice. As a simple example, the term professors in the above text could be changed to lecturers. Such changes make it more difficult for checking software to detect that the text was not written by a human. The use of AI is not restricted to essays. As an example, ChatGPT can generate computer code. While AICheatCheck initially identified the code as written by AI it failed to do so when the explanatory text was removed (see Appendix 3). ChatGPT can also be used to deliberately fool ChatGPT checkers (an example is provided in Appendix 4). Meanwhile, while the attention has been focused on detecting content generated by ChatGPT, the content generated by other AI applications could be overlooked (Appendix 5 presents an example).

It can be said that AI Detection tools may or may not be reliable or effective, they themselves alone will not be accurate and effective in detecting AI-generated content. We need to look at other measures as well, including:

- Asking students to show their drafts, the process of their work, research evidence, and collected literature.
- Checking the references of the paper (in many cases, the references provided/generated by ChatGPT are not correct).
- Paying attention to content to see whether it addresses specific assignment requirements and whether it reflects the student's usual writing style and knowledge level.
- Interviewing students with suspected AI-related Academic Misconduct cases and ask them to elaborate and explain the content in their report.
- The best way of dealing with AI-led Academic Misconduct is education (e.g., educating students about the positive and negative impacts of ChatGPT discussed earlier in this chapter) and prevention (e.g., redesigning assessment items and reviewing teaching practices discussed previously in this chapter).

References

Abecina, M. (2023). How ChatGPT will impact the future of education. McCrindle. Accessed on April 6, 2023. Available at https://mccrindle.com.au/article/how-chatgpt-will-impact-the-future-of-education/.

Abramson (2023). How to use ChatGPT as a learning tool. American Psychological Association, June 1, 2023. Accessed on July 10, 2023. Available at https://www.apa.org/monitor/2023/06/chatgpt-learning-tool.

Arasa, D. (2023). Schools struggle to ChatGPT — Proof exams and assignments. Inquiry Technology, August 15, 2023. Accessed on August 19, 2023. Available at https://technology.inquirer.net/126972/schools-chatgpt-proof-exams-and-assignments#:~:text=ChatGPT%20disrupted%20the%20global%20education,it%20may%20not%20be%20enough.

Australian Academic Integrity Network (AAIN) (2023). AAIN generative artificial guidelines. AAIN Generative AI Working Group, March 2023, pp. 1–6.

Australian National University (2023). ChatGPT and other generative AI tools: What ANU academics need to know. ANU Center for Learning and Teaching, pp. 1–6.

Buehler, K., Dooley, R., Grennan, L. & Singla, A. (2021). Getting to know and manage your biggest ai risks. McKinsey Analytics, May 2021, pp. 1–6.

Chin, L.K. (2023). A new buzz in teaching and learning: ChatGPT. eLearning Industry, February 5, 2023. Accessed on May 15, 2023. Available at https://elearningindustry.com/a-new-buzz-in-teaching-and-learning-chatgpt.

Chui, M., Roberts, R. & Yee, L. (2022). Generative AI is here: How tools like ChatGPT could change your business. Quantum Black, AI by McKinsey, pp. 1–5.

Confino, P. (2023). IBM CEO who plans hiring pause for 7,800 jobs due to A.I. says the world will be worse without the technology. Otherwise quality of life is going to fall. Yahoo Finance, 23 August 2023. Accessed on August 24, 2023. Available at https://finance.yahoo.com/news/ibm-ceo-plans-hiring-pause-183135825.html.

Cotton, D. R., Cotton, P.A. & Reubin Shipway, J. (2023). Chatting and cheating: Ensuring academic integrity in the era of ChatGPT. *Innovations in Education and Teaching International*, May 13, 2023, pp. 1–12.

Craig, R. (2021). How higher Ed can prepare students for today's digital jobs. *Harvard Business Review*, November 24, 2021. Accessed on January 20, 2023. Available at https://hbr.org/2021/11/how-higher-ed-can-prepare-students-for-todays-digital-jobs.

Davis, W. (2023). Sarah Silverman is suing OpenAI and meta for copyright infringement. *The Verge*, July 10, 2023. Accessed on August 20, 2023. Available at https://www.theverge.com/2023/7/9/23788741/sarah-silverman-openai-meta-chatgpt-llama-copyright-infringement-chatbots-artificial-intelligence-ai.

Davis, W. & Peters. J. (2023). The *New York Times* blocks OpenAI's web crawler. *The Verge*, August 22, 2023. Accessed on August 23, 2023. Available at: https://www.theverge.com/2023/8/21/23840705/new-york-times-openai-web-crawler-ai-gpt.

Entrepreneur Staff (2023). How will ChatGPT change education and teaching entrepreneur, February 16, 2023. Accessed on 28 April 2023. Available at https://www.entrepreneur.com/science-technology/how-will-chatgpt-change-education-and-teaching/445018.

Flinders University (2023). Good practice guide-Designing assessment for artificial intelligence and academic integrity. Assessed on August 20, 2023. Available at https://staff.flinders.edu.au/learning-teaching/good-practice-guides/good-practice-guide-designing-assessment-for-artificial-intell.

Fowler, G.A. (2023). We tested a new ChatGPT detector for teachers. It flagged an innocent student. *The Washington Post*, April 3, 2023. Accessed on June 15, 2023. Available at https://www.washingtonpost.com/technology/2023/04/01/chatgpt-cheating-detection-turnitin/.

Gallagher, S. (2023). Investing in talent with work-integrated learning. Forbes, 28 August 2023. Accessed on August 29, 2023. Available at https://www.forbes.com/sites/stand-together/2023/08/28/investing-in-talent-with-work-integrated-learning/?sh=5340c3cc782f.

Gecker, J. & The Associated Press (2023). College professor are in "full-on crisis mode" as they catch one "ChatGPT plagiarist" after another. Fortune, August 11, 2023. Accessed on 14 August 2023. Available at https://fortune.com/2023/08/10/chatpgt-cheating-plagarism-college-professors-full-on-crisis-mode/.

Gleason, N. (2022). ChatGPT and the rise of AI writers: How should higher education respond. *Times Higher Education*, December 9, 2022. Accessed on March 20, 2023. Available at https://www.timeshighereducation.com/campus/chatgpt-and-rise-ai-writers-how-should-higher-education-respond.

Gordon, C. (2023). How are educators reacting to ChatGPT? Forbes, April 30, 2023. Accessed on May 15, 2023. Available at https://www.forbes.com/sites/cindygordon/2023/04/30/how-are-educators-reacting-to-chat-gpt/?sh=586815d22f1c.

Hall, S., Schmautzer, D., Tmiri, S. & Tschupp, R. (2022). Reimagining higher education in MENAP. Education Practices, May 2022, McKinsey & Company, pp. 1–8.

Heaven, W.D. (2023). ChatGPT is going to change education, not destroy it. *MIT Technology Review*, April 6, 2023. Accessed on June 16, 2023. Available at https://www.technologyreview.com/2023/04/06/1071059/chatgpt-change-not-destroy-education-openai/.

Helsper, A. (2023). How to use ChatGPT in the classroom — Without abandoning critical thinking. Ball State University, May 31, 2023. Accessed on July 16, 2023. Available at https://blogs.bsu.edu/teaching-innovation/2023/05/31/how-use-chatgpt-classroom-without-abandoning-critical-thinking/.

Hulik, K. (2023). How ChatGPT and similar AI will disrupt education. *Science News*, April 12, 2023. Accessed on May 18, 2023. Available at https://www.sciencenews.org/article/chatgpt-ai-artificial-intelligence-education-cheating-accuracy.

Javaid, M., Haleem, A., Singh, R.P., Khan, S.M. & Khan, I.H. (2023). Unlocking the opportunities through ChatGPT tool towards ameliorating the education system. *BenchCouncil Transactions on Benchmarks, Standards and Evaluations*, 3, 1–12.

Kahn, J. (2023). Elon Musk and Apple Cofounder Steve Wozniak among over 1,100 who signed open letter calling for 6-month ban creating powerful AI.

Fortune, 29 March (2023). Accessed on May 10, 2023. Available at https://fortune.com/2023/03/29/elon-musk-apple-steve-wozniak-over-1100-sign-open-letter-6-month-ban-creating-powerful-ai/.

Kirk, T. (2023). ChatGPT (we need to talk). University of Cambridge, 5 April 2023. Accessed on July 10, 2023. Available at https://news.educ.cam.ac.uk/230403-chat-gpt-education.

Kunerth, V. (2023). ChatGPT-3.5 vs ChatGPT-4: A comparison of the latest GPT-based Chatbot web apps. LinkedIn, May 5, 2023. Accessed on August 20, 2023. Available at https://www.linkedin.com/pulse/chatgpt-35-vs-chatgpt-4-comparison-latest-gpt-based-chatbot-kunerth#:~:text=%5B3%5D%20%22Compared%20to%20GPT,restrictions%20GPT%2D4%20does.%22.

Liu, D. (2023). GPT-4 is here. What is it, and what does this mean for higher education. Teaching@Sydney, March 16, 2023. Accessed on May 10, 2023. Available at https://educational-innovation.sydney.edu.au/teaching@sydney/gpt-4-is-here-what-is-it-and-what-does-this-mean-for-higher-education/#:~:text=Perhaps%20most%20strikingly%2C%20GPT%2D4,scores%20in%20the%20bottom%20decile.

Liu, D., Ho, E., Weeks, R. & Bridgeman, A. (2023). How AI can be used meaningfully by teachers and students in 2023. Teaching@ Sydney, January 20, 2023. Accessed on May 16, 2023. Available at https://educational-innovation.sydney.edu.au/teaching@sydney/how-ai-can-be-used-meaningfully-by-teachers-and-students-in-2023/#:~:text=Get%20creative%20and%20incorporate%20AI%20into%20assessment&text=For%20example%2C%20AI%20could%20generate,commentary%20supported%20with%20key%20references.

Marr, B. (2023). The top 10 limitations of ChatGPT. Forbes, 3 March 2023. Accessed on July 10, 2023. Available at https://www.forbes.com/sites/bernardmarr/2023/03/03/the-top-10-limitations-of-chatgpt/?sh=4b7f15288f35.

Monash University (2023). Using artificial intelligence-student academic success. Accessed on August 10, 2023. Available at https://www.monash.edu/student-academic-success/build-digital-capabilities/create-online/using-artificial-intelligence.

Northen Illinois University (2023). ChatGPT and education. Center for Innovative Teaching and Learning. Accessed on August 18, 2023. Available at https://www.niu.edu/citl/resources/guides/chatgpt-and-education.shtml.

NSW Department of Education (2023). Guidelines regarding use of generative AI (ChatGPT), June 1, 2023. Available at https://education.nsw.gov.au/teaching-and-learning/education-for-a-changing-world/guidelines-regarding-use-of-generative-ai-chatgpt.

OpenAI (2023). Educator consideration for ChatGPT. Accessed on 17 August 2023. Available at https://platform.openai.com/docs/chatgpt-education.

Pappas, C. (2023). *The Ultimate AI in eLearning Guide*. E-Learning Industry, pp. 1–31.

Rim, C. (2023). Don't ban ChatGPT — Teach students how to use it. Forbes, March 3, 2023. Accessed on May 15, 2023. Available at https://www.forbes.com/sites/christopherrim/2023/05/03/dont-ban-chatgpt-teach-students-how-to-use-it/?sh=2828559245b0.

Rose, J. (2023). ChatGPT as a teaching tool, not a cheating tool. Times Higher Education, February 21, 2023. Accessed on July 10, 2023. Available at https://www.timeshighereducation.com/campus/chatgpt-teaching-tool-not-cheating-tool.

Rouse, M. (2023). "ChatGPT", August 16, 2023. Techopedia. Accessed on August 20, 2023. Available at: https://www.techopedia.com/definition/34933/chatgpt.

Sadler, K. (2023). What to do about ChatGPT. *AEU News*, April 3, 2023. Accessed on June 10, 2023. Available at https://news.aeuvic.asn.au/what-to-do-about-chatgpt/#:~:text=Be%20transparent%20and%20outline%20expectations,the%20technology%20can%20fall%20short.

Sanghvi, S. & Westhoff, M. (2022). Five trends to watch in the edtech industry. Education Practice, November 2022, pp. 1–5.

Serrels, M. (2023). AI's teachable moment: How ChatGPT is transforming the classroom. CNET, June 30, 2023. Accessed on July 20, 2023. Available at https://www.cnet.com/tech/features/ais-teachable-moment-how-chatgpt-is-transforming-the-classroom/.

Smith, G. (2023). Use ChatGPT to enhance learning experiences and revolutionize your classroom. THIS IS GRAEME, May 10, 2023. Accessed on May 26, 2023. Available at https://thisisgraeme.me/2023/05/10/use-chat-gpt-to-enhance-learning/#:~:text=Use%20Chat%20GPT%20to%20generate%20ideas%20for%20rubrics%20to%20assess,and%20accessible%20for%20all%20students.

Tech Business News (2023). ChatGPT may lead to the downfall of education and critical thinking, July 7, 2023, Editorial Desk. Accessed on August 10, 2023. Available at https://www.techbusinessnews.com.au/blog/chatgpt-may-lead-to-the-downfall-of-eduction-and-critical-thinking/#:~:text=Reduces%20creativity%3A%20Chat%20GPT%20generates,learn%20and%20understand%20the%20material.

TEQSA (2023). Artificial intelligence: Advice for students, April 4, 2023. Accessed on June 20, 2023. Available at https://www.teqsa.gov.au/students/artificial-intelligence-advice-students.

UNESCO (2023). ChatGPT and Artificial Intelligence in Higher Education. Paris: UNESCO, pp. 1–14.

UNESCO (2023b). World Teachers' Day: UNESCO sounds the alarm on the global teacher shortages crisis. Accessed on August 20, 2023. Available at https://www.unesco.org/en/articles/world-teachers-day-unesco-sounds-alarm-global-teacher-shortage-crisis#:~:text=New%20UNESCO%20figures%20unveiled%20for,set%20by%20the%202030%20Agenda.

University of Rhode Island (2023). Teaching with ChatGPT and other AI. Office of the Advancement of Teaching and Learning. Accessed on 20 August 2023. Available at https://web.uri.edu/atl/teaching-with-chatgpt-other-ai/.

University of Illinois Urbana-Champaign (2023). ChatGPT: Artificial intelligence implications in teaching and learning. Center for Innovation on Teaching & Learning, Center for Innovation in Teaching & Learning, June 13, 2023. Accessed on July 10, 2023. Available at https://citl.illinois.edu/citl-101/instructional-spaces-technologies/teaching-with-technology/chatgpt.

University of Washington (2023). ChatGPT and other AI-based tools. Center for Teaching and Learning. Assessed on March 10, 2023. Available at https://teaching.washington.edu/course-design/chatgpt/.

University of Waterloo (2023). Frequently asked questions: ChatGPT and generative AI in teaching and learning at the University of Waterloo. Accessed on August 20, 2023. Available at https://uwaterloo.ca/associate-vice-president-academic/frequently-asked-questions-chatgpt-and-generative-ai.

Vaughan-Nicholas, S. (2023). GPT-3.5 vs GPT-4: Is ChatGPT plus worth is subscription fee? ZDNET, June 12, 2023. Accessed on August 20, 2023. Available at https://www.zdnet.com/article/gpt-3-5-vs-gpt-4-is-chatgpt-plus-worth-its-subscription-fee/.

Webster, B. (2023). How can we teach students to use ChatGPT responsibly. teaching assistant, June 1, 2023. Assessed on July 20, 2023. Available at https://www.teachingaissistant.co.uk/blog/n8lp0kmnlt515z7n7dmxnvxw2exfdd#:~:text=By%20modelling%20responsible%20and%20critical,to%20get%20into%20good%20habits.

Wilichowski, T. & Cobo, C. (2023). How to use ChatGPT to support teaches: The good, the bad, and the ugly. World Bank, May 2, 2023. Accessed on June 10, 2023. Available at https://blogs.worldbank.org/education/how-use-chatgpt-support-teachers-good-bad-and-ugly.

Woodland, T. (2023). ChatGPT for improving medical education: Proceed with caution. *Mayo Clinic Proceedings: Digital Health*, 3, pp. 294–295.

Appendix 1: Sample Curriculum and Teaching Resources Generated by ChatGPT 3.5

ChatGPT can also be used by teachers to generate curriculum and teaching material as shown in the following example of a fictitious subject "Introduction to Web Design". The ethical implications of this are for future discussion. Subject outline and learning outcomes (note — the learning outcomes would need some human input to be acceptable (e.g., how do you measure "understand" or "learn"). Nevertheless, the generated content provides a useful starting point). In addition, you can re-generate a response if you are not happy with the initial response.

> Write a subject overview and 5 learning outcomes for a university subject on Introduction to Web Design

> Subject Overview: Introduction to Web Design
>
> This subject provides students with an introduction to the principles and techniques of web design. Students will learn about the key concepts and technologies involved in creating effective and engaging websites, including user experience design, graphic design, HTML, CSS, and JavaScript. The subject will cover the design process from start to finish, including the development of user personas, wireframing, prototyping, and testing. Throughout the course, students will be encouraged to experiment and take creative risks, while also developing a solid understanding of the technical skills required to create and maintain websites.
>
> Learning Outcomes:
>
> 1. Understand the basics of user experience design and how it affects the success of a website
> 2. Develop skills in graphic design and be able to create visually appealing layouts for websites
> 3. Acquire proficiency in HTML and CSS, and understand how to use these technologies to create structured and stylized web pages
> 4. Learn the basics of JavaScript and be able to implement simple interactivity into websites
> 5. Develop the ability to plan, design, and prototype a functional website using a design process that incorporates user-centered design principles and best practices for web design.

Weekly Topics (Week 12 Is Set Aside Revision)

Write an 11 week topic schedule for a university subject on Introduction to Web Design

Week 1: Introduction to Web Design and User Experience Design

- Overview of the course and learning outcomes
- Introduction to user experience design and its importance in web design
- Understanding user personas and user journeys

Week 2: Graphic Design Fundamentals

- Overview of graphic design principles and techniques
- Design elements and principles, including color, typography, and composition
- Creating visual design mockups for websites

Week 3: HTML and CSS Basics

- Introduction to HTML and its role in web design
- Basic HTML tags and attributes
- Introduction to CSS and its role in styling web pages

Week 4: HTML and CSS Advanced

- Advanced HTML tags and attributes
- CSS selectors, properties, and values
- Understanding the box model in CSS and its impact on layout

Week 5: JavaScript Basics

- Introduction to JavaScript and its role in web design
- Basic JavaScript syntax and data types
- Manipulating HTML elements using JavaScript

Week 6: JavaScript Advanced

- Advanced JavaScript concepts, including functions, loops, and conditional statements
- Understanding the Document Object Model (DOM) and how to interact with it using JavaScript
- Creating interactive elements for websites using JavaScript

Week 7: Responsive Web Design

- Understanding the importance of responsive design for modern websites
- Using CSS media queries and responsive design techniques to create websites that adapt to different screen sizes and devices

Week 8: Website Prototyping

- Overview of the website design and development process
- Creating wireframes and prototypes to communicate design ideas and test functionality
- Using tools and resources to create effective prototypes

Week 9: Testing and Debugging

- Understanding the importance of testing and debugging in the web design process
- Debugging HTML, CSS, and JavaScript errors and resolving compatibility issues
- Testing websites for functionality and user experience

Week 10: Website Deployment and Maintenance

- Overview of website deployment and hosting options
- Understanding the importance of website maintenance and security
- Deploying websites to a live server and updating content and functionality over time

Week 11: Final Project

- Bringing together all of the concepts and techniques covered in the course
- Working in groups or individually to design, build, and deploy a functional website
- Presenting final projects and reflecting on the course and personal learning outcomes.

Multiple Choice Exam Questions

> Write a multiple choice exam with 5 questions for a university subject on Introduction to Web Design

1. What is the purpose of user experience design in web design?
   A) To create visually appealing websites
   B) To make websites easy to use and accessible to all users
   C) To make websites fast and efficient to load
   D) To make websites compatible with all browsers
2. What are the basic design elements and principles in graphic design for websites?
   A) Color, typography, and composition
   B) Speed, functionality, and compatibility
   C) User experience, accessibility, and security
   D) User journeys, wireframes, and prototypes
3. What is the role of HTML in web design?
   A) To provide structure and content for web pages
   B) To add interactivity and animation to web pages
   C) To style and visually enhance web pages
   D) To manage website hosting and deployment
4. What is the purpose of CSS in web design?
   A) To add interactivity and animation to web pages
   B) To manage website hosting and deployment
   C) To style and visually enhance web pages
   D) To provide structure and content for web pages
5. What is the role of JavaScript in web design?
   A) To style and visually enhance web pages
   B) To provide structure and content for web pages
   C) To add interactivity and animation to web pages
   D) To manage website hosting and deployment

Answers:

1. B
2. A
3. A
4. C
5. C

Exam Questions That Are Not Multiple Choice

Write an exam with 5 questions for a university subject on Introduction to Web Design. The questions must not be multiple choice.

1. Define the purpose of user experience design in web design and give an example of a website that demonstrates good user experience design. (10 points)
2. Discuss the basic design elements and principles in graphic design for websites, including color, typography, and composition. Provide an example of a website that effectively uses these elements and principles. (15 points)
3. Explain the role of HTML in web design and provide an example of a web page that demonstrates a well-structured HTML document. (10 points)
4. Describe the purpose of CSS in web design and provide an example of a web page that effectively uses CSS for styling and visual enhancement. (10 points)
5. Discuss the role of JavaScript in web design and provide an example of an interactive element on a website that was created using JavaScript. (15 points)

Bonus Question: (10 points)
Analyze the design and user experience of your favorite website and provide suggestions for how it could be improved. Be specific and include examples of design elements and principles that could be applied to enhance the user experience.

Case Study Assignment

Write a case study assignment for a university subject on Introduction to Web Design

Case Study Assignment: Website Redesign for a Local Non-Profit Organization

Objective:
To design and develop a new website for a local non-profit organization that improves their online presence and helps them achieve their goals.

Instructions:

1. Choose a local non-profit organization and research their mission, goals, and target audience.
2. Analyze the current website of the organization and identify areas for improvement in terms of user experience, design, and functionality.
3. Create a user persona and user journey to understand the needs and behaviors of the target audience.
4. Design and develop a new website for the organization, incorporating principles of graphic design, HTML, CSS, and JavaScript.
5. Use responsive design techniques to ensure that the website is accessible and usable on a variety of devices and screen sizes.
6. Test the website for functionality and user experience and make any necessary revisions.
7. Deploy the website to a live server and submit the final project, including all design mockups, code, and a brief report detailing the design process and decision-making.

Grading Rubric:

- Design Process (25%)
- Graphic Design (25%)
- HTML, CSS, and JavaScript Implementation (25%)
- User Experience and Functionality (20%)
- Deployment and Maintenance (5%)

Notes:

- The website should be designed with accessibility and inclusive design principles in mind.
- The website should be developed using best practices for HTML, CSS, and JavaScript and be free of any major errors or compatibility issues.
- The website should be visually appealing, intuitive to use, and effective in communicating the mission and goals of the organization.

Appendix 2: Test of AI Generated Content by GPTZero and AICheatCheck

ChatGPT content discussed in Section 5 in this chapter was correctly identified as AI generated by AICheatCheck, but not another checker GPTZero.

AICheatCheck

Our tool offers a reliable solution for professors, teachers and universities to verify the authenticity of student's work. By analyzing sentence structure and readability, our tool accurately detects the presence of a GPT model, ensuring academic integrity in the age of AI.

Below you can find a demo of our AICheatCheck model. We are currently working with universities on integrating with Learning Management Systems such as Canvas and other internal systems.

Interested in using our tool within your university or company? Send us an e-mail at contact@aicheatcheck.com.

> Higher education institutions may be concerned about the use of ChatGPT by their students for several reasons, including:
>
> Cheating: One of the main concerns is that students may use ChatGPT or similar AI technology to cheat on exams or assignments. For example, a student could use a chatbot to generate answers to exam questions or to complete homework assignments without truly understanding the material.
>
> Lack of critical thinking: By relying on ChatGPT to provide answers to their questions, students may not be developing their own critical thinking and problem-solving skills.
>
> Misinformation: Another concern is that ChatGPT and other AI technology may not always provide accurate or reliable information, especially when it comes to complex or specialized topics. If

Please note that our system currently only works with the English language and is most accurate above 50 words.

[Check] [Clear]

100% certain the text was written by an AI

GPTZero

Humans Deserve the Truth

Try it out 👆

> Higher education institutions may be concerned about the use of ChatGPT by their students for several reasons, including:
>
> Cheating: One of the main concerns is that students may use ChatGPT or similar AI technology to cheat on exams or assignments. For example, a student could use a chatbot to generate answers to exam questions or to complete homework assignments without truly

or, choose a file to upload

CHOOSE FILE No file chosen

Accepted file types: pdf, docx, txt

✓ I agree to the **terms of service**   **GET RESULTS**

Your text may include parts written by AI

114 *Teaching and Learning in the Digital Era: Issues and Studies*

Appendix 3: AI to Develop Computer Code (and How to Fool the Checkers)

> Write a javascript program to develop random passwords

> Here's a simple program to generate random passwords in JavaScript:
>
> ```javascript
> function generatePassword(length) {
>     const characters = "abcdefghijklmnopqrstuvwxyzABCDEFGHIJKLMNOPQRSTUVWXYZ0123456789";
>     let password = "";
>     for (let i = 0; i < length; i++) {
>         password += characters.charAt(Math.floor(Math.random() * characters.length));
>     }
>     return password;
> }
>
> console.log(generatePassword(10));
> ```
>
> In this program, `generatePassword` is a function that takes in the desired length of the password as an argument. It then defines a string of characters that can be used in the password and generates a password by randomly selecting characters from this string. The for loop runs `length` times, each time adding a randomly selected character to the password string. Finally, the password string is returned as the output of the function.
>
> You can adjust the length of the password and the set of characters used by modifying the `length` argument and the `characters` string in the code.

If the explanatory text is left in, AICheatCheck correctly identifies this as being written by AI.

```
    return password;
}

console.log(generatePassword(10));
```

In this program, generatePassword is a function that takes in the desired length of the password as an argument. It then defines a string of characters that can be used in the password and generates a password by randomly selecting characters from this string. The for loop runs length times, each time adding a randomly selected character to the password string. Finally, the password string is returned as the output of the function.

You can adjust the length of the password and the set of characters used by modifying the length argument and the characters string in the code.

Please note that our system currently only works with the English language and is most accurate above 50 words.

[Check]

[Clear]

100% certain the text was written by an AI

However, if this text is removed and only the code is left then AICheatCheck suggests it was probably human generated.

```
function generatePassword(length) {
    const characters =
"abcdefghijklmnopqrstuvwxyzABCDEFGHIJKLMNOPQRSTUVWXYZ0123456789!@#$%^&*";
    let password = "";
    for (let i = 0; i < length; i++) {
        password += characters.charAt(Math.floor(Math.random() * characters.length));
    }
    return password;
}

console.log(generatePassword(10));
```

Please note that our system currently only works with the English language and is most accurate above 50 words.

[Check]

[Clear]

82% certain the text was generated by a Human

Appendix 4: Using ChatGPT to Fool ChatGPT Checkers

By asking ChatGPT to deliberately make mistakes AICheatCheck can be fooled.

> Generate 200 words on Macbeth. Your answer should include at least five spelling errors, two errors in punctuation, two further grammatical errors, and and least one error of fact.

> Macbeth is a tragedy play by William Shakesphere, written in the early 1600s. The play revolves around the titular character Macbeth, a nobleman who is propted by the prophesies of three withes to take matters into his own hands and kill King Duncan. Macbeth succeds in his plan, but is tormented by guilt and fear of being discovered. This eventually leads to a downward spiral, as Macbeth becomes more and more power hungry, commiting more and more crimes to maintain his power.
>
> One of the most famous quotes from the play is "to be, or not to be: that is the question". Macbeth is often seen as a cautionary tale about the dangers of unchecked ambition, and is one of Shakespeare's most popular works, due in no small part to its intense character development and powerful themes.
>
> Desptie its popularity, the play has been the subject of much controversy, with some critices claiming that it is overly violent and morbid, while others argue that it is a masterpiece of literature. Regardless, Macbeth remains a staple of high school curriculums and is widely performed on stages all over the world.

Macbeth is a tragedy play by William Shakesphere, written in the early 1600s. The play revolves around the titular character Macbeth, a nobleman who is propted by the prophesies of three withes to take matters into his own hands and kill King Duncan. Macbeth succeds in his plan, but is tormented by guilt and fear of being discovered. This eventually leads to a downward spiral, as Macbeth becomes more and more power hungry, commiting more and more crimes to maintain his power.

One of the most famous quotes from the play is "to be, or not to be: that is the question". Macbeth is often seen as a cautionary tale about the dangers of unchecked ambition, and is one of Shakespeare's most popular works, due in no small part to its intense character development and powerful themes.

Desptie its popularity, the play has been the subject of much controversy, with some critices claiming that it is overly violent and morbid, while others argue that it is a masterpiece of literature. Regardless,

Please note that our system currently only works with the English language and is most accurate above 50 words.

Check

Clear

100% certain the text was generated by a Human

Appendix 5: Comparison of Text Generated by ChatGPT and a Commercial Package (HelloScribe)

It may be that current checkers are focused on ChatGPT, but there are other packages using different algorithms. In this example, the same prompt was used (a story about a student from Nepal) but only the output from ChatGPT was detected as written by AI.

HelloScribe Generation

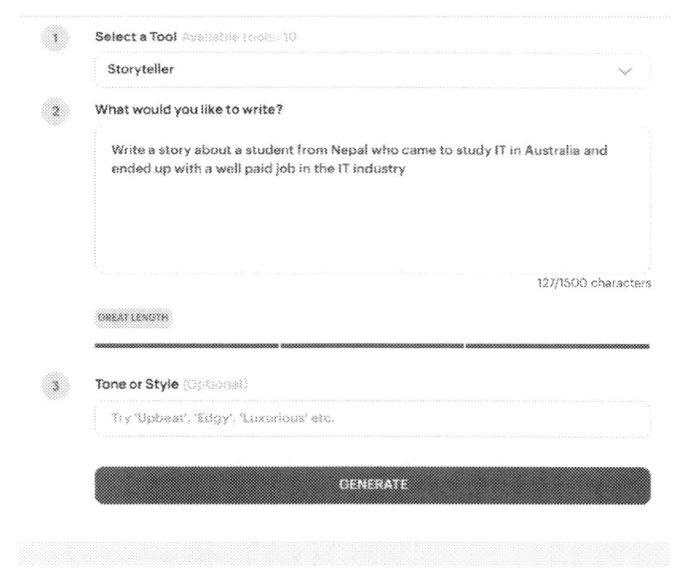

1. Select a Tool Available tools: 10

Storyteller

2. What would you like to write?

Write a story about a student from Nepal who came to study IT in Australia and ended up with a well paid job in the IT industry

127/1500 characters

GREAT LENGTH

3. Tone or Style (Optional)

Try 'Upbeat', 'Edgy', 'Luxurious' etc.

GENERATE

When Shyam arrived in Australia from Nepal, he was filled with ambition and excitement. He had come to study IT at one of the top universities in Australia, eager to use his skills to make a better life for himself.

But when he started university, Shyam found that his dreams of success felt further away than ever. The courses were far more challenging than he expected, and he often felt out of place amongst his peers.

Still, Shyam kept going. He studied hard and managed to finish his degree at the top of his class. But even then, getting a job in the IT industry seemed impossible. Until one day, a friend told him about an upcoming coding competition that offered a generous cash prize and the chance to be employed by one of the biggest IT companies in the world.

The competition was daunting, but Shyam was determined to try. He spent all of his free time practicing and working on new projects. Finally, the day of the competition arrived, and Shyam was ready. Against all odds, he won first place!

With the prize money and newfound recognition, Shyam was able to achieve his dream: a well-paid job in the IT industry. But it wasn't just money that made his success so meaningful - it was knowing that all of his hard work had paid off. Shyam could finally see how far he'd come since coming to Australia from Nepal. A brand-new future lay ahead of him.

HelloScribe Check Output

contact@aicheatcheck.com.

Still, Shyam kept going. He studied hard and managed to finish his degree at the top of his class. But even then, getting a job in the IT industry seemed impossible. Until one day, a friend told him about an upcoming coding competition that offered a generous cash prize and the chance to be employed by one of the biggest IT companies in the world.

The competition was daunting, but Shyam was determined to try. He spent all of his free time practicing and working on new projects. Finally, the day of the competition arrived, and Shyam was ready. Against all odds, he won first place!

With the prize money and newfound recognition, Shyam was able to achieve his dream: a well-paid job in the IT industry. But it wasn't just money that made his success so meaningful - it was knowing that all of his hard work had paid off. Shyam could finally see how far he'd come since coming to Australia from Nepal. A brand-new future lay ahead of him.

Please note that our system currently only works with the English language and is most accurate above 50 words.

Check

Clear

93% certain the text was generated by a Human

ChatGPT Generation

Write a story about a student from Nepal who came to study IT in Australia and ended up with a well paid job in the IT industry

---

Once upon a time, there was a young man named Raj from Nepal. He was an ambitious and hardworking student who dreamed of making a successful career in the field of Information Technology. He worked hard in his studies and eventually received a scholarship to study IT in Australia.

Raj was very excited about this opportunity and arrived in Australia with high hopes. He threw himself into his studies and worked hard to master the latest technologies. He also made new friends and became a well-respected member of the student community. Despite the many challenges he faced as an international student, Raj remained focused on his goal and was determined to succeed.

After he graduated from university, Raj began applying for IT jobs in Australia. It was a competitive market, but he persevered and eventually landed a job with a leading IT company. His hard work and dedication quickly caught the attention of his superiors, and he was promoted to a higher position within the company.

As his career progressed, Raj continued to demonstrate his skills and expertise, and he soon became one of the most sought-after IT professionals in the industry. He was offered many job offers from companies around the world, but he decided to stay in Australia, where he had found his home.

Years passed, and Raj's hard work and determination paid off. He became a successful and well-respected figure in the IT industry, earning a very high salary and enjoying a comfortable lifestyle. He never forgot his humble beginnings in Nepal and remained grateful for the opportunities that had come his way.

Raj's story is a testament to the power of hard work and determination. He came to Australia as a student, but he left as a successful IT professional with a bright future ahead of him. His journey serves as an inspiration to others who may be facing similar challenges, reminding us that anything is possible with the right mindset and a strong work ethic.

ChatGPT Check Output

As his career progressed, Raj continued to demonstrate his skills and expertise, and he soon became one of the most sought-after IT professionals in the industry. He was offered many job offers from companies around the world, but he decided to stay in Australia, where he had found his home.

Years passed, and Raj's hard work and determination paid off. He became a successful and well-respected figure in the IT industry, earning a very high salary and enjoying a comfortable lifestyle. He never forgot his humble beginnings in Nepal and remained grateful for the opportunities that had come his way.

Raj's story is a testament to the power of hard work and determination. He came to Australia as a student, but he left as a successful IT professional with a bright future ahead of him. His journey serves as an inspiration to others who may be facing similar challenges, reminding us that anything is possible with the right mindset and a strong work ethic.

Please note that our system currently only works with the English language and is most accurate above 50 words.

Check

Clear

100% certain the text was written by an AI

© 2024 World Scientific Publishing Company
https://doi.org/10.1142/9789811285622_0004

Chapter 4

Online Education: Challenges, Tools, and Emerging Trends

Sweta Thakur[*], Farzaneh Mayabadi[*], Fariza Sabrina[†], and Shaleeza Sohail[‡]

[*]*King's Own Institute, Australia*

[†]*Central Queensland University, Australia*

[‡]*University of Newcastle, Australia*

Abstract

The advancement of new technology in the education system has significantly impacted teaching and learning approaches in both online and face-to-face environments. The education systems are anticipating the future and adopting different modes of delivery for learning (e.g., online learning, face-to-face learning, hybrid learning) in simultaneous and asynchronous ways. Online education has acquired significant recognition recently due to the pandemic when the education industry underwent a transition from face-to-face to online mode as a spontaneous solution to prevail in this uncertainty. It is feasible to teach and learn from anywhere in the world at any time, with unlimited access to resources, which play a significant role in effective and efficient teaching and learning. This study provides an enhanced comprehension of online education. To upgrade the teaching and learning process many tools and resources are used in different circumstances.

This chapter elaborates on educational tools and how they can be used to enhance the quality of education. Given that it is of utmost importance to understand the current demands, this chapter provides an overview of the emerging trends in online education.

Keywords: Online education, Online learning, E-learning, COVID-19 pandemic, Tools for online education, Emerging trends.

1. Introduction

The educational system has made continuous advancements for decades. Technological development and online tools revolutionized the education system by providing new avenues for teaching and learning in both face-to-face and online environments. However, COVID-19 was a turning point for educational institutes as they had to shift from face-to-face education to online education as an immediate response to the pervasive lockdown.

Online education, simultaneous and asynchronous, is also known as eLearning, is a new educational concept using Internet technology. According to Hassenburg (2009: 1), "E-Learning covers a wide set of applications and processes, including multimedia online activities such as the web, Internet video CD-ROM, TV and radio" which facilitate self-study for students as per their convenience at their own pace (Titthasiri, 2013). As stated by Papanis (2005: 1) "the components of online/E-Learning include content delivery in multiple formats, management of the learning experience, a networked community of learners, and content developers and experts".

Even after the pandemic, online education remains prevalent as it provides an interactive learning experience and increases students' engagement. It provides students with an opportunity to access educational resources from anywhere at any time. At the same time, acknowledging different dimensions of online and face-to-face education, studies suggest that there are no remarkable differences in students' and teachers' performance in these two modes of delivery (Maware *et al.*, 2023; Peimani & Kamalipour, 2021).

Pervasiveness of online education improved the role of online tools significantly in providing high-quality education. Considering the importance of online tools in the education system, this chapter aims to shed light on the opportunities and challenges of online education, and its key platforms and tools. Moreover, to identify any gap for online delivery to enhance the learning process and experiences, emerging trends in online education are also discussed.

2. Opportunities and Challenges of Online Education

This section explores the benefits and challenges of online education from the teacher and student's perspective. Findings provided through various studies (e.g., Arkorful & Abaidoo, 2015; Hameed, 2008; Klein & Ware, 2003; Marc, 2002; Yuhanna, 2020; Zylfiu et al., 2020) are discussed in this section.

From the teacher's viewpoint, many advantages have been identified. They can effortlessly become accustomed to the technology and keep enhancing their skills. The utilization of different means of online learning also helps them to improve their teaching. It is stated that a shortage of academics, lecturers, tutors, facilitators, etc., is never a matter of concern anymore with online teaching and learning. Another aspect is its cost-effectiveness whether it is about travel or infrastructure or even if we talk about the cost of hardware, software, and Internet service that is counted as negligible and always disregarded. The teacher can have experience of teaching a small cohort to a significant number of students.

For students, the most significant fact is navigation, without even moving from your computer you can access any resources anytime anywhere. It helps to strengthen the effectiveness of knowledge as a large amount of information can be accessed without any difficulty. This mode of learning can help the learners save time and money by avoiding traveling, which is a subject of critical interest. The student also has an opportunity for comfortable and convenient communication with their instructors at any time through email, they can exchange ideas with ease and acquire consultation from an expert.

Though there are many benefits, different studies have revealed the associated challenges of online teaching and learning. The teachers have highlighted that there is a serious lack of motivation and engagement, student–student cooperation, insufficient student–teacher cooperation, learners should always be under inspection. The students could have difficulties with technologies, sometimes they may face obstruction due to heavy dependency on websites. Lack of quality control can be a major issue as the information can be accessed without any difficulty but maybe without knowledge of whether it's accurate or false.

Assessment plays a major role, and if not properly designed it can initiate a big impact on learning. For the tests/exams, because of unsupervised invigilation it is difficult to control cheating, piracy, plagiarism, and academic misconduct. These limitations can be managed and overcome effortlessly with the help of educational tools as discussed in the next section.

3. Key Tools for Online Education

Online teaching heavily depends on the use of educational tools for effective, engaging, and timely delivery of teaching material. Online teaching tools can be of four categories based on their use. In this section firstly, a brief description of each category is provided and then a detailed discussion and analysis of some recent and emerging tools for online assessment, evaluation, and feedback are provided.

3.1. *Course Management*

Learning Management Systems (LMS) are online centralized platforms where educators can create, organize, and share course content with students in a timely manner. The use of LMS like Moodle (Moodle, 2017), Blackboard (www.blackboard.com, n.d.), and Canvas (Instructure, n.d.) is very common in higher education these days irrespective of the mode of course delivery (face-to-face, online, or hybrid). These platforms play a pivotal role in modern education, but when it comes to online education, proper and effective utilization of LMS is critical to providing an engaging learning experience for online learners. LMS enables educators to organize teaching material and assessments in one digital space to simplify course management and distribution. LMS platforms are very effective for enhancing student engagement through interactive features, discussion forums, and multimedia integration. In addition, LMS provides very effective tools for tracking student progress, enabling timely interventions and tailored support. Lastly, LMS systems can promote collaboration among students by creating a virtual classroom environment that can result in productive teamwork and peer learning.

3.2. Communication and Collaboration Tools

One of the most important factors considered for online teaching is the effectiveness of communication and collaboration among students and educators. An engaging virtual classroom experience can be provided by using platforms like Zoom (Zoom, 2022), Microsoft Teams (www.microsoft.com, n.d.), and Google Meet (workspace.google.com, n.d.) that enable real-time interactions among the participants for recreating classroom ambiance in online mode. Different features of these tools like screen sharing, breakout rooms, virtual whiteboards, and file sharing gauge student understanding and maintain engagement. Collaboration can be enhanced by using messaging tools like Slack (Slack, n.d.) and Discord (Discord, 2022) by employing different discussion boards for peer learning and teamwork. Google Workspace (workspace.google.com, n.d.) and Microsoft 365 (www.microsoft.com, n.d.) provide means for collaborative document editing to facilitate real-time group work, knowledge sharing and brainstorming activities in an online environment.

3.3. Multimedia Tools and Content Creation

Online educators need to cater to diverse needs of the learners for which multimedia content can play a significant role. Podcasting and video creation tools like Audacity (Audacity, 2019) and iMovie (Apple, 2011) can help in preparing engaging audio and video content. Screen capturing tools like OBS Studio (Obsproject.com, 2012) and Loom (Loom, 2019) provide an excellent option for preparing easy-to-follow guided tutorials and software walkthroughs. VR platforms like Engage and AltspaceVR can provide an immersive learning experience for exploring complex concepts. Lecture content can be improved significantly by using interactive presentation tools like Google Slides and Prezi (Prezi, 2009) that allow embedding of multimedia content.

3.4. Online Assessment, Evaluation, and Feedback Tools

In online delivery of courses, assessment setting and evaluation is the most challenging aspect that requires careful planning and significant effort and time. Most LMS contain some features to facilitate assessment setting like question banks, randomizing questions, and answers, etc.

However, when it comes to assessment evaluation limited options are available for essay questions. Blackboard Learn (www.blackboard.com, n.d.) and Moodle plugins (Moodle, 2017) provide some functionality for automated assignment grading and feedback. Online quizzing tools like Kahoot (Kahoot!, 2019) and Quizlet (Quizlet, 2019) provide options for creating interactive quizzes where instant feedback can be provided, and feedback discussion can also be incorporated. For monitoring online exams, proctoring tools like ProctorU (ProctorU, 2018) and Proctorio (proctorio.com, n.d.) are applied to ensure exam integrity. Artificial intelligence is effectively used in Gradescope and FeedbackFruits for assessment evaluation that allows educators to set up custom rubrics for automated grading.

3.4.1. Tools for Evaluation and Feedback

Most of the assessments in higher education are criterion-referenced. This type of assessment assesses students' performance against certain criteria which have a direct relation to the unit learning outcomes. One of the challenges of criterion-referenced assessments is that they could be very time-consuming. The online tools that can be used to create and apply rubrics to students' work are beneficial to students and teachers and can enhance the quality of online pedagogy.

Two widely used LMS platforms that can be utilized for criterion-referenced assessments are Gradescope and FeedbackFruits. These digital assessment tools can be used by educators to assess students' work and provide feedback efficiently and effectively, which can have positive impacts on students' engagement and performance.

3.4.1.1. Gradescope

It is a web-based assessment tool that allows educators to create, distribute, and grade different types of assessments. Dr. Sara A. Atwood argues that this digital assessment tool helps educators provide feedback that is "prompt, equitable, flexible and formative" (2018).

Students received meaningful and formative feedback in Gradescope. In addition to their predetermined rubrics, feedback, and annotated comments can be used to provide students with an in-depth understanding of their performance.

Comments on one student's work can be used for other students, and there is no need to rewrite the comment for the same mistake. This streamlines the grading process which enhances the formative impact of feedback. Giving timely feedback to students helps them to make meaning of received feedback in relation to their response (Reif, 2008).

Rather than grading one student at a time, in Gradescope educators can mark one question at a time. This increases the consistency and fairness of grading as students lose the same marks for the same mistake (McDonald, 2016).

Gradescope is a flexible tool for educators and students. They can give and receive feedback respectively from anywhere. Multiple markers can work at the same time, and rubrics can be modified at any time and be applied to all the works graded previously. This helps with "creating a reliable real-time standard for all students" (www.turnitin.com, 2019). It is also flexible for students as it allows them to submit their assessments written on paper or online or a combination of both.

In online education, the authenticity of assessments is crucial for the students. Higher education has shifted its focus from traditional assessment, where students' knowledge of topics and theories is measured, to authentic assessments and constructive feedback to nurture lifelong skills that will help them in their lives and future careers.

3.4.1.2. FeedbackFruits

It is an online platform that provides a series of tools for online learning and student engagement. The tools it offers for authentic assessment and peer feedback include Peer Review, Group Member Evaluation, Automated Feedback, Assignment Review, Skill Review, and Self-Assessment.

- *PeerReview*: This tool helps students submit their work, receive feedback from their peers against predetermined criteria and reflect on their peers' feedback.
- *Group Member Evaluation*: This tool allows students to assess their peers' contribution to a group work assessment, based on predetermined criteria developed by their teacher.
- *Automated Feedback*: This is an AI tool that streamlines marking by automatically picking up structural, formatting, and referencing mistakes and allows teachers to focus on concepts and arguments.

- *Assignment Review*: This allows teachers to give meaningful feedback to students' work by using rubrics. This streamlines the process of marking and makes teachers' feedback more meaningful. At the same time, students can benefit from timely feedback.
- *Skill Review*: Teachers can use their rubrics to mark students' work. They can reuse the same comments and feedback for the same mistakes rather than rewriting them. It also allows interactive feedback between students and instructors by allowing students to respond to the received feedback. This "leads to a useful conversation that shows that students understand the feedback and are prepared to revise effectively" (Siegal & Gilliland, 2021: 144).
- *Self-Assessment*: This is for students to assess their own work against the criteria and rubrics developed by the teacher. Alongside improving students' critical thinking, self-assessment allows them to identify and reflect on their own strengths and weaknesses.

4. Emerging Trends in Online Education

The landscape of educational tools and technologies for online delivery is rapidly evolving, offering new and exciting opportunities to enhance learning experiences. Technologies like AI, Blockchain, AR/VR, and gamification are reshaping education by making it more accessible, engaging, and effective. As educators and institutions embrace these trends, the potential to revolutionize education and meet the needs of diverse learners becomes more tangible than ever before.

4.1. *Emerging Trends in Learning Management System (LMS)*

By using LMS effectively it is possible to address the varying requirements of higher education learners and transform students' learning experience into an interactive and student-centered process (Veluvali & Surisetti, 2022). With features such as AI, Blockchain, multimedia integration, discussion forums, and real-time assessment, LMS offers a comprehensive solution for delivering engaging online courses. This trend aligns with the growing demand for flexible, remote learning options, allowing educators to seamlessly transition from traditional classrooms to virtual environments. By incorporating emerging technologies, LMS can transform online teaching by enhancing accessibility, personalization, and the overall learning experience for both students and instructors.

Haque *et al.* (2022) present their proposed Machine Learning-based LMS Model designed to efficiently address students' problems and challenges during online classes, especially during the COVID-19 pandemic in 2019. The paper suggests that a Machine Learning-based LMS Model can effectively handle students' issues and challenges in online classes.

Rahardja *et al.* (2022) proposed a Blockchain-based Learning Management System at Raharja University. The authors emphasized that blockchain technology can enhance the traditional educational data management system model, making it easier for students to access learning materials for their lectures.

Legarde (2022) suggested that Google Classroom enables the swift and effortless completion of academic tasks and could be beneficial for faculty members when utilized as an LMS.

4.2. *AI-Powered Adaptive Learning*

Artificial Intelligence is leading the way in personalized education. AI-driven algorithms analyze learners' performance and behavior to tailor content to individual needs (Chen, 2023; St-Hilaire *et al.*, 2022). Adaptive learning platforms could adjust the difficulty and pacing of lessons, ensuring that each learner progresses at their optimal pace. This approach maximizes learning efficiency and minimizes frustration, fostering a more positive learning experience.

Dogan *et al.* (2023) argue that there is an increasing use of a wide range of artificial intelligence technologies in online distance education, and the use of these technologies could significantly improve students' learning experience.

Marappan & Bhaskaran (2022) argue that employing soft computing strategies, such as the ontology-based approach, association mining, self-organizing maps, Long Short-Term Memory (LSTM), content-based filtering etc., could be very effective in personalizing students' learning.

4.3. *Gamification for Engagement*

Gamification, an emerging trend of using game mechanisms for educational purposes, has proven to be an effective way to improve students' learning. Gamification techniques, such as leaderboards, badges, and interactive quizzes, introduce an element of competition and fun into the learning process. These elements enhance engagement and motivation, transforming the educational experience into an interactive and enjoyable journey (Kuo & Chuang, 2016; Mohamad *et al.*, 2018; Nieto-Escamez & Roldán-Tapia, 2021).

Kuo and Chuang (2016) investigated the impact of gamification on enhancing online academic dissemination. In this work, the authors designed, developed, and implemented eight-game designs and demonstrated the positive impact of gamification on the promotion of academic dissemination in an online context.

Mohamad *et al.* (2018) emphasized that using a gamification approach in education to increase student participation and interaction, improved the overall learning experience. This study delved into six distinct categories of gamification for educational purposes. The findings derived from the research indicate a predominant preference among the participants for receiving rewards like levels, avatars, and points during the learning journey.

Nieto-Escamez and Roldán-Tapia (2021) provided a concise review of using gamification as an online teaching strategy in response to the COVID-19 pandemic. The research emphasizes that the integration of gamification with traditional lectures can be a very valuable tool for enhancing online delivery.

Gordillo *et al.* (2022) investigated the effectiveness of video-based learning vs. game-based learning in online software engineering education using teacher-authored video games. The study compares these two approaches to understand their impact on student engagement and learning outcomes within the context of online education for software engineering. The findings indicated that utilizing educational video games created for game-based learning was more effective compared to video-based learning. This method exhibited superior results regarding both gaining knowledge and enhancing motivation.

4.4. *Video-Based Learning*

Video content is becoming a dominant and effective medium for students' learning in online education (Joko, 2021; Mao *et al.*, 2022). Video lectures, tutorials, and demonstrations provide visual and auditory learners with an immersive experience and are very effective in conveying complex concepts.

Sablić *et al.* (2021) provided a review of research on video-based learning (VBL) and concluded that video has been proven as an effective educational medium for disseminating information. It can create an engaging learning environment in which students can comprehensively grasp and retain knowledge.

Yee *et al.* (2020) introduced a video-based learning framework in surgery that uses videos of varying durations, aiming to improve surgeon engagement. The study explores the effectiveness of using surgical videos as a learning tool and investigates how surgeons engage with and benefit from videos of different lengths for educational purposes. The authors suggest that YouTube improved engagement and achieved good international exposure.

Pal & Patra (2021) explored university students' perception of video-based learning during the COVID-19 pandemic, utilizing the Technology Acceptance Model (TAM) and Task-Technology Fit (TTF) framework. The findings of this research, conducted on 232 students, indicate that students see video-based learning as a good match and use it in a positive way for remote education.

4.5. *Data Analytics for Personalization*

There is an emerging trend in educational institutions to utilize data analytics to gain insights into students' learning patterns and performance. By using data analytics, educators can gather information from students' interactions, performance, and preferences in online courses. These insights enable the creation of personalized learning pathways, adaptive content, and timely interventions, enhancing engagement, comprehension, and overall learning outcomes.

4.6. *Collaborative and Social Learning*

Online learning platforms are increasingly incorporating social and collaborative features, enhancing the learning experience. Collaborative learning, a pedagogical approach that unites students to deliberate on course-relevant subjects, plays a crucial role (Ng *et al.*, 2022). Discussion forums, group projects, and peer assessments facilitate meaningful interactions among learners, cultivating a sense of community and shared learning experiences.

Gupta *et al.* (2022) highlighted the significance of 3D networking and collaborative environments in the context of online education. Their study highlights the potential of these innovative technologies to enhance the virtual learning experience, offering promising avenues for the future development of interactive and engaging online educational platforms.

Kalmar *et al.* (2022) emphasized the efficacy of online collaborative learning (OCL) during the COVID-19 pandemic. The authors found that there are noteworthy connections among online collaborative tools, OCL activities, student engagement, and student learning and performance. Their conclusion highlights how OCL encourages student engagement and teacher participation, thereby enhancing group discussions and ultimately improving student learning outcomes.

5. Conclusion

- The educational system has a consequential influence because of the innovation of new technology. To enhance the performance of the teaching and learning process and make it more effective and efficient in face-to-face and online education, it is important to understand the current gap and demands of the advancement of technology. Nevertheless, online education captured attention due to the pandemic as it offers a resolution to conquer unpredictability. It provides students with the possibility to access educational resources without confines from their computer at any moment from any location. Due to this, it helps to reinforce the efficacy of knowledge as a considerable amount of information can be retrieved effortlessly. It has been observed from studies that there are no exceptional differences in students' academic performance and the skills and knowledge they have acquired through face-to-face or online education.
- Online teaching excessively relies on the use of educational tools for constructive, engaging, and on-time delivery of teaching material. The role of online tools is more significant in providing high-quality education to perpetuate online teaching and learning. These online tools can be used in different aspects of online education which is beneficial to students and teachers and can enhance the quality of online pedagogy. As educators and institutions, it is essential to recognize the trends, the prospective to restructuring education and fulfill the demands of diverse learners

becomes more substantial than ever before. Consequently, it has been highlighted how the emerging trends in online education can be used for online delivery to enhance the learning process and experiences.

References

Apple (2011). iMovie. Apple (Australia). Available at https://www.apple.com/au/imovie/.

Arkorful, V. & Abaidoo, N. (2015). The role of e-learning, advantages and disadvantages of its adoption in higher education. *International Journal of Instructional Technology and Distance Learning*, 12(1), 29–42.

Atwood, S.A. & Singh, A. (2018). *Improved Pedagogy Enabled by Assessment Using Gradescope*. Atlanta, GA: Association for Engineering Education, Engineering Library Division Papers, American Society for Engineering Education-ASEE.

Audacity (2019). Free, open source, cross-platform audio software for multitrack recording and editing. Audacityteam.org. Available at https://www.audacityteam.org/.

Chen, Z. (2023). Artificial intelligence-virtual trainer: Innovative didactics aimed at personalized training needs. *Journal of the Knowledge Economy*, 142, pp. 2007–2025.

Discord (2022). A new way to chat with friends & communities. *Discord*. Available at https://discord.com/.

Dogan, M.E., Goru Dogan, T. & Bozkurt, A. (2023). The use of artificial intelligence (AI) in online learning and distance education processes: A systematic review of empirical studies. *Applied Sciences*, 13(5), 3056.

Gordillo, A., Lopez-Fernandez, D. & Tovar, E. (2022). Comparing the effectiveness of video-based learning and game-based learning using teacher-authored video games for online software engineering education. *IEEE Transactions on Education*, 65(4), 1–9.

Gupta, Y.P., Chawla, A., Pal, T., Reddy, M.P. & Yadav, D.S. (2022). 3D networking and collaborative environment for online education. *The Institute of Electrical and Electronics Engineers, Inc. (IEEE) Conference Proceedings*, The Institute of Electrical and Electronics Engineers, Inc. (IEEE), Piscataway.

Hameed, S. Badii, A. & Cullen, A.J. (2008). Effective e-learning integration with traditional learning in a blended learning environment. *European and Mediterranean Conference on Information System*, pp. 25–26.

Haque, M.A., Sonal, D., Haque, S., Rahman, M. & Kumar, K. (2022). Learning management system empowered by machine learning. *AIP Conference Proceedings*, American Institute of Physics, Melville.

Hassenburg, A. (2009). Distance education versus the traditional classroom. *Berkeley Scientific*, 13(1).
Instructure. (n.d.). Canvas Overview. Available at https://www.instructure.com/en-au/canvas.
Joko Prayudha, S. (2021). Video-based learning as a media for teaching English during pandemic Covid-19. *Journal of Language Intelligence and Culture*, 2(1), 1–11.
Kahoot! (2019). Learning Games. Make Learning Awesome! *Kahoot!* Available at https://kahoot.com/.
Kalmar, E., Aarts, T., Bosman, E., Ford, C., de Kluijver, L., Beets, J., Veldkamp, L., Timmers, P., Besseling, D., Koopman, J., Fan, C., Berrevoets, E., Trotsenburg, M., Maton, L., van Remundt, J., Sari, E., Omar, L.-W., Beinema, E., Winkel, R. & van der Sanden, M. (2022). The COVID-19 paradox of online collaborative education: When you cannot physically meet, you need more social interactions. *Heliyon*, 8(1), e08823–e08823.
Klein, D. & Ware, M. (2003). E-learning: New opportunities in continuing professional development. *Learned Publishing*, 16(1), 34–46.
Kuo, M.-S. & Chuang, T.-Y. (2016). How gamification motivates visits and engagement for online academic dissemination — An empirical study. *Computers in Human Behavior*, 55, 16–27.
Legarde, M.A.A. (2022). The adoption of learning management system in teaching and learning in the new normal. *International Journal of Multidisciplinary Research and Analysis*, 5(3).
Loom (2019). Video recording, simplified. Available at https://www.loom.com/.
Mao, B.P., Teichroeb, M.L., Lee, T., Wong, G., Pang, T. & Pleass, H. (2022). Is online video-based education an effective method to teach basic surgical skills to students and surgical trainees? A systematic review and meta-analysis. *Journal of Surgical Education*, 79(6), 1536–1545.
Marappan, R. & Bhaskaran, S. (2022). Analysis of recent trends in e-learning personalization techniques. *The Education Review*, 6(5), 167–170.
Marc, J.R. (2002). Book review: E-learning strategies for delivering knowledge in the digital age. *Internet and Higher Education*, 5, 185–188.
McDonald, D. (2016). Grading and providing feedback: Consistency, effectiveness, and fairness. Center for Teaching and Learning, Wiley Education Services. Available at https://ctl.wiley.com/grading-and-providing-feedback-consistency-effectiveness-and-fairness (Accessed 30 August 2023).
Moodle (2017). Moodle. Available at https://moodle.com/.
Nieto-Escamez, F.A. & Roldán-Tapia, M.D. (2021). Gamification as online teaching strategy during COVID-19: A mini-review. *Frontiers in Psychology*, 12, 648552–648552.

Ng, P.M.L., Chan, J.K.Y. & Lit, K.K. (2022). Student learning performance in online collaborative learning. *Education and Information Technologies*, 27(6), 8129–8145.

Obsproject.com. (2012). Open Broadcaster Software. OBS. Available at https://obsproject.com/.

Pal, D. & Patra, S. (2021). "University students" perception of video-based learning in times of COVID-19: A TAM/TTF perspective. *International Journal of Human-Computer Interaction*, 37(10), 903–921.

Papanis, E. (2005). Traditional Teaching versus e-learning. *Experimental Approach, Statistical Review*, 1(1), 19–35.

Peimani, N. & Kamalipour, H. (2021). Online education and the COVID-19 outbreak: A case study of online teaching during lockdown. *Education Sciences*, 11(2), 72.

Prezi (2009). Presentation software. Online presentation tools. *Prezi*. Available at https://prezi.com/.

proctorio.com. (n.d.). A comprehensive learning integrity platform — *Proctorio*. Available at https://proctorio.com/.

ProctorU. (2018). ProctorU — The leading proctoring solution for online exams. Available at https://www.proctoru.com/.

Quizlet (2019). Quizlet. Available at https://quizlet.com/en-gb.

Rahardja, U., Aini, Q., Khairunisa, A. & Millah, S. (2021). Implementation of blockchain technology in Learning Management System (LMS). *APTISI Transactions on Management (ATM)*, 6(2), 112–120.

Reif, F. (2008). *Applying Cognitive Science to Education: Thinking and Learning in Scientific or Other Complex Domains*. Cambridge, MA: MIT Press.

Sablic, M., Mirosavljevic, A. & Skugor, A. (2021). Video-based learning (VBL) — Past, present and future: An overview of the research published from 2008 to 2019. *Technology, Knowledge and Learning*, 26(4), 1061–1077.

Siegal, M. & Gilliland, E. (2021). *Empowering the Community College First-Year Composition Teacher: Pedagogies and Policies*. Ann Arbor, MI: University of Michigan Press.

Mohamad, S.N.M., Sazali, NS.S. & Salleh, M.A.M. (2018). Gamification approach in education to increase learning engagement. *International Journal of Humanities, Arts and Social Sciences*, 4(1), 22.

Slack (n.d.). Slack is your digital HQ. *Slack*. Available at https://slack.com/intl/en-au.

St-Hilaire, F., Vu, D.D., Frau, A., Burns, N., Faraji, F., Potochny, J., Robert, S., Roussel, A., Zheng, S., Glazier, T. & Romano, J.V. (2022). A new era: Intelligent tutoring systems will transform online learning for millions. Glossary of terms. Tertiary Education Quality and Standards Agency. Available at https://www.teqsa.gov.au/guides-resources/glossary-terms#e.

Titthasiri, W. (2013). A comparison of e-learning and traditional learning: Experimental approach. *International Conference on Mobile Learning, E-Society and E-Learning Technology (ICMLEET)* — Singapore on November, pp. 6–7.

Veluvali, P. & Surisetti, J. (2022). Learning management system for greater learner engagement in higher education — A review. *Higher Education for the Future*, 9(1), 107–121.

workspace.google.com. (n.d.). Google Workspace. Business Apps & Collaboration Tools. Available at https://workspace.google.com/intl/en_au/.

workspace.google.com. (n.d.). Online video conferencing with Google Meet and Duo — Google Workspace. Available at https://workspace.google.com/intl/en_au/resources/video-conferencing/.

www.blackboard.com. (n.d.). Educational technology solutions. Blackboard. Asia Pacific. Available at https://www.blackboard.com/group/136.

www.microsoft.com. (n.d.). Microsoft 365 overview. Secure, Integrated Office 365 Apps. Available at https://www.microsoft.com/en-au/microsoft-365.

www.microsoft.com. (n.d.). Microsoft Teams. Group Chat. Free Chat. Available at https://www.microsoft.com/en-au/microsoft-teams/group-chat-software.

www.turnitin.com (2019). 10 ways Gradescope helps improve teaching and learning. Available at https://www.turnitin.com/blog/10-ways-gradescope-helps-improve-teaching-and-learning/ (Accessed 30 August 2023).

Yee, A., Padovano, W.M., Fox, I.K., Hill, E.J.R., Rowe, A.G., Brunt, L.M., Moore, A.M., Snyder-Warwick, A.K., Kahn, L.C., Wood, M.D., Coert, J.H. & Mackinnon, S.E. (2020). Video-based learning in surgery: Establishing surgeon engagement and utilization of variable-duration videos. *Annals of Surgery*, 272(6), 1012–1019.

Yuhanna, I., Alexander, A. & Kachik, A. (2020). Advantages and disadvantages of online learning. *Journal Educational Verkenning*, 1(2), 13–19.

Zoom (2022). Video conferencing, web conferencing, webinars, screen sharing. Zoom Video. Available at https://zoom.us/.

Zylfiu, D.B.G. & Rasimi, D.A. (2020). Challenges and advantages of online learning: The case of Kosovo. *International Journal of Management*, 11(10), 1873–1880.

Chapter 5

Assessment Integrity and Assessment Security in the Digital Era

Smitha Shivshankar

King's Own Institute, Australia

Abstract

Educational institutions have raised paramount concerns over assessment integrity and security in the evolving landscape of the digital era and the transition to online and hybrid learning environments. This chapter starts by exploring the significance of assessment integrity and security and emphasizing their imperative role in preserving the value of academic qualification and genuine knowledge acquisition. It unfolds by presenting a detailed exploration of the multifaceted challenges in online exam settings ranging from cheating to unauthorized access to information. It then sheds light on the strategies and digital tools for addressing the challenges, and concerns and issues associated with the digital tools are also discussed.

Keywords: Assessment integrity, Assessment security, Assessment fraud, Academic integrity, Academic cheating, Online exam.

1. Introduction

The unexpected event of COVID-19 in 2020 showed the need to deal with unexpected challenges and forced a number of stakeholders to enter into a domain that required iterative experimentation to acquire new knowledge and learn from mistakes (Fischer, 2021). The education industry was forced to change its educational practices (e.g., making distance learning a necessity rather than a choice). The last two decades have experienced a serious shift from offline to online settings due to various reasons, such as ease of access, time flexibility, and scalability (Garg, 2022). Online learning has made a significant impact during and post the pandemic, and the number of learners enrolled in online courses increased from 300,000 to 220 million accelerating the growth by 92% (Diaz-Infante, 2022), but the future of online education is not a bleak (Harve, 2023).

While digital technologies are changing every aspect of life (Fischer, 2021), the academic industry is not being an exceptional environment, significant changes have taken place, and technology has been increasingly seen as an important enabler/tool for teaching and learning (Akour, 2022). Voogt (2018) discussed the education systems in the digital age with a focus on: "the need for alignment; informal learning for technology; professional development for technology-enhanced learning leaders; digital agency to empower equity in the classroom; formative assessment supported by technology; developing creativity in teachers and learners; learning from national policy experiences; upbringing in a digital world; sustainability and scalability of technology integration initiatives." Digital technologies can enable some key aspects of assessment processes (e.g., datafication of learning, feedback and scaffolding, peer assessment, and peer feedback) (Voogt, 2018).

The fundamental goal of education is to prepare students to act independently which is measured by how well the students are prepared to do an ideal assessment (Schwartz, 2009). Assessments are an integral component of education and learning, and it is vital to see how well students are prepared to do an ideal assessment irrespective of the mode of learning. The appropriate design of assessment tasks to evaluate student learning determines the effective design of any course. Almost one-third of the time, teachers have engaged in assessment-related tasks (e.g., emphasizing the importance of aligning subject learning outcomes to the design of formative and summative assessments) (Meccawy, 2021; Sewell, 2010). Formative assessment assists student learning during a course while summative assessments are high-stake assessments measuring the student achievement at the end of learning with a final mark awarded for the assessment.

Assessments in an online education setting are no exception and are an integral component of teaching and learning. Examples of some types of assessments used in online study programs are: "paper/essay, written assignment, exam/quiz, online discussion, projects/simulations/case study, reflection, presentation, fieldwork, portfolio, peer evaluation" (Sabrina, 2022). Online assessments nevertheless offer several benefits including the ease of evaluation, reduced cost, and time. However, these benefits are accompanied by certain challenges, including the risk of academic dishonesty learning experience concerns, and validity and trust issues in online assessments (Costley, 2019). Academic dishonesty (also called academic integrity) refers to academic offenses that break the code of honor to achieve credit that does not rely on learning (Garg, 2022). The risk of academic dishonesty is accompanied by serious challenges in addressing the security and integrity of assessments, as in many circumstances, it is difficult to assess if it's the student's original work. Academic integrity entails commitment to the fundamental values of honesty, trust, fairness, respect, responsibility, and courage defining ethical academic behavior and creating a community dedicated to learning and exchange of ideas (Fishman, 2014).

Following sections of this chapter will take a closer look at the current state of assessment integrity and assessment security, threats, and challenges in addressing assessment integrity and security, and strategies and tools applied to address assessment integrity and security. The chapter will also include a discussion on the ethical considerations of the deployment of technological tools in addressing assessment integrity and assessment security.

2. Assessment Integrity and Assessment Security

Academic integrity is central to the process of learning, and the institutions offering the curriculum need to take the responsibility of creating a culture that maintains academic integrity. The assessment design should incorporate instructions that give little or no opportunity for students to violate academic integrity (Ahadiat & Gomaa, 2020; Swartz, 2013: 7). Students who cheat are eventually graduated as ones that lack knowledge and also considered unethical citizens. Hence, there is a strong need to address dishonesty, as what is acceptable professionally depends on what is an acceptable behavior. Academic integrity focuses on creating policies, procedures, and pedagogies that integrate integrity and encourage students not to cheat, and build foundational capability to work with integrity and value the right thing.

Academic integrity does not primarily focus on detecting cheating and/or punishing students who cheat. It includes student's awareness of honesty, trustworthiness, and consequences of malpractices. Academic integrity means students need to complete the tasks on their own and submit their work, without having unauthorized collaboration, external help, or undue advantage. It could be looked at from three different dimensions such as: understanding why students cheat, identifying how students cheat, and employing practices to safeguard academic integrity. Academic integrity entails providing a foundation for learners to develop capabilities and values necessary to conduct ethical scholarship, and assessment security focuses on strengthening assessments against attempts to cheat and detecting any cheating that has occurred. Assessment security starts where assessment integrity finishes, and it also includes measures to detect cheating and approaches to make cheating more difficult. Making possible changes to the authentic assessments is one of the vital requirements to address integrity (Bearman *et al.*, 2023; Nieminen, 2023). Assessment security is a multidisciplinary field focusing on detecting and stopping those who cheat, and it is about knowing the current practices and what we would like to do to stop academic cheating (e.g., by asking questions such as: How well does this anti-cheating approach actually stop cheating? Are we prepared to accept the limitations/drawbacks that comes with it?) (Dawson, 2020b).

An assessment is secure when we have absolute certainty on who undertook the assessment and did their own work in the precise circumstances that would be difficult to solve. Two key operational features of assessment security are as follows (Butler-Henderson, 2020; Chao, 2012):

- *Authentication refers to student identification to know that they are the ones who take the exam themselves*: There is a primary and vital reason for the need of physical attendance for the validation and authentication of the student taking the assessment. For example, checking students' ID cards during the traditional face-to-face exam is an attempt to achieve authentication that determines if the student being assessed is the one who had completed the assessment to overcome common problems of authentication such as (1) Exam impersonators who present their own fake ID cards is a common problem in assessment security and (2) Task outsourcing where the answers to the exam questions are dictated and the student who is physically present is just reproducing. Academic integrity in an online setting is a major concern arising from an increased potential of cheating due to the limited control of the test settings and inability to effectively monitor the students taking tests (Palloff cited in Meccawy, 2021: 5). Assessments designed for online courses should be given serious consideration as academic integrity and test security are real issues of concern. According to the United States Higher Education Opportunity Act (HEOA) 2008 (Sabrina, 2022), it is imperative that educational institutions verify the identity of students in an online setting using either a secure login, proctored exams, or any other tool to verify the identity of the student. Some of the current technology-based authentication options available for the online exam settings include:

- Fingerprint reading.
- Authenticating student cohorts by media streaming and follow-up identification.
- Subsidiary products and plugins incorporated into the learning management systems (such as Moodle proctoring plugin to support authentication process).
- Keystroke authentication, stylometry for linguistics, extraction of unique data and recording for decision-making using biometric features.

- Control of circumstances ensures that the assessment conditions are enforced and the work is produced under the conditions. This adds to the validity of assessment security as authentication may fail to protect from the range of free online resources available for a closed-book examination. This creates a difference in the judgment as the assessor is no longer confident in knowing who is taking the exam. The extent to which the circumstances of the exam conditions can be enforced depends on:
  - Students being able to access proscribed information leaves the assessor of not being capable of judging on how the students can perform without the access to information as the security highly depends on restricting access to information.
  - Assessors' awareness of the range of tools available and whether the students are allowed to use these tools for completing the assessments.
  - Ensuring all resources are accessible to the students as intended.

The COVID crisis led to the transition to online assessment and the transition from face-to-face exams to online exams (Cramp *et al.*, 2019; Day & Lawrence, 2020; Hillier, 2014; Ladyshewsky, 2015 as cited by Reedy *et al.*, 2021: 2). While the transition had a lot of evident benefits such as temporal and spatial flexibility, cost reduction, and reduced administrative burden, online examination was accompanied by a set of challenges such as privacy concerns, technical and digital equity issues, and academic integrity concerns. Hence, the assessment types and practices that evaluate competencies and capabilities and their relationship to learning in the digital age should be revisited (Boitshwarelo *et al.*, 2017).

The validity of the execution process of online proctored exams is argued to be lower than supervised on-campus exams. The online exams rely on bring-your-own-device models and use software on personal devices or classroom/lab resources (Okojie cited in Ananou, 2014: 17). It could be very challenging to deliver perfect assessment security, but we can take an incremental approach (e.g., improving gradually). It is believed that technology can provide a great learning experience for students when orchestrated properly and has become an active element in students.

3. Assessment Fraud

Face-to-face practices are a commonly used approach for assessment, and online assessments are considered to be challenging (Bailey cited in Meccawy *et al.*, 2021: 3). The pandemic has given an opportunity to embrace the digital academic experience (Mishra, 2020: 2) and improve "technological educational skills (Elzainy *et al.*, 2020 as cited by Reedy *et al.*, 2021: 2). While many of the learning and teaching transactions such as lecture delivery and communication are handled exceptionally well by the contemporary online learning technologies, assessing learning outcomes are fraught with challenges as the academics raise concerns about cheating.

3.1. *Common Forms of Academic Dishonesty*

An international problem of assessment present in the current classroom settings is academic fraud and dishonesty with a variation in methods and severity. Some possible ways to violate academic integrity include (Sabrina *et al.*, 2022; St. Petersburg College, 2022):

- Bribery (Bribing for academic advantage (e.g., student offering goods or services in exchange for marks) and using an academic advantage (e.g., professor offering student a passing grade in exchange for money/goods/services)).
- Misrepresentation (e.g., lying to an instructor to ask for a grade increase or being confronted with allegations of academic dishonesty).
- Collusion (e.g., working together on an individual assessment without permission).
- Cheating (e.g., copying from other students' work, allowing other students to copy, using formulas without permission, collaborating in a take-home exam, outsourcing the work).
- Duplicate submission (e.g., submitting the same paper for two different classes).
- Conspiracy (e.g., working together to commit academic dishonesty).
- Fabrication (e.g., creating or altering experimental data).
- Academic misconduct (e.g., violations of policies, tampering with grades, or obtaining/distributing assessment/test paper).
- Improper computer/calculator use (e.g., unauthorized use of computer or calculator).
- Improper behavior (e.g., accepting or providing outside help on online assessment without permission).
- Plagiarism (e.g., representing another person's work as your own, failing to cite information from a source).
- Social networks assisting students to share assignments and solutions and to involve in group cheating.

The determination of students to be involved in cheating falls under the below identified reasons:

- New technologies making it easier.
- Less than 10% are caught.
- No serious penalties: The byword appears to have changed from "Don't cheat to Don't get caught" (Lathrop cited in Ananou, 2014: 23).

4. Threats and Challenges to Maintaining Assessment Integrity in the Digital Era

Technological advancements have revolutionized students' approach to assessments. The motivation to cheat has grown stronger, motivation levels have gone high, and the myriad of tools and platforms have made cheating not only easier but also attractive. The perceived likelihood of academic dishonesty has imposed a series of threats and challenges (Ananou, 2014: 12) among educators in terms of identifying cheating and measuring the effectiveness of learning (Kleeman, n.d.).

4.1. Possible Tech-Driven and Behavioral Threats to Assessment Integrity

The convergence of the advancing technology and the change in students' behaviors and their approach to assessments presents a unique set of challenges for the educators. While it is certain that technology provides powerful and sophisticated tools for learning and assessment, it also opens venues for cheating. Technology being one of the main enablers of cheating makes it easier to locate information and not synthesize it, and it in turn impacts the student's ability to achieve success in learning. The latest form of contract cheating involves in using AI-driven text generation or AI-assisted writing (e.g., ChatGPT) (Brown, 2020; Cotton, 2023 cited in Cotton, 2023; Ryan, 2023).

As a simple tool to use, students simply need to prompt ChatGPT with the problem statement rather than generating their own ideas by undertaking research and building argument skills based on analysis and reflection. According to the leading industry expert, George Veletsianos, Professor of Education and Canada Research Chair in Innovative Learning and Technology at Royal Roads University, educators reckon that rather than banning digital tools, we should acknowledge and brace new technology (Gordon, 2023; Lindsay, 2023). Meanwhile, intentional and unintentional use of ChatGPT and AI tools to cheat can vary in severity. Some examples in which these tools are used to cheat include (1) AI-assisted plagiarism (e.g., submitting g AI-generated text as their own work (such as essays, assignments or take-home exams); (2) Plagiarism (e.g., using the tool to rephrase content and passing it as their own work; (3) Self-plagiarism (e.g., using the tool to rewrite an assessment report previously submitted with an intention to resubmit it); and (4) Data Fabrication (e.g., using ChatGPT to generate false data and presenting them as genuine findings to support the work).

Assessments are often referred to as a critical intersection of learning and teaching that evaluates teaching efficiency and learning outcomes. The changes required to the assessments are hiking as there is a need to conduct assessments that are compatible with changing teaching and learning environments. The digital assessments could be classified into two broad categories (Sabrina, 2022): (1) Non-exam assessments (e.g., similarity checking tools could be used to identify collusion and plagiarism with the assessments submitted on LMS. However, detecting and addressing contract cheating is a limitation of these tools. Turntin's AI writing detection capabilities argue that the false positive rate of the document is less than 1% with a series of updates to the detection module (Turnitin, 2023). Viva or oral examinations could be applied to check and verify the students' understanding of the assessment tasks as a form of authentic assessment to prevent misconduct in both online and face-to-face settings) and (2) Online exams (e.g., closed book exams need to be administered under strict exam conditions and require invigilators/proctors to maintain integrity. Even with online exam conditions the requirement for invigilation or proctoring cannot be overlooked). On a related note, assessment integrity could revolve around several perspectives in an online setting such as assessment security measures, technical issues, inadequate training, and vague guidelines (Almoosa, 2022).

4.2. *Challenges in Addressing Assessment Integrity*

The major limitation experienced in addressing assessment integrity in online learning is the lack of clear guidelines and required information. There are noticeable challenges experienced by the educators along these lines:

- Increased workload to secure assessment and redesign tasks to fit the online learning.
- Challenges in identifying and confirming assessment integrity incidents (e.g., time-consuming process, students creating groups for cheating, lack of skills in detecting, and verifying suspected cases).
- Technical issues (e.g., having no access to computing equipment, Internet access issues).
- AI-related issues (e.g., higher possibility of plagiarism, over-reliance on digital tools thus losing research and thinking skills).

The interaction between technological advancements and the shifting of students' behaviors toward academic cheating emphasizes the complexity of assessment standards. As the potential vulnerabilities of the digital tools and the changing students' mindsets are acknowledged, it becomes a pressing need for educators, institutions, and policymakers to adapt, innovate, and reinforce measures that preserve academic integrity which does not only aim at preventing academic cheating but also focuses on ensuring fairness, sustaining educational value, and fostering an environment of legitimate learning.

According to the Forbes School of Business & Technology's Dean, Dr. Maja Zelihic, and Dr. Karen Lynne-Faniels Ivy, Department Chair and Professor of technology studies, we should embrace new technologies and explore how those new tools can be integrated into modifying curriculum methods to design more complex assignments that require interview or video presentations where they have to use their research and speech capabilities. Educational institutions should think about investing in AI plagiarism toolkits, and their curriculum should ensure that students are building critical thinking and judgment skills.

5. Strategies and Tools to Improve Assessment Integrity and Security

The traditional on-campus face-to-face exams offered a great degree of confidence with respect to authentication, however, it has limitations (such as scheduling inconveniences, traveling time and other potential associated costs, multiple students being monitored by a single proctor, poor training, becoming tired, distracted or overwhelmed, and being more subjective or biased (Kolski, 2020). However, the shift to online learning and teaching environment requires the need for additional methods is place to address the requirements of assessment integrity and security.

5.1. *Strategies and Tools for Redesigning Online Assessments*

Education dynamics evolving with the new addition of online and hybrid learning adds the need to redesign assessments in order to provide opportunities to efficiently align with the goals of learning and teaching by minimizing academic cheating. The literature presents a series of processes in place to design exams that minimize cheating such as

(Kolski, 2020; Marcus *et al.*, 2008; Rios & Liu, 2017 as cited in Aisyah *et al.*, 2018; Kolski, 2020; Mohanna & Patel, 2016; Sabrina *et al.*, 2022):

- Incorporating the institution's academic integrity policy into the subject curriculum.
- Defining academic dishonesty and specifying the consequences reduces academic cheating.
- Developing awareness of the educators/academic staff and providing the support and tools required for cheating detection.
- Supplementing policies and awareness with a variety of measures of detection, deterrence, and correction.
- Designing using question banks with true/false, matching, and multiple-choice questions and allowing randomization of questions.
- Conducting more frequent and shorter quizzes and setting up questions based on the previous work for formative knowledge development.
- Setting up quiz questions including materials from lecture discussions and avoiding generic questions.
- Providing detailed marking criteria for students to have a complete understanding of the assessment requirements.
- Adopting progressive assessment (later assessment tasks are progressions of the previous assessment tasks) and reflective assessments requiring students to reflect on tasks performed during group work in class or project work making it hard for third parties to complete a task who have little knowledge about what happened in class or in a project.
- Deploying authentication and conducting post-hoc assessments to search for cheating.
- Developing authentication systems that authenticate at the pre and post-examination periods from the examinee's perspective and validating the examinee by accessing photographic authentication from the pre and intra-examination periods.
- Using open book open web as they apply authentic assessment and placing the learner as a decision-maker and expert witness, with validation by avoiding any question that could have a generic answer and evaluate conceptual understanding.
- Applying the Smart Authenticated Fast Exams application.
- Implementing synchronous online exams as an alternative to traditional proctored exams while manually authenticating.

- Progressively extracting learning from the curriculum wherever the final exam may not be appropriate.
- Changing one-third of the assessment items every semester.
- Incorporating a minimum fixed time window to start and finish an exam to overcome the possibilities of collaborative cheating and high exam scores in large time duration online and /or take-home exams.
- Adding a time limit for each question.

While the above discussion lists a number of different approaches, there is no single design or method in place to eliminate all forms of academic integrity violations. The commitment to the development of authentic assessment environments requires real-life learning processes and unstructured problem-solving. Some fundamental considerations for designing quality learning-oriented assessments are as follows (University of Wollongong Australia, 2023):

- Aligning assessment with learning outcomes: Constructively aligned assessments enable students to understand the purpose of the assessment and how it is related to their learning.
- Designing authentic assessments: Requiring students to perform real-world tasks to demonstrate meaningful application of knowledge and skills appropriate to the discipline.
- Designing assessment to ensure that the student's effort and intellectual engagement are spread evenly across the subject.
- Including a variety of assessment types to enhance students' interest and provide them with opportunities to demonstrate learning, examples include a mix of individual and collaborative tasks and assessment tasks that require to use oral or video artifacts.
- Designing assessments that involve the development of students' evaluative judgment where they have the capability to make decisions about the quality of work of self and others (Tai cited in University of Wollongong Australia, 2023).

While a number of strategies have been discussed in the literature with regard to redesigning assessments as above, tracking student progress is still a challenge in an online setting. The efficiency in assessing student learning depends on the real-time feedback available from the student learning enabled by the benefits of flexibility, personalization, and engagement. With the rise of technology, traditional assessment methods likely fail to meet the needs of today's learners. The digital assessment tools extend significant support and transform how educators and learners approach learning and evaluation. Table 1 presents a list of some examples of digital assessment tools for improving student learning experience, and the educators should consider incorporating them into their teaching

Table 1: Digital assessment tools.

Name	Features	Assessment Types
Hurix	Creating, delivering, and grading assessment	Multiple choice, True or False, and short answer questions
Socrative	Creating and delivering assessments; Real-time analytics allowing teachers to track student performance	Multiple choice, True or False, and short answer questions
Mentimeter	Creating engaging and interactive assessments; Can be integrated with the LMS and presentation software such as PowerPoint and Google slides	Multiple choice, True or False, and open-ended questions and rating scales
Kahoot	Game-based learning platform	Quiz with multiple choice, True or False, or open-ended questions
Quizlet	Converts information into flashcards, quizzes, and games; Can include images and audio	True or False, multiple choice, matching and constructed response questions (such as short answer questions and essays)
Thinglink	Creating interactive images and videos for the students; Multimedia options including text, images, audio, and video	Interactive timelines, maps, and infographics to enhance students' learning experience; Students interact with images and video by clicking on the links that lead to content or activities
Google Forms	Creating and delivering assessments online although requiring a lot of manual effort due to the limited templates available; Real-time analytics and reporting features for student performance and progress	Multiple-choice, True or False, and open-ended questions
Moodle	Open source LMS for creating and delivering online courses	Quizzes, Assignments, workshops, multiple choice, True/False, and essay questions

Source: Developed from Harve (2023).

strategy (Harve, 2023; Quizlet, n.d.). A combination of the above-listed tools can be used by educators to evaluate student learning. There are other tools available for specific discipline and particular categories of assessments (e.g., Jambot, Mote, Padlet, Parlay, PearDeck, PlayPosit, Seesaw, Flip, Edutastic, ASSISTments) (Bell, 2021; Deignan, 2022).

5.2. *Strategies and Tools for Detecting Academic Cheating*

While we closely look at the series of strategies and tools to minimize cheating and enhance student learning, it is equally vital to include measures to detect cheating and address academic misconduct to preserve academic integrity. A set of approaches applied to the learning environments are as follows:

- *Detecting Cheating Collecting Evidence and Applying Penalties*: Contract cheating includes different types of behaviors where students outsource their work or contracts it out (Medway, 2018). According to TEQSA, contract cheating as "when students outsource their assessments to a third party, whether that is a commercial provider, current or former student, family member or acquaintance. It includes the unauthorized use of file-sharing sites, as well as organizing another person to take an examination" and about 8% of students may be engaged in contract teaching (TEQSA, 2022). Contract cheating is usually not reported as it is hard to prove (Harper cited in Reedy, 2021) and it depends on how acceptable is the evidence to the decision-makers. In addition, a detection with 100% accuracy cannot provide real assessment security. Lastly, penalties should fit the circumstances. Cotton (2023) presents five considerations for universities and colleges on how to contract cheating and continue to develop institutional strategies for academic integrity:
    - Determining academic integrity strategy to ensure a "systematic approach" for addressing the issue of contract cheating. It is vital to have an in-depth consideration of how an institutional strategy can be integrated and augmented to different forms of academic misconduct involving third parties and outsourcing.
    - Reviewing institutional policies that include details of academic misconduct and measures in place to record, monitor, and identify whether penalties are consistently applied (QAA as cited in Cotton, 2023).

- Understanding students' motivation in engaging in contract cheating.
  - Revisiting and redesigning assessment practices to minimize opportunities for academic misconduct.
  - Providing training to staff on identifying contract cheating and processing identified contract cheating cases.
  - Facilitating effective student discussions on academic integrity.
- Another category of exams that needs attention is the online "high-stakes summative assessment events. To address the requirements of assessment integrity and security, it is vital that these exams are mediated by digital technologies, which take place in a defined place or time, conducted under restrictions of access to course materials, and in secure condition such as invigilation" (Allan, 2020). Digital platforms not only contribute to educational delivery and examinations they also assist in monitoring students' behavior. This can be achieved with the use of biometric features such as fingerprints, digital signatures, facial features, or voice recognition (Sabrina *et al.*, 2020). Some practices include (Aditya, 2021; Decuypere *et al.*, 2021; Juola, 2017; Komljenovic, 2022; Udechukwu, 2020):
  - *Content Matching*: Text matching tools can compare student's assignments against a large database (e.g., Turnitin). The limitations of the text matching tools are that the matches are subject to a degree of permutation making them less effective against cheating by paraphrasing. With the increasing level of sophistication and adoption of paraphrasing tools, the text-matching tools may need to adopt semantic approaches otherwise may be able to detect only the most blatant copy-paste plagiarism.
  - Stylometric approach uses a range of tools to build content profiles produced by students using linguistic markers that include readability scores, punctuation preferences, complexity, sentence length, vocabulary diversity, and other computable features. However, the limitations with such tools are: What if the student has substantially improved writing? What about different genres of work? What if the student uses the same contract cheating writer throughout the entire degree? In addition, these tools do not involve real-time monitoring of student's work processes.
  - Lockdown approach that disables certain functionalities to stop students from doing wrong things. This includes the use of

restricted web browsers, live-boot operating systems that take control of a computer, apps for mobile operating systems that prevent other device functions from being used and block networks to prevent access to part of all of the Internet. The lockdown approach can be adopted either as a ban-list model where everything is accessible except the one on the ban list, or an allow-list model where nothing is accessible except what is on the allow-list. This approach focuses on the control of circumstances to enhance security.
- Stealth assessments measure learning in the background while they play video games and require continual monitoring of students' activities to identify problematic behavior. The approach is banned due to reasons such as demonstrated distrust toward students, students' dislike of being monitored, and concerns about over-the-shoulder cheating.
- Digital Proctoring/e-proctoring/virtual proctoring/remote proctoring tools that aim at addressing both authentication and control of circumstances to ensure that exam-takers adhere to prescribed guidelines to verify the authenticity and authorship of exams and protect and detect any unauthorized or unacceptable activities during online exams. Such approach uses two components: web camera for recording the video and locking to prevent students from opening other tabs in the browsers. These systems focus on periodic authentication of the exam taker, behavior monitoring, multifactor, and biometric authentication (Slusky cited in Sabrina, 2022). The proctoring activity is efficiently scaled with the use of AI tools. The efficiency of the surveillance approaches depends to what extent the surveillance is effective and the degree of bypassing the surveillance. Digital proctoring could be classified into three main categories (Arnò et al., 2021; Das, 2022; Duncan & Joyner, 2022; González-González et al., 2020):
    - *Live Proctoring (LP)*: It involves human invigilators authenticating exam takers and monitoring their activities of around 10–12 exam-takers via screensharing and requiring additional invigilators for larger groups. This requires exams to be scheduled at a specific time depending on the availability of a proctor on a given date and time (ex., ProctorU, ProctorEdu, ExamRoom.AI, TestInvite, ExamMonitor, SpeedExam, MeritTrac).

Assessment Integrity and Assessment Security in the Digital Era

- *Recorded Proctoring (RP)*: It has no human invigilator present during the exam, and human intervention is required for reviewing the recordings. The students' behaviors in the exam are recorded and reviewed to identify potential instances of cheating or misconduct. This approach involves reviewing video recordings and student logs at a later time to assess the integrity. An example of available tools is MeritTrac.
- Automated Proctoring (AP) can be used in conjunction with LP and RP and applies AI to monitor exams in real time. The system is scalable as the human component is replaced by artificial intelligence and hence considered the most effective. Some available tools include Proctortrack, Mercer Mettl, MapleLMS, and Examus.

Table 2 presents a list of some of the proctoring tools that can be used in online exams.

Table 2: Online exam proctoring tools.

Name	Working Features	Data Collection and Processing
Proctortrack	Students download software after verifying their identity by scanning their face, a valid ID and knuckles; Instructors set up the proctoring restrictions to meet the required standards.	Uses an AI program to process the recorded feed and device activity. When the exam concludes, the processed data appears on the instructor's dashboard.
Mettl	Automatic proctoring and human-based review of recorded sessions.	AI observes and flags unusual activities like ID mismatch, student not present, presence of devices or external human voice and creates a report for human editor.
ProctorExam	Computer and smartphone for a 360-degree view of the test-takers' environment. Complete security is ensured using webcams and microphones. Allows use of resources as decided by the instructors.	Exams monitoring options include recording and reviewing, live monitoring, and integrating with a learning management system (LMS).

(*Continued*)

Table 2: (*Continued*)

Name	Working Features	Data Collection and Processing
ProctorEdu	Uses multimedia and remote collaboration technologies for proctors to intervene when required. Human proctors are randomly assigned. Monitor up to 30 students. Proctor student interaction done via chat, video, or audio.	Live monitoring and flag fraudulent activities in real-time and send a credibility report when the exam concludes.
MapleLMS	Includes live and automated proctoring. Monitors up to 10,000 students in a single exam setup by activating a Monitor AI program; Observes face, motion, keyboard activities, device activities and mouse movements.	AI generates reports automatically without distracting the test takers. Data collection also includes random facial recognition, face missing, hiding the camera, multiple faces, and browser activities while the live proctoring relies on video, audio, and screen activities.
ExamRoom. AI	Provides a 6:1 or 1:1 proctoring for live sessions; Offers recorded and review proctoring.	Flags fraudulent activities with time spans and visual evidence and the report.
Test Invite	Uses a lockdown, real-time candidate monitoring; Records webcam feed and device screen, time limiting the tests, restrictions on navigations, and validating the student with pin code, student ID, and invitation code.	Reports on fraudulent activities from the webcam feed and the device screen.
Examus	Uses a blend of AI-based and human-led proctoring for maximum security; Uses face recognition, reads test-takers emotional status, detects tab changes and strangers close to the exam taker, and alerts proctor or flags time stamp if the student is absent.	Detects and flags events of students gazing at cheating materials and tab changes and strangers and generates report.

Table 2: (*Continued*)

Name	Working Features	Data Collection and Processing
Honorlock	Students are verified using the student ID and continue with the exams.	Reports on illicit exam content, barred activities, unusual activities informed to the proctor for real-time intervention.
Proctorio	Deploys a robust toolbox into the LMS tool; Consists of proctoring algorithms, identity verification system, content protection and plagiarism detection. Protects the entire test screen from being copied. Blocks re-entry into assessment and thus candidates cannot switch seats after the identity verification process.	Encrypted report of video, audio, and computer screen from the start of the exam until the exam is shut down and accessible through the Blackboard/Canvas systems.
ExamSoft	Utilizes audio and video monitoring technologies to deliver online proctoring. Includes AI detecting abnormal behavior, screen monitoring and recording, requires internet for logging in and uploading exam Proctors review the exam data and flogs cheating attempts of the students.	Audio and video recordings of the exam taker (both webcam and screen capture) uploaded to Examsoft after the completion of the exam (Examsoft, 2020).
MeriTrac (CodeTrack, Pariksha, and SmartTest)	Includes live proctoring, recorded proctoring, and automated proctoring; Ensures exam integrity by monitoring students' movements, device activities, mouse movements, browser activities, etc. Easily integrates with LMS.	Generates a comprehensive report of the student movements, device activities, mouse movements, and browser activities for the proctor or recruiter for judgments about the integrity of the candidates' performance results.

Source: Developed from Das (2022).

The accuracy of detecting the misconduct during online exams have been significantly improved with the use of such tools thereby enhancing academic integrity and security. The remote-proctoring companies such as Proctorio, ProctorU, Examity, and ExamSoft gained significant benefits from the shutdown in March 2020. ProctorU, had administered roughly 4 million exams in 2020 and increased from 1.5 million in 2019, and Examity's growth increased by 35%. Proctorio's client base grew more than 500%, from 400 in 2019 to 2500 in 2021, administering an estimated 21 million exams in 2020, compared with 4 million in 2019 (Caplan-Bricker, 2021). Higher education institutions in the United States and Europe have embraced proctoring systems such as Examity, ProctorU, Proctorio, Proctortrack and Inspera Exam Portal. In Australia and New Zealand, ProctorU and Inspera are commonly used, while Examsoft and RPNow are prevalent in Asian countries (Arnò et al., 2021).

6. Challenges in the Use of AI-Based Digital Proctoring Tools

The use of digital tools is on the rise as educational institutions continue to switch to the online learning model. A study conducted by Educause in April 2020 found that 54% of educational institutions are using online or remote proctoring to proctor students taking online exams by embracing AI-based tools to automate the process. However, the next question for us to consider is: "Is AI good enough as the sole method of remote proctoring?" To answer this question, it is necessary to take a look at some challenges presented by AI-based proctoring (EnFuse, 2021; HireQuotient, 2022):

- *Multiple Prerequisites*: The pre-requisite list includes the need for a functional laptop, high-resolution webcams, high-speed Internet, and other software like voice detection and browser locks. This can limit the learner group from remote areas with limited infrastructure or poor connectivity (EnFuse, 2021; HireQuotient, 2022; Swauger, 2020). Some tools automatically shut down the exam due to poor connectivity (e.g., ProctorU).
- *False Flagging*: While these tools can detect most instances of dishonest activity, chances of false flagging of suspicious behavior are high. For example, AI flagging when exam taker looks away from the

Table 3: Summary of the European Commission Framework for the digital competence of educators.

Professional Engagement: Technological tools for communication, collaboration, and professional development	
Competence Element	Potential Indicators
Critically describes the positive and negative impacts of AI in Education and understand the basics of AI and learning analytics	Continuous professional learning on AI and learning analytics, Ethical use and assessing ethical impact of AI systems, Strategies to promote ethical and responsible use of AI and data, and Awareness on AI working principles.
Digital Resources: Sourcing, creating and sharing digital resources	
Data Governance and AI Governance	Awareness of the forms of personal data used, Maintaining data security and privacy with respect to data access. Knows that AI systems regulations, key principles of data quality, and incorporating AI edited/manipulated digital content in one's own work and to be credited.
Teaching and Learning: Digital technologies in teaching and learning	
Models of Learning, Education Objectives, Human Agency, Fairness and Humanity, and Practices learning practices that use AI	Understand how to measure learning and address the objectives of education, impact on teacher autonomy, professional development, and educational innovation, emotional dependency and student self-image when using these systems, impact on students' community, the influence of the use of technology, and the ethical principles in design of learning practices.
Assessment: Technologies and strategies to enhance assessment	
Personal differences, Cognitive focus and Misuse of technology	Be aware of student reactions to automated feedback, inability of AI systems to assess collaboration, social competencies or creativity ways to manipulate assessment.
Empowering Learners: Enhance inclusion, personalization and learner's active engagement	
AI addressing learners' diverse learning needs and justified choice	Know how personalized learning systems can adapt their behavior, explain how a system can benefit all students independent of their cognitive, cultural, economic, or physical differences, understand how the system treats student groups differently, consider impact on the development of student self-efficiency, self-image, mindset, and cognitive and affective self-regulation skills, recognises the need for constant monitoring of AI outcomes and learn from unexpected outcomes.

(*Continued*)

158 Teaching and Learning in the Digital Era: Issues and Studies

Table 3: (Continued)

Facilitating learners' digital competence: Use of digital technologies for information, communication, content creation, wellbeing and problem solving	
AI and Learning Analytics ethics	Be able to use AI projects and deployments for students to learn about the AI ethics and data use in education

Source: Developed from European Commission (2022).

device screen. Without human intervention, AI has the power to raise a false flag for "inappropriate behaviour" that can lead to unnecessary disciplinary action against the student leading to students getting stressed due to constant monitoring and inability to talk to human proctors (EnFuse, 2021; HireQuotient, 2022).

- *Bias in Facial Recognition*: These tools have also been alleged to show biases against black or marginalized students and students being denied access to an exam when the tool could not verify their identity.
- *Continuous Monitoring of Students*: While AI tools use facial recognition and eye-tracking, it also recognize noises and count that as cheating which can be a pain for students who do not have a quiet private space to take the test. This can lead to test anxiety in students.
- *Data Privacy Concerns*: Companies offering remote proctoring services are known to collect sensitive information like their device's IP address and biometrics including fingerprints and retina scans. While the data collection is required for delivering the services, there is not enough clarity on how long the data will be retained thereby raising concerns on data privacy (EnFuse, 2021; Swauger, 2020).

7. Ethical Considerations in the Use of Digital Tools

With the technological advancement and the move to online and hybrid models, the use of chatbots and AI proctoring tools are becoming prevalent which is accompanied by a number of ethical concerns (such as privacy, security, and accessibility). While assisting students with quick and convenient access to content and information, it is important to ensure that ethical and relevant guard rails are created for using digital tools (King, 2023). Educators play a central role in realizing the benefits of AI systems and successfully adopting AI systems into their teaching practices. The

European Framework (European Commission, 2022) for the Digital Competence of Educators (DigCompEdu) provides a general reference framework to support the development of educator-specific digital competences which considers a set of competence elements and the potential indicators for the ethical use of AI and data in teaching and learning listed (see Table 3).

References

Aditya, D.S. (2021). Embarking digital learning due to COVID-19: Are teachers ready? *Journal of Technology and Science Education*, 11(1), 104–116.

Ahadiat, N. & Gomaa, M.I. (2020). Online accounting education: How to improve security and integrity of students' performance assessments. *Journal of Instructional Pedagogies*, 24.

Ananou, T.S. (2014). *Academic Honesty in the Digital Age*. Pennsylvania: Indiana University of Pennsylvania.

Almossa, S.Y. & Alzahrani, S.M. (2022). Lessons on maintaining assessment integrity during COVID-19. *International Journal for Educational Integrity*, 18(1), 1–17.

Arnò, S., Galassi, A., Tommasi, M., Saggino, A. & Vittorini, P. (2021). State-of-the-art of commercial proctoring systems and their use in academic online exams. *International Journal of Distance Education Technologies (IJDET)*, 19(2), 55–76.

Bearman, M., Nieminen, J.H. & Ajjawi, R. (2023). Designing assessment in a digital world: An organising framework. *Assessment & Evaluation in Higher Education*, 48(3), 291–304.

Bell, K. (2021). 27 Formative Assessment Tools for Your Classroom. 6 July. Accessed August 25, 2023. Available at https://shakeuplearning.com/blog/20-formative-assessment-tools-for-your-classroom/.

Boitshwarelo, B., Reedy, A. & Billany, T. (2017). Envisioning the use of online tests in assessing twenty-first century learning: A literature review. *Research and Practice in Technology Enhanced Learning*, 12(16): 1–16.

Butler-Henderson, K. & Crawford, J. (2020). A systematic review of online examinations: A pedagogical innovation for scalable authentication and integrity. *Computers & Education*, 159, 104024.

Caplan-Bricker, N. (2021). Is Online Test-Monitoring Here to Stay? *The New Yorker*.

Chao, K.J., Hung, I.C. & Chen, N.S. (2012). On the design of online synchronous assessments in a synchronous cyber classroom. *Journal of Computer Assisted Learning*, 28(4), 379–395.

Chin, M. (2021). University will stop using controversial remote-testing software following student outcry. *The Verge*.

Costley, J. (2019). Student perceptions of academic dishonesty at a cyber-university in South Korea. *Journal of Academic Ethics*, 17(2), 205–217.

Cotton, D.R., Cotton, P.A. & Shipway, J.R. (2023). Chatting and cheating: Ensuring academic integrity in the era of ChatGPT. *Innovations in Education and Teaching International*, 1–12.

Cramp, J., Medlin, J.F., Lake, P. & Sharp, C. (2019). Lessons learned from implementing remotely invigilated online exams. *Journal of University Teaching & Learning Practice*, 16(1), 10.

Das, T. (2022). Top 14 proctoring software to secure your online exams/tests. 25 November. Accessed August 25, 2023. Available at https://geekflare.com/exam-proctoring-software/.

Dawson, P. (2020a). Strategies for using online invigilated exams. Academic integrity experts advice hub. *TEQSA*.

Dawson, P. (2020b). *Defending Assessment Security in a Digital World: Preventing e-cheating and Supporting Academic Integrity in Higher Education*. Abingdon: Routledge.

Day, K. & Lawrence, J. (2020). Implementing remotely invigilated online exams at scale. Transforming assessment webinar series. 25 March 2020. Available at http://transformingassessment.com/sites/default/files/files/TA_webinar_25_mar_2020_slides_ extended.pdf.

Decuypere, M., Grimaldi, E. & Landri, P. (2021). Introduction: Critical studies of digital education platforms. *Critical Studies in Education*, 62(1), 1–16.

Deignan, S. (2022). Interactive Classrooms — 8 Best Assessment Tools for Educators. 01 September. Available at https://www.mentimeter.com/blog/interactive-classrooms/best-assessment-tools (Accessed 25 August 2023).

Diaz-Infante, N. Lazar. M, Ram. S. & Ray. A. (2022). Demand for online education is growing. Are providers ready? 20 July. Available at https://www.mckinsey.com/industries/education/our-insights/demand-for-online-education-is-growing-are-providers-ready (Accessed 26 August 2023).

Duncan, A. & Joyner, D. (2022). On the necessity (or lack thereof) of digital proctoring: Drawbacks, perceptions, and alternatives. *Journal of Computer Assisted Learning*, 38(5), 1482–1496.

Enfuse (2021). AI-Based Proctoring Presents both Challenges and Opportunities. 25 August. Available at https://www.enfuse-solutions.com/ai-based-proctoring-presents-both-challenges-and-opportunities/. (Accessed 25 August 2023).

Examsoft (2020). ExamMonitor: Remote Proctor. https://examsoft.com/resources/exammonitor-remote-proctor/.

European Commission, Directorate-General for Education, Youth, Sport and Culture (2022). Ethical guidelines on the use of artificial intelligence (AI) and data in teaching and learning for educators. Publications Office of the European Union. Available at https://data.europa.eu/doi/10.2766/153756 (Accessed 26 August 2023).

Fischer, G. (2021). Challenges and opportunities of COVID-19 for rethinking and reinventing learning, education, and collaboration in the digital age. *merz| medien+ erziehung*, 65(1), 30–36.

Garg, M. & Goel, A. (2022). A systematic literature review on online assessment security: Current challenges and integrity strategies. *Computers & Security*, 113, 102544.

González-González, C.S., Infante-Moro, A. & Infante-Moro, J.C. (2020). Implementation of e-proctoring in online teaching: A study about motivational factors. *Sustainability*, 12(8), 3488.

Gordon, C. (2023). How are educators reacting to ChatGPT. 30 April. Available at https://www.forbes.com/sites/cindygordon/2023/04/30/how-are-educators-reacting-to-chat-gpt/?sh=664a1b592f1c (Accessed 15 August 2023).

Han, S., Nikou, S. & Yilma Ayele, W. (2023). Digital proctoring in higher education: A systematic literature review. *International Journal of Educational Management*.

Harve, A. (2023). 10 best digital assessment tools that are useful for both students as well as teachers, Higher Education, 11 July. Accessed August 26, 2023. Available at https://www.hurix.com/best-digital-assessment-tools-that-are-useful-for-both-students-as-well-as-teachers/.

Hillier, M. (2014). The very idea of e-Exams: student (pre) conceptions. *Proceedings of ASCILITE 2014-Annual Conference of the Australian Society for Computers in Tertiary Education*, pp. 77–88.

HireQuotient (2022). AI proctoring: What you need to know. 7 December. Accessed August 25, 2023. Available at https://www.hirequotient.com/blog/ai-proctoring-what-you-need-to-know.

Holden, O.L., Norris, M.E. & Kuhlmeier, V.A. (2021). Academic integrity in online assessment: A research review. In *Frontiers in Education*, Vol. 6, p. 639814. Frontiers Media SA. https://www.newyorker.com/tech/annals-of-technology/is-online-test-monitoring-here-to-stay.

Hussein, M.J., Yusuf, J., Deb, A.S., Fong, L. & Naidu, S. (2020). An evaluation of online proctoring tools. *Open Praxis*, 12(4), 509–525.

Juola, P. (2017). Detecting contract cheating via stylometric methods. *Proceedings on the Conference on Plagiarism across Europe and Beyond*, pp. 187–198.

King, M.R. (2023). ChatGPT: A conversation on artificial intelligence, chatbots, and plagiarism in higher education. *Cellular and Molecular Bioengeering*, 16(1), 1–2.

Kleeman, J. (n.d.). To be perfectly honest: How AI and technology could impact test cheating. Available at https://learnosity.com/edtech-blog/to-be-perfectly-honest-how-ai-and-technology-could-impact-test-cheating/.

Kolski, T. (2020). *Virtual Proctoring and Academic integrity. Learning in the Digital Age.* Oklahoma: Oklahoma State University.

Komljenovic, J. (2022). The future of value in digitalised higher education: Why data privacy should not be our biggest concern. *Higher Education*, 83(1), 119–135.

Lindsay K.T. (2023). ChatGPT and the future of university assessment. 16 January. Accessed August 10, 2023. Available at https://katelindsayblogs.com/2023/01/16/chatgpt-and-the-future-of-university-assessment/.

Meccawy, Z., Meccawy, M. & Alsobhi, A. (2021). Assessment in "survival mode": Student and faculty perceptions of online assessment practices in HE during COVID-19 pandemic. *International Journal for Educational Integrity*, 17, 1–24.

Medway, D., Roper, S. & Gillooly, L. (2018). Contract cheating in UK higher education: A covert investigation of essay mills. *British Educational Research Journal*, 44(3), 393–418.

Mishra, L., Gupta, T. & Shree, A. (2020). Online teaching-learning in higher education during lockdown period of COVID-19 pandemic. *International Journal of Educational Research Open*, 1, 100012.

Nieminen, J.H., Bearman, M. & Ajjawi, R. (2023). Designing the digital in authentic assessment: is it fit for purpose? *Assessment & Evaluation in Higher Education*, 48(4), 529–543.

Reedy, A., Pfitzner, D., Rook, L. & Ellis, L. (2021). Responding to the COVID-19 emergency: Student and academic staff perceptions of academic integrity in the transition to online exams at three Australian universities. *International Journal for Educational Integrity*, 17(1), 1–32.

Ryan, E. (2023). Is Using ChatGPT Cheating? 21 August. Available at https://www.scribbr.com/ai-tools/chatgpt-cheating/

Sabrina, F., Azad, S., Sohail, S. & Thakur, S. (2022). Ensuring academic integrity in online assessments: A literature review and recommendations.

Schwartz, D.L. & Arena, D. (2009). Choice-based assessments for the digital age. MacArthur 21st Century Learning and Assessment Project. Stanford: Stanford University, School of Education.

Selwyn, N., O'Neill, C., Smith, G., Andrejevic, M. & Gu, X. (2023). A necessary evil? The rise of online exam proctoring in Australian universities. *Media International Australia*, 186(1), 149–164.

Sewell, J.P., Frith, K.H. & Colvin, M.M. (2010). Online assessment strategies: A primer. MERLOT *Journal of Online Learning and Teaching*, 6(1), 297–305.

St. Petersburg College (2022). Plagiarism and academic integrity, library resources and services, 20 May. Accessed August 10, 2023. Available at https://spcollege.libguides.com/c.php?g=254383&p=1695452#:~:text=Bribery%20takes%20on%20two%20forms,a%20professor%20accepts%20this%20bribe.

Swartz, L.B. & Cole, M.T. (2013). "Students" perception of academic integrity in online business education courses. *Journal of Business & Educational Leadership*, 4(1), 102–112.

Swauger, S. (2020). Software that monitors students during tests perpetuates inequality and violates their privacy. 7 August. Accessed August 25, 2023. Available at https://www.technologyreview.com/2020/08/07/1006132/software-algorithms-proctoring-online-tests-ai-ethics/.

TEQSA (2022). What is contract cheating and method to reduce it. 13 October. Accessed August 26, 2023. Available at https://www.teqsa.gov.au/preventing-contract-cheating/what-contract-cheating-and-methods-reduce-it.

Turnitin (2023). AI writing detection capabilities — Frequently asked questions. Accessed August 26, 2023. Available at https://www.turnitin.com/products/features/ai-writing-detection/faq.

Turnitin (2023). The launch of Turnitin's AI writing detector and the road ahead. 4 April. Accessed August 26, 2023. Available at https://www.turnitin.com/blog/the-launch-of-turnitins-ai-writing-detector-and-the-road-ahead.

Udechukwu, J. (2020). Digital proctoring: Challenges and prospects in computer-based assessment in Nigeria. *European Academic Research Journal*, 7(12), 6259–6273.

University of Wollongong (2023). The role of quality assessment design in strengthening academic integrity. https://ltc.uow.edu.au/hub/article/assessment-design-to-strengthen-academic-integrity.

Voogt, J. & Knezek, G. (2018). Rethinking learning in a digital age: Outcomes from EDUsummIT 2017. *Technology, Knowledge and Learning*, 23(3), 369–375.

Williamson, B., Eynon, R. & Potter, J. (2020). Pandemic politics, pedagogies and practices: Digital technologies and distance education during the coronavirus emergency. *Learning, Media and Technology*, 45(2): 107–114.

Chapter 6

Designing Effective Online Assessment

Shima Forughi

King's Own Institute, Australia

Abstract

This chapter delves into the realm of online assessments, shedding light on their advantages, prerequisites, and the critical role of student perspectives. Online peer assessments offer anonymity, flexibility, and reduced teacher workload. However, fostering positive student attitudes and providing thorough training are essential requisites. Online examinations, including platforms like Google Forms, streamline grading processes and minimize costs, albeit challenges related to Internet access and digital literacy persist. Notably, the present chapter emphasizes the pivotal influence of student attitudes, motivations, and emotions on the outcomes of online assessments. In addition, this chapter provides a scope to the online evaluation by looking into assessment types, consideration of academic integrity, alternative ways of the learners' evaluation and different aspects of online examinations.

Keywords: Formative assessment, Summative assessment, Online assessment, Peer assessment, Online examination, Emotion.

1. Introduction

There is no consensus on the definition of "assessment" within the relevant literature because of the variety of approaches/applications of educational testing and versatile interpretations of the concept (Bachman, 2004; Menyani et al., 2022). Throughout the literature, assessment is defined as any act of interpreting data on student performance that has been gathered using a range of methods or practices (Brown, 2004). In the same vein, when assessment is considered, it is frequently associated with exams and homework, as well as evaluating students' performance to determine whether they are qualified to "pass" a certain subject or portion of it (Benson & Brack, 2010). As a clearer definition, assessment is the systematic gathering, analysis, and use of data concerning educational programs carried out with the intention of enhancing student learning and development (Palomba & Banta, 1999). Online assessments, on the other hand, can be characterized as any procedure or course of action for rating students' performance on learning tasks, giving feedback, or advancing learners in their learning processes in entirely online courses (Weleschuk et al., 2019). This diversified range of definitions of assessment necessitates the designer of the assessments to have it defined at the inception of the assessment task (Menyani et al., 2022).

In order to comprehend what a student has learned, assessment is a crucial feedback mechanism, and teachers may utilize a variety of assessments in the courses they teach (Vellanki et al., 2023). This chapter presents an overview of the methods of assessment used in online learning, considering the increased risk of academic integrity violations. Also, the design of assessment to effectively improve the students' learning outcomes and minimize cheating will be elaborated. Following a discussion of the two primary methods of assessment in Section 2, Section 3 will concentrate further on online teaching and learning. The effective evaluation design and the relevant factors to consider are discussed in Section 4. Section 6 will elaborate on online examination after discussing online peer assessment as an alternate evaluation method in Section 5. Through Sections 7 and 8, the impact of students' attitudes on the online assessment will be discussed. Section 9 concludes the chapter.

2. Assessment Types

It is important to distinguish between formative and summative assessments given the various definitions of assessment. Formative assessment is mainly concerned with the learning process and advancement of the students and is defined as "the iterative processes of determining what, how much, and how well students are learning in relation to the learning goals and expected outcomes to inform tailored formative feedback and support further learning. This definition is consistent with the idea that formative assessment is a pedagogical strategy that is more effective when the role is shared among the teacher, peers, and the individual learner" (Gikandi et al., 2011: 2337 as cited in Menyani et al., 2022: 197).

Thus, this kind of feedback is essential since it enables students to pinpoint their strong points and areas for development. According to Senel & Senel (2021) for the student to identify flaws and errors, feedback is necessary. Feedback is also necessary to ensure interaction between instructors and students in distance education given the situation in distance learning. It is also argued that monitoring and feedback, which is an aspect of formative evaluation in distance education, is becoming more important as it is also a method of contact and communication between students and teachers (Menyani et al., 2022).

A summative assessment, on the other hand, aims to compare students' learning to a benchmark at the end of a course of instruction. Summative evaluation has a directing influence because it provides the incentive for making significant decisions like passing a course, enrolling in a higher education program, and getting a diploma or certificate. Similar to this, summative assessment is also defined as a summation of what a student has succeeded with at the end of a term, relative to the learning aims and the relevant state/national standards (Biesta, 2009; Mogboh & Okoye, 2019 as cited in Menyani et al., 2022). The writers are used to have mentioned both sorts of assessments in the same sentence:

Formative assessments, to monitor students' development, and summative assessments, to grade learners based on compliance with a set of standards or criteria (Menyani et al., 2022).

Summative assessment, for instance, is used to determine if students have grasped a particular concept or have met the course's expectations for learning outcomes. High-stakes exams are typically a component of summative evaluations, the outcomes of which may determine whether a student is advanced to another level of study or is allowed to graduate. On the other hand, formative assessment aids in monitoring students' understanding and development through official tests and assignments, as well as more informal methods like in-class exercises, presentations, peer evaluation, etc. During the formative assessment phase, teachers provide students with a variety of feedback, such as written, audio, or video feedback (Johnson & Cooke, 2016). It may also be recommended for students to evaluate their own learning to see how they are doing. In order to increase student accomplishment, formative assessment is used to manage instruction and learning and to modify learning activities in order to change teaching methods (Baleni, 2015; Looney, 2005). Additionally, it serves the purpose of accelerating student growth as teachers gather and analyze data on student accomplishments to improve their education. The majority of the time, it affects students' final course marks (Black & Wiliam, 2009; Vellanki et al., 2023).

3. Online Education: Teaching and Learning

The Internet is becoming more and more popular as a tool for teaching and learning, and it can assist students in learning content independently and boost their confidence in their capacity to function as independent learners. Since at least 2002, technologies for conducting several online experiments in science and engineering have been developed (Ammari & Slama, 2006; Gillet et al., 2005; Kian-Sam et al., 2003; Salzmann et al., 2000 as cited in Rane & MacKenzie, 2020). The availability of e-journals, documents, and references on the Internet, which can be shared and kept in vast numbers for references, has aided engineering education (Allen & Seaman, 2008).

This phenomenon has led to new debates regarding the most effective ways to assist students in learning course material as technology and the Internet have created new ways for both students and educators to teach. Students can comprehend course information better by using well-designed online modules (Henson et al., 2002; Rane & MacKenzie, 2020).

Although teachers spend a lot of time and effort creating coursework and courses that will benefit students in their future jobs, most students find it difficult to remember what they are taught in lectures. Recognizing a student's difficulty grasping the content, giving them helpful criticism, letting them practice the material, and evaluating student learning can all support student learning (Lyle & Crawford, 2011; Rane & MacKenzie, 2020).

Many nations used social isolation to stop the COVID-19 uncontrollable global pandemic from spreading. According to Bunyan (2020), the Movement Control Order, which forbade all national activities involving large gatherings, including the closing of all schools, was initially put into effect in March 2020. This forced the Education authorities of various countries to launch online instruction until schools could resume (Tan *et al.*, 2021). Employment of technology in education is now a crucial component of the present system and no longer plays the opulent supporting function it once did. The way we view education as a whole is altered by these fusions. It removes the constraint of conventional classroom teaching and learning and creates new possibilities. This includes the choice to conduct assessments without paper, such as those that are knowledge-based, performance-based, or practice-based (Crisp, 2007). However, as with any assessment process, planning for an e-assessment requires careful consideration of the type of assessment that will be needed, how it will relate to the immediate learning objectives, learning outcomes, and the rest of the curriculum, and whether it will be completed electronically at all (Ellaway & Masters, 2009 as cited in Tan *et al.*, 2021).

In order to modernize and prepare for the future, online teaching and learning must be implemented. This pandemic around the world has accelerated the adoption of this conversion. Despite how effective this approach is at preventing the spread of disease, social isolation will persist, and it is also a barrier to the delivery of regular classroom instruction. The transition to online learning would necessitate rearranging a lesson plan to meet the demands of the syllabus at the time. In the future, we can fully utilize online exams as a method of evaluation thanks to the technology that is currently available (Povera & Yunus, 2020; Tan *et al.*, 2021).

3.1. *Online Assessment*

Online assessment is described as a methodical way of using Information and Communications Technology (ICT) to acquire data or artifacts about a student and their learning processes in order to make assumptions about their character (Baker *et al.*, 2016). The extent to which assessments, when implemented in online contexts, can simultaneously fulfill the interests of students, teachers, and the educational organization is, in our opinion, one of the biggest difficulties facing the future of assessment. Gikandi *et al.* (2011 as cited in Heil & Ifenthaler, 2023) highlighted the advantages of using online tests to enable meaningful feedback and offer interactive help for students. Nguyen *et al.* (2017 as cited in Heil & Ifenthaler, 2023) have conducted an empirical study on online assessment identifies potential factors that may have an impact on learner engagement and academic outcomes. Empirical studies have concentrated on various online assessment implementations, such as online formative assessments (Baleni, 2015 as cited in Heil & Ifenthaler, 2023), digital game-based assessments (Kim & Ifenthaler, 2019 as cited in Heil & Ifenthaler, 2023), or online peer- and self-assessments, as a result of the increased use of online learning environments and the stronger presence of distance education program (Admiraal *et al.*, 2014; Moore & Kearsley, 2011 as cited in Heil & Ifenthaler, 2023).

Students can learn more efficiently by tailoring the curriculum to their needs and changing the present instructional design. Particularly in the Internet era, traditional in-person exams may not be the most effective approach to evaluate students or aid in their learning. Research has looked into using tests to aid learning rather than just assessing students for more than a century (Gates, 1917; Jones, 1923; Lyle & Crawford, 2011; Passerini & Granger, 2000; Zacharis, 2010 as cited in Rane & MacKenzie, 2020). Technology, including computers, can be effective in the teaching and learning process (Rane & MacKenzie, 2020).

3.2. *Assessment Reform to Accommodate Online Learning*

There have been modifications to assessments as of COVID-19. The most frequently invigilated assessment types employed in different courses for a significant period of time have been in-class quizzes or tests, mid-semester tests or examinations, and final exams, all of which are typically performed in a face-to-face setting. As a result, when the shift to online learning was initiated in response to COVID-19, the first move was to implement substitute online tests. Assessments were transformed into evaluations for various courses of different education levels quickly. The invigilated tests and exams were replaced with substitute online evaluations. Alternative tests were taken into consideration in this situation to allow students more freedom and control over their learning and assessment (Ali *et al.*, 2022).

Actions taken by education providers to minimize instances of plagiarism/cheating included:

- To substitute the exams with the open-book online alternative assessments

- The assessment was to be finished and submitted through the learning management system within 24 hours. The time was not limited to 3 hours as in the typical face-to-face exams. For various reasons such as students having problems with computers and/or the Internet, concerns with equity in terms of technology and digital literacy, and other obligations students were likely to have as a result of the epidemic (Ali *et al.*, 2022).
- Students who sought for special consideration due to various causes, such as conflicts with evaluations of other courses and health and home concerns, were granted additional extensions for up to five working days.
- Instead of using multiple-choice questions based on numeracy in the final examinations, more skills-based questions were employed. It was thought that when answers called for justifications and explanations, students were less likely to replicate them (Ali *et al.*, 2022).
- Turnitin anti-plagiarism software was required for submission of the answer papers so that any plagiarism could be quickly found. According to the faculty academic integrity guidelines policy, staff members warned students about the repercussions of cheating, which might include failing the course or being expelled from the university, depending on how serious the infraction was (Ali *et al.*, 2022).

It is asserted that although the pandemic has expedited this tendency, the shift from conventional to online accounting education was already underway as a result of digital revolution (Reyneke *et al.*, 2021 as cited in Ali *et al.*, 2022). Universities were forced to switch from traditional face-to-face evaluations to online assessments because of the pandemic's shift to online learning (White 2021 as cited in Ali *et al.*, 2022). Fundamentally, any teaching system must include learning assessment. Reports, essays, and case studies completed through the learning management system were among the non-invigilated assessments used in some courses. Most of the invigilated assessments were tests, mid-semester examinations, and end-of-semester exams that were taken in a face-to-face invigilated setting. As the face-to-face tests and exams were switched to online assessments, the 2020 shift to online learning created a number of problems and difficulties for the teaching team. We all had the opportunity to learn as we experimented with designing and implementing online assessments because the majority of the teaching staff lacked the necessary expertise to administer online tests and exams (Ali *et al.*, 2022; Kuh and Ewell, 2010).

After we switched to online evaluation, a number of problems and difficulties appeared. These included issues with conducting online group assessments, increased workloads for students and staff, inconsistent pass rates across courses, and student cheating. There was also a lack of some necessary technology, such as e-proctoring tools. One of the main difficulties in the development and delivery of online exams was the lack of knowledge and expertise in some of the technology capabilities already in use (Ali *et al.*, 2022).

4. Effective Online Assessment Design

A high-quality instructional design includes assessment, which must be closely related to the desired learning outcomes (Judi, 2022). Clear learning objectives, prudently organized content, balanced student workloads, use of unified media, appropriate student activities, and assessment are signs of the remaining instructional design. The process of organizing, implementing, and evaluating education is known as instructional design. This is especially true when dealing with the standard learning tasks (Bane, 2019; Donmez & Cagiltay, 2016 as cited in Judi, 2022).

Despite the difficult period following the pandemic, assessment continues to serve its primary function of fostering learning (Judi, 2022). Digital assessment is defined by Shraim (2019 as cited in Judi, 2022) as a system that evaluates students online or as a part of a learning management system, such as Moodle or Sakai. In comparison to traditional assessment, instructional design appears to be more important in digital assessment. Digital assessment necessitates the explicit use of some form of design process to integrate and coordinate numerous learning components, unlike face-to-face assessment where the underlying model of instructional design appears to be implicit in the decision-making processes (Rapanta *et al.*, 2020).

4.1. *Is Online Assessment an Invite to Cheat (Okada et al. 2019)?*

The educators are now faced with a new challenge: How can they ensure that students have attempted the assessment's work on their own? These worries bring up challenges with assessment security and academic honesty. Both are essential to ensuring that students who graduate from universities have achieved the requisite results. Education with a strong moral and ethical foundation is emphasized in academic honesty. Assessment security is a different idea that prioritizes tightening up student evaluation to thwart any efforts at deception and deal with any wrongdoing (Judi, 2022).

Consideration of technical, organizational, and pedagogical needs to support the modified interaction style and learning method while preserving high-quality education is one of the issues faced by educational institutions and instructors when conducting online education. There are inherent issues in the new educational paradigm as well as in the digital assessment (Bojović *et al.*, 2020; Judi, 2022).

Assessment plays a significant part in the learning process at higher education institutions in order to provide observable indicators of learning, managing student development, and ascertaining mastery of the curriculum. How an institution views future generations and conceptualizes learning plus how it develops and implements evaluation affects education (Oldfield & Timmis, 2013).

The cornerstone of education is academic integrity. Academic integrity is defined by six core principles by the International Centre for Academic Integrity: honesty, fairness, truth, respect, responsibility, and courage (Khan *et al.*, 2022).

A variety of behaviors have been classified as violations of academic integrity, such as electronic cheating and other examined assessment designs and more (Khan *et al.*, 2022). Also, 21 such behaviors were identified that can be considered as cheating, such as cheating in exams, impersonating someone else to sit for exams, using unapproved material during exams, collusion, fraud, impersonating others, using someone else's work as their own, paying someone to get their own work done, and so forth (Harmon *et al.*, 2010 as cited in Khan *et al.*, 2022).

Academic misconduct is the practice of engaging in behavior that conflicts with certain commitments and beliefs. The term "academic integrity" is frequently used in the more particular context of helping students to stay away from academic misconduct (Amrane-Cooper *et al.*, 2022). In these discussions, it appears that there are two main themes that are far from complimentary. One theme entails encouraging innovative assessment design while applying the core assessment values of authenticity, inclusivity, validity, and dependability. Additionally, it requires giving students explicit instructions on what institutions anticipate in terms of citing, plagiarism, and cooperation. The second thread discusses practical and technological safeguards to preserve academic integrity, including online invigilation software (proctoring systems), text-matching software that finds similar or exact matches between submitted student work and other digital content and moderation of marking to validate student academic work (Amrane-Cooper *et al.*, 2022).

Technical difficulties rather than moral and societal concerns have received the majority of attention in research on academic misconduct. Some academics appear to combine the two themes mentioned previously by suggesting online synchronous assessments as a replacement for conventional proctored exams while retaining the option of human authentication (Chao *et al.*, 2012 as cited in Amrane-Cooper *et al.*, 2022).

According to Sullivan (2016), quizzes are to test factual knowledge, practice tests are to test procedural knowledge, essays are to test conceptual knowledge, and oral tests are to evaluate metacognitive knowledge. Offering random access to various question banks or essay questions as a technique to lessen the inclination to cheat by lowering the stakes through several delivery attempts is another measure that has benefited academic honesty. Each option's key objective has been to maintain the importance and integrity of accomplishing learning outcomes while balancing student authentication (Amrane-Cooper *et al.*, 2022).

Students can cheat online by texting answers, copying and pasting concepts without giving credit, or buying professionally written essays to pass off as their own. Utilizing new technologies to encourage more authentic assessments is one strategy for solving this issue (Ali *et al.*, 2022).

Despite having clear policies for academic integrity in place, staff members expressed worries about students' use of "ghostwriters" and other forms of cheating on online tests (Ali *et al.*, 2022). Given that they were all completed without supervision, it was challenging to tell if the assessments had been completed by the students. Due to the lockdown scenario as an instance, or for the big cohorts, several students who were suspected of using ghostwriters to complete their written assessments were not penalized for several reasons, including the fact that the Turnitin plagiarism detection tool could not find any plagiarism matches (Ali *et al.*, 2022).

4.2. *How to Investigate Cheating?*

As studied by Harmon and Lambrinos (2008), students with more maturity and experience in the classroom are less prone to cheat. Additionally, this group was discovered to be more receptive to e-Authentication systems, as they felt that they would guarantee the integrity of the online test and contribute to a positive assessment experience (Okada *et al.*, 2019).

Also, the study of Underwood & Szabo (2003 as cited in Okada *et al.*, 2019) on UK students revealed that there is a connection between a person's tendency to engage in academic misconduct and their gender, how frequently they use the Internet, their age, and maturity. New undergraduates are more prone to cheat and plagiarize than students in their ending years of study.

Reliable exams, trustworthy technology, and authentic assessments are crucial for quality assurance (limiting cheating) in formative and summative assessments (Okada *et al.*, 2019).

"The Trust-based e-Assessment System for Learning (TeSLA) system was designed to check student authentication and authorship through a combination of the following instruments:

- *Biometrics*: facial recognition (analyzing the face and facial expressions), voice recognition (analyzing audio structures), and keystroke analysis (analyzing how the user uses the keyboard).
- *Textual analysis*: anti-plagiarism (using text matching to detect similarities between documents) and forensic (to verify the authorship of written documents).
- *Security*: digital signature (to authenticate) and timestamp (to identify when an event is recorded by the computer)" (Okada *et al.*, 2019: 862).

The findings of the study of Okada *et al.* (2019) highlight the need for educational teams and e-authentication system developers to notice and respond to the vastly different nature of examinees while also supporting the usage of cutting-edge technologies in assessment. The solution can be found through comprehending students' attitudes toward and experiences with electronic assessment methods. High-quality assurance will be possible thanks to a trust-based system for e-authentication that combines a number of tools and reduces plagiarism and cheating in online assessments (Okada *et al.*, 2019).

Considering the crucial role of academic integrity in the future, Amrane-Cooper *et al.* (2022) the shift to the online assessment will necessitate the following:

- A thorough overhaul of exams to make them functional for meeting the demands of students in an online context. Since open book exams significantly aid students in avoiding academic dishonesty, there has been a considerable push towards them in terms of academic integrity.
- Students must be innovatively prepared for online assessment by adopting practices for online exams that prevent collaboration and plagiarism. From a technological and educational standpoint, this comprises training materials and introducing students to online evaluation.
- Developing strategies to help students work with assessments in a wider range of durations and formats than standard fixed-time exams in testing facilities. This should include the capacity to manage time properly and work efficiently under pressure (Amrane-Cooper *et al.*, 2022).

The adoption of alternative evaluation methods gave rise to chances to rethink institutional and assessment frameworks that support students' growth and success. Worldwide attitudes towards online testing are very likely to improve as network infrastructure advances and staff and student comfort levels with remote work rise. Higher education institutions now have the option to move exams to the Internet on a scheduled and ongoing basis. But the risk to academic integrity must be taken into account and minimized (Amrane-Cooper *et al.*, 2022).

5. Online Peer Assessment, an Alternative Evaluation Method

Online peer assessment has been suggested by the literature as a successful method for encouraging critical thinking in college students (see Dominguez *et al.*, 2015; Filius *et al.*, 2018; Gambrill *et al.*, 2017; Guiller *et al.*, 2008; Novakovich, 2016; Puig *et al.*, 2019 as cited in Zhan, 2021). It is widely believed that critical thinking can be taught and learned. According to research, critical thinkers are better equipped to make judgments and judgments in challenging situations, do better academically, engage in social issues more intelligently and actively, and obtain employment more readily (Zhan, 2021).

Peers are involved in social interactions and bargaining during online peer assessment, which invariably involves sociocultural aspects. Some scholars have noted cultural resistance to peer review in environments with a Confucian past. It should be made clear what factors instructors should consider when designing assignments to ensure that online peer assessment is successful in fostering students' critical thinking (Zhan, 2021).

Previous research frequently referred to three efficient design components for online peer assessments. These components seem to improve peer interaction, which is essential for the growth of critical thinking. First, a key component of preparing students is online peer assessment training. Online peer assessment training makes the desired results of student learning and the standards of evaluation clearer, making the quality of peer interaction more likely to be ensured (Zhan, 2021).

Second, students' growth in critical thinking can be guided and supported by teachers' advice during the online peer assessment process. As a result, when students evaluate one another's work, teachers guiding questions give them something to think about, which tends to improve the quality of peer interaction (Zhan, 2021).

Third, it is crucial to define the kind of peer feedback that students are encouraged to provide since the substance of peer feedback is intimately tied to its effects on students' development of critical thinking. Novakovich's (2016 as cited in Zhan, 2021) study established that participants' critical remarks and justifications were substantially connected with the growth of their critical thinking skills. The findings of another study (Filius *et al.*, 2018 as cited in Zhan, 2021) found that the participants considered peer feedback with ideas that forced them to consider, ponder, and examine their responses would be helpful. Therefore, constructive criticism accompanied by justification from peers can help resolve any cognitive conflicts that arise during peer interaction, fostering the growth of students' critical thinking (Zhan, 2021).

Peer evaluation takes many distinct forms, depending on the learners, learning contexts, and assessment implementation characteristics. These forms include writing, portfolios, oral presentations, performance tasks, and other skilled behaviors. Both formative and summative aims can be served by this type of evaluation (Bolzer *et al.*, 2015; Chinn, 2005; DiGiovanni & Nagaswami, 2001; Panadero *et al.*, 2018; Patchan et al., 2018; Topping et al., 2009 as cited in Wang et al., 2020). Peers exchange ideas and review one other's work by assigning marks or ratings in accordance with the evaluation criteria or by providing written or oral comments. Students are reflectively involved in critical thinking about their peers' work while providing comments, which improves their learning (Wang et al., 2020). Students who participate in peer assessment also have a deeper comprehension of the evaluation process and, as a result, improve their learning and assessment-related skills (Wang et al., 2020).

5.1. Online Peer Assessments: Advantages

- Online peer evaluation makes ensuring anonymity simple.
- With the aid of the learning platform, peer assessment may be carried out at flexible times and locations, and teachers can more carefully monitor students' progress and activities.
- To ensure that each student gets several peers' input on their work.
- Online peer assessment allows teachers to do the same task more quickly and efficiently, which lessens their workload, especially when they have a high number of students.
- With the use of technology, online peer assessment can be used in traditional classrooms and is not necessarily exclusive to online courses (Wang et al., 2020).

5.2. Online Peer Assessments: Requisites

The attitudes of students matter in encouraging successful outcomes and the educational advantages of peer assessment. While students who have unfavorable views toward peer assessment may not be motivated to participate, those who have positive attitudes are more likely to take the assessment process seriously and to benefit academically. They might have negative learning outcomes from peer assessment, feel bored and frustrated, and not finish the work for peer assessment (Wang et al., 2020).

To encourage good student attitudes, online peer assessment should educate students about learning objectives, foster positive attitudes toward activities, and inspire them to perform well on the cognitive, emotional, and behavioral levels. Prior to the peer assessment activity, students should receive rigorous online peer assessment training in order to increase the quality of peer comments (Wang *et al.*, 2020).

6. Online Examination

As early as 2009, the introduction of online exams was documented, and it resulted in successful outcomes. Online tests have a great chance to be the answer to this issue. This online exam's administration has raised a few technical issues that need to be resolved. A prerequisite is having sufficient knowledge of fundamental computer abilities, which may be quickly fixed with time and familiarity. This would imply that not just any academic personnel are qualified to carry the burden of responsibility in handling the online exam preparation. The skilled staff must be able to assist any candidate who needs technical assistance in addition to transferring the questions to an online format. Therefore, appropriate coaching for professors is required if online exams are to be used to their full potential (Tan *et al.*, 2021).

6.1. Online Examination: Advantages

- The choice to use Google Form for exams is based on a number of variables. Despite its straightforward design, the software's friendliness toward users makes it desirable.
- The multiple-choice questions are automatically graded by the system in real time, which saves time and encourages helpful criticism from the students to boost performance (Tan *et al.*, 2021).
- Conducting a professional exam typically needs extensive financial preparations. This platform reduces overhead expenses while eliminating the cost of pointless activities. Due to the exam's minimal use of physical goods, there is less financial strain (Tan *et al.*, 2021).

Online assessments can be used for practice and to give students immediate feedback (unlike traditional examination) so they can correct their errors. Scores increase when students repeatedly practice with the same or comparable test variants (Rane & MacKenzie, 2020). Inadequate academic performance can be attributed to anxiety. Students who are anxious may have panic attacks, mental fogginess before exams, a sense of helplessness when studying, and a rapid heartbeat. Students studying engineering may be especially prone to worry. Because the majority of courses only have a few exams during the semester and most of the student's mark depends on how well they perform on each exam, traditional in-class exams can make students more anxious (Rane & MacKenzie, 2020).

6.2. *Online Examination: Limitations*

The core functionality of an online system may be jeopardized by slow speed and poor Internet access. Some online video or instructional platforms are being supplied for free in an effort to provide a more affordable choice, but at the expense of all the limitations put in place. This obstacle may have an impact on how the system is delivered by, for example, limiting the number of participants, the number of questions that may be created, or even the length of a video chat. As a result, an institution will need to think about joining a platform of their choosing and, if possible, consider spending extra money to invest in a reliable security system to protect the assessment. For people who are not tech-savvy, preparing the questions might require some basic computer abilities, which could be difficult. Due to a lack of certain characteristics, the conversion from the original format to an online platform may not always go as planned. Even after a successful conversion, numerous repetitive trial runs must be carried out to guarantee that the system functions properly (Snodgrass *et al.*, 2014; Walsh, 2015 as cited in Tan *et al.*, 2021). To find any potential problems, it is essential to do this tiresome work. The software's ability to regularly back up the data in order to prevent data loss in the case of an Internet connection outage is a crucial factor to take into account when taking an online exam. Unfortunately, if a user presses the browser's refresh button, Google Form is unable to save the data (Tan *et al.*, 2021).

Longer reaction time requirements in assessments caused difficulties for both teaching professionals and students. Given that we have a sizable cohort of overseas students for whom English is a second language, writing longer comments in numerically oriented courses was a particular problem for pupils. These pupils struggle with queries that call for lengthy written responses and prefer problems and questions that are math-based. Staff had to read longer replies when students were asked to submit longer written responses as part of online exams, which increased their workload.

The teaching team had already spent numerous hours studying new procedures and preparing for lessons. In place of more conventional assessments like midterm exams and in-class tests, alternative assessments like essays and reports took more time to complete and had higher non-completion rates (Ali *et al.*, 2022).

6.3. *Online Examination: Types*

Three general types of online exams were utilized in the shift to online assessment: proctored exams, fixed-time unseen closed-book exams, and unseen but open-book exams with a longer response time. An evaluation technique known as open-book examination enables students to use their class notes and summaries, textbooks, or other authorized sources while responding to questions in an invigilated environment (Amrane-Cooper *et al.*, 2022). The submission window, or the amount of time students had to finish and submit their answers, was referred to as the response time. The majority of the time, content adjustments included switching to open-book exams and restructuring questions to deter plagiarism (including self-plagiarism from previously graded student work). By creating submission windows of varying lengths, it was hoped to lessen the emphasis on memorization, add some flexibility, and lighten anxiety. Due to the rising use of online exams, the shift to online assessment has encouraged innovations and inventive practice in assessment methodologies (Amrane-Cooper *et al.*, 2022).

7. Online Assessment: Students' View

Since motivation is a prerequisite for and a byproduct of effective education, students' attitudes and motivation toward assessments are crucial factors for success in online learning. Because they involve new expectations with regard to their learning, the literature urge student participation in the development of their learning spaces through the distributed pedagogy (Makina, 2022).

Students desire support because they want to have a say in how they are taught and evaluated. They want their suggestions incorporated into course designs and into fresh teaching methods created for their instructors to support efficient online learning. Successful formative online assessment experiences with the students depend on their motivation.

Understanding and critically thinking about the many online formative assessment methodologies utilized in an open distance learning environment can contribute to motivating student experiences (Makina, 2022).

This is especially true in open distance learning settings in higher education. Education scholars have been examining formative assessment methodologies' effects on student motivation to study more and more (e.g., Andersson & Palm, 2017; Gikandi *et al.*, 2011, McLaughlin & Yan, 2017 as cited in Makina, 2022). However, the study on online assessment has not been particularly interested in features of students' demotivation to participate online. The background of online formative assessment practices that demotivate students; how students approach assessment activities is heavily influenced by how lecturers convey to them the goals of learning using online formative assessment procedures are investigated by Makina (2022). In this study, demotivating online formative assessment procedures in an open distance learning context are examined from the perspective of students. The purpose is to consider how online formative evaluation techniques might improve the motivation and caliber of students' online learning experiences.

A feed-out function of assessment, assessment of learning, and assessment as learning, which fosters rigorous learning processes in which the learner can engage with tasks that will eventually be assessed, are just a few of the characteristics of formative assessment. In order to make specific educational judgments, formative assessment is regarded to be the gathering of student data and their learning processes (Gikandi *et al.*, 2011; Makina, 2022). Effective formative assessment integration in online learning environments has the potential to provide a suitable framework for ongoing meaningful interactions between students and the instructor as well as to promote the growth of productive learning communities that support meaningful learning and assessment. One cannot help but notice the evident difficulties in its execution while studying the literature on online formative assessment and its educational consequences because this calls for well-structured procedures that are unfamiliar to the majority of online educators (Makina, 2022).

One of the key elements for success in e-learning has frequently been identified as a student's motivation to participate in online assessment and learning. It is crucial to keep students' interest and engagement levels high; else, involvement from students would be low. The process by which goal-directed behavior is initiated, sustained, and controlled by a construct that can result from the interaction of conscious and unconscious elements is known as motivation. Participation in online formative assessment represents a true feature of motivation because it requires a behavior that, once started, must be maintained (Makina, 2022).

Motivated students are more inclined to take on difficult tasks that promote active engagement, enjoyment, and the adoption of a deep learning philosophy. They will perform better and be more persistent and creative. These elements could be the intensity of the need or want, the incentive or reward value of the objective, or the person's expectations. Motivated students are those who voluntarily continue to complete learning assignments that advance their academic objectives. Tasks in online settings that are motivated by goals are goal-oriented, and course instructors should be able to alter online formative assessment techniques to meet those goals. This is so because motivation can affect what students learn, how they learn, and when they decide to learn in online learning settings (Makina, 2022).

Designing more effective assessment tactics that encourage students to stick with their studies may be aided by identifying characteristics of online formative assessment strategies. An individual student's method of learning is typically a reaction to the perceived demands of any learning task rather than a quality of the student. In other words, a student's aptitude or method of learning is determined by how they react to an evaluation, whether they like it or not. Therefore, in order to encourage students to learn in online environments, lecturers in those contexts need new attitudes, knowledge, abilities, and operational methods (Makina, 2022).

8. Online Assessment: Emotions

Although there is research on assessment-related emotions, there is little on student emotion in online assessments or on contrasting feelings in various assessment formats. In the past, the majority of research has been on anxiety, showing that students are less stressed and anxious while taking summative exams online. However, while students with low classroom-test anxiety experienced higher anxiety online, those with high classroom-test anxiety exhibited equal levels of anxiety. Positive associations between positive affect, such as comfort and confidence, and online evaluation have been reported in a few research that examined positive affect. More recently, it was discovered that students felt more positively than negatively after finishing a computer-based exam (Riegel & Evans, 2021).

It is also important to account for student variations in order to more fully understand how online assessments affect students' emotions. Research to date has shown that women are more likely than men to experience anxiety connected to assessments. Males tend to report more positive feelings and lesser negative emotions, according to the few research that have looked into other emotions. Positive emotions, as previously mentioned, frequently correlate favorably with performance, whereas negative emotions frequently do not. Additionally, there is considerable evidence linking anxiousness to subpar performance in online assessments. Studies must take into account factors like gender and prior achievement because the field of study on emotions in online assessment settings is still developing. This is crucial to determine which student groups online evaluations favor or ignore (Riegel & Evans, 2021).

There is a need for further research, as evidenced by the scant amount of literature on emotions in online evaluation and the disregard for good emotions in this setting. This study explores the complex emotional landscape of university students' assessment experiences by separating the connections between their reported feelings in an online quiz and a conventional classroom test. It is not just focused on assessment anxiety. Additionally, the online tests used in this study differ significantly from previous studies in terms of the frequency, time allotted for each question, and weight of the grade, which reflects contemporary trends in society. We investigated the effect online assessment played on students' assessment-related emotions in a sizable sample of undergraduate students using the complementary power of a mixed-methods approach, allowing for more generalizable and transferrable conclusions. In this way, we have contributed to the research on practical and successful methods of performing online assessment, which is a crucial component of contemporary higher education (Riegel & Evans, 2021).

The study conducted by Senadheera & Kulasekara (2022) proved that students have experienced deep learning as a result of the thoughtful design of online formative assessments, making them the main agents of their own learning. The assessment's design increased students' engagement with the material and encouraged them to think outside the box, according to an analysis of their replies. The results of the assessment tasks clearly demonstrated the presence of self-determined learning, despite the fact that the tests' design was more biased toward constructive alignment than heutagogy principles or self-determined learning. This example also illustrates how several learning strategies can help the students to learn skills. It further supports the idea of convergence in learning strategies for developing higher-order cognitive abilities. Additionally, examiners must take great care to format their questions so that they are readable on a variety of displays, including the small ones used by students' devices (Senadheera & Kulasekara, 2022).

Technically, the compatibility of these queries with different browsers needs to be tested. The authors advise colleges to pay attention to developing the necessary infrastructure facilities and student accessibility of information communication technology for assessments given that online exams are more flexible and offer some advantages over paper-based tests. Many academics are still improving their online assessment techniques, and they frequently create online exams with a paper-based mindset in mind. This early strategy jeopardizes the authenticity, integrity, and intended learning results of the exam. It is a major risk to the development of online tests as an effective teaching tool to have poor infrastructure and poorly educated human resources in online assessment systems (Senadheera & Kulasekara, 2022).

9. Conclusion

With regard to improving the design of online examinations and formative and summative assessment procedures, teachers and scholars came up with the following suggestions for helping ensure academic integrity:

- Design tests and quizzes so that students can only see one question per page and have one chance to respond to each one (this feature is available in the majority of learning management systems).
- Make the questions random so that every student sees a different one at once. There should be multiple test versions so that teachers can alter the questions or response choices, for example, in multiple-choice questions. This would make it impossible for students to distribute and reproduce questions to their classmates by photocopying, sharing, or other means.
- To make online exams harder, develop a variety of question types fitting the students' degree of proficiency. The majority of the learning management systems on the market allow for the development of multiple-choice, matching, fill-in-the-blank, dropdown, true/false, short answer, and essay questions with ease.

- Students at more advanced levels are given more subjective questions than objective questions in comparison to pre-elementary and elementary level children. With this addition, the problem of plagiarism would be somewhat resolved, and advanced-level students would have more of a challenge. This opinion runs counter to Alghammas's (2020 as cited in Vellanki *et al.*, 2023) research, which showed that respondents preferred objective over subjective questions.
- Online tests should not be too long so that pupils don't have too much time. Teachers believe that because students have so much time to finish tests, they frequently consult one another for the answers. They suggest holding quick multiple-choice exams that last no longer than 30 minutes in order to discourage pupils from conferring and exchanging answers.
- Use a secure browser setting to stop students from accessing other websites while taking tests (Vellanki *et al.*, 2023).

References

Admiraal, W., Huisman, B. & van de Ven, M. (2014). Self- and peer assessment in massive open online courses. *International Journal of Higher Education*, 3(3), 119–128.

Alghammas, A. (2020). Online language assessment during the COVID-19 pandemic: University faculty members' perceptions and practices. *Asian EFL Journal*, 27(44), 169–195.

Ali, Narayan, A.K. & Gedera, D. (2022). Transforming assessment in accounting education to align with online learning. *Pacific Accounting Review*, 34(4), 536–547.

Allen, I.E. & Seaman, J. (2008). *Staying the Course: Online Education in the United States*. Sloan Consortium. Eric Collection.

Ammari, A.C. & Slama, J.B.H. (2006). The development of a remote laboratory for internet-based engineering education. *Journal of Asynchronous Learning Networks*, 10(4), 3–13.

Amrane-Cooper, Hatzipanagos, S. & Tait, A. (2022). Developing student behaviours that support academic integrity in distance learning. *Open Praxis*, 13(4), 378–384.

Andersson, C. & Palm, P. (2017). Characteristics of improved formative assessment practice. *Education Inquiry*, 8(2), 104.

Bachman, L.F. (2004). *Statistical Analyses for Language Assessment*. Cambridge: Cambridge University Press.

Baker, E., Chung, G. & Cai, L. (2016). Assessment, gaze, refraction, and blur: The course of achievement testing in the past 100 years. *Review of Research in Education*, 40, 94–142.
Baleni, G.Z. (2015). Online formative assessment in higher education: Its pros and cons. *The Electronic Journal of e-Learning*, 13(4), 228–236.
Baleni, Z. (2015). Online formative assessment in higher education: Its pros and cons. *Electronic Journal of e-Learning*, 13(4), 228–226.
Bane, J.A. (2019). Academic integrity in the online classroom. eLearn July (Emerging technologies. https://elearnmag.acm.org/featured.cfm?aid=3343233).
Benson, R. & Brack, C. (2010). *Online Learning and Assessment in Higher Education: A Planning Guide*. Cambridge: Chandos Publishing.
Biesta, G. (2009). Good education in an age of measurement: On the need to reconnect with the question of purpose in education. *Educational Assessment, Evaluation and Accountability*, 21(1), 33–46.
Black, P. & Wiliam, D. (2009). Developing the theory of formative assessment. *Educational Assessment, Evaluation and Accountability*, 21(1), 5–31.
Bojović, Ž., Bojović, P. D., Vujošević, D. & Šuh, J. (2020). Education in times of crisis: Rapid transition to distance learning. Computer Applications in Engineering Education (August).
Bolzer, M., Strijbos, J.W. & Fischer, F. (2015). Inferring mindful cognitive-processing of peer-feedback via eye-tracking: Role of feedback-characteristics, fixation-durations and transitions. *Journal of Computer Assisted Learning*, 31(5), 422–434.
Brown, H.D. (2004). *Language Assessment: Principles and Classroom Practices*. London: Pearson Education.
Bunyan, J. (2020). PM: Malaysia under movement control order from wed until March 31, all shops closed except for essential services. Malay Mail. Available at www.malaymail.com/news/malaysia/2020/03/16/pm-malaysia-in-lockdown-from-wed-until-march-31-all-shops-closed-except-for/1847204.
Chao, Hung, I.-C. & Chen, N.-S. (2012). On the design of online synchronous assessments in a synchronous cyber classroom: Design of online synchronous assessments. *Journal of Computer Assisted Learning*, 28(4), 379–395.
Chinn, D. (2005). Peer assessment in the algorithms course. *Acm Sigcse Bulletin*, 37(3), 69–73.
Crisp, G. (2007). *E-Assessment Handbook*, 1st edn. London: Continuum International Publishing Group Ltd.
DiGiovanni, E. & Nagaswami, G. (2001). Online peer review: An alternative to face-to face? *ELT Journal*, 55(3): 263–272.

Dominguez, C., Nascimento, M.M.R., Payan-Carreira, G., Cruz, H., Silva, H.J., Lopes, M.F.A. & Morais, E. (2015). Adding value to the learning process by online peer review activities: Towards the elaboration of a methodology to promote critical thinking in future engineers. *European Journal of Engineering Education*, 40(5), 573–591.

Donmez, M. & Cagiltay, K. (2016). A review and categorization of instructional design models. *E-Learn* 2016, 370–384.

Ellaway, R. & Masters, K. (2009). AMEE Guide 32: e-Learning In Medical Education Part 1: Learning, Teaching And Assessment. *Medical Teacher*, 30(5), 455–473.

Filius, R.M., de Kleijn, R.A., Uijl, S.G., Prins, F.J., van Rijen, H.V. & Grobbee, D.E. (2018). Strengthening dialogic peer feedback aiming for deep learning in SPOCs. *Computers & Education*, 125, 86–100.

Gambrill, E. (2006). *Critical Thinking in Clinical Practice: Improving the Quality of Judgments and Decisions*. New Jersey: John Wiley & Sons.

Gates, A.I. (1917). *Recitation as a Factor in Memorizing*. No. 40. Beijing: Science Press.

Gikandi, J.W., Morrow, D. & Davis, N.E. (2011). Online formative assessment in higher education: A Review of the Literature. *Computers & Education*, 57(4), 2333–2351.

Gikandi, J.W., Morrow, D. & Davis, N.E. (2011). Online formative assessment in higher education: A review of the literature. *Computers & Education*, 57(4), 2333–2351.

Gillet, D., Ngoc, A.V.N. & Rekik, Y. (2005). Collaborative web-based experimentation in flexible engineering education. *IEEE Transactions on Education*, 48(4), 696–704.

Guiller, J., Durndell, A. & Ross, A. (2008). Peer interaction and critical thinking: Face-to-face or online discussion?" *Learning and Instruction*, 18(2): 187–200.

Harmon, L. & Buffolino, J. (2010). Assessment design and cheating risk in online instruction. *Online Journal of Distance Learning Administration*, 13(3).

Harmon, O.R. & Lambrinos, J. (2008). Are online exams an invitation to cheat? *The Journal of Economic Education*, 39, 116–125.

Heil, J. & Ifenthaler, D. (2023). Online assessment in higher education: A systematic review. *Online Learning*, 27(1), 187–218.

Henson, A.B., Fridley, K.J., Pollock, D.G. & Brahler, C.J. (2002). Efficacy of interactive Internet-based education in structural timber design. *Journal of Engineering Education*, 91(4),371–378.

Johnson, G.M. & Cooke, A. (2016). An ecological model of student interaction in online learning environments. In Kyei-Blankson, L., Blankson, J., Ntuli, E. & Agyeman, C. (eds.), *Handbook of Research on Strategic*

Management of Interaction, Presence, and Participation in Online Courses (pp. 1–28). Pennsylvania: IGI Global.

Jones, H. (1923). The effects of examination on the performance of learning. *Archives of Psychology*, 10, 1–70.

Judi, H.M. (2022). Integrity and security of digital assessment: Experiences in online learning. *Global Business and Management Research*, 14(1), 97–107.

Khan, P.J. & Tuffnell, C. (2022). Culture of integrity — Institutional response to integrity during COVID19. *International Journal for Educational Integrity*, 18(1), 1–38.

Kian-Sam, H., Abang Ahmad, R. & Ming-Koon, K. (2003). Students' attitudes toward the use of the Internet for learning: A study at a university in Malaysia. *Journal of Educational Technology & Society*, 6(2), 45–49.

Kim, Y.J. & Ifenthaler, D. (2019). Game-based assessment: The past ten years and moving forward. In Ifenthaler, D. & Kim, Y.J. (eds.), *Game-Based Assessment Revisted* (pp. 3–12). Berlin: Springer.

Kuh, G.D. & Ewell, P.T. (2010). The state of learning outcomes assessment in the United States. *Higher Education Management and Policy*, 22(1), 1–20.

Looney, J. (Ed.) (2005). *Formative Assessment: Improving Learning in Secondary Classrooms*. Paris: Organization for Economic Cooperation and Development.

Lyle, K.B. & Crawford, N.A. (2011). Retrieving essential material at the end of lectures improves performance on statistics exams. *Teaching of Psychology*, 38(2), 94–97.

Makina (2022). Students experiences of demotivating online formative assessment strategies at an open distance learning university. *Perspectives in Education*, 40(2), 32–51.

McLaughlin, T. & Yan, Z. (2017). Diverse delivery methods and strong psychological benefits: A review of online formative assessment. *Journal of Computer Assisted Learning*, 33, 562–574.

Menyani, Boumehdi, A. & El Jaadi, O. (2022). Online assessment in the digital era: Moroccan EFL university students' experiences, perceptions and challenges. *IAFOR Journal of Education*, 10(1), 193–210.

Mogboh, V. & Okoye, A.C. (2019). Formative and summative assessment: Trends and practices in basic education. *Journal of Education and Practice*, 10(27), 39–45.

Moore, M.G. & Kearsley, G. (2011). *Distance Education: A Systems View of Online Learning*. Boston: Wadsworth Cengage Learning.

Nguyen, Q., Rienties, B., Toetenel, L., Ferguson, R. & Whitelock, D. (2017). Examining the designs of computer-based assessment and its impact on student engagement, satisfaction, and pass rates. *Computers in Human Behavior*, 76, 703–714.

Novakovich, J. (2016). Fostering critical thinking and reflection through blog-mediated peer feedback. *Journal of Computer Assisted Learning*, 32(1), 16–30.

Okada, Whitelock, D., Holmes, W. & Edwards, C. (2019). e-Authentication for online assessment: A mixed-method study: e-Authentication for online assessment. *British Journal of Educational Technology*, 50(2), 861–875.

Oldfield, A. & Timmis, S. (2013). Assessment in a Digital Age: A Research Review. Http://Www.Bristol.Ac.Uk/Media-Library/Sites/Education/Documents/Researchreview.Pdf.

Palomba, C.A. & Banta, T.W. (1999). *Assessment Essentials: Planning, Implementing, and Improving Assessment in Higher Education. Higher and Adult Education Series*. Hoboken: JosseyBass, Inc., Publishers.

Panadero, E., Jonsson, A. & Alqassab, M. (2018). Providing Formative Peer Feedback: What Do We Know? In Lipnevich, A.A. & Smith, J.K., *The Cambridge Handbook of Instructional Feedback*. Cambridge: Cambridge University Press.

Passerini, K. & Granger, M.J. (2000). A developmental model for distance learning using the Internet. *Computers & Education*, 34(1), 1–15.

Patchan, M.M., Schunn, C.D. & Clark, R.J. (2018). Accountability in peer assessment: Examining the effects of reviewing grades on peer ratings and peer feedback. *Studies in Higher Education*, 43(12), 2263–2278.

Povera, A. & Yunus, A. (2020). Education ministry to organise home-based learning during MCO [NSTTV]. New Straits Times. Available at www.nst.com.my/news/nation/2020/04/583180/education-ministry-organise-home-based-learning-during-mco-nsttv.

Puig, B., Blanco-Anaya, I., Bargiela, M. & Crujeiras-Perez, B. (2019). A systematic review on critical thinking intervention studies in higher education across professional fields. *Studies in Higher Education*, 44(5), 860–869.

Rane, V. & MacKenzie, C.A. (2020). Evaluating students with online testing modules in engineering economics: A comparison of student performance with online testing and with traditional assessments. *The Engineering Economist*, 65(3), 213–235.

Rane, V. & MacKenzie, C.A. (2020). Evaluating students with online testing modules in engineering economics: A comparison of student performance with online testing and with traditional assessments. *The Engineering Economist*, 65(3), 213–235.

Rapanta, C. *et al.* (2020). Online university teaching during and after the COVID-19 crisis: Refocusing teacher presence and learning activity. *Postdigital Science and Education*, 2(3), 923–945.

Reyneke, Y., Shuttleworth, C.C. & Visagie, R.G. (2021). Pivot to online in a post-COVID-19 world: Critically applying BSCS 5E to enhance plagiarism awareness of accounting students. *Accounting Education*, 30(1), 1–21.

Riegel, K. & Evans, T. (2021). Student achievement emotions: Examining the role of frequent online assessment. *Australasian Journal of Educational Technology*, 37(6), 75–87.

Salzmann, C., Gillet, D. & Huguenin, P. (2000). Introduction to real-time control using LabVIEW (TM) with an application to distance learning. *International Journal of Engineering Education*, 16(3), 255–272.

Senadheera, P. & Kulasekara, G.U. (2022). A formative assessment design suitable for online learning environments and its impact on students' learning. *Open Praxis*, 13(4), 385–396.

Senel, S. & Senel, H.C. (2021). Remote assessment in higher education during COVID-19 pandemic. *International Journal of Assessment Tools in Education*, 8(2), 181–199.

Shraim, K.Y. (2019). Online examination practices in higher education institutions: Learners' perspective. *Turkish Online Journal of Distance Education*, 20(4), 185–196.

Snodgrass, S.J., Ashby, S.E., Anyango, L., Russell, T. & Rivett, D.A. (2014). Electronic practical skills assessments in the health professions: A review. *The Internet Journal of Allied Health Science and Practice*, 12(1), 1–10.

Sullivan (2016). An Integrated Approach to Preempt Cheating on Asynchronous, Objective, Online Assessments in Graduate Business Classes. Online Learning (Newburyport, Mass.), 20(3).

Tan, Swe, K.M.M. & Poulsaeman, V. (2021). Online examination: A feasible alternative during COVID-19 lockdown. *Quality Assurance in Education*, 29(4), 550–557.

Topping, K.J. (2009). Peer assessment. *Theory into Practice*, 48(1), 20–27.

Underwood, J. & Szabo, A. (2003). Academic offences and e-learning: Individual propensities in cheating. *British Journal of Educational Technology*, 34, 467–477.

Vellanki, M.S. & Khan, Z.K. (2023). Promoting academic integrity in remote/online assessment — EFL teachers' perspectives. *TESL-EJ*, 26(4), 1–20.

Walsh, K. (2015). Point of view: Online assessment in medical education — Current trends and future directions. *Malawi Medical Journal*, 27(2), 71–72.

Wang, Gao, R., Guo, X. & Liu, J. (2020). Factors associated with students' attitude change in online peer assessment — A mixed methods study in a graduate-level course. *Assessment and Evaluation in Higher Education*, 45(5), 714–727.

Weleschuk, A., Dyjur, P. & Kelly, P. (2019). *Online Assessment in Higher Education*. Calgary: Taylor Institute for Teaching and Learning Guide Series. Calgary, AB Taylor Inst. Teach. Learn. Univ. Calgary.

White, A. (2021). May you live in interesting times: A reflection on academic integrity and accounting assessment during COVID-19 and online learning. *Accounting Research Journal*, 34(3), 304–312.

Zacharis, N.Z. (2010). Innovative assessment for learning enhancement: Issues and practices. *Contemporary Issues in Education Research (Cier))*, 3(1), 61–70.

Zhan (2021). What matters in design? Cultivating undergraduates' critical thinking through online peer assessment in a Confucian heritage context. *Assessment and Evaluation in Higher Education*, 46(4), 615–630.

© 2024 World Scientific Publishing Company
https://doi.org/10.1142/9789811285622_0007

Chapter 7

Academic Integrity and Online Teaching and Learning

Yuxi Lan, Nora Bhangi, and Jun Xu

King's Own Institute, Australia

Abstract

Higher education institutions have undergone a remarkable transformation in course delivery and assessment arrangements over the last two decades, and online learning has become more and more popular. Literature has broadly suggested that online course delivery and digital technologies will lead to greater potential for academic misconduct. This chapter starts with a brief illustration of academic integrity and online assessment arrangements, including exams. It then proceeds to explore the factors associated with academic misconduct, followed by a discussion on various measures and digital tools that can be utilized to cope with academic integrity. This chapter also provides current practices of deterring academic misconduct examples at King's Own Institute (KOI), Australia.

Keywords: Academic integrity, Academic dishonesty, Academic misconduct, Online teaching and learning, Artificial intelligence (AI), King's Own Institute.

1. Introduction

Over the last 20 years, higher education institutions have experienced a remarkable transition and have embarked on online teaching and learning journey to deal with issues such as large-class teaching and remote/distance learning (Dendir & Maxwell, 2020; Hilliger et al., 2022; Mahabeer & Pirtheepal, 2019; Rahmani, 2021; Tolman, 2017; Ullah et al., 2019). Digital technologies have been playing significant roles in the evolution of online teaching and learning, and it can be expected that the same trend will continue (Nguyen et al., 2020). Online teaching and learning have created significant flexibility for learners looking to further their education while balancing work and life demands (Ladyshewsky, 2015). In view of that, there is a need to adjust the way teaching and assessment are administered to suit the online delivery, particularly in the interactions with learning materials and undertaking examinations from remote locations (Baso et al., 2023; Montenegro-Rueda et al., 2021; Ullah et al., 2019).

As the number of students studying online increases, there is a natural assumption that academic dishonesty would potentially occur at the same rate or even greater than traditional face-to-face teaching (Tolman, 2017). While there is some research suggesting the possibility that cheating is greater in online teaching and learning (Arnold, 2022; Judi, 2022; Tolman, 2017) and concerns regarding the greater potential for academic dishonesty in online courses (Cronan et al., 2018; Dendir & Maxwell, 2020; Ladyshewsky, 2015; Ullah et al., 2019), there is a lack of conclusive evidence to suggest that new technologies adopted in teaching and learning have led to an increase in cheating (Hope et al., 2021; Ladyshewsky, 2015; Tolman, 2017).

With the exponential growth of technologies in an online teaching and learning environment, maintaining academic integrity is a significant challenge that education faculties and administrators will need to address (Sefcik et al., 2020; Tolman, 2017). Cheating through the ease of accessing and utilizing technology in particular, is one of the main concerns in upholding academic integrity. Providing cheating services via websites, promoting cheating to students via social media, or employing Artificial Intelligence (AI) to generate student essays are some examples of how technology could cause academic integrity issues (Dawson, 2021). Hence, it is important to examine the notion of academic dishonesty in online learning and the factors that contribute to its occurrence. In view of that, this chapter aims to reveal a deeper understanding of the digital violations of academic integrity and discuss technological possibilities for coping with academic integrity within the sphere of online learning.

2. Online Assessment and Academic Integrity

Assessment is undoubtedly important in the process of learning and cannot be removed. Online assessments encompass both online assignments and online exams, and they are essential components of online learning settings (Ullah *et al.*, 2019). Assessment serves several key purposes in higher education, including assessing students' knowledge and abilities to ensure educational quality, evaluating whether students have achieved learning outcomes, and determining the performance of the teaching and learning process (Judi, 2022; Mahabeer & Pirtheepal, 2019; Rahmani, 2021). There is an increasing shift toward online assignments, which is driven by various advantages, such as the convenience associated with grading, the flexibility to schedule and manage assignments (Chuang *et al.*, 2017; Ladyshewsky, 2015), a decrease in instructional time (Ladyshewsky, 2015), the capability to apply to a wide range of subjects (Munoz & Mackay, 2019), and the faster delivery of feedback between both teachers and students (Ladyshewsky, 2015). In addition, research evidence indicate that students prefer digital assignments than the written ones (Munoz & Mackay, 2019).

Academic integrity is a deeply rooted, culturally dependent, universal phenomenon in the education field (Peled *et al.*, 2019). Defining academic integrity may appear simple, but there is substantial empirical evidence highlighting a lack of understanding among both students and educators concerning the boundaries between academic misconduct and academic integrity, which are often blurrier (Dawson, 2021; Tatum & Schwartz, 2017). Academic integrity serves as the ethical foundation of higher education, embodying a commitment to values of "honesty, trust, fairness, respect, responsibility, and courage" in supporting the university's goals, protecting one's knowledge, and ensuring that all students are guided in the best integrity learning behaviors (Mahabeer & Pirtheepal, 2019; Sefcik *et al.*, 2020). In contrast, academic misconduct encompasses various forms and behaviors aimed at gaining an unfair advantage and misrepresenting students' capabilities and knowledge (Baso *et al.*, 2023; Dendir & Maxwell, 2020; Mahabeer & Pirtheepal, 2019; Munoz & Mackay, 2019).

Acting with academic integrity ensures the quality of teaching, learning, and assessment while engaging in academic dishonesty harms the credibility of the student, the educators, and the education faculties. On the other hand, it also can be said that the behavior of breaching academic integrity leads to academic misconduct (i.e., two sides of the same coin). Common types of academic misconduct include:

- Cheating, which encompasses actions that involve unauthorized assistance or materials in assignments or exams (Mahabeer & Pirtheepal, 2019; Tatum & Schwartz, 2017). It also extends to the inappropriate use of advanced AI writing tools when it is specifically restricted by the teacher for a particular assignment (Anders, 2023).
- Contract cheating, which poses a significant threat to academic integrity (Eaton & Christensen, 2022; Rettinger & Bertram, 2022), and often involves students seeking an unauthorized party to complete their assignment (Garg & Goel, 2022; Ullah et al., 2019; White, 2021), or even substitute themselves for an examination (Eaton & Christensen, 2022; Luck et al., 2022; Rettinger & Bertram, 2022). It can occur with payment (e.g., buying a contract cheating service from an agent), without charge (e.g., family members or friends assisting for free), or with profit exchange (e.g., exchanging assignment answers or any other benefits). The availability of contract cheating services is widespread in education settings, with a specific focus on non-English-speaking students (Rettinger & Bertram, 2022).
- Fabrication, which entails the falsification of information, such as making up data for research, doctoring an experiment report, or providing fake references for a paper (Tatum & Schwartz, 2017).
- Plagiarism that encompasses both cribbing and presenting other people's ideas, words, or statements as one's own, as well as submitting the same assignment work for two different subjects without the teacher's permission (i.e., self-plagiarism) (Mahabeer & Pirtheepal, 2019; Tatum & Schwartz, 2017). Students can plagiarize materials through various ways. One of the hot topics could probably be the use of online translator software (e.g., Google Translator) and writing-assistant applications (e.g., Grammarly). The argument lies in such perspectives as whether the students have used online translator software and writing-assistant applications for generating essay content or for checking the writeup. Meanwhile, similar arguments can go to artificial intelligence applications (e.g., whether ChatGPT is used for

generating ideas vs. generating essay content?). On a related note, using digital tools for paraphrasing could reduce the likelihood of plagiarism detection since they only replace words without altering the overall syntax of the sentence (Garg & Goel, 2022).
- Collusion, also referred to as collaboration, represents an organized form of cheating that involves two or more students working together and aiding each other in assignments, such as sharing papers, exam questions, or answers (Garg & Goel, 2022; Tatum & Schwartz, 2017).

Academic misconduct has been highlighted in past studies as a serious threat to the validity of online assignments and is a major issue in an unsupervised environment (Dendir & Maxwell, 2020; Hylton *et al.*, 2016; Munoz & Mackay, 2019; Ullah *et al.*, 2019). Assignment grades should represent students' real level of knowledge, abilities, and attitudes, but academic misconduct behavior can mislead these signals and perceptions (Gotzmann *et al.*, 2017; Munoz & Mackay, 2019). Factors such as lack of awareness and responsibility, easy access to online content & assessment answers as well as online assistance (including unauthorized help), and challenges in identifying and confirming AI-assisted writing and contract cheating all call for the implementation of policies, procedures, and tools to ensure the integrity and security of online assessments (Blau *et al.*, 2021; Davies & Sharefeen, 2022; Dendir & Maxwell, 2020; Judi, 2022; Hylton *et al.*, 2016; Khan *et al.*, 2021; Ladyshewsky, 2015; Ng, 2020).

3. Reasons for Committing Academic Misconduct

In the changing landscape of cheating and misconduct, students engage in academic dishonesty for a range of reasons (Harris *et al.*, 2020). Reddy *et al.* (2022) pointed out that opportunity, extrinsic stimulation, and intrinsic attitude are necessary for cheating to occur. Common reasons are as follows:

(1) Students are unsatisfied with their current teaching and learning practices and arrangements (White, 2021), which include assignment design (Reddy *et al.*, 2022; Surahman & Wang, 2022), teaching quality, learning outcomes and the class delivery method (Kaktins, 2019; Mahabeer & Pirtheepal, 2019). Students intend to act dishonesty when they feel the quality of the teaching and assessment design is poor (Mahabeer & Pirtheepal, 2019). Teaching large classes can result

in students becoming less interested in the class and having less interactions with their teachers and less time engaged in class activities, and feeling neglected and alienated (Kaktins, 2019; Mahabeer & Pirtheepal, 2019), which could lead to more academic misconduct cases (Tolman, 2017).

(2) Inadequate preparation for an assignment and/or lack of drive to learn can be another reason (Chuang et al., 2017; Cronan et al., 2018; Dendir & Maxwell, 2020; Ladyshewsky, 2015).

(3) Poor time management skills and ineffective study strategies could play a role as well (Blau et al., 2021; Ladyshewsky, 2015; Luck et al., 2022; Verhoef & Coetser, 2021).

(4) Personal moral values, which are associated with a sense of shame and remorse, could also have a significant impact on academic dishonesty (Chudzicka-Czupala et al., 2016; Gotzmann et al., 2017; Orosz et al., 2013; Peled et al., 2019, as cited in Dendir & Maxwell, 2020).

(5) Lack of clarity in academic integrity policy and assignment instructions or expectations could also be responsible for students' academic misconduct behavior (Blau et al., 2021; Cronan et al., 2018; Dendir & Maxwell, 2020; Peled et al., 2019; Sefcik et al., 2020).

(6) High pressure, including the need to meet high standards of performance (Dendir & Maxwell, 2020; Kaktins, 2019; Peled et al., 2019) or deadlines (Ladyshewsky, 2015); fear of punishment (Blau et al., 2021; Ladyshewsky, 2015; Peled et al., 2019); unfamiliar with new technology and procedures (Verhoef & Coetser, 2021); severe competition between peers (Luck et al., 2022; Surahman & Wang, 2022; Verhoef & Coetser, 2021), particularly among non-native speakers or ethnic minority students, could also contribute to students' behavior of academic misconduct (Blau et al., 2021; Luck et al., 2022; White, 2021); and high expectations from others (Ladyshewsky, 2015).

(7) Personal perspectives and values in relation to success (Chuang et al., 2017; Dendir & Maxwell, 2020; Ladyshewsky, 2015; Mahabeer & Pirtheepal, 2019) (such as desire for social acceptance, professional development, pleasing friends and family members, or subsistence income) could have impact on students' attitude toward academic misconduct (Luck et al., 2022; Mahabeer & Pirtheepal, 2019; Peled et al., 2019).

(8) Social acceptance and culture are also found to play a role in academic misconduct (Chuang et al., 2017; Dendir & Maxwell, 2020; Davies & Sharefeen, 2022; Reddy et al., 2022). A culture of academic

dishonesty implies that students are not only accepting of cheating but also believe it is a necessary means to attain success, which makes them perceive that peers around them are engaging in dishonesty practices (Abd-Elaal *et al.*, 2022; Dendir & Maxwell, 2020; Tolman, 2017). When students observe their peers cheating and consider it socially acceptable, they are more inclined to engage in misconduct themselves (Cronan *et al.*, 2018; Dendir & Maxwell, 2020; Luck *et al.*, 2022; Mahabeer & Pirtheepal, 2019; Tatum & Schwartz, 2017).

(9) Currently, various user-friendly artificial intelligence applications (such as Chat GPT, Socratic, word spinner, ProWritingAid, QuillBot, Google Translator), along with big data and other emerging technologies, have made it convenient for students to engage in breaches of academic integrity (Hylton *et al.*, 2016; Khan *et al.*, 2021). This is especially pronounced when there is insufficient guidance on how to uphold academic integrity while utilizing these tools (Dawson, 2021). Students often misuse these technologies for academic tasks like conducting online researches, generating essay contents, paraphrasing sentences, and checking and correcting grammar, spelling, and punctuation (Dawson, 2021; Eysenbach, 2023; Khan *et al.*, 2021; McCarthy, 2023; Rettinger & Bertram, 2022; Skavronskaya *et al.*, 2023).

4. Measures for Maintaining Academic Integrity

A diverse discussion has been held on how institutions can embrace cost-effective academic integrity solutions while ensuring the accessibility and flexibility of online delivery (Judi, 2022). Maintaining academic integrity should be a multi-faceted approach (Khan *et al.*, 2021).

4.1. *Developing Strong Academic Integrity Policies*

TEQSA (Tertiary Education Quality and Standards Agency) in Australia mandates higher education providers in Australia to establish policies for academic integrity, risk mitigation, and guidance on good practices (TEQSA 2017, as cited in Sefcik *et al.*, 2020). Developing and implementing robust academic integrity policy frameworks with consequences for academic misconduct is crucial to academic integrity education (Abd-Elaal *et al.*, 2022; Blau *et al.*, 2021; Davies & Sharefeen, 2022; Golden & Kohlbeck, 2020; Ladyshewsky, 2015; Sando *et al.*, 2021;

Striepe *et al.*, 2023; Tatum & Schwartz, 2017). Academic integrity policies should be available online (Luck *et al.*, 2022), comprehensively cover academic integrity values (Sefcik *et al.*, 2020), involve multiple stakeholders (Judi, 2022), address categories of academic misconduct, outline processes for handling breaches, and be regularly updated (Eaton & Christensen, 2022; Luck *et al.*, 2022; Nguyen *et al.*, 2020; Rettinger & Bertram, 2022; Sefcik *et al.*, 2020). With the advancement of technology (such as the emergence of ChatGPT), it is essential to update academic integrity policies to include warnings regarding the use of new digital tools (Abd-Elaal *et al.*, 2022). Rather than prescribing a "ban-list" of forbidden activities, prescribing an "allow-list" may be more preferable (Dawson, 2021). Prevention and education should be guiding principles for policy development (Chuang *et al.*, 2017; Luck *et al.*, 2022) and extra care and support for students should be provided rather than purely from a punitive approach (Rettinger & Bertram, 2022). Penalties for academic misconduct can vary from severe (expulsion) to softer penalties (reprimand) and education for minor cases (Eaton & Christensen, 2022; Striepe *et al.*, 2023). Students should have the right to appeal, and in the appeal process, a follow-up interview is strongly recommended for asking students to describe their ideas and processes when conducting the assignment (Abd-Elaal *et al.*, 2022).

4.2. *Fostering a Culture of Academic Integrity*

The cultural climate within an institution significantly shapes students' values and behaviors (Davies & Sharefeen, 2022; Judi, 2022; Sefcik *et al.*, 2020; Striepe *et al.*, 2023). To combat a culture of cheating, higher education institutes must be careful of their campus culture and promptly address dishonesty culture (Tolman, 2017), and foster a healthy academic environment (Luck *et al.*, 2022). Measures such as positive peer pressure (Sefcik *et al.*, 2020), focusing on establishing longer and formal honor codes (Blau *et al.*, 2021; Cronan *et al.*, 2018; Golden & Kohlbeck, 2020; Hylton *et al.*, 2016), strengthening students' ethical beliefs, showing trust and respect for students, and expressing clear expectations about academic integrity (Corrigan-Gibbs *et al.*, 2015), may help achieve a culture of academic integrity. Increasing students' investment in the honor code, it could, in turn, reduce likelihood of misconduct. Improving teachers' awareness of the cultural and situational stresses among students would assist staff in creating learning environments that promote the importance of academic integrity.

4.3. Providing Academic Integrity Training and Education

Continuous education and reminders about academic integrity are essential (Gamage *et al.*, 2022; Judi, 2022). Academic integrity educational courses for tudents and staff have a wide-ranging scope and are associated with a positive influence on the development of academic integrity competence (Davies & Sharefeen, 2022; Judi, 2022; Sefcik *et al.*, 2020; Striepe *et al.*, 2023), which should be addressed early on (McCarthy, 2023). Higher education institutions can offer training courses/programs to communicate essential information (Eaton & Christensen, 2022; Judi, 2022; Rettinger & Bertram, 2022), and such training programs should focus on values, practical skills and the quality of outcomes along with rules, regulations and policy (Sefcik *et al.*, 2020). Meanwhile, teachers are in the best position to have a more intimate conversation with students about discovering and shaping their academic integrity (Cronan *et al.*, 2018; Judi, 2022).

In light of the fact that plagiarism is a common misconduct behavior (Tatum & Schwartz, 2017), teachers can incorporate in-class activities on citing original sources and asking students to identify content that is considered plagiarism, as well as content that demonstrates appropriate paraphrasing and citations (Eaton & Christensen, 2022; Karizaki, 2021; Tatum & Schwartz, 2017; White, 2021) as well as critiquing the content generated by ChatGPT and other AI applications. Higher education institutions should be proactive in observing technological development & trends and training on how to work with new digital tools should be provided to both teachers and students (Abd-Elaal *et al.*, 2022). Learning management systems (LMS) (such as Moodle) can play important roles as platforms for disseminating academic integrity-related information (e.g., best practices, case studies, examples) and providing training to both staff and students (Luck *et al.*, 2022).

4.4. Working on Quality of Course and Assignment Design

It would be beneficial to allow teaching staff to plan and design effective courses and assignment tasks (Davies & Sharefeen, 2022; Luck *et al.*, 2022; Striepe *et al.*, 2023). Teachers should consider diversifying the types of questions posed, randomizing questions from a large pool (Chuang *et al.*, 2017; Golden & Kohlbeck, 2020; Gotzmann *et al.*, 2017; Hilliger *et al.*, 2022; Judi, 2022; Karizaki, 2021), and imposing stricter time constraints (Golden & Kohlbeck, 2020; Khan *et al.*, 2021; Ladyshewsky, 2015; Munoz & Mackay, 2019; Verhoef & Coetser, 2021). Furthermore, enhancing the authenticity of assessments can be pivotal (Blau *et al.*, 2021; Dawson, 2021; Judi, 2022; Ng, 2020), it requires the application of knowledge, reflection on personal experiences, and the use of oral presentations, where students must tailor their responses to specific scenarios. Classroom-based assessment activities can also be employed to foster authenticity (Choi *et al.*, 2023; Hilliger *et al.*, 2022; Luck *et al.*, 2022; Ng, 2020). Increasing task cooperation and social learning activity in learning courses also could strengthen social attributes (Munoz & Mackay, 2019; Peled *et al.*, 2019), and designing the criteria for grading assignments together with students (Thomas and Scott 2016, as cited in Blau *et al.*, 2021) that may further reduce academic misconduct. The lower-stake assessment tasks could decrease the students' desire to cheat (Nguyen *et al.*, 2020). In addition, teachers should explore the potential of using ChatGPT and other AI applications in their curriculum and assessment design (Skavronskaya *et al.*, 2023).

4.5. *Selecting Tools for Deterring Academic Misconduct*

Many universities require students to submit their work through Turnitin before grading (Luck *et al.*, 2022). Turnitin has an international reach and can compare students' submitted assignments with those retained in repositories in participating institutions across the globe, along with other databases of scholarly articles and internet-based resources (Luck *et al.*, 2022; Mahabeer & Pirtheepal, 2019; Vasilopoulos & Bangou, 2022). The disadvantages of Turnitin software are that it does not detect material that is password protected or texts produced by paraphrasing tools (Dawson, 2021; Luck *et al.*, 2022; Velliaris & Breen, 2016). It requires a high degree of human intervention to assess the similarity reports and determine if there are any instances of plagiarism (Mahabeer & Pirtheepal, 2019).

Advanced online proctoring biometric technologies, including 360-degree camera, fingerprint, voice recognition checking mechanisms, retinal scanning (Dendir & Maxwell, 2020; Eaton & Christensen, 2022; Golden & Kohlbeck, 2020; Luck *et al.*, 2022; Montenegro-Rueda *et al.*, 2021) and secure software/webcam-based Proctoring (Hylton et al., 2016) offer the potential to enhance assessment integrity by monitoring student activity while they complete assessments (Richardson, 2022).

Other live-boot operating systems can be helpful as well, which make students to be locked into the online assignment environment once they log in (Dawson, 2021; Davies & Sharefeen, 2022; Ladyshewsky, 2015; Vasilopoulos & Bangou, 2022) and restrict web browsers to a specific website and limits computer functionalities, including print, copy and paste, screen sharing, and capture devices until students submit their assignments for marking (Dawson, 2021).

AI tools can also be used to detect academic breaches. Several technology companies have been developing new AI-assisted cheating detection software (Dawson, 2021). However, since AI lacks a sufficiently complex and nuanced social understanding of the nature of academic misconduct, human intervention is always required.

5. Current Academic Integrity Practices at King's Own Institute (KOI)

5.1. *Current Practices for Online Assignments at KOI*

KOI has strict academic integrity policies and procedures to guide academic integrity. KOI Academic Integrity Policy and Procedure have been updated regularly and posted on its website. In 2023, the policy has been updated to categorize "using Gen AI to do assessment tasks without proper acknowledgement" as cheating behaviors. If a teacher identifies a student who is accused of academic misconduct, the teacher will report it to the academic integrity officer for investigation. All misconduct cases must be reported within two weeks of the assessment due date. The academic integrity officer invites involved students to respond to allegations and discusses matters with heads of program and subject coordinators when necessary.

The KOI Academic Misconduct Recommended Penalties Guideline is used for determining academic misconduct penalties. For students with first offence in their first trimester, a resubmission opportunity is offered. For cases related to AI tools, the respective teacher will arrange interviews with relevant alleged students, demonstrate how to use Gen AI tools with proper reference citations, and offer a resubmission chance. For repeated cases, the penalties range from a 30% reduction in an assignment mark to a failed grade, depending on the severity of the offense. Upon receiving the official outcome letter from the academic integrity officer, the subject coordinator must confirm that the penalty has been applied to the student's grade. All these students with confirmed academic misconduct cases have to undergo a learning skill workshop to mitigate future risks.

Students are given very clear warnings regarding the risks associated with any breaches of academic integrity, with particular emphasis on contract cheating. And all new students have to complete online academic integrity module within first four weeks of their first trimester. These warnings are posted online each trimester, displayed regularly on the monitors in waiting areas of our campuses, and also provided prior to students attempting assessment tasks such as the middle-term exam or final exam. The library has posted a "Turnitin can now identify the use of ChatGPT in assessments" notification on the Moodle home page. KOI also requires students to submit their assignments through Turnitin.

If KOI recognized an increasing trend of academic misconduct cases in a particular subject, the assessments of that subject will be reviewed and the pattern of assessments in that subject would be completely changed. Every trimester, KOI analyses the results and the factors affecting academic integrity, then makes the necessary changes in the assessment for the upcoming trimester. It is a mandatory requirement. The teachers, SCs (subject coordinators), and HOPs (heads of program) discuss feedback prior to any changes in the subjects (including assessment tasks) to avoid academic misconduct.

KOI's course assignments involve problem-based questions where students need to consider issues, reflection on the experience of completing the assessment, and oral presentations that could be video-recorded versions (especially for online delivery). KOI now sets questions that are not easily answered just by using Google. In some assignments, each individual student or group (in group assignments) gets a different question, but with an equal level of difficulty. KOI utilizes features in Moodle where numerous questions with as many as 80 different varieties based on the same formula can be created. Where there is an assessment with 10 questions requiring calculations and legal principles, students are faced with 80 variations of the 10 questions, i.e., $(10 \times 80) = 800$ varieties of questions. Each student gets a different question and can't copy or compare answers in the restricted timeframe.

There is a valid argument for allowing students to use online assessment with open computers as well as open books, particularly in subjects such as taxation law, where it is much more important that students learn to find the latest tax regulations and learn how to apply the formula to cope with their future working environments. Therefore, KOI embraces it while acknowledging the challenges. For some subjects, there is weekly or biweekly progress to be present in the class for the major assessments, which helps the teacher understand whether it is the student's own work or not.

5.2. *Current Practices for Online Exams at KOI*

Question banks are used for multiple-choice questions. The questions shuffle and create a different set of questions for each individual student. Question banks are updated regularly, KOI adds new questions to the question banks every trimester. Considering academic misconduct, the major part of the exam (each exam), say 25%–30%, is case-study-based questions (online exams). To deal with academic misconduct issues in the exam (especially online exams), case-based questions, scenario-based tasks, and questions requiring reflection on their knowledge are included in the exam. The MCQs (multiple choice questions) only accounted for 5% of the total exams. For deferred or supplementary exams, new/different exam papers are required. Meanwhile invigilation is required for both face-to-face and online exams. For online exam invigilation, tools such as proctoring software and Zoom will be adopted to assist the invigilation process. In addition, students' photos are uploaded into the student portal before the online exam by the IT team and the Library Team.

6. Conclusion

The rapid evolution of online education over the past two decades has significantly transformed the landscape of higher education. Even though this transition has led to various benefits, it has also given rise to new challenges, particularly in maintaining academic integrity in the higher education landscape. This chapter has explored the various facets of academic integrity in online learning environments, highlighting the issues and plausible solutions to address them. Students engage in academic misconduct for various reasons, including dissatisfaction with the learning environment, inadequate preparation, poor time management, and external pressures. Social factors such as the cheating culture also contribute to academic misconduct. Additionally, the accessibility of advanced digital tools has made it easier for students to engage in breaches of academic integrity. This chapter also provided insights into the current academic integrity practices at KOI, illustrating how institutions can implement these measures effectively.

There is no single solution to treat all academic dishonesty problems at once. Students, teachers, and higher education institutions should collectively engage in maintaining academic integrity. Higher education institutions should build a strong policy framework for dealing with academic misconduct issues and fostering a positive culture of integrity by offering training courses and forming honor codes in schools. Teachers could design their courses and assignments in such a way as to enhance their teaching qualities and prevent academic misconduct. Students could improve their study attitude and develop a sense of academic integrity towards their education. Various technologies, such as the Turnitin software, online proctoring programs, Zoom, and even AI tools can be used to help ensure that academic integrity is upheld. Future research can investigate additional factors that drive student violations and implement appropriate measures to better address the continuous challenges of maintaining academic integrity.

References

Abd-Elaal, E., Gamage, S.H.P.W. & Mills, J.E. (2022). Assisting academics to identify computer generated writing. *European Journal of Engineering Education*, 47(5), 725–745.

Anders, B.A. (2023). Is using ChatGPT cheating, plagiarism, both, neither, or forward thinking? *Patterns*, 4(3), 100694.

Arnold, I.J.M. (2022). Online proctored assessment during COVID-19: Has cheating increased? *The Journal of Economic Education*, 53(4), 277–295.

Baso, Y.S., Murtadho, N., Syihabuddin, Maulani, H., Agussalim, A., Haeruddin, Ahmad Fadlan, & Ramadhan, I. (2023). Reducing cheating in online exams through the proctor test I. *International Journal of Advanced Computer Science & Applications*, 14(1).

Benuyenah, V. (2023). Commentary: ChatGPT use in higher education assessment: Prospects and epistemic threats. *Journal of Research in Innovative Teaching & Learning*, 16(1), 134–135.

Blau, I., Goldberg, S., Friedman, A. & Eshet-Alkalai, Y. (2021). Violation of digital and analog academic integrity through the eyes of faculty members and students: Do institutional roles and technology change ethical perspectives? *Journal of Computing in Higher Education*, 33(1), 157–187.

Choi, E.P.H., Lee, J.J., Ho, M.-H., Kwok, J.Y.Y. & Lok, K.Y.W. (2023). Chatting or cheating? The impacts of ChatGPT and other artificial intelligence language models on nurse education. *Nurse Education Today*, 125, 105796–105796.

Chuang, C.Y., Craig, S.D. & Femiani, J. (2017). Detecting probable cheating during online assessments based on time delay and head pose. *Higher Education Research and Development*, 36(6), 1123–1137.

Corrigan-Gibbs, H., Gupta, N., Northcutt, C., Cutrell, E. & Thies, W. (2015). Deterring cheating in online environments. *ACM Transactions on Computer-Human Interaction*, 22(6), 1–23.

Cotton, D.R.E., Cotton, P.A. & Shipway, J.R. (2023). Chatting and cheating: Ensuring academic integrity in the era of ChatGPT. *Innovations in Education and Teaching International*, ahead-of-print, 1–12.

Cronan, T.P., Mullins, J. K. & Douglas, D.E. (2018). Further understanding factors that explain freshman business students' academic integrity intention and behavior: Plagiarism and sharing homework. *Journal of Business Ethics*, 147(1), 197–220.

Davies, A. & Sharefeen, R.A. (2022). Enhancing academic integrity in a UAE safety, security defence emergency management academy the Covid-19 response and beyond. *International Journal for Educational Integrity*, 18(1), 1–18.

Dawson, P. (2021). *Defending Assessment Security in a Digital World: Preventing E-Cheating and Supporting Academic Integrity in Higher Education*. Abingdon: Routledge.

Dendir, S., & Maxwell, R. S. (2020). Cheating in online courses: Evidence from online proctoring. Computers in Human Behavior Reports, 2, 100033.

Eaton, S.E., & Christensen Hughes, J. (2022). *Academic Integrity in Canada: An Enduring and Essential Challenge*. Berlin: Springer Nature.

Eysenbach, G. (2023). The role of ChatGPT, generative language models, and artificial intelligence in medical education: A conversation with ChatGPT and a call for papers. *JMIR Medical Education*, 9, e46885–e46885.

Fergus, S., Botha, M. & Ostovar, M. (2023). Evaluating academic answers generated using ChatGPT. *Journal of Chemical Education*, 100(4), 1672–1675.

Gamage, K.A.A., Pradeep, R.G.G.R. & de Silva, E.K. (2022). Rethinking assessment: The future of examinations in higher education. *Sustainability (Basel, Switzerland)*, 14(6), 3552.

Garg, M., & Goel, A. (2022). A systematic literature review on online assessment security: Current challenges and integrity strategies. *Computers & Security*, 113, 102544.

Golden, J., & Kohlbeck, M. (2020). Addressing cheating when using test bank questions in online Classes. *Journal of Accounting Education*, 52, 100671.

Gotzmann, A., De Champlain, A.F., Homayra, F., Fotheringham, A., De Vries, I., Forgie, M.A. & Pugh, D. (2017). Cheating in OSCEs: The impact of simulated security breaches on OSCE Performance. *Teaching and Learning in Medicine*, 29(1), 52–58.

Harris, L., Harrison, D., McNally, D. & Ford, C. (2020). Academic Integrity in an Online Culture: Do McCabe's Findings Hold True for Online, Adult Learners? *Journal of Academic Ethics*, 18(4), 419–434.

Hilliger, I., Ruipérez-Valiente, J.A., Alexandron, G. & Gašević, D. (2022). Trustworthy remote assessments: A typology of pedagogical and technological strategies. *Journal of Computer Assisted Learning*, 38(6), 1507–1520.

Hope, D., Davids, V., Bollington, L. & Maxwell, S. (2021). Candidates undertaking (invigilated) assessment online show no differences in performance compared to those undertaking assessment offline. *Medical Teacher*, 43(6), 646–650.

Hylton, K., Levy, Y. & Dringus, L.P. (2016). Utilizing webcam-based proctoring to deter misconduct in online exams. *Computers and Education*, 92–93, 53–63.

Judi, H. M. (2022). Integrity and security of digital assessment: Experiences in online learning. *Global Business and Management Research*, 14(1), 97–107. http://www.gbmrjournal.com/pdf/v14n1/V14N1-9.pdf.

Kaktins, L. (2019). Does Turnitin support the development of international students' academic integrity? *Ethics and Education*, 14(4), 430–448.

Karizaki, V.M. (2021). Different approaches for reducing cheating in online assessments. *Journal of Medical Imaging and Radiation Sciences*, 52(4), 650–651.

Khan, Z.R., Sivasubramaniam, S., Anand, P. & Hysaj, A. (2021). "E"-thinking teaching and assessment to uphold academic integrity: Lessons learned from emergency distance learning. *International Journal for Educational Integrity*, 17(1), 1–27.

Ladyshewsky, R.K. (2015). Post-graduate student performance in "supervised in-class" vs. "unsupervised online" multiple choice tests: implications for cheating and test security. *Assessment and Evaluation in Higher Education*, 40(7), 883–897.

Luck, J.A., Chugh, R., Turnbull, D. & Pember, E.R. (2022). Glitches and hitches: sessional academic staff viewpoints on academic integrity and academic misconduct. *Higher Education Research and Development*, 41(4), 1152–1167.

Mahabeer, P. & Pirtheepal, T. (2019). Assessment, plagiarism and its effect on academic integrity: Experiences of academics at a university in South Africa. *South African Journal of Science*, 115(11–12), 32–39.

McCarthy, C. (2023). ChatGPT use could change views on academic misconduct. *Student Affairs Today*, 26(2), 3–6.

McCarthy, C. (2023). Take a closer look at how ChatGPT could change teaching, learning. *Campus Legal Advisor*, 23(9), 1–6.

Montenegro-Rueda, M., Luque-de la Rosa, A., Sarasola Sánchez-Serrano, J.L. & Fernández-Cerero, J. (2021). Assessment in Higher Education during the COVID-19 Pandemic: A Systematic Review. *Sustainability (Basel, Switzerland)*, 13(19), 10509.

Munoz, A., & Mackay, J. (2019). An online testing design choice typology towards cheating threat minimisation. *Journal of University Teaching & Learning Practice*, 16(3), 54–70.

Ng, C.K.C. (2020). Evaluation of academic integrity of online open book assessments implemented in an undergraduate medical radiation science course during COVID-19 pandemic. *Journal of Medical Imaging and Radiation Sciences*, 51(4), 610–616.

Nguyen, J.G., Keuseman, K.J. & Humston, J.J. (2020). Minimize online cheating for online assessments during COVID-19 pandemic. *Journal of Chemical Education*, 97(9), 3429–3435.

Ofgang, E. (2023). How to prevent ChatGPT cheating: ChatGPT has a lot of potential for teaching, say educators, but it can also be used to cheat. Here are strategies to prevent ChatGPT cheating. *Tech & Learning*, 10. https://link-gale-com.ezproxy.cqu.edu.au/apps/doc/A743668041/AONE?u=cqu&sid=bookmark-AONE&xid=d38af4c9.

Peled, Y., Eshet, Y., Barczyk, C. & Grinautski, K. (2019). Predictors of academic dishonesty among undergraduate students in online and face-to-face courses. *Computers and Education*, 131, 49–59.

Rahmani, A. (2021). Shifting towards online assessment: A new promising gate in the higher educational level. *Arab World English Journal*, 7(1), 217–238.

Reddy, L., Letswalo, M.L., Sefage, A.P., Kheswa, B.V., Balakrishna, A., Changundega, J.M., Mvelase, M.J., Kheswa, K.A., Majola, S.N.T., Mathe, T., Seakamela, T. & Nemakhavhani, T.E. (2022). Integrity vs. quality of assessments: Are they compromised on the online platform? *Pedagogical Research*, 7(2), em0121.

Rettinger, D.A. & Bertram, G.T. (2022). *Cheating Academic Integrity: Lessons from 30 years of Research.* John Wiley & Sons, Inc.

Richardson, S. (2022). Mathematics assessment integrity during lockdown: Experiences in running online un-invigilated exams. *International Journal of Mathematical Education in Science and Technology*, 53(3), 662–672.

Sando, K., Medina, M.S., & Whalen, K. (2021). The need for new guidelines and training for remote/online testing and proctoring due to COVID-19. *American Journal of Pharmaceutical Education*, 8545.

Sefcik, L., Striepe, M. & Yorke, J. (2020). Mapping the landscape of academic integrity education programs: what approaches are effective? *Assessment and Evaluation in Higher Education*, 45(1), 30–43.

Skavronskaya, L., Hadinejad, A. & Cotterell, D. (2023). Reversing the threat of artificial intelligence to opportunity: A discussion of ChatGPT in tourism education. *Journal of Teaching in Travel & Tourism*, ahead-of-print, 1–6.

Sotiriadou, P., Logan, D., Daly, A., & Guest, R. (2020). The role of authentic assessment to preserve academic integrity and promote skill development and employability. *Studies in Higher Education (Dorchester-on-Thames)*, 45(11), 2132–2148. https://doi.org/10.1080/03075079.2019.1582015.

Striepe, M., Thomson, S., & Sefcik, L. (2023). Understanding academic integrity education: Case studies from two Australian universities. *Journal of Academic Ethics*, 21(1), 1–17. https://doi.org/10.1007/s10805-021-09429-x.

Surahman, E., & Wang, T. (2022). Academic dishonesty and trustworthy assessment in online learning: A systematic literature review. *Journal of Computer Assisted Learning*, 38(6), 1535–1553. https://doi.org/10.1111/jcal.12708.

Taneja, V. (2023, Mar 03). ChatGPT: Future of cheating or future of teaching. Business World. https://ezproxy.cqu.edu.au/login?url=https://www.proquest.com/magazines/chatgpt-future-cheating-teaching/docview/2781463884/se-2.

Tatum, H. & Schwartz, B.M. (2017). Honor codes: Evidence based strategies for improving academic integrity. *Theory into Practice*, 56(2), 129–135.

Tiong, L.C.O., Lee, H.J. & Lim, K.L. (2022). Online assessment misconduct detection using internet protocol and behavioural classification.

Tolman, S. (2017). Academic dishonesty in online courses: Considerations for graduate, reparatory programs in higher education. *College Student Journal*, 51(4), 579–584.

Ullah, A., Xiao, H. & Barker, T. (2019). A study into the usability and security implications of text and image based challenge questions in the context of online examination. *Education and Information Technologies*, 24(1), 13–39.

Vasilopoulos, E. & Bangou, F. (2022). Intersections of Student engagement and academic integrity in the emergency remote "english for academic purposes" assemblage. *Language & Literacy*, 24(1), 6–23.

Velliaris, D.M. & Breen, P. (2016). An institutional three-stage framework: Elevating academic writing and integrity standards of international pathway students. *Journal of International Students*, 6(2), 565–587.

Verhoef, A.H. & Coetser, Y. M. (2021). Academic integrity of university students during emergency remote online assessment: An exploration of student voices. *Transformation in Higher Education*, 6(1), e1–e12.

White, A. (2021). May you live in interesting times: A reflection on academic integrity and accounting assessment during COVID19 and online learning. *Accounting Research Journal*, 34(3), 304–312.

Part 2
Studies

© 2024 World Scientific Publishing Company
https://doi.org/10.1142/9789811285622_0008

Chapter 8

Creating Engaging Online Lessons

Graeme Salter

King's Own Institute, Australia

Abstract

This chapter examines the benefits and challenges of creating engaging lessons in an online learning environment. Suggestions for increasing student engagement online are provided. The importance of gaining attention, demonstrating relevance, and providing state changes during a lesson are highlighted. The reader is encouraged to adopt and trial any suggested techniques which fit with their particular teaching style. As this list cannot be exhaustive, the reader is also encouraged to use these as a prompt to further investigate and reflect on the myriad ways to engage students in their online classes.

Keywords: Engaging lessons, Learner engagement, Online learning, Active learning, Passive learning, Attention, Motivation.

1. The Benefits of Creating Engaging Lessons

Engaging lessons can lead to improved student achievement. In a meta-analysis of more than 75 separate studies, Marzano (2007) showed that students in highly engaging classrooms outperform students in unengaging classrooms by nearly 30 percentile points. Students may also benefit from increased motivation and ownership of learning. If done well, engaging classes can simply be more fun to attend.

If students are motivated, enjoying class, and achieving better results, teachers are likely to have greater job satisfaction. They may also receive evidence of good teaching such as better student evaluations and unsolicited testimonials. This evidence can then be used for award, promotion, and employment applications. The institution may also benefit through increased attendance, retention, and completion.

2. The Challenge of Creating Engaging Lessons

Creating engaging lessons is a challenge in both face-to-face and online learning environments. In a pre-pandemic survey of more than 20,000 academic staff, in response to the question "What's your biggest teaching challenge?", the principal concern was "Students not paying attention or participating in class". When asked "What's most important to you in your lectures?", the largest response was "Increasing student participation and engagement" (TopHat, 2016).

COVID-19 thrust educational systems worldwide into a "hard reset" leaving many academics and students in uncharted territory (Klein *et al.*, 2023). The expensive, acoustically balanced lecture halls were suddenly replaced with the experience of watching many academics attempting online teaching for the first time using a $20 webcam (Ofgang, 2021). Making classes engaging and encouraging students to want to be there takes on extra importance with online teaching (Dick, 2021). The challenge lies in creating engaging online lessons that captivate learners' attention, foster active participation, and promote meaningful learning experiences.

The good news is that a move to online teaching can prompt "pedagogical re-engineering" where teachers reevaluate their current teaching methods and perhaps adopt improved techniques (Baker, 2020; Salter, 2004; Thaker-King, 2023).

"Teachers often need to rethink their course design and adopt different education, engagement, and evaluation strategies in an online environment" (Sharma, 2022).

The bad news is that the speed of change caused by the pandemic led some to embrace "panic-gogy" (Baker, 2020). Fortunately, in a post-pandemic world we can take time to reflect on the experiences of teaching online, review the literature, and put best practice (or at least better practice) in place.

3. The Benefits of Online Learning

Online learning can provide a range of benefits for students. Convenience and flexibility are often cited as major benefits allowing students to attend from anywhere and, when asynchronous, at any time. In a survey of over 1,200 students at King's Own Institute in 2021 (during COVID), the self-reported benefits (in order of number of responses) included:

- Not having to travel
- Time management
- Recorded lectures
- Interaction
- Flexibility
- New experience
- Health & Safety (during COVID)
- Personalized learning
- Good communication
- Cost saving
- Initiative of teachers
- Less disturbance

Responses such as not having to travel, flexibility, and cost-saving were to be expected. However, it was pleasing to note that students were positive about the new learning experience and the initiative of teachers. Sharma (2022) notes that a potential benefit of online learning is in "providing novel, creative and entertaining learning contexts".

The flexibility and convenience noted by students are also applicable to teachers. During lockdowns, many teachers took the time and made the effort to learn more about how to engage the students online. Quite a number invested in their own home studios as part of their response to an extended period of online teaching. The following is an example from one of the teachers at KOI (with permission to include here).

4. The Challenge of Online Learning

Online learners also face a range of challenges including distractions, lack of face-to-face interaction, limited accountability, and isolation. Sumalinog (2022) identified a range of barriers which include:

- technological barriers (poor Internet connectivity, lack of devices, and technical skills);
- attitudinal barriers (procrastination, poor time management, and lack of motivation);
- environmental barriers (lack of workspaces, noise, and other distractions).

In the survey of KOI students noted in the previous section, the self-reported challenges (in order of number of responses) included:

- Time management
- Interaction between student and teacher
- Distractions (microphones not muted)
- Prefer live lectures
- Issues related to zoom links
- Connection issues
- Initiative of teachers
- Lecture class duration
- Attendance process
- Video quality
- Interaction between students
- Online presentations

Again, some of the challenges, such as distractions caused by unmuted participants, were to be expected. What is interesting is that some of the same factors found in the list of benefits, such as interaction, initiative of teachers, and time management were also perceived as challenges by others. When observing the teachers, it was clear that some continued to use the more familiar chalk-and-talk "talking head" approach while others embraced the challenge and experimented with new ways to collaborate and interact. It is quite possible that the teaching methods chosen may have played a large role in the perception of students.

The students in this survey were located in a major city and still reported connection issues. Such frustrations become magnified in rural areas where Internet connections may be slow and, at times, absent.

The challenges for students are not insignificant. Studies have found that students report feeling overwhelmed and isolated in online courses and that the withdrawal rate can be 10%–20% higher than face-to-face courses (Wills and Grimes, 2020).

Teachers face similar technical, attitudinal, and environmental challenges. There can also be logistical issues, such as dealing with students located in different time zones. In particular, with the abundance of distractions available to students "it can be difficult or impossible to verify whether learners are engaged" (Charles, n.d.).

5. Theoretical Frameworks

A range of educational theories focus explicitly on student engagement. These include the engagement theory of learning (Kearsley and Schneiderman, 1998) and Kolb's experiential learning theory. Many other frameworks may be less explicit but still recognize the importance of student engagement.

There is no consensus as to what constitutes "engaged learning" and there are varied definitions for engagement (Bond *et al.*, 2020). Johnson (2013) provides a simple, but workable definition in that "engaged means students are active".

"If true learning is to occur, then students have to be at the very least participants in the process, and not merely products" (Johnson, 2013).

Active learning, which fits within a broader constructivist framework (University of Washington, 2022), can be a major contributor to creating engagement. Baker provides a wide list of evidence demonstrating student engagement including — performing/presenting, inquiring, exploring, explaining, evaluating, and experimenting. Nevertheless, there are times when students will be passive but still engaged such as paying attention during teacher-directed learning (Johnson, 2013).

Theoretical models aimed at increasing motivation can also provide useful insights into how to engage students. These include models from within education, such as the ARCS Model of Motivational Design Theories (Keller, 2010), as well as models from other disciplines, such as the AIDA marketing model (Bean, 2014; Polk, 2018).

6. Getting Attention before You Start

Attention is a prerequisite for learning (Sylwester & Cho, 1992). Motivation is also a prerequisite for learning (Naastrom *et al.*, 2021). This implies a "chicken and egg" conundrum. Do the students pay attention because they are motivated or do they become motivated after paying attention? It may be best to view this as cyclical rather than linear (Figure 1).

6.1. *First Impressions Count*

It is likely that the first encounter a student has with a new online subject will happen even before classes start. Many (but probably not all) students will review the materials provided in the Learning Management System (LMS) prior to the start of a semester. This is a critical point for an online class, but the aim is not just to get students to attend the first class. While some students may not attend any classes this probably doesn't reflect on the quality of the materials provided as these students are often not "genuine" students and never log into the LMS.

Beyond promoting initial attendance, these resources can be used to increase the motivation to study this particular subject. In light of this, practical steps that might be taken can be informed by the ARCS Model of Motivational Design. This model is based on four components (Figure 2):

The components can be summarized as:
A — *Attention*: Arouse and sustain a learner's curiosity and interest
R — *Relevance*: Link a learner's needs, interests, and motives
C — *Confidence*: Develop positive expectations for achieving success
S — *Satisfaction*: Provide reinforcement and reward for learners

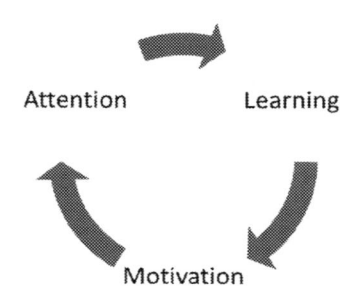

Figure 1: Attention, learning, and motivation model (developed for this study).

Creating Engaging Online Lessons 221

Figure 2: ARCS model (developed for this study).

Extrinsic motivation provides the initial "attention" prompting the students to view the available subject materials. Given that we already have the student's attention we can look at the next components — relevance and confidence. In relation to these, the questions a new student may have include:

Relevance:

- Have I made the right subject choice (even if it is core or mandatory)?
- Will this subject help me with more advanced subjects?
- Will this subject help me in my career?
- What's in it for me (WIIFM)?

Confidence:

- Where do I find information and resources?
- Can I interact with and get help from the teacher?
- Can I Interact with and get help from other students?
- Will I be able to form relationships and networks with others?
- Is it clear how I can get the grade I want?

The practical steps that can be taken to answer these questions include:

Recording a personal video introduction: In order to connect with students online, teachers need to be visible. This includes "seeing our faces as well as hearing our voices" (Wills & Grimes, 2020). An introductory video can focus on the questions that students are likely to have as noted above. For example, an introduction might start with something like:

"Hi, I'm [name]. Congratulations on joining this subject — you've made a great choice! The reasons this is a great choice are [discuss benefits]"

The term "benefits" in the example above is very important. When we introduce a new subject we often focus on features. For example, we might discuss how many assessments there are and when they are due. Benefits refer to the actual benefits for the student in studying this subject. The aim is to answer the question that is at the top of each student's mind — what's in it for me. For example, we might note that this subject is necessary to attain professional accreditation.

Being seen should not be restricted to an introductory video. Wills and Grimes (2020) recommend setting video-based consultations (electronic office hours) as well as adding camera recordings of the teacher in the corner of screencasts. Recording from a webcam and a presentation at the same time can be done using software such as Loom or recent versions of PowerPoint. If the thought of having a talking head during an entire presentation is not appealing, this could be reserved for intros and/or outros as a way of maintaining a more personal connection with the students.

Add testimonials to demonstrate relevance: Testimonials are often used by marketing to promote a course, but they are less frequently used within a subject that students are already enrolled in. Nevertheless, they can add considerable value. They help build trust, credibility and most importantly demonstrate relevance, i.e., that the content is a good fit with the learners' goals. Students expect a teacher to sing the praises of the subject they are teaching. An endorsement from a previous graduate or someone from industry who is applying these skills in the workplace is likely to have much greater impact. Imagine someone from industry commenting along the lines of:

"I studied [this subject] in my undergraduate degree and wondered if I would ever use this in the real-world. Now that I am working in industry

I am so glad I did [this subject] because I'm using these skills all the time".

Written testimonials are relatively easy to obtain through email requests, but video testimonials carry more weight. However, as these don't need high production value they can be obtained fairly easily by capturing a brief Zoom meeting.

Set expectations: Expectations should be set before the first class (although they will probably need to be reinforced throughout the course). Examples in an online environment might include "keeping cameras on, muting microphones when not speaking, and, when possible, minimize environmental distractors" (Klein *et al.*, 2023).

Make navigation easy: If students have trouble finding the material they want they may become frustrated and give up searching (Dick, 2021). The LMS should be set up so that it is easy to navigate. This may include sign posts such as "Start here" and "Next steps". A navigation tour as a written guide or video screencast could also be provided.

Guide to netiquette: Students tend to be familiar with a very informal (and sometimes inappropriate) way of communicating using technology. It is important for them to be able to distinguish between private/social communication and professional communication. In particular, students should be shown how to argue a case rather than make a personal attack. Again, this assistance could be in the form of a written guide or screencast.

Provide clear instructions: Students desire clear communication (Klein *et al.*, 2023). As with navigation, instructions should be easy to follow. The level of language used should be appropriate for the particular student cohort. For example, accommodations may need to be made if English is not the first language of the students.

All instructions should be clear, but given that assessment drives learning it is especially important that students understand what is required of them in assignments and exams. Extra support (or scaffolding) can be supplied to assist. For example, in some situations it may be appropriate to provide exemplar answers that give students an indication of best and worst practices (taking care not to provide a means of copying or plagiarism).

"Exemplars are a very useful way in which students can be helped to gain a firm understanding, in a concrete, contextual, and non-threatening fashion, of exactly what it is that is required of them in order to succeed to their desired level of achievement within a particular unit or in any particular assessment task." (Newlyn , 2013)

Encourage questions: Students should be encouraged to ask questions. Such encouragement can be promoted in an introductory video. In an online environment you also need to make spaces where questions can be easily asked at any time. Forums are one mechanism which allow teachers and/or fellow students to post answers in a timely manner. However, care needs to be taken to set appropriate expectations regarding "timeliness". Students may expect teacher-generated answers 24/7. To avoid such unrealistic expectations you can set electronic office hours where you make it explicit when you will respond to questions. Where the same question is asked by many students it may be better handled by adding it to an FAQ and responding with a link to the single answer.

Email and written discussion boards have the potential to be viewed as "old-fashioned" by students. Fortunately, there are more modern alternatives which can be made use of. For example, Wills & Grimes (2020) used Flipgrid (now known as Flip) to set up a video discussion board and found that student engagement was higher than traditional forums.

Encourage community: "Feeling welcome and greeted are the first steps to building community and a sense of belonging. This is especially true at the beginning of an online program" (Wills & Grimes, 2020).

Surveys by TopHat have found that students are far more likely to be motivated by teachers who create a sense of community and belonging (TopHat, 2021). As well as the opportunity to post and respond to academic questions in forums it can be valuable to provide a social rather than academic "café" space where students can form connections and network. However, you may want to consider making the study of netiquette a prerequisite for entry into such a space.

7. Getting Attention in an Online Class

When we move to the virtual classroom, the challenge becomes — how can we gain attention in online lessons?

"Students don't owe you their attention. Once you internalize this, you can embrace the fact that it's your responsibility to keep your audience engaged" (Kao, 2021).

First impressions count — every time: While it is important to set the scene for a subject with the resources available in an LMS, you should aim to engage your students at the beginning of every class.

One way to do this is to use a "hook". A hook is a tactic used by presenters to instantly engage an audience. Five examples are shown below, but there are a plethora to choose from (simply Google "how to hook an audience").

Use a contrarian approach: Take a well-known piece of conventional knowledge and contradict it. For example, "You know the phrase 'buy low and sell high'. Well, it's WRONG. Let me show you why …"

'Did you know that …'

Tell a startling fact. For example, 'Did you know that there are about 55 earthquakes around the Earth every day?'

'Imagine …'

Paint a picture of a preferred future. For example, 'What if you were debt free?'

Tell a story

"The human species thinks in metaphors and learns through stories." Mary Catherine Bateson (in Flickinger, 2021)

There is an apocryphal quote that states that "a fact wrapped in a story is 22 times more memorable than facts alone". Patience-Davies investigated and could not locate an original source for this oft-used quote. Nevertheless, she found other references to the power of stories. For example, one study found the "stories are about 12 times as memorable as statistics" (Patience-Davies, 2021). While it is probably impossible to quantify the benefit, stories can definitely be used to create engagement as attested to by the popularity of books, television, and movies. Contextual stories relating to current affairs, real-life case studies and personal experience are likely to have greater relevance.

Open a loop: "Open loops work. All you have to do is start a thought, idea or question and then complete it somewhere else. It's the in-between space that drives more curiosity, interest and consumption" (McLaren, n.d.).

An open loop introduces a topic, but doesn't give it all away. For example, you could set an intriguing question at the beginning of a class and then add "by the end of the lesson you will have enough information to solve this mystery". You can also open a loop at the end of one lesson to act as a "cliffhanger" for the next.

No matter what opening techniques are used, it is helpful to demonstrate the relevance to the students of the learning outcomes at the beginning of each particular lesson. To do this, reflect on the question 'What's in it for me'? from a student's perspective.

8. Engagement — Maintaining Attention

"Your audience's attention will fade over time unless you take specific steps to keep them engaged" (Mitchell, n.d.).

Attention levels over the course of a didactic style of presentation vary. Typically, attention is highest at the start, but rapidly declines. It often shows a slight increase nearing the end (Bligh, 1998; Medina, 2014; Mitchell, n.d.).

Fortunately, the decline can often be arrested and attention levels restored (or at least improved) by using a state change (Kao, 2021) or as Mitchell (n.d.) describes it — by hitting the "attention reset button".

Kao (2021) suggests using a state change every 3–5 minutes, while Mitchell recommends hitting the reset button every 10 minutes. John Medina in his book *Brain Rules* is even more specific and facetiously states that "at 9 minutes and 59 seconds, something must be done to regain attention and restart the clock" (Medina, 2014). Of course, there is nothing magical about 10 minutes as there are many variables involved. For example, speakers tend to dread the reduced attention levels associated with the "after-lunch" time slot.

In a face-to-face class we can often judge when to include a state change by monitoring the class. (I avoided the use of the term "audience" rather than class as this tends to reinforce the notion of students being passive). When you are online you lose the ability to read the room. Some will look bored, some excited and "a bunch of people where you can't quite tell what they're thinking" (Kao, 2021). This, of course, presumes that the students even have their cameras turned on. Miller (2020) notes that we should accept that some students may not have "eyes on you at all times in all of your synchronous meetings, and that's okay".

Given this difficulty it may be best to schedule regular changes when planning the lesson. The focus then becomes on what to include as a state change. Mitchell (n.d.) warns against continuing to repeat the same type of activity to avoid the students becoming habituated to the change and it consequently having a lower impact on restoring attention level.

Kao (2021) provides an example of how a Zoom session could be revised using state changes going from a monologue to one interspersed with activities such as "Ask a question" and go to a "Breakout Group". Kao provides limited activities in his example, but adds that when teaching live on Zoom you should "reach into your toolkit of active learning options and pepper them in" (Kao, 2021).

9. Active Learning Strategies

Most students place great importance on learning experiences that are active and engaging. They want instructors who promote discussion and collaboration — and who make learning relevant by applying learnings to real-world issues. They also want opportunities to develop transferable skills, which is important to a generation that increasingly equates higher education with securing a good job (TopHat, 2021).

There isn't a standard definition for active learning (Chitanana, 2022). For the purposes of this discussion, active learning will be considered as a pedagogical approach that encourages students to engage in the learning process actively. It goes beyond passive listening or reading and focuses on involving learners in meaningful activities that promote critical thinking, problem-solving, and knowledge construction.

There are a vast variety of active learning strategies that can be employed in an online environment. They include:

Effective questioning: While most, if not all, teachers incorporate questioning in their repertoire, the effectiveness can vary depending on the approach. Only asking closed questions that require a "Yes/No" or simple recall response can promote surface learning. Open follow-up questions, such as "Why do you think that?" allow for more in-depth responses. Another common technique is for teachers to answer questions themselves when the students are unresponsive. On its own this is not necessarily bad, but if this is the pattern, students soon learn that they do not need to engage with the questions being asked.

Discussions: In-class discussion and asynchronous discussion forums can both be used to facilitate meaningful discussions, debates, and knowledge exchange among students. By posing thought-provoking questions, providing clear instructions, and actively taking part in the conversations teachers can encourage critical thinking and help to cultivate a sense of community in the virtual classroom.

Gamification: Gamification involves applying game-design principles to non-gaming contexts to increase engagement and motivation. In online lessons, this can be achieved by incorporating elements such as points, badges, leaderboards, and challenges. Gamification promotes a sense of achievement, fosters healthy competition, and encourages learners to actively participate.

Online quizzes and polls: There are many tools available to incorporate quizzes and polls online. Some increase engagement by including gamification elements such as leaderboards and time limits for answering. When not part of formal assessment, quizzes allow students to receive formative feedback. Real-time quizzes and polls also provide the teacher with immediate feedback to gauge student understanding of the material and to recast if needed.

Collaborative projects: Cooperative learning activities designed for teams "help students improve empathy, collaboration, and the ability to understand others' perspectives" (Leman & Mott, 2023). Students can collaborate on tasks, share documents, and negotiate ideas. Such activities enhance their ability to work in diverse teams, a valuable skill in the modern workplace.

Virtual simulations and virtual field trips: Apart from the cost savings, simulations of real-world scenarios allow students to apply theoretical knowledge, make decisions, and witness the consequences of their actions in a risk-free environment. Virtual field trips allow students to become immersed in alternative cultures and places. As with collaborative projects this may assist in gaining alternative perspectives.

Interactive tutorial activities: There are tools that allow the teacher to monitor the progress of students as they complete online activities. This allows the teacher to give help when students need it and interact with them according to their needs. Some also allow students to provide assistance to each other. Other tools allow you to set up interactive activities where personalized feedback can be provided automatically. Some tools go beyond this and provide adaptive learning — where students get custom learning experiences adapted to their individual needs.

Interactive videos: Active learning can be incorporated into the passive act of viewing a video by adding interactivity. Typical interactive elements include hotspots, drag and drop, links, summaries, and quizzes. More advanced tools also allow branching so that customized paths can be taken.

Guest speakers and industry experts: For face-to-face classes, attracting guest speakers and industry experts can be difficult given travel requirements and time constraints. However, in the post-pandemic world, most people have familiarity with video-conferencing tools such as Zoom. External participants now have the opportunity to join the class from their home or office and are more likely to accept invitations (particularly if the duration is not too long). Listening to a guest speaker isn't active. However, students will appreciate the opportunity to ask questions in real-time if an interactive Q&A session is included.

Student generated content: Students can be encouraged to create and share their own content, such as writing blog posts, recording podcasts, or designing graphics. This empowers students to take ownership of their learning and contribute to the course community. Fatayer (2016) describes how student-generated content can be used to generate open education resources such as interactive activities for use in future classes.

Host virtual office hours: Virtual office hours can be scheduled in order to connect with students one-on-one or in small groups. Students can ask questions, seek clarifications, or discuss specific topics, fostering a personalized and interactive learning experience.

10. Passive Learning

Active learning lends itself toward engaged learning, but not all learning can take place in this format. Passive learning has a somewhat undeserved bad reputation, as it has advantages and is a component of most learning situations. For example, passive learning occurs when listening to a TED talk, reading a book, or watching a video. Russell (2021) states that "as a life-long learner, I know that passive learning is where I find comfort". Her advice on whether to use active or passive learning is … use both! The question then becomes "How can we make passive learning more engaging"?

One of the techniques already mentioned is breaking passive learning up with segments of active learning. However, even within a longer duration of passive learning there are techniques we can use to make it more engaging.

"Rule #4: We don't pay attention to boring things" (Medina, 2014).

Engaging presentations: Most people have experienced "Death by PowerPoint" on more than one occasion. Fortunately, there are techniques that can be used to lessen the chances of providing a boring presentation.

Many authors argue that presentation slides should primarily use images with limited text (Horvath, 2019; Dick, 2021). Horvath (2019) argues for this position using evidence from neuroscience. He gives details of research into the "Broca/Wernicke bottleneck" which demonstrates that the ability to understand verbal information is limited to one form at any time. Images should be contextually relevant and Dick (2021) advises that some effort should be put into choosing suitable images.

Based on other biological evidence, Horvath also recommends using a consistent format except for times when you want to focus attention. Like many others, he also recommends the use of stories to guide understanding and help create memory "landmarks" (Horvath, 2019).

Presentation length: Recorded videos of lecture-style presentations should be limited in duration. There is no set optimal duration. Berg *et al.* (2014) recommend less than 15 minutes. Guo suggests 6 minutes or shorter but notes that the real takeaway is that lectures should be broken up into small, 'bite-size pieces' (Guo,2013). Cordiner (2021) recognizes that longer videos are not necessarily "bad". However, with an average video viewing time of 1–4 minutes she notes that students may not get all the way to the end of a long video. Adding interaction to videos (as described in a previous section) is likely to increase the average viewing time.

Curated content: Teachers can share articles, blog posts, research papers, YouTube videos, or other relevant resources on the LMS. This helps students explore additional content, gain diverse perspectives, and delve deeper into the subject matter. As always, relevance needs to be demonstrated whether this be a link to assessment or future careers. Length of resources also needs to be considered. Using the LMS as a repository for large amounts of reading or hours-worth of video without some context or guidance is a sure recipe for students not to engage.

11. Technology and Online Teaching

"Technology can amplify great teaching but great technology cannot replace poor teaching" (OECD, 2015).

It is recognized that educational technology has the potential to improve student engagement. However, there is no guarantee that the use of technology will result in active engagement (Bond *et al.*, 2020). I have had the privilege of observing many online teaching sessions. During these sessions I have seen poor lessons using great technology and great lessons using relatively simple technology such as Zoom with breakout rooms. The naming of specific online learning tools has been avoided in this chapter because "without careful planning and sound pedagogy, technology can prompt disengagement" (Bond *et al.*, 2020). In addition, the available technology is changing and improving at a rapid rate so any references are likely to be quickly outdated. It may be better to focus on the pedagogy first and then evaluate which of the (then current) technology tools fit with these pedagogical requirements.

12. Next Steps

The ideas and examples given in this chapter are not exhaustive. In addition, not all suggestions will fit with every teaching style. Hopefully, though, they might inspire you to apply techniques that fit your personal teaching philosophy and prompt you to investigate other ways to engage students in online classes.

When choosing how to teach online you may want to consider the following (scary) question:

If I was a student in my own class, would I find it engaging?

References

Baker, K.J. (2020). Panic-gogy: A conversation with Sean Michael Morris. *The National Teaching & Learning Forum*, 29, 1–3.

Bean, C. (2014). *The Accidental Instructional Designer*. Alexandria: Astd Press.

Berg, R., Brand, A., Grant, J., Kirk, J. & Zimmerman, T. (2014). Leveraging recorded mini-lectures to increase student learning. *Course Design*, 14(2), 5–8.

Bligh (1998). *What's the Use of Lectures*. Exeter: Intellect.

Bond, M., Buntins, K., Bedenlier, S. *et al.* (2020). Mapping research in student engagement and educational technology in higher education: A systematic evidence map. *International Journal of Educational Technology in Higher Education*, 17, 2.

Charles, B. (n.d.). Leveraging Learning Theories in eLearning. Available at https://www.flarelearning.com/post/22-leveraging-learning-theories-in-elearning.

Chitanana, L. (2022). Enhancing student engagement and active learning in online learning environments: Lesson learnt during the COVID-19 lockdown. In Keengwe, J. (ed.), *Handbook of Research on Active Learning and Student Engagement in Higher Education*. Pennsylvania: IGI Global, pp. 128–152.

Cordiner, S. (2021). How long should your online course videos be? Sarah Cordiner. Available at https://sarahcordiner.com/getting-perfect-online-course-video-duration/.

Dick, G. (2021). Teaching online: Creating student engagement. *Communications of the Association for Information Systems*, 48, 65–72.

Fatayer, M.M. (2016). *Towards a Sustainable Open Educational Resources Development Model: Tapping into the Cognitive Surplus of Student-Generated Content*. Thesis (Ph.D.). Available at: http://hdl.handle.net/1959.7/uws:38470.

Guo, P. (2013). Optimal video length for student engagement [web log post]. Available at https://blog.edx.org/optimal-video-length-student-engagement.

Horvath, J.C. (2019). *Stop Talking Start Influencing: 12 Insights from Brain Science to Make Your Message Stick*. Sorrento: Exisle Publishing.

Johnson, B. (2013). How do we know when students are engaged? Edutopia; George Lucas Educational Foundation. Available at https://www.edutopia.org/blog/student-engagement-definition-ben-johnson.

Kao, W. (2021). The state change method: how to deliver engaging live lectures on Zoom. Available at https://www.weskao.com/blog/the-state-change-method?utm_source=coursecreatorsweekly.

Kearsley, G. & Shneiderman, B. (1998). Engagement theory: A framework for technology-based teaching and learning. *Educational Technology*, 38(5), 20–23.

Keller, J.M. (2010). *Motivational Design For Learning And Performance: The ARCS Model Approach*. Berlin: Springer.

Klein, K., Galantino, M., Crowell, T. & Cavazza, R. (2023). The abrupt educational switch: Impact of COVID-19 and lessons learned for health science faculty and students. *The Internet Journal of Allied Health Sciences and Practice*, 21(2), Article 14.

Leman, A. & Mott, R. (2023). Evaluating the outcomes of human-centered design in a virtual program development higher education course. *Journal of Human Sciences and Extension*, 11(1), 15.

Marzano, R.J. (2007). The art and science of teaching: A comprehensive framework for effective instruction. Association For Supervision And Curriculum Development.

Mclaren, S. (n.d.). Open loops and where to use them. Available at https://www.marketingyourbusiness.com/podcast/open-loops.

Medina, J. (2014). *Brain Rules: 12 Principles for Surviving and Thriving at Work, Home and School*. Washington: Pear Press.

Miller, M. (2020). This professor says radical availability will make the fall a success. *Top Hat*. Available at https://tophat.com/blog/michelle-miller-guest-lecture/.

Mitchell, O. (n.d.). What to do when you're losing your audience. Speaking about Presenting. Available at https://speakingaboutpresenting.com/audience/losing-audience/.

Näsström, G., Andersson, C., Granberg, C., Palm, T. & Palmberg, B. (2021). Changes in student motivation and teacher decision making when implementing a formative assessment practice. *Frontiers in Education*, 6. https://www.frontiersin.org/articles/10.3389/feduc.2021.616216.

Newlyn, D. (2013). Providing exemplars in the learning environment: The case for and against. *Universal Journal of Educational Research*, 1(1), 26–32.

OECD (2015). *Students, Computers and Learning*. PISA: OECD Publishing. Available at http://www.oecd-ilibrary.org/education/students-computers-and-learning_9789264239555-en.

Ofgang, E. (2021). Research: Video learning may be more effective than in-person lectures. *TechLearningMagazine*. Available at https://www.techlearning.com/news/research-video-learning-may-be-more-effective-than-in-person-lectures.

Patience-Davies, H. (2021). Where did the claim that stories are 22 times more memorable come from? Available at https://patiencedavies.com/2021/01/27/the-case-of-the-missing-author-just-where-did-the-claim-that-stories-are-22-times-more-memorable-than-facts-alone-come-from/.

Polk, X. (2018). Marketing: The key to successful teaching and learning. *Journal of Marketing Development and Competitiveness*, 12(2), 49–57.

Russell, K. (2021). Active vs. passive learning: What's the difference? Graduate Programs for Educators. Available at https://www.graduateprogram.org/2021/06/active-vs-passive-learning-whats-the-difference/.

Salter, G. (2004). A constructivist approach to online learning: Encouraging pedagogical re-engineering. Student thesis: Professional doctorate — CDU. Available at: https://doi.org/10.25913/2w07-0b88.

Sharma, L.R. (2022). Identifying the benefits and challenges of digital technology and online learning. *International Research Journal of MMC*, 3(2), 26–32. https://doi.org/10.3126/irjmmc.v3i2.46297.

Sumalinog, G.G. (2022). Barriers of online education in the new normal: Teachers' perspectives. *International Journal of Learning, Teaching and Educational Research*, 21(1), 33–50. https://doi.org/10.26803/ijlter.21.1.3.

Sylwester, R. & Cho, J. (1992). What brain research says about paying attention. *Educational Leadership*, 50(4), 71–75.

Thacker-King, J.S. (2023). Global educational ramifications of COVID-19 on minorities and students living in poverty or extreme poverty: A literature review. *Journal of Global Education and Research*, 7(3), 226–233.

TopHat (2016). Professor pulse survey. Available at https://tophat.com/wp-content/uploads/2017/09/2016-Top-Hat-Professor-Pulse-Survey.pdf.

TopHat (2021). 3,052 college students on the good, the bad, and learning post-COVID. Available at https://tophat.com/thank-you/winter-2021-student-survey-report-thank-you/.

University of Washington (2022). Active learning. Center for Teaching and Learning. Available at https://teaching.washington.edu/topics/engaging-students-in-learning/promoting-student-engagement-through-active-learning/.

Wills, S. & Grimes, R. (2020). Developing relationships in an online environment. *The European Conference on Language Learning 2020: Official Conference Proceedings*.

Chapter 9

Effectiveness of Game-Based Learning for Programming Courses

Mubashir Hussain

King's Own Institute, Australia

Abstract

In this technological era, programming skill has become highly valuable across IT and non-IT sectors. Teaching programming can be challenging, requiring a deep understanding of the subject and effective communication skills. Traditional pedagogy, focused on lectures, textbooks, and written assessments, tends to emphasize content over student-centered learning, resulting in limited practical application and knowledge retention. This chapter explores the potential of "Game-Based Learning" (GBL) and gamification as an alternative pedagogy to improve learner's engagement, problem-solving skills, and learning skills. This chapter provides insights on GBL and its application in programming education, which enables instructors to make better decisions in their teaching practices for programming courses and improve students' learning experiences.

Keywords: Game-based learning, Gamification, Programming, Cognitive learning, Constructive learning, Case studies.

1. Introduction

In today's world, programming has become a valuable skill to have, and it is impacting a wide variety of fields. It is used in business, finance, healthcare, automotive, aerospace, manufacturing, education, gaming, entertainment, music, architecture, and many more. Programming helps people solve complex problems, automate mundane tasks, and create new systems. There is an increasing demand in each industry for graduates with analytical, technical, and programming capabilities (Mathrani *et al.*, 2016).

However, teaching programming to students can be challenging. It requires a good understanding of the material and the ability to communicate complex concepts in an engaging and understandable way (Panskyi & Rowińska, 2021). In addition, it is crucial to tailor the teaching techniques according to the different learning levels of students.

Traditional pedagogy typically involves lecture-focused teaching, textbook-centric learning, and written assessments. This kind of teaching is heavily content-focused rather than student-focused (Puranik, 2020). Using such approaches has the following disadvantages.

(1) *Lecture-focused teaching*: Delivery of programming content using only lecture slides in the classroom can deliver theoretical concepts to the student but doesn't provide its link to practical implementation. It also limits the opportunity to interact with the student.
(2) *Textbook-centric learning*: Students follow a prescribed textbook during the course. The textbooks provide in-depth explanations of the lecture material but can be overwhelming for students new to programming due to their complexity.
(3) *Written assessments*: The students are asked to write the codes in the exam that only measure students' retention of information.

Traditional teaching methods do not provide enough opportunities for students to practice their learning. This can lead to students forgetting what they have learned, and many who enroll in programming courses often find it challenging to apply their knowledge to new or real-world problems.

Furthermore, the traditional approaches don't promote collaboration among students. As a result, students' motivation and interest in learning drop, and it becomes challenging for the lecturer to keep them engaged in the class (Prensky, 2003; Sarkar, 2006). During the last decade, a different approach to teaching called game-based learning (GBL) has gained more popularity as it boosts student's motivation and interest in learning (Gordillo *et al.*, 2022). In this chapter, we will discuss the theoretical foundations of GBL, the benefits and challenges of using GBL in programming, the implementation of GBL, case studies, limitations, and using GBL in programming subjects.

2. Theoretical Foundations for GBL

2.1. *What Is GBL?*

A word game refers to a play with certain rules, challenges, and goals to achieve for entertainment purposes (Cheng *et al.*, 2015). GBL is a pedagogical approach that uses games as a medium for teaching and learning. The aim of GBL is for students to achieve predefined learning outcomes (Shaffer *et al.*, 2005). Designing and developing learning games involves balancing of subject content and entertainment aspect of the game. GBL can be applied to various subjects, but it is especially relevant for programming, which is a skill that requires creativity, problem-solving, critical thinking, and collaboration. With the popularity of GBL a new term "gamification" has emerged and gained increasing relevance since 2010 (Deterding *et al.*, 2011; Seaborn and Fels, 2015). Gamification involves using different game elements, such as incentive systems (levels, points, leaderboards, certificates, or badges) to motivate players to engage in learning tasks and solve problems (Zainuddin *et al.*, 2020).

GBL vs. Gamification: The fundamental difference between gamification and GBL is that GBL is the learning experience, however, gamification is adding the game component to the traditional teaching pedagogy (Kapp, 2012).

In GBL, the instructor needs to design learning activities while considering the game's principles and characteristics. However, gamification adds game elements to exciting learning activities. The differences are summarized in Table 1. The interactivity and engagement intrinsic to games create a conducive environment for learning complex subjects like programming.

In this section, we discuss what is GBL and the theoretical foundations that make GBL a powerful tool for students to acquire knowledge.

Table 1: Difference between GBL and gamification.

Feature	Game-Based Learning	Gamification
Definition	The game-like learning activities need to be designed for learners	Adding game elements to existing learning activities
Goals	To teach concepts and skills in an engaging way	To make traditional learning more engaging
Immersion	More immersive	Less immersive
Engagement	More engaging	Can be engaging
Cost	More expensive	Less expensive
Development Time	More time-consuming	Less time-consuming

Source: Kapp (2012) and Zainuddin *et al.* (2020).

2.2. Learning Theories for GBL

Learning theories provide a basic framework for understanding how individuals acquire knowledge and skills. According to Smith (1999) there are four main learning theories as follows:

- Behaviorism is a learning theory that emphasizes the role of external stimuli and rewards in shaping behavior. In the context of GBL, behaviorist principles can be applied to design games that provide clear goals and objectives, immediate feedback, and the use of rewards to encourage desired behaviors.
- Cognitivism is a learning theory that focuses on the mental processes involved in learning, such as attention, memory, and problem-solving. In the context of GBL, cognitive principles can be applied to design games that engage learners' attention, provide opportunities for practice and feedback, and challenge learners to solve problems.
- Constructivism is a learning theory that emphasizes the active role of learners in constructing their knowledge. In the context of GBL, constructivist principles can be applied to design games that allow learners to explore and experiment, make mistakes, and reflect on their learning.
- Humanism is a learning theory that focuses on the individual learner's needs, interests, and motivations. In the context of GBL, humanistic principles can be applied to design games that are engaging, challenging, and fun, and that allow learners to express themselves and take ownership of their learning.

Many educational games were designed according to behaviorist theory in the past (Rugelj & Lapina, 2019). These games, often following programmed instruction, presented students with questions or tasks (stimuli). The students immediately select from provided answers that lead to positive feedback for correct answers, reinforcing the association between questions and correct responses. Incorrect answers triggered negative feedback, weakening the associations. Point-and-click games and quizzes exemplify this approach, embedding drill and practice within behaviorism-based gameplay. These types of games are only suitable for basic memorization or understanding.

The games based on cognitive learning theory focus on optimally managing the learning by providing mental models to manage cognitive load. The students learn the fundamental concepts and then use logical deduction to gain new insights. These games are designed to adapt to the learner's level by providing an incremental level of complexity. Strategy games are examples of cognitive theory-based games. Some of these games can provide personalized learning based on students' behavioral profiles.

Another type of game for teaching students may involve constructive learning theory. According to Woolfolk the main ideas are:

> ... students actively construct their knowledge: the mind of the student mediates input from the outside world to determine what the student will learn. Learning is active mental work, not passive reception of teaching" (Woolfolk, 1993).

The games developed based on this theory used immersive environments where students take on roles, make different decisions, and experience the outcomes of those decisions. This encourages students to actively engage and build their knowledge. The challenges in the games help students refine their understandings through iterative attempts and employing different strategies.

3. GBL for Programming Courses

GBL for teaching programming concepts has been popular since the 1990s (Suzuki & Kata, 1995). According to Kanika *et al.* (2020), there are two types of techniques that are used for teaching programming concepts.

(1) The learners are instructed to write programs to develop games and play games (Corral et al., 2014).
(2) The learners are instructed to develop simple games using the graphical libraries representing the programming concepts (Dolgopolovas et al., 2018; Martins et al., 2018).

These approaches have a positive impact on the learners and improve their understanding of programming concepts. In Kato and Ide (1995), the learners were taught programming concepts by writing programs to control wrestlers. Many studies taught programming concepts by instructing students to write programs and play games (Bierre & Phelps, 2004; Chaffin et al., 2009; Jiau et al., 2009). In the study by Miljanovic and Bradbury (2016), a game is introduced to teach fundamental concepts of C++ programming to students without prior coding experience. They introduced an evaluation strategy aimed at comprehensively assessing the game's effects on learning outcomes and user engagement. However, the study did not provide conclusive results from the evaluation phase.

Similarly, Mathrani et al. (2016) used GBL in diploma computing courses to evaluate the impact on the programming courses. They found that GBL improved the engagement of the learners. Also, it was easier for the learner to map game elements with the programming concepts.

Seaborn et al. (2012) conducted a pilot study, incorporating GameMaker, a game development engine, in a high school computer science course. This course comprised three modules, each involving student teams that perform different roles (designers, artists, and programmers) contributing to game proposals and development. The approach was effective in enhancing learners' understanding of programming concepts.

Zhi et al. (2018) examined instructional support design within educational programming. Dicheva and Hodge (2018) introduced a Stack Game to help learners grasp the concept of stack data structure. The game notably improved students' understanding of stacks and garnered positive attitudes toward GBL. López-Fernández et al. (2021) conducted randomized control trials, noting increased student motivation with GBL. Similarly Miljanovic & Bradbury (2020) introduced GidgetML, an adaptive serious game for debugging, revealing reduced performance variability. These studies collectively highlight GBL's potential to enhance programming learning through innovative strategies and adaptive approaches, although further research is needed to draw definitive conclusions. Some research works implemented GBL into the programming courses, which are discussed in Table 2.

Table 2: GBL for teaching programming.

Research Work	Tools	Contribution	Target Users	Sample Size
Kato and Ide (1995)	AlgoBlok	Students were made to write programs to control wrestlers in a game	UG (Undergraduate) students	10+
Pane (2002)	HANDS	Students developed simple games	School kids	10+
Bierre and Phelps (2004)	Multi-User Programming Pedagogy (MUPPETS)	Student wrote programs to display and manipulate 3D objects	UG Students	10+
Leutenegger and Edgington (2007)	Game-based exercise (no name given in the literature)	Games used to teach programming	UG Students	100+
Sung et al. (2008)	Game-based assessments (no name given in the literature)	Game-based assessments are used to teach programming	UG Students	10+
Chaffin et al. (2009)	EleMental	Teaching advanced programming concepts using programming	Senior UG Students	10+
Jiau et al. (2009)	Game-based assessments (no name given in the literature)	Assessments used to identify learners styles of programming	UG Students	10+
Li and Watson (2011)	Board game (no name given in the literature)	Taught programming use board games	School kids/UG Students	10+
Fowler et al. (2012)	Kodu Game Lab	Taught programming using 3D game	School kids	10+

Source: Kanika et al. (2020).

4. Benefits of GBL in Programming

Several studies showed that GBL offers significant advantages over traditional teaching and improves the learning experience (Mathrani *et al.*, 2016; Rugelj & Lapina, 2019; Zhan *et al.*, 2022).

- *Engagement*: The GBL learning improves the engagement of the students. Games inherently possess a quality to engage players for a long period. The challenges and interactive elements don't let students be passive and only consume instructions. The elements such as feedback, collaboration, and choice motivate students to learn (Serrano, 2019).
- *Problem-solving skills*: GBL helps students to improve their problem-solving skills. The games provide challenges of different levels and complexity to the students. The students need to use their logical and decision-making skills to solve those problems. In the process, they also understand the impact of decisions in different scenarios. Problem-solving is an essential skill for programmers.
- *Critical thinking*: GBL requires new and innovative solutions from the students. Students are presented with coding challenges and logical puzzles that enhance their critical thinking skills. The research (Cicchino, 2015) shows that GBL helps to improve students' critical thinking skills.
- *Immediate feedback*: Providing timely feedback to the students significantly improves learning outcomes (Hattie & Timperley, 2007). GBL provides immediate feedback to accelerate the learning curve of the students. In programming courses, providing feedback related to logical issues will help students to understand programming concepts more effectively.
- *Self-directed learning*: GBL makes students more independent and helps them to become self-directed learners. Researchers Palaniappan & Noor (2022) show that the introduction of gamification improved students' self-directed learning levels. In programming games students at different levels can choose their own learning pace, the order in which they tackle challenges, and provide them to do additional practice.
- *Collaboration*: The real-world programming projects require different teams from different locations to work together to build the software systems. GBL can replicate this by encouraging students to

collaborate to succeed. For example, the games can be designed to ask students to write different parts of the code that as a whole make a solution.
- *Real-world simulations*: GBL can help in designing and developing complex programming challenges that students will face in the real world. The simulations of such scenarios help students to gain insights into the practical applications. This helps to reduce the gap between theoretical knowledge and practical implementation.

5. Challenges and Limitations

Most of the researchers discussed the advantages of GBL, but some researchers have highlighted the interrelated disadvantages of GBL for both learners and instructors. If instructors face challenges with GBL, it will have negative consequences for the learners (Jääskä & Aaltonen, 2022). The challenges faced during the implementation of GBL by the instructors and learners are as follows:

- *Time commitment*: GBL may be time-consuming as it requires significant time commitment from students (Boghian *et al.*, 2019). Games can take a long time to play and can also require a significant amount of time to learn how to play. Furthermore, some students may have a steep learning curve, compared to others.
- *GBL design*: Instructors require specific skills and technical knowledge of implementing game theory to design GBL for their courses (Sánchez-Mena & Martí-Parreño, 2017). Instructors need to consider the technological infrastructure to support the GBL practices (Vu & Feinstein, 2017).
- *Assessment*: Within the GBL environment it would become difficult to assess student learning (Jong, 2016). The main reason is that the learners are on different levels and learn at different pace and time. The instructors need to be trained to design effective assessments for GBL.
- *Motivation*: Some learners find games to be distracting or challenging. For learners, incomplete implementation of GBL practices in the curriculum leads to distraction from learning objectives and causes frustration. Some students regard gamification classes as demanding and lose motivation (Domínguez *et al.*, 2013).

- *Cost*: GBL is expensive to implement, especially for games that are designed and developed for the subjects. The cost may include hiring a professional game developer or purchasing off-the-shelf games. Furthermore, setting up the technology infrastructure to support the GBL and training instructors will incur additional costs (Kaimara *et al.*, 2021).
- *Accessibility*: One of the least discussed challenges of implementing GBL is to provide equal learning opportunities to all students. Some students may have limited access to the hardware required for GBL or the Internet. Others may have some disabilities that make it difficult for them to get the maximum benefit from GBL. The instructors need to consider this while using GBL strategies.

In summary, there are numerous challenges in implementing the GBL in classrooms. It includes lack of financial resources, incomplete GBL design due to lack of required skill, lack of knowledge to achieve learning goals or developing assessment items, technology learning curve, and created for all types of students. GBL still needs to be studied in more detail by the researchers. If it is not implemented properly, both the instructors and learners will have a poor experience.

6. Implementation of GBL

The implementation of GBL for programming courses requires careful planning and execution. Many studies indicate the effectiveness of GBL, but some studies also highlight that GBL may not be effective in achieving learning outcomes (O'Neil *et al.*, 2005). It has been noted that some of the learners don't like the game and simulation-based learning (De Freitas, 2006b). While implementing GBL consider the following points mentioned by De Freitas (2006a):

(1) *Conduct background research on effective GBL*: Before integrating GBL into the programming course, conduct a thorough literature review on how to achieve effective learning outcomes through games. Explore studies that highlight the cognitive benefits of GBL and can improve problem-solving skills in programming tasks.
(2) *Context and learning objectives*: Carefully consider the context of GBL for programming courses. No contextualizing the games into a

meaningful learning context would lead to the failure of GBL. Identify clear learning objectives for your programming course. Determine the specific programming skills you want learners to develop through the GBL approach.

(3) *Understand learners*: Analyze the ICT skills and expectations of learners. Choose the games that match with learner's skill levels and align with the learning objectives. For example, a novice programmer can benefit from games that provide detailed coding guidance and feedback.

(4) *Select an appropriate pedagogy*: Consider an appropriate pedagogy that aligns with the programming concepts to be taught. For example, problem-based learning is used to solve different parts of programming projects.

(5) *Examine game-based aspects*: Assess the games whether they provide challenges of the same complexity as real-world programming scenarios before designing the learning activities for the students.

(6) *Address technical support*: Identify the technical support needed to run the games. Test the games on institution computers to ensure it is compatible and function as intended. Check if there are network restrictions that could prevent students from accessing the game.

(7) *Evaluate costs and funding*: Calculate the financial implications of using the games for your learners. Seek funding related to expenses, licensing, or technical support.

(8) *Provide guidance and support*: Guide learners and make sure they understand the rules and objectives of the games. Develop tutorials, guides, and FAQs to assist them. It is very important to identify that all learners are equally supported by GBL. Also, the games should be accessible remotely for better learning.

(9) *Comprehensive learning activity planning*: Plan a sequence of learning activities that help learners to progressively build programming skills. These activities can range from solving coding puzzles to collaborating on complex programming challenges. Ensure that the activities are designed to enhance understanding, critical thinking, and practical application of programming concepts.

(10) *Integrate games into the learning process*: Add the GBL activities into the curriculum at specific locations. Make the game a part of learning rather than an end in itself. Explain to the learners the importance of each game and how it contributes to their programming skills.

(11) *Monitor progress and provide feedback*: Regularly monitor students' progress based on the activities completed and provide timely feedback on their performance. The game's built-in feedback can be used to offer immediate guidance on code correction and problem-solving approaches.
(12) *Encourage collaboration*: Promote collaboration among learners. Develop group-based activities that encourage teamwork and learners can devise strategies and solutions together.
(13) *Assess learning outcomes*: Assess learners based on the skills acquired and if they achieve the learning objectives. Evaluation can be done based on the performance of learners within the game and assessments.
(14) *Continuous improvements*: Incorporate the learners' comments to improve the GBL implementation. Adjust the games, develop, or modify in-game activities and improve supporting material to enhance the learning experience and for better mapping of learning objectives.

7. Case Studies on GBL for Programming Courses

In this section, we discuss a few case studies related to the implementation of GBL in programming courses and their findings.

7.1. *Case Study 1*

In this case study, Mathrani *et al.* (2016) focus on a non-university education provider to see the impact of the GBL approach on teach introductory programming concepts. Before the experiment, the IT tutors were interviewed to identify challenges faced by ICT students. The tutors raised the following concerns:

(1) Difficulty in converting the theoretical concepts to practical implementation.
(2) Difficulty in understanding programming constructs.
(3) Lack of interest in the content.

Based on the feedback the authors have selected the programming constructs such as sequential logic flow, conditional statements, functions, loops, and recursions for the GBL experiment. The study involved two student cohorts: The first cohort that had not started the programming course, and the second cohort that had completed the programming course but needed to be assessed. The results of the study highlight the following points:

(1) Students find programming more interesting after the use of GBL.
(2) The understanding of programming constructs improved after the introduction of GBL.
(3) The first cohort performed better in assessment than the second cohort.

The study results suggest that using GBL can help students learn programming concepts more effectively than traditional methods. However, implementing the GBL for advanced programming concepts will be challenging and require more complicated games.

7.2. Case Study 2

In Maskeliūnas *et al.* (2020), the researcher used GBL to teach the introductory JavaScript programming course at the university. The researchers identify pedagogical objectives, students' skills, and content to teach. A mobile game has been developed for students to solve programming problems and visualize the actions performed based on their algorithm.

Game idea: The game is based on ecological problems and environmental awareness. The learners will act as commercial advisors to solve puzzles to increase city revenue by avoiding excessive pollution. The game is used to provide visual feedback to students for the implementation of common programming algorithms and concepts: linear algorithms, branching algorithms, sorting algorithms, searching algorithms, recursion, and graph algorithms.

Evaluation and results: The study involving 54 undergraduate students at Kaunas University of Technology in Lithuania aimed to evaluate the effectiveness of a programming game. Participants were randomly divided into two groups: a game group and a control group, both attending a traditionally delivered programming course, but the game group was introduced to the game.

To assess the game's effectiveness, pre-test and post-test evaluations were conducted. These tests, covering the same programming topics and content complexity, were created by computer science teachers. The pre-test, administered before the course, aimed to gauge students' initial programming knowledge. The post-test, given after the course, assessed their knowledge improvement.

The results show that there was no significant difference in pre-test scores between the game and control groups. Even the control group had slightly better results than the game group. However, in the post-test, the game group significantly outperformed the control group, indicating a substantial learning gain in the game group.

These findings show that including GBL in the programming courses can improve students' programming skills. Also, students are more willing to use serious games for learning purposes.

7.3. Case Study 3

In the study by Zhao *et al.* (2022), the efficacy of game-based teaching in programming modules is explored within the context of the EU-funded NEWTON project (https://www.newtonproject.eu/), which aims to advance learning technologies. The project focuses on developing technologies to improve the learning process. The researchers investigate usability, learning experience, knowledge acquisition, and students' perception of the games used in their course.

Game idea: There are two games used in this study, which are related to the programming concepts of "variables" and "loops". These games are designed with JavaScript and C programming principles in mind.

Variable game: The first game uses a warehouse scenario to teach the concept of variables, data type size, and type conversions. This game has three levels and each level taught new concepts related to variables.

Loop game: The second game introduces the for-loop concept through a coin collection task. The game focuses on the concepts related to for-loop with continue and break statements.

Evaluation and results: The study spans three institutions — Dublin City University Ireland, Slovak Technical University for Bratislava, and the National College of Ireland — with over 100 participants. These participants encompass mature students, first-year undergraduates, and second-year undergraduates, hailing from diverse academic backgrounds. This sample selection serves two main purposes:

(1) Evaluating the perception of learning games for different age groups and varying academic backgrounds.
(2) Investigating the difference between using games for revision or first-time learning.

The knowledge tests were taken by the students before and after playing the game to evaluate learning outcome levels. After finishing each game students were asked about the usability, knowledge acquisition, and user experience. The study's findings can be summarized as follows:

(1) Educational games are particularly effective for novice programming learners. This is because understanding abstract programming concepts is difficult for first-time learners.
(2) Simple concept-oriented games are not suited for advanced learners.
(3) Personalizing games to accommodate varying levels of student knowledge enhances their effectiveness.
(4) Lack of in-game instructions affects user experience and causes confusion and frustration. Therefore, it is important to provide detailed instructions before or within the games.

7.4. Key Takeaways

The case studies collectively demonstrate that GBL can enhance students' understanding of programming concepts, increase their interest in programming, and improve their performance in assessments. GBL is especially effective for beginners when personalized and clear instructions are provided for optimizing the learning experience.

8. Games to Learn Programming Concepts

Many studies have explored the effectiveness of various games in teaching programming concepts as discussed in Section 3. Implementing GBL using these games requires careful consideration. Mostly these games are categorized based on specific programming concepts, target learners, pedagogical approaches, or types of games (Lindberg et al., 2019; Miljanovic & Bradbury, 2018). Some of the selection criteria are as follows:

- *Programming concepts*: Games may be categorized based on the specific programming concepts they aim to teach, such as loops, conditionals, variables, functions, algorithms, data structures, and more.
- *Target learners*: Games can be categorized according to the target audience, such as elementary school kids, middle school, high school, or university-level students.

- *Pedagogical approach*: Some games may follow a text-based programming approach, where students write code using textual languages, while others use block-based programming, where students use visual blocks to create code.
- *Types of games*: Games can be grouped into genres like puzzles, simulations, adventure games, role-playing games, strategy games, etc., based on the type of gameplay and learning experience they provide.
- *Skill level*: Games can be categorized based on whether they are designed for beginners with no prior programming experience or for more advanced learners looking to deepen their understanding.
- *Learning objectives*: Serious games may have different learning objectives, such as problem-solving, logic development, algorithmic thinking, or collaboration.

8.1. *Types of Games*

In this section, we will explore the game types in more detail.

(1) *Puzzle games*: Puzzle games present learners with challenges that require logical thinking and problem-solving to progress. In the context of programming education, puzzle games can offer coding puzzles where students must apply programming concepts to solve challenges.

(2) *Simulations*: Simulation games replicate real-world scenarios, allowing players to manipulate variables and observe the outcomes. For programming education, simulations provide a dynamic environment where students can experiment with code to understand cause-and-effect relationships. Simulations can enhance students' ability to comprehend complex concepts through hands-on experiences.

(3) *Adventure games*: Adventure games immerse players in narrative-driven experiences where exploration and decision-making play a pivotal role. In the realm of programming education, adventure games can introduce coding challenges as part of the storyline. Students must code solutions to advance in the game, which contextualizes programming concepts within an engaging narrative framework.

(4) *Role-playing games (RPGs)*: RPGs enable players to assume roles within fictional worlds, making choices that impact the game's outcome. In the context of programming learning, RPGs can be adapted

to teach coding by having students code actions or interactions for characters. This dynamic approach immerses students in active coding practices, enhancing their understanding of programming logic.
(5) *Strategy games*: Strategy games emphasize tactical planning and decision-making. In programming education, strategy games can present coding challenges that require students to strategies coding solutions to achieve in-game objectives.

8.2. Examples of Games to Teach Programming

In Miljanovic & Bradbury (2018) and Lindberg *et al.* (2019), researchers performed a detailed review of many games to teach programming concepts. Some examples of those games are discussed below:

- *Robocode* (https://robocode.sourceforge.io): A programming game where players design robot tanks using Java to battle against each other.
- *LightBot* (https://lightbot.com/): Teaches programming logic using a robot to solve puzzles through programming sequences of commands.
- *CodeCombat 9* (https://codecombat.com/): An online platform where players learn programming by guiding characters through levels using coding.
- *Human Resource Machine* (https://tomorrowcorporation.com/humanresourcemachine): A puzzle game that teaches assembly language programming concepts using visual programming.
- *Screeps* (https://screeps.com/): An MMO strategy game where players program their units in JavaScript to compete for resources and territory.
- *Alice* (http://www.alice.org/): A 3D programming environment that teaches programming concepts by creating animations and stories.
- *Kodable* (https://www.kodable.com/): A programming game for young learners that introduces basic coding concepts using visual blocks.

9. Conclusion

In this chapter, we discuss the effectiveness of GBL compared to traditional teaching methods, especially for programming courses. Programming is a valuable skill that impacts many industries and requires critical thinking and problem-solving skills. Traditional teaching methods, which often revolve around lectures, textbooks, and written assessments, do not provide effective learning experiences for programming concepts. Such approaches are content-focused rather than student-focused, potentially hindering practical application and retention of knowledge.

The emergence of GBL offers a promising solution to these challenges. GBL improves engagement and a deeper understanding of programming concepts. It encourages collaboration and focuses on problem-solving skills through diverse challenges. It also provides immediate feedback that reduces learning time and simulation games can bridge the gap between theoretical understanding and practical implementation. These factors collectively enhance learners' motivation and interest in learning programming.

While GBL has been widely acknowledged for its positive impacts on learners, the correct implementation of GBL is a challenge. A key challenge is the time commitment required for both development and learning. The instructors designing GBL need technical skills, knowledge of game theory, and technological support. Incomplete integration of GBL into the curriculum can lead to distractions and frustration among learners. Ensuring equal access for all students, considering hardware, Internet, and disabilities, remains challenging.

To address such complexities, a comprehensive approach to implementing GBL is crucial. The instructor needs a thorough background research to understand and align the desired objectives with appropriate games. Learners' skill levels must be considered, and pedagogical strategies need to be chosen accordingly. Regular assessment of learners' skills acquisition and feedback collection are essential to refining GBL integration in the course. Puzzle, simulation, role-playing, and strategy games offer diverse options to consider while implementing GBL for programming courses. These games help teach concepts like variables, conditions, loops, functions, and objects to different levels of learners.

In conclusion, GBL can be an effective and innovative way to teach programming if applied with careful planning and evaluation. It enhances students' understanding of programming concepts, increases their interest in programming, and improves their performance in assessments. GBL proves particularly beneficial for novice learners. It must be customized to suit varying skill levels and provide comprehensive in-game instructions to enhance the overall learning experience.

References

Bierre, K.J. & Phelps, A.M. (2004). The use of MUPPETS in an introductory java programming course. In *Proceedings of the 5th Conference on Information Technology Education*, pp. 122–127.

Boghian, I., Cojocariu, V.-M., Popescu, C.V. & Mâță, L. (2019). Game-based learning. Using board games in adult education. *Journal of Educational Science & Psychology*, 9, 51–57.

Chaffin, A., Doran, K., Hicks, D. & Barnes, T. (2009). Experimental evaluation of teaching recursion in a video game. In *Proceedings of the 2009 ACM SIGGRAPH Symposium on Video Games*. pp. 79–86.

Cheng, M.-T., Chen, J.-H., Chu, S.-J. & Chen, S.-Y. (2015). The use of serious games in science education: A review of selected empirical research from 2002 to 2013. *Journal of Computers in Education*, 2, 353–375.

Cicchino, M.I. (2015). Using game-based learning to foster critical thinking in student discourse. *The Interdisciplinary Journal of Problem-Based Learning*, 9, 1–19.

Corral, J.M.R., Balcells, A.C., Estévez, A.M., Moreno, G.J. & Ramos, M.J.F. (2014). A game-based approach to the teaching of object-oriented programming languages. *Computers & Education*, 73, 83–92.

De Freitas, S.I. (2006a). Learning in Immersive Worlds. A Review of Game-based Learning Prepared for the JISC e-Learning Programme. *JISC ELearning and Innovation*, 3, 73.

De Freitas, S.I. (2006b). Using games and simulations for supporting learning. Learn. *Media Technology*, 31, 343–358.

Deterding, S., Dixon, D., Khaled, R. & Nacke, L. (2011). From game design elements to gamefulness: Defining "gamification". In *Proceedings of the 15th International Academic MindTrek Conference: Envisioning Future Media Environments*, pp. 9–15.

Dicheva, D. & Hodge, A. (2018). Active learning through game play in a data structures course. In *Proceedings of the 49th ACM Technical Symposium on Computer Science Education*, pp. 834–839.

Dolgopolovas, V., Jevsikova, T. & Dagiene, V. (2018). From android games to coding in C — An approach to motivate novice engineering students to learn programming: A case study. *Computer Applications in Engineering Education*, 26, 75–90.

Domínguez, A., Saenz-de-Navarrete, J., De-Marcos, L., Fernández-Sanz, L., Pagés, C. & Martínez-Herráiz, J.-J. (2013). Gamifying learning experiences: Practical implications and outcomes. *Computer & Education*, 63, 380–392.

Fowler, A., Fristce, T. & MacLauren, M. (2012). Kodu Game Lab: A programming environment. *Computer Games Journal*, 1, 17–28.

Gordillo, A., López-Fernández, D. & Tovar, E. (2022). Comparing the effectiveness of video-based learning and game-based learning using teacher-authored video games for online software engineering education. *IEEE Transactions on Education*, 65, 524–532.

Hattie, J. & Timperley, H. (2007). The power of feedback. *Review of Educational Research*, 77, 81–112.

Jääskä, E. & Aaltonen, K. (2022). Teachers' experiences of using game-based learning methods in project management higher education. *Project Leadership & Society*, 3, 100041.

Jiau, H.C., Chen, J.C. & Ssu, K.-F. (2009). Enhancing self-motivation in learning programming using game-based simulation and metrics. *IEEE Transactions on Education*, 52, 555–562.

Jong, M.S. (2016). Teachers' concerns about adopting constructivist online game-based learning in formal curriculum teaching: The VISOLE experience. *British Journal of Educational Technology*, 47, 601–617.

Kaimara, P., Fokides, E., Oikonomou, A. & Deliyannis, I. (2021). Potential barriers to the implementation of digital game-based learning in the classroom: Pre-service teachers' views. *Technology, Knowledge & Learning*, 26, 825–844.

Kanika, Chakraverty, S. & Chakraborty, P. (2020). Tools and techniques for teaching computer programming: A review. *Journal of Educational Technology Systems*, 49, 170–198.

Kapp, K.M. (2012). *The Gamification of Learning and Instruction: Game-Based Methods and Strategies for Training and Education*. Hoboken, NJ: John Wiley & Sons.

Kato, H. & Ide, A. (1995). Using a game for social setting in a learning environment: AlgoArena — A tool for learning software design. In Schnase, J.L. & Cunnius, E.L. (eds.), *CSCL '95: The First International Conference on Computer Support for Collaborative Learning*. Bloomington, IN: Lawrence Erlbaum Associates, Inc., pp. 195–199.

Kazimoglu, C., Kiernan, M., Bacon, L. & MacKinnon, L. (2012). Learning programming at the computational thinking level via digital game-play. *Procedia Computer Science*, 9, 522–531.

Lee, M.J., Ko, A.J. & Kwan, I. (2013). In-game assessments increase novice programmers' engagement and level completion speed. In *Proceedings of the Ninth Annual International ACM Conference on International Computing Education Research*, pp. 153–160.

Leutenegger, S. & Edgington, J. (2007). A games first approach to teaching introductory programming. In *Proceedings of the 38th SIGCSE Technical Symposium on Computer Science Education*, pp. 115–118.

Li, F.W. & Watson, C. (2011). Game-based concept visualization for learning programming. In *Proceedings of the Third International ACM Workshop on Multimedia Technologies for Distance Learning*, pp. 37–42.

Lindberg, R.S., Laine, T.H. & Haaranen, L. (2019). Gamifying programming education in K-12: A review of programming curricula in seven countries and programming games. *British Journal of Educational Technology*, 50, 1979–1995.

López-Fernández, D., Gordillo, A., Alarcón, P.P., Tovar, E. (2021). Comparing traditional teaching and game-based learning using teacher-authored games on computer science education. *IEEE Transactions on Education* 64, 367–373.

Malliarakis, C., Satratzemi, M. & Xinogalos, S. (2014). CMX: Implementing an MMORPG for learning programming. In *Proceeding of the European Conference on Games-Based Learning*, pp. 346–355.

Martins, V.F., de Almeida Souza Concilio, I. & de Paiva Guimarães, M. (2018). Problem based learning associated to the development of games for programming teaching. *Computer Applications in Engineering Education*, 26, 1577–1589.

Maskeliūnas, R., Kulikajevas, A., Blažauskas, T., Damaševičius, R. & Swacha, J. (2020). An interactive serious mobile game for supporting the learning of programming in Javascript in the context of eco-friendly city management. *Computers*, 9, 102.

Mathrani, A., Christian, S. & Ponder-Sutton, A. (2016). PlayIT: Game based learning approach for teaching programming concepts. *Journal of Educational Technology & Society*, 19, 5–17.

Miljanovic, M.A. & Bradbury, J.S. (2020). GidgetML: An adaptive serious game for enhancing first year programming labs. In *Proceedings of the ACM/IEEE 42nd International Conference on Software Engineering: Software Engineering Education and Training*, pp. 184–192.

Miljanovic, M.A. & Bradbury, J.S. (2018). A review of serious games for programming. In *Serious Games: 4th Joint International Conference*, JCSG 2018, Darmstadt, Germany, pp. 204–216.

Miljanovic, M.A. & Bradbury, J.S. (2016). Robot on! A serious game for improving programming comprehension. In *Proceedings of the 5th International Workshop on Games and Software Engineering*, pp. 33–36.

O'Neil, H.F., Wainess, R. & Baker, E.L. (2005). Classification of learning outcomes: Evidence from the computer games literature. *The Curriculum Journal*, 16, 455–474.

Palaniappan, K. & Noor, N.M. (2022). Gamification strategy to support self-directed learning in an online learning environment. *International Journal of Emerging Technologies in Learning*, 17, 104–116.

Pane, J.F. (2002). *A Programming System for Children that is Designed for Usability*. Carnegie: Carnegie Mellon University.

Panskyi, T. & Rowińska, Z. (2021). A holistic digital game-based learning approach to out-of-school primary programming education. *Informatics in Education*, 20(2), 255–276.

Papadakis, S. & Kalogiannakis, M. (2019). Evaluating the effectiveness of a game-based learning approach in modifying students' behavioural outcomes and competence, in an introductory programming course. A case study in Greece. *International Journal of Teaching and Case Studies*,10, 235–250.
Prensky, M. (2003). Digital game-based learning. *Computers in Entertainment*, 1, 21–21.
Puranik, S., (2020). Innovative teaching methods in higher education. *BSSS Journal of Education*, 9, 67–75.
Rugelj, J. & Lapina, M. (2019). Game design based learning of programming. In *Proceedings of SLET-2019 — International Scientific Conference Innovative Approaches to the Application of Digital Technologies in Education and Research*, pp. 20–23.
Sánchez-Mena, A., Martí-Parreño, J. (2017). Drivers and barriers to adopting gamification: Teachers' perspectives. *Electronic Journal of e-Learning*, 15, 434–443.
Sarkar, N.I. (2006). Teaching computer networking fundamentals using practical laboratory exercises. *IEEE Transactions on Education*, 49, 285–291.
Seaborn, K. & Fels, D.I. (2015). Gamification in theory and action: A survey. *International Journal of Human Computer Studies*, 74, 14–31.
Seaborn, K., Seif El-Nasr, M., Milam, D. & Yung, D. (2012). Programming, PWNed: Using digital game development to enhance learners' competency and self-efficacy in a high school computing science course. In *Proceedings of the 43rd ACM Technical Symposium on Computer Science Education*, pp. 93–98.
Serrano, K. (2019). The effect of digital game-based learning on student learning: A literature review. *Graduate Research Papers*, 943.
Shaffer, D.W., Halverson, R., Squire, K.R. & Gee, J.P. (2005). *Video Games and the Future of Learning*. WCER Working Paper No. 2005-4. Wisconsin Center for Education Research, 92, 102599.
Smith, M.K. (1999). Learning Theory. In *The Encyclopaedia of Informal Education*. Available at https://infed.org/mobi/learning-theory-models-product-and-process/.
Sung, K., Panitz, M., Wallace, S., Anderson, R. & Nordlinger, J. (2008). Game-themed programming assignments: The faculty perspective. In *Proceedings of the 39th SIGCSE Technical Symposium on Computer Science Education*, pp. 300–304.
Suzuki, H. & Kata, H. (1995). Interaction-level support for collaborative learning: AlgoBlock — an open programming language. In *CSCL '95: The First International Conference on Computer Support for Collaborative Learning*. Bloomington, IN: Lawrence Erlbaum Associates, Inc., pp. 349–355.

Tillmann, N., De Halleux, J., Xie, T., Gulwani, S. & Bishop, J. (2013). Teaching and learning programming and software engineering via interactive gaming. In *2013 35th International Conference on Software Engineering (ICSE). IEEE*, pp. 1117–1126.

Vu, P. & Feinstein, S. (2017). An exploratory multiple case study about using game-based learning in STEM classrooms. *International Journal of Research in Education and Science*, 3, 582–588.

Woolfolk, A.E. (1993). *Educational Psychology.* Boston, MA: Allyn and Bacon.

Zainuddin, Z., Chu, S.K.W., Shujahat, M. & Perera, C.J. (2020). The impact of gamification on learning and instruction: A systematic review of empirical evidence. *Educational Research Review*, 30, 100326.

Zhan, Z., He, L., Tong, Y., Liang, X., Guo, S. & Lan, X. (2022). The effectiveness of gamification in programming education: Evidence from a meta-analysis. *Computers and Education: Artificial Intelligence*, 3, 100096.

Zhao, D., Chis, A., Muntean, G. & Muntean, C. (2018). A large-scale pilot study on game-based learning and blended learning methodologies in undergraduate programming courses. In *Edulearn18 Proceedings. IATED*, pp. 3716–3724.

Zhao, D., Muntean, C.H., Chis, A.E., Rozinaj, G. & Muntean, G.-M. (2022). Game-based learning: Enhancing student experience, knowledge gain, and usability in higher education programming courses. *IEEE Transactions on Education*, 65, 502–513.

Zhi, R., Lytle, N. & Price, T.W. (2018). Exploring instructional support design in an educational game for K-12 computing education. In *Proceedings of the 49th ACM Technical Symposium on Computer Science Education*, pp. 747–752.

© 2024 World Scientific Publishing Company
https://doi.org/10.1142/9789811285622_0010

Chapter 10

Monitor and Predict Student Engagement and Retention Using Learning Management System (LMS)

Behnaz Rezaie Ortakand

King's Own Institute, Australia

Abstract

The survival and economic equilibrium of Higher Education institutions are heavily contingent on student retention. Predictive models for retention play a crucial role in identifying students at risk of attrition during the early phases, thereby aiding the financial sustainability of these educational establishments. In recent times, scholars have employed a range of data sources, including robust ones like the Learning Management System (LMS), which are meticulously examined and incorporated into these models by researchers to mitigate the perils of attrition.

Keywords: Attrition rate, Data mining, Higher education institution, Learning analytics, Learning management system (LMS), Predictive learning analytics, Student retention.

1. Introduction

The survival and financial sustainability of Higher Education providers highly depend on student retention. In line with this need, learning analytics, educational data mining, and machine learning techniques assist researchers and subsequently higher education providers in detecting at-risk students at early stages by predicting retention models. A variety of data sources, including the Learning Management System (LMS), are analyzed and implemented in student retention predictive models to reduce the attrition risk by the researchers.

Higher educational institutions focus on maintaining the student retention ratio for their financial and organizational success. The private sector cannot financially sustain itself without student fees, while the public sector mostly relies on government funding programs. The literature identifies a significant number of studies on understanding the reasons for attrition in the educational sector (Aljohani, 2016a, 2016b; Bean, 1980; Burke & University, 2019; Mason et al., 2018; McCarthy, 2019; Naylor et al., 2018; Webster & Showers, 2011).

2. Private Higher Education, Competition, and Attrition

Higher education has recently become more vital due to its important role in the economy, employment rate, and revenue generation in Australia. In 2017, the higher education sector generated AU$38 billion in revenue (What we do, 2021), and the total number of academic staff across the sector increased by 23% between 2009 and 2018 (Australian Government — Department of Education, 2020). Considering a 50% increase in student numbers and 79% growth in the international students' market share between 2013 and 2017. The private sector generated AU$570.9 million in revenue in 2017 (TEQSA, 2018b, 2019). According to TEQSA (2019), the number of overseas (international) students increased by 85% between 2013 and 2017 in the Australian private higher education sector.

Higher education institutions experience an increasingly competitive market year after year that causes attrition problems for the providers as some students might not leave their studies entirely and could only change their institutions. General customer relationship research has revealed that preserving current customers can be five to seven times less costly than attracting new customers (Gemme, 1997; Leigh & Marshall, 2001). Focusing on student retention rather than new student recruitment and a 10% improvement in retention rates could increase higher education revenues by 22% (Ackerman & Schibrowsky, 2007; Webster & Showers, 2011). The higher education provider's sustainability and reputation are highly dependent on both the number of enrolled students and student retention thus attrition has become their high priority (Shah, 2018).

Higher education establishments would struggle to maintain financial viability in the face of substantial attrition rates, making student fees and government funding the primary pillars of their financial sustenance. "TEQSA defines attrition as the ratio of first-year higher education commencing students in a year who neither completed nor returned to study in the following year, to the total commencing students in that year" (TEQSA, 2017). Among Australian tertiary students engaged in full or part-time study, approximately 46% never completed their degree in nine years, between 2005 and 2016 (Australian Government — Department of Education, 2020).

Student retention rate is vital for all higher education providers, but the private sector is at a bigger risk due to its high reliance on students, particularly international students. The private and public sectors are different in the source of financing so they require different scopes of study and student retention modeling. The public sector is under less financial pressure than the private sector due to receiving research funding, government funding, and support. However, private higher education institutions must survive primarily by the students' payments, mainly international students. Although the Australian private sector's attrition rate is distinctly higher than that of universities, due to the complexity of measurement, their attrition rates are not easily measured and remain unclear (TEQSA, 2018a). The private higher education student attrition rate data is not publicly available as the providers avoid publishing their attrition rates to their competitors. Furthermore, the reasons for attrition and related variables affecting that, are not the same for domestic/international students or public/private sectors. Consequently, the private sector shareholders and the Australian economy could be disadvantaged by the lack of this information.

3. Student Retention, Variables, and Methods

Past studies applied a number of different variables in the predictive models as determinants of student retention to control the attrition risk. Variables such as assessment grades, submissions, LMS data, student demographics, student previous academic background, and social networking-based data have been used by scholars for student retention studies. Thomas (2002) and Tinto (2006) used socioeconomic background, and academic integration/preparedness variables to develop their retention systems. Bakharia *et al.* (2009) applied social (Network) integration retention system variables in their model. Student attendance, grades, demographics, and commitments are adopted variables for developing retention systems by Picciano (2012), Bin Mat *et al.* (2013), and He *et al.* (2015). LMS activity has been also examined to some extent by Boston and Ice (2010), Smith *et al.* (2012), and Arnold and Pistilli (2012). A comprehensive five-yearly survey has been done on eight diverse Australian universities by Naylor *et al.* (2018) and variables such as belongings, intellectual engagement, support from staff, and workload stress were introduced. Australian Teaching and Learning Council Ltd. funded a large project, Empirical Study of Student Attrition, which was conducted by five Australian universities to study university-level students' persistence by adopting demographic variables (Hodges *et al.*, 2013). Saa *et al.* (2019) provided a list of the most commonly used categories of public university student performance variables by scholars.

4. Learning Management System (LMS)

The LMS serves as a valuable information source, continuously producing data that can be further examined and explored within student retention models. Students generate various amounts of data while they leave their digital paths in their LMS (Hooda & Rana, 2020) such as Moodle. LMS can be considered as one of the decent data sources that act as a repository of student information and available built-in tools: LMS such as Moodle logs, reports, and results can be translated to valuable information about student engagement and eventually about student retention (Akçapınar & Bayazit, 2019).

Early alert systems involving LMS, as a best practice in identifying at-risk students, are in place during the 21st century to address higher education providers' retention issues (Jokhan *et al.*, 2019). Commercial early detection systems (e.g., Starfish, Aviso, MAP-Works, SEAtS, Oracle, and DropGuard) could enhance a higher education provider's revenue by early detection of the at-risk student. However, the systems are not designed for a specific country or institution and might not be cost-efficient enough for an average private provider (Berens *et al.*, 2019; Mangold *et al.*, 2003). What's more, not many early alert platforms available in the market disclose detailed algorithms or provide proper tools for the end-user to personalize and adjust the product for their custom circumstance (Berens *et al.*, 2018).

Adding time dimension to the data and using LMS that produces data dynamically and continuously generates "big data". Big data is vast in terms of volume, variety, velocity, and complexity and thus cannot be processed by applying traditional database analysis tools (Stark, 2018; Weiss & Indurkhya, 1998). Predictive Modeling which is more action-oriented has been extensively applied to educational data analysis lately. Predictive models, unlike explanatory models, set up a scenario that describes outcomes by using historical data as well as correlations among variables (Sclater *et al.*, 2016). To achieve success in applying machine learning models in educational predictive analytics, we need to consider some key issues including selecting data sources, dealing with missing data, validating models, choosing effective techniques, and checking the accuracy of the model (Cui *et al.*, 2019; Kotsiantis *et al.*, 2007).

5. Theoretical Linkage

During 19th and 20th centuries, student retention models have been under the influence of classical theories such as Marx's ideology of alienation, Mead's theory of social psychology of I, me, and generalized others, and Durkheim's suicide theory (Kerby, 2015). The following are some theories that are used by the researchers who developed their retention models.

One of the key socio-psychological theories vital in forming retention models is the theory of social identity by Tajfel and Turner (1979). The two fundamental processes of the social identity theory are categorization and self-enhancement (Stets & Burke, 2000). These two processes establish that individuals could be assigned to groups according to innumerable major or minor characteristics such as sex, nationality, and age (Kerby, 2015). Another theoretical ideology is the complementary theory of Lawrence *et al.* (1966) which influenced Spady (1970) to demonstrate that some students' academic achievement could compensate for their insecurities. Balance theory is another important theory according to the work of Newcomb (1961), Festinger (1957), and Fritz (1958), and is the foundation of Spady's student attrition model. This model highlights how attraction between individuals in a relationship is subject to a third influence such as social systems and institutions (Spady, 1971).

Scholars during the 1970s primarily utilized social classical theories except Spady (1970), who instead found a link between Durkheim's suicide theory, one of the major psychological theories, and his attrition model (Kerby, 2015). Considering higher education institutions as a society, Spady (1970) believed that the student dropout can be called an academic suicide. Therefore, the conditions that lead the individuals to commit suicide in social system are comparable to dropping out of academic institutions (Spady, 1970; Tinto, 1975). Classical theories continued to be utilized by researchers up until the 1990s (Kerby, 2015). Pascarella and Terenzini (1991) used Marx's alienation theory in a first-year student study to explain how the student's de-socialization could cause alienation and eventually attrition.

During the last eight decades, researchers have developed retention models by including academic, non-academic, socio-economic, and institutional variables (Manyanga et al., 2017). Since the 1970s, theoretical models mostly employed students' background, characteristics, and goal commitments; however, Tinto (1975) introduced a new retention variable, the student's motivation. For three decades, starting from the 1970s, two major models were developed named student attrition and student integration while from 2000 onward, the researchers focused more on student advising/engagement and integrated strategies (Manyanga et al., 2017). More recently, Kerby (2015) introduced his model that implicates the impact of external factors such as politics and economy on the environmental, sociocultural, and individual factors.

6. Empirical Studies

Student retention studies and theoretical models have been developed and well-documented in the literature during the last four decades. There are six student retention theoretical models which are cited extensively by the researchers. Spady (1970) initiated the systematic student retention models by introducing the Undergraduate Dropout Process Model which was adopted from psychological studies. It was followed by Tinto (1975) who developed the Institutional Departure Model which included both academic and social systems and was extensively tested and cited by many scholars (Aljohani, 2016a). Demographic characteristic variables of the students and their institutions were applied by Bean (1980) to conduct another student attrition model. Durkheim's Suicide model, which was the foundation of Spady and Tinto's models, was criticized by Bean (1980). However, Spady and Tinto's models which focused on the student interaction with faculty members were expanded by Pascarella (1980) to establish the Student–Faculty Informal Contact Model. Pascarella's model employed other institutional and individual variables for instance the capabilities, goals, educational history, family, and personalities (Aljohani, 2016a; Pascarella, 1980). The non-traditional Student Attrition Model was built by Bean and Metzner (1985) to add a new variable of student interaction with the external environment. Cabrera *et al*. (1993) integrated Tinto and Bean's models with the statistical analysis to emphasize the important variables and to propose intervention strategies to the institutions (Aljohani, 2016a).

In summary, some of the major variables used by the researchers in their retention models are; Socio-Economic Background, Individual Attributes, Pre-College Schooling, Student Commitment, Academic Integration, Social Integration, and Residence (Bean, 1983; Bean & Metzner, 1985; Bean, 1980; Kelly *et al.*, 2012; Kuh *et al.*, 2008; Murtaugh *et al.*, 1999; Pascarella, 1980; Tinto, 1975). Considering the important theoretical models, a combination of variables including demographics, student performance, course/program/institution, and instructor-related variables could be considered to improve the student retention rates within higher education institutions.

7. Predictive Learning Analytics, Factors, and Variables

The Society for Learning Analytics Research (SoLAR) defines learning analytics as "measurement, collection, analysis, and reporting of data about learners and their contexts, for purposes of understanding and optimizing learning and the environments in which it occurs" (Joksimović *et al.*, 2019). Predictive learning analytics offers solutions for one of the significant issues of higher education providers, attrition rate and detecting at-risk students. Business Intelligence (BI) is the process of applying mathematical models and methods to variables to create important information that could affect complex decisions (Vercellis, 2009). Big data analytics requires BI techniques to be analyzed and the massive educational data could be processed by BI techniques to generate more accurate retention predictive models. Some of the most popular algorithms in literature which detect the relationship between different variables are

Decision Tree Classifier, Multilayered Perceptrons (Artificial Neural Networks), Naive Bayes classifiers, Support Vector Machines (Chaudhuri, 1998; Gardner & Dorling, 1998; Rish, 2001; Vapnik *et al.*, 1995).

Predictive learning analytic models and statistical analysis provide information to the users (e.g., institutions, instructors, and students) by modeling different types of data (Na & Tasir, 2017). Some studies have examined the effect of access level to Information Technology, high school GPA, and socioeconomic status on student success and retention (Papamitsiou & Economides, 2016; Williams, 2014). Most of the initial learning analytic studies have used fixed factors and simple integration of student characteristics to create the predictors for a one-time point model with an acceptable accuracy level, though inadequate when assessing risk factors and interventions (Larrabee Sønderlund *et al.*, 2019; Williams, 2014). As a result, dynamic models are under scrutiny by researchers to involve data fluidity over time and allow more broad predictions (Agudo-Peregrina *et al.*, 2014; De Freitas *et al.*, 2015). Machine learning, data and computer science, education, statistics, and a few more scientific areas have offered a variety of theories in Learning Analytics (Baker & Inventado, 2014). Worldwide web, distance, and online learning improved learning and teaching effectiveness in the 1990s, subsequently, LMS offered the chance to aggregate technology and data analytics and to develop tailored learning models (Gašević *et al.*, 2015; Joksimović *et al.*, 2019). The impact of student social network communication interactions on the higher education environment, studied by Dawson (2008), was quantitative research based on a student-reported online survey, and student-online behavior data from the LMS, sourced from unit discussion forum logs (Dawson, 2008; Dawson *et al.*, 2010).

8. Tools and Techniques

Arnold and Pistilli (2012) designed an early detection learning analytic tool namely Course Signals which was a predictive model accompanied by a traffic light dashboard for detecting at-risk students. The Course Signal software was designed using a range of variables, however, the details of the model and algorithm behind the software are not disclosed; so, there is no evidence of examining the software adoption level and its outcomes (Arnold & Pistilli, 2012). Machine learning technologies have caused multimodal learning analytics that has been noteworthy for recent researchers as they offer different learning design options and more precise learning models (Joksimović et al., 2019). Unlike conventional learning analytic approaches, multimodal learning analytics is capable of involving data from different sources and recognizing data streams that could track the student's engagement (Joksimović et al., 2019; Ochoa, 2017). However, integrating data from different sources or platforms has become one of the significant challenges that require developing software (Shankar et al., 2018).

Learning analytics has been expanding in developing models, techniques, and other areas. However, most higher education institutions fail to fully adopt the learning analytic models or just employ them at a basic level while the majority of them are conscious of the advantages but not still entirely aware of its capacities (Colvin et al., 2015; Drachsler & Greller, 2016; Haythornthwaite, 2017; Tsai & Gasevic, 2017). Furthermore, the recent tendency of learning analytics, rather than technology developments, is mostly moved to teaching and learning principles; for instance, student learning support, student feedback, intervention, and emotions (Joksimović et al., 2019). Matcha et al. (2019) argued that although learning analytics dashboards could simplify data presentation, they are not led by existing educational theories. Moreover, the current dashboards are not effective enough to provide learning strategies and feedback (Matcha et al., 2019). To shift the focus of learning analytics from just improving student learning and grades, recent studies on detecting at-risk students are significant (Jayaprakash et al., 2014; Mullis, 2019; Ours, 2020; Penaloza, 2015; Tampke, 2013; Villano et al., 2018).

According to Aldowah et al. (2019), Educational learning analytics involves data mining techniques and data-based models to achieve developing efficiency and teaching/learning quality in the higher education sector by collecting, processing, reporting, and manipulating digital data. Although some data mining techniques (e.g., clustering, classification, statistics, association rule, visual data mining, and regression) are regularly applied to the higher education sector some of which are not commonly used due to complexity (e.g., sequential pattern mining, text mining, correlation mining, outlier detection, causal mining, and density estimation) (Aldowah et al., 2019). Thus, more consideration is still demanded on the application of data mining in higher education to connect educational problems, educational data mining techniques, and learning analytics.

The growing number of dropouts has directed learning analytic studies to investigate the factors and explore a broad range of prediction tools but there is no agreement on the best way to understand them due to their varying nature (Aldowah et al., 2019). Some studies on student retention have conducted applying learning analytics, for instance, predicting dropout rates for distance learning courses (Cambruzzi et al., 2015), detecting at-risk students based on their academic performance (Das & Kizhekkethottam, 2015), predicting dropouts using student social behavior (Bayer et al., 2012), and predicting dropout rate by studying first-semester (Dekker et al., 2009).

Data mining methods are adopted by educational researchers to develop early warning systems and predictive models to detect at-risk students (Howard et al., 2018). Learning analytics demand for good data sources has led researchers to employ LMS tools to predict student performance lately (Bravo-Agapito et al., 2021). So, Moodle logs accompanied by a variety of models including exploratory factor analysis, multiple linear regressions, cluster analysis, and correlation have been utilized by Bravo-Agapito et al. (2021) for fully online courses.

LMS data (Blackboard) for the first half of the semester (optimal time) was employed by Howard et al. (2018) to predict the final grade of STEM undergraduate students. One effective study on developing an early warning system for high school completion by Knowles (2015) applied the longitudinal data system to the entire Wisconsin, USA. Saa et al. (2019) has summarised the most common data mining algorithms and their frequency of usage in educational studies including Neural network, Decision tree, K-Nearest Neighbor, Logistic regression and Naive Bayes Classifiers.

Current retention and learning analytic studies are conducted either at course-level to help instructors detect at-risk students and forecast the student success rate with almost 85% accuracy or at program-level to predict student GPA and retention or degree completion with the variables (Cui et al., 2019).

Course definition in this research is "a series of lectures or classes taken to fulfill requirements of a subject" and program definition is "a series of lectures or courses to complete a program or attain a degree" (difference between, 2020).

The majority of studies have focused on course-level, have used variables such as assessment grades and submissions and LMS data, e.g., Moodle logs, which are positively correlated with the student's course performance (Tempelaar et al., 2015). Contrary to course-level studies, program-level ones focus mostly on student demographics (e.g., age at admission, gender, city of origin), student previous academic background (e.g., high school type, level of Maths, English), and social networking-based data (e.g., Facebook, Instagram) (Uddin & Lee, 2017). Although course-level student performance is studied by applying models to multiple courses, there is a lack of comprehensive studies that combine course-level and program-level variables with learning analytics to examine their correlation and their effect on student retention. In summary, finding student study patterns and footprints on LMS for individual courses could provide a model to assess the risk of both course and program dropouts. Additionally, it is crucial for institutions to track at-risk students and provide early intervention support. Therefore, cohort analysis could provide good information on which group of students needs more support.

A significant number of papers have failed to provide details of their applied methods, such as the process of checking accuracy level before modeling and that of specifying important student features and how those features are interrelated and could affect predicting student outcomes (Cui *et al.*, 2019). According to Ifenthaler (2017) and Ifenthaler and Schumacher (2019), large-scale studies have not yet been done to provide enough evidence that learning analytics can support students to succeed in their study. Although some researchers have already introduced variables, algorithms, and methods, new researchers could utilize them and further expand the design and application of learning analytics systems. For instance, large-scale longitudinal, or quasi-experimental studies are good to focus on further (Ifenthaler & Yau, 2020).

References

Ackerman, R. & Schibrowsky, J. (2007). A business marketing strategy applied to student retention: A higher education initiative. *Journal of College Student Retention: Research Theory*, 9(3), 307–336.

Agudo-Peregrina, Á.F., Iglesias-Pradas, S., Conde-González, M.Á. & Hernández-García, Á.J.C. i.h.b. (2014). Can we predict success from log data in VLEs? Classification of interactions for learning analytics and their relation with performance in VLE-supported F2F and online learning. *Computers in Human Behavior*, 31, 542–550.

Akçapınar, G. & Bayazit, A. (2019). MoodleMiner: Data mining analysis tool for Moodle Learning Management System. *Ilköğretim online*, 18(1), 406–415. doi:10.17051/ilkonline.2019.527645.

Aldowah, H., Al-Samarraie, H. & Fauzy, W.M. (2019). Educational data mining and learning analytics for 21st century higher education: A review and synthesis. *Telematics and Informatics*, 37, 13–49.

Aljohani, O. (2016a). A comprehensive review of the major studies and theoretical models of student retention in higher education. *Higher Education Studies*, 6(2), 1–18.

Aljohani, O. (2016b). A review of the contemporary international literature on student retention in higher education. *International Journal of Education Literacy Studies*, 4(1), 40–52.

Arnold, K.E. & Pistilli, M.D. (2012). Course signals at Purdue: Using learning analytics to increase student success. Paper presented at the *Proceedings of the 2nd International Conference on Learning Analytics and Knowledge*.

Australian Government — Department of Education, S. A. E. (2020, 17 September 2020). Selected Higher Education Statistics-2019. Available at https://www.education.gov.au/student-data.

Baker, R.S. & Inventado, P.S. (2014). Educational data mining and learning analytics. In *Learning Analytics*. Berlin: Springer, pp. 61–75.

Bakharia, A., Heathcote, E. & Dawson, S. (2009). *Social Networks Adapting Pedagogical Practice*. SNAPP. Citeseer.

Bassi, J.S., Dada, E.G., Hamidu, A.A. & Elijah, M.D. (2019). Students graduation on time prediction model using artificial neural network. *Journal of Computer Engineering*, 21(3), 28–35.

Bayer, J., Bydzovská, H., Géryk, J., Obsivac, T. & Popelinsky, L. (2012). *Predicting Drop-Out from Social Behaviour of Students*. International Educational Data Mining Society.

Bean, J. (1983). The application of a model of turnover in work organizations to the student attrition process. *The Review of Higher Education*, 6(2), 129–148.

Bean, J. & Metzner, B. (1985). A conceptual model of nontraditional student attrition undergraduate. *Review of Educational Research*, 55(4), 485–540.

Bean, J.P. (1980). Dropouts and turnover: The synthesis and test of a causal model of student attrition. *Research in Higher Education*, 12(2), 155–187.

Bean, J.P. (1985). Interaction effects based on class level in an explanatory model of college student dropout syndrome. *American Educational Research Journal*, 22(1), 35–64.

Berens, J., Schneider, K., Gortz, S., Oster, S. & Burghoff, J. (2019). Early detection of students at risk — Predicting student dropouts using administrative student data from German universities and machine learning methods. *Journal of Educational Data Mining*, 11(3), 1–41.

Berge, Z.L. & Huang, Y. (2004). A model for sustainable student retention: A holistic perspective on the student dropout problem with special attention to e-Learning. DEOSNEWS Distance Education, 13(5).

Bin Mat, U., Buniyamin, N., Arsad, P.M. & Kassim, R. (2013). An overview of using academic analytics to predict and improve students' achievement: A proposed proactive intelligent intervention. Paper presented at the *2013 IEEE 5th Conference on Engineering Education (ICEED)*.

Boston, W. & Ice, P. (2010). Comprehensive assessment of student retention in online learning environments. Paper presented at the *E-Learn: World Conference on E-Learning in Corporate, Government, Healthcare, and Higher Education*.

Bravo-Agapito, J., Romero, S.J. & Pamplona, S. (2021). Early prediction of undergraduate Student's academic performance in completely online learning: A five-year study. *Computers in Human Behavior*, 115.

Brooks, C., Thompson, C. & Teasley, S. (2015). A time series interaction analysis method for building predictive models of learners using log data. Paper presented at the *Proceedings of the Fifth International Conference on Learning Analytics and Knowledge*.

Burke, A.J.C. & University (2019). Student retention models in higher education. *A Literature Review*, 94(2), 12–21.

Cabrera, A.F., Nora, A. & Castaneda, M.B. (1993). College persistence: Structural equations modeling test of an integrated model of student retention. *The Journal of Higher Education*, 64(2), 123–139.

Cambruzzi, W.L., Rigo, S.J. & Barbosa, J.L. (2015). Dropout prediction and reduction in distance education courses with the learning analytics multi-trail approach. *UCS*, 21(1), 23–47.

Chaudhuri, S. (1998). Data mining and database systems: Where is the intersection? *IEEE Data Engineering Bulletin*, 21(1), 4–8.

Chen, W., Brinton, C.G., Cao, D., Mason-Singh, A., Lu, C. & Chiang, M. (2018). Early detection prediction of learning outcomes in online short-courses via learning behaviors. *IEEE Transactions on Learning Technologies*, 12(1), 44–58.

Colvin, C., Rodgers, T., Wade, A., Dawson, S., Gasevic, D., Shum, S.B. *et al.* (2015). Student retention and learning analytics: A snapshot of Australian practices and a framework for advancement. Final report. University of South Australia.

Conijn, R., Snijders, C., Kleingeld, A. & Matzat, U. (2016). Predicting student performance from LMS data: A comparison of 17 blended courses using Moodle LMS. *IEEE Transactions on Learning Technologies*, 10(1), 17–29.

Cui, Y., Chen, F., Shiri, A. & Fan, Y. (2019). Predictive analytic models of student success in higher education. *Information Learning Sciences*, 120(3), 208–227.

Dawson, S. (2008). A study of the relationship between student social networks and sense of community. *Journal of Educational Technology Society*, 11(3), 224–238.

Dawson, S., Bakharia, A. & Heathcote, E. (2010). SNAPP: Realising the affordances of real-time SNA within networked learning environments.
De Freitas, S., Gibson, D., Du Plessis, C., Halloran, P., Williams, E., Ambrose, M. et al. (2015). Foundations of dynamic learning analytics: Using university student data to increase retention. *British Journal of Educational Technology*, 46(6), 1175–1188.
Dekker, G.W., Pechenizkiy, M. & Vleeshouwers, J.M. (2009). *Predicting Students Drop Out: A Case Study*. International Working Group on Educational Data Mining. Eindhoven: Eindhoven University of Technology. difference between. (2020). Available at http://www.differencebetween.info/difference-between-course-and-programme.
Drachsler, H. & Greller, W. (2016). Privacy and Analytics: It's a DELICATE Issue a Checklist for Trusted Learning Analytics. *Proceedings of the Sixth International Conference on Learning Analytics & Knowledge*.
Dreiseitl, S. & Ohno-Machado, L. (2002). Logistic regression and artificial neural network classification models: A methodology review. *Journal of Biomedical Informatics*, 35(5–6), 352–359.
Ferguson, R., Brasher, A., Clow, D., Cooper, A., Hillaire, G., Mittelmeier, J. et al. (2016). *Research Evidence on the Use of Learning Analytics: Implications for Education Policy*. Seville: Joint Research Center.
Ferguson, R. & Clow, D. (2017). Where is the evidence? A call to action for learning analytics. Paper presented at the *Proceedings of the Seventh International Learning Analytics & Knowledge Conference*.
Fischer, C., Pardos, Z.A., Baker, R.S., Williams, J.J., Smyth, P., Yu, R. et al. (2020). Mining big data in education: Affordances and challenges. *Sage Journals*, 44(1), 130–160.
Festinger, L. (1957). *A Theory Of Cognitive Dissonance*, Vol. 2. Stanford, CA: Stanford University Press.
Fritz, H. (1958). *The Psychology Of Interpersonal Relations*. New York: John Wiley & Sons.
Fitzmaurice, G., Davidian, M., Verbeke, G. & Molenberghs, G. (2008). *Longitudinal Data Analysis*. Boca Raton, FL: CRC Press.
Gardner, M.W. & Dorling, S. (1998). Artificial neural networks (the multilayer perceptron) — A review of applications in the atmospheric sciences. *Atmospheric Environment*, 32(14–15), 2627–2636.
Gašević, D., Dawson, S. & Siemens, G. (2015). Let's not forget: Learning analytics are about learning. *TechTrends*, 59(1), 64–71.
Gemme, E.M. (1997). Retaining customers in a managed care market. *Marketing Health Services*, 17(3), 19.
Harrison, S., Villano, R., Lynch, G. & Chen, G. (2016). Measuring financial implications of an early alert system. Paper presented at the *Proceedings of the Sixth International Conference on Learning Analytics & Knowledge*.

Haythornthwaite, C. (2017). An information policy perspective on learning analytics. Paper presented at the *Proceedings of the Seventh International Learning Analytics & Knowledge Conference*.

He, J., Bailey, J., Rubinstein, B. & Zhang, R. (2015). Identifying at-risk students in massive open online courses. Paper presented at the *Proceedings of the AAAI Conference on Artificial Intelligence*.

Hernández, C.F.R. (2020). *An Artificial Neural Network Analysis of Academic Performance in Higher Education*. Leuven: KU Leuven.

Hodges, B., Bedford, T., Hartley, J., Klinger, C., Murray, N., O'Rourke, J., & Schofield, N. (2013). Enabling retention: Processes and strategies for improving student retention in university-based enabling programs. Final Report 2013: Australian Government Office for Learning and Teaching.

Hooda, M. & Rana, C. (2020). Learning analytics lens: Improving quality of higher education. *International Journal*, 8(5), 1626–1646.

Howard, E., Meehan, M. & Parnell, A. (2018). Contrasting prediction methods for early warning systems at undergraduate level. *The Internet Higher Education Studies*, 37, 66–75.

Ifenthaler, D. (2017). Are higher education institutions prepared for learning analytics? *TechTrends*, 61(4), 366–371.

Ifenthaler, D. & Schumacher, C. (2019). Releasing personal information within learning analytics systems. In Sampson, D.G., Spector, J.M., Ifenthaler, D., Isaias, P. & Sergis, S. (eds.), *Learning Technologies for Transforming Large-Scale Teaching, Learning, and Assessment*, pp. 3–18.

Ifenthaler, D. & Yau, J. (2020). Utilising learning analytics to support study success in higher education: A systematic review. *Educational Technology Research & Development*, 68, 1–30.

Jayaprakash, S.M., Moody, E.W., Lauría, E.J., Regan, J.R. & Baron, J.D. (2014). Early alert of academically at-risk students: An open source analytics initiative. *Journal of Learning Analytics*, 1(1), 6–47.

Jokhan, A., Sharma, B. & Singh, S. (2019). Early warning system as a predictor for student performance in higher education blended courses. *Studies in Higher Education*, 44(11), 1900–1911.

Joksimović, S., Kovanović, V. & Dawson, S. (2019). The journey of learning analytics. *HERDSA Review of Higher Education*, 6, 27–63.

Kelly, K., Patrocínio, C. & Marshall, C. (2012). Prediction of student performance in engineering programs. *Engineering Education*, 23, 26.

Kent, R. (2009). Rethinking data analysis-part two: Some alternatives to frequentist approaches. *International Journal of Market Research*, 51(2), 1–16.

Kerby, M.B. (2015). Toward a new predictive model of student retention in higher education: An application of classical sociological theory. *Journal of College Student Retention : Research, Theory & Practice*, 17(2), 138–161.

Knowles, J.E. (2015). Of needles and haystacks: Building an accurate statewide dropout early warning system in Wisconsin. *Journal of Educational Data Mining*, 7(3), 18–67.

Kotsiantis, S.B., Zaharakis, I. & Pintelas, P. (2007). Supervised machine learning: A review of classification techniques. *Emerging Artificial Intelligence Applications in Computer Engineering*, 160(1), 3–24.

Kuh, G.D., Cruce, T.M., Shoup, R., Kinzie, J. & Gonyea, R.M. (2008). Unmasking the effects of student engagement on first-year college grades and persistence. *The Journal of Higher Education*, 79(5), 540–563.

Larrabee Sønderlund, A., Hughes, E. & Smith, J. (2019). The efficacy of learning analytics interventions in higher education: A systematic review. *British Journal of Educational Technology*, 50(5), 2594–2618.

Lawrence, P.A., Reik, L.E. & Dalrymple, W. (1966). *The CollegeDropout and the Utilization of Talent*. Princeton, NJ: Princeton University Press.

Leahy, M., Polesel, J. & Gillis, S. (2020). *Escher's Staircase: Higher Education and Migration in Australia*. Cham: Springer International Publishing, pp. 25–38.

Leigh, T.W. & Marshall, G.W. (2001). Research priorities in sales strategy and performance. *Journal of Personal Selling Sales Management*, 21(2), 83–93.

Mangold, W.D., Bean, L. & Adams, D. (2003). The impact of intercollegiate athletics on graduation rates among major NCAA Division I universities: Implications for college persistence theory and practice. *The Journal of Higher Education*, 74(5), 540–562.

Mason, C., Twomey, J., Wright, D. & Whitman, L. (2018). Predicting engineering student attrition risk using a probabilistic neural network and comparing results with a backpropagation neural network and logistic regression. *Research in Higher Education*, 59(3), 382–400.

Manyanga, F., Sithole, A., & Hanson, S.M. (2017). Comparison of student retention models in undergraduate education from the past eight decades, *Journal of Applied Learning in Higher Education*, 7, 30–42.

Matcha, W., Gasevic, D. & Pardo, A. (2019). A systematic review of empirical studies on learning analytics dashboards: A self-regulated learning perspective. *IEEE Transactions on Learning Technologies*, 99, 1.

McCarthy, J. (2019). *A Data Driven Approach to Student Retention: The Impact on Leadership Behaviour*. Cork: University College Cork.

Mullis, K.J. (2019). *Early Alert Practices in North Carolina Community Colleges*. Carolina: East Carolina University.

Murtaugh, P.A., Burns, L.D. & Schuster, J. (1999). Predicting the retention of university students. *Research in Higher Education*, 40(3), 355–371.

Musso, M.F., Kyndt, E., Cascallar, E.C. & Dochy, F. (2013). Predicting general academic performance and identifying the differential contribution of participating variables using artificial neural networks. *Frontline Learning Research*, 1(1), 42–71.

Na, K.S. & Tasir, Z. (2017). Identifying at-risk students in online learning by analysing learning behaviour: A systematic review. Paper presented at the 2017 *IEEE Conference on Big Data and Analytics (ICBDA)*.

Naylor, R., Baik, C. & Arkoudis, S. (2018). Identifying attrition risk based on the first year experience. *Higher Education Research Development*, 37(2), 328–342.

Newcomb, T.M. (1961). *The Acquaintance Process As A Prototype Of Human Interaction*. Boston: Holt, Rinehart & Winston.

Ochoa, X. (2017). Multimodal learning analytics. In Charles Lang, George Siemens, Alyssa Wise, and Dragan Gašević (eds.) *The Handbook of Learning Analytics*, USA: Society for Learning Analytics Research pp. 1, 129–141.

Ours, A.R. (2020). *Assessment of Technology Use Data Contribution to Early Alert Efforts at an Access Based Institution*. Valdosta: Valdosta State University.

Papamitsiou, Z. & Economides, A.A. (2016). Learning analytics for smart learning environments: A meta-analysis of empirical research results from 2009 to 2015. *Learning, Design, Technology: An International Compendium Of Theory, Research, Practice, Policy*, 1–23.

Pascarella, E.T. (1980). Student-faculty informal contact and college outcomes. *Review of Educational Research*, 50(4), 545–595.

Pascarella, E.T. & Terenzini, P.T. (1991). *How College Affects Students: Findings and Insights from Twenty Years of Research*. San Francisco, CA: Jossey-Bass.

Penaloza, F. (2015). Effectiveness of retention software on retention and graduation rates. (D.M.), Colorado Technical University, Ann Arbor. Available at https://search.proquest.com/docview/1731233686?pq-origsite=gscholar&fromopenview=trueProQuestDissertations&ThesesGlobaldatabase. (3733964).

Picciano, A.G. (2012). The evolution of big data and learning analytics in American higher education. *Journal of Asynchronous Learning Networks*, 16(3), 9–20.

Pradeep, A., Das, S. & Kizhekkethottam, J.J. (2015). Students dropout factor prediction using EDM techniques. Paper presented at the 2015 *International Conference on Soft-Computing and Networks Security (ICSNS)*.

Rish, I. (2001). An empirical study of the naive Bayes classifier. Paper presented at the *IJCAI 2001 Workshop on Empirical Methods in Artificial Intelligence*.

Romero, C. & Ventura, S. (2013). Data mining in education. *Wiley Interdisciplinary Reviews: Data Mining Knowledge Discovery*, 3(1), 12–27.

Saa, A.A., Al-Emran, M. & Shaalan, K. (2019). Factors affecting students' performance in higher education: A systematic review of predictive data mining techniques. *Technology, Knowledge and Learning*, 24(4), 567–598.

Sclater, N., Peasgood, A. & Mullan, J. (2016). *Learning Analytics in Higher Education*. London: Jisc, p. 176.

Shah, T.H. (2018). Big data analytics in higher education. In Perry, S.M. (ed.), *Maximizing Social Science Research Through Publicly Accessible Data Sets Database*. Pennsylvania: IGI Global.

Shankar, S.K., Prieto, L.P., Rodríguez–Triana, M.J. & Ruiz-Calleja, A. (2018). A review of multimodal learning analytics architectures. Paper presented at the 2018 *IEEE 18th International Conference on Advanced Learning Technologies (ICALT)*.

Smith, V.C., Lange, A. & Huston, D.R. (2012). Predictive modeling to forecast student outcomes and drive effective interventions in online community college courses. *Journal of Asynchronous Learning Networks*, 16(3), 51–61.

Somers, M.J. & Casal, J.C. (2009). Using artificial neural networks to model nonlinearity: The case of the job satisfaction — Job performance relationship. *Organizational Research Methods*, 12(3), 403–417.

Spady, W.G.J.I. (1970). Dropouts from higher education: An interdisciplinary review and synthesis. *Interchange*, 1(1), 64–85.

Spady, W. (1971). Dropouts from higher education: Toward an empirical model. *Interchange*, 2(3), 38–62.

Stark, J. (2018). Opportunities and challenges for big data analytics in US higher education. *Industry & Higher Education*, 32(3), 169–182.

Stets, J.E., & Burke, P.J. (2000). Identity theory and social identity theory. *Social Psychology Quarterly*, 63(3), 224–237.

Tajfel, H. & Turner, J. (1979). Social Identity Theory. Available at dikutip dari www.Learning-theories.Com, diakses, p. 20.

Tampke, D.R. (2013). Developing, implementing, and assessing an early alert system. *Journal of College Student Retention: Research, Theory & Practice*, 14(4), 523–532.

Tempelaar, D.T., Rienties, B. & Giesbers, B. (2015). In search for the most informative data for feedback generation: Learning analytics in a data-rich context. *Computers in Human Behavior*, 47, 157–167.

TEQSA (2017). Characteristics of Australian Higher Education Providers and Their Relation to First-Year Student Attrition. Available at https://www.teqsa.gov.au/for-providers/resources/characteristics-australian-higher-education-providers-and-th.

TEQSA (2018a). Improving Retention, Completion and Success in Higher Education (1760511560). Retrieved from https://www.dese.gov.au/uncategorised/resources/higher-education-standards-panel-final-report-improving-retention-completion-and-success-higher

TEQSA (2018b). Key Financial Metrics On Australia's Higher Education Sector, December 2018.

TEQSA (2019). Statistics report on TEQSA Registered Higher Education Providers 2019. Available at https://www.teqsa.gov.au/sites/default/files/statistics-report-2019.pdf?v=1572233269.

TEQSA (2021). Renewing Course Accreditation. Available at https://www.teqsa.gov.au/renewing-course-accreditation.

Thomas, L. (2002). Student retention in higher education: the role of institutional habitus. *Journal of Education Policy*, 17(4), 423–442.

Tinto, V. (1975). Dropout from higher education: A theoretical synthesis of recent research. *Review of Educational Research*, 45(1), 89–125.

Tinto, V. (1987). *Leaving College: Rethinking the Causes and Cures of Student Attrition.* Chicago, IL: University of Chicago Press.

Tinto, V. (2006). Research and practice of student retention: What next?, *Sage Journals*, 8(1), 1–19.

Tsai, Y.-S. & Gasevic, D. (2017). Learning analytics in higher education — Challenges and policies: A review of eight learning analytics policies. Paper presented at the *Proceedings of the Seventh International Learning Analytics & Knowledge Conference.*

Twisk, J.W. (2013). *Applied Longitudinal Data Analysis for Epidemiology: A Practical Guide.* Cambridge: Cambridge University Press.

Uddin, M.F. & Lee, J. (2017). Proposing stochastic probability-based math model and algorithms utilizing social networking and academic data for good fit students prediction. *Social Network Analysis Mining*, 7(1), 29.

Vapnik, V., Guyon, I., & Hastie, T. (1995). Support vector machines. *Machine Learning*, 20(3), 273–297.

Vercellis, C. (2009). *Business Intelligence: Data Mining and Optimization for Decision Making.* Hoboken, NJ: Wiley Online Library.

Viberg, O., Hatakka, M., Bälter, O. & Mavroudi, A. (2018). The current landscape of learning analytics in higher education. *Computers in Human Behavior*, 89, 98–110.

Villano, R., Harrison, S., Lynch, G. & Chen, G. (2018). Linking early alert systems and student retention: A survival analysis approach. *Higher Education Research Development*, 76(5), 903–920.

Webster, A.L. & Showers, V.E. (2011). Measuring predictors of student retention rates. *American Journal of Economics and Business Administration*, 3(2), 301–311.

Weiss, S.M. & Indurkhya, N. (1998). *Predictive Data Mining: A Practical Guide.* Burlington, MA: Morgan Kaufmann.

What We Do. (2021). Available at https://www.teqsa.gov.au/what-we-do.

Williams, P. (2014). Squaring the circle: A new alternative to alternative-assessment. *Teaching in Higher Education*, 19(5), 565–577.

Xian, L. (2016). Chapter 2 — *Traditional Methods of Longitudinal Data Analysis.* Amsterdam: Elsevier Inc.

Chapter 11

Enhancing Student Engagement by Using Machine Learning Algorithms

Mehrdad Razmjoo

King's Own Institute, Australia

Abstract

Student engagement is an important factor toward academic success, and machine learning techniques are valuable tools for predicting and improving it. This chapter explores some applications of machine learning to predict student engagement by using different data sources, particularly in the context of online education. The chapter discusses different machine learning algorithms, including, logistic regression, decision trees, support vector machines, Naïve Bayes, deep learning, K-nearest neighbors, and random forests. It also dives into the importance of student engagement, the challenges involved, and the utilization of learning analytics in the educational process. The findings highlight the potential of machine learning in identifying at-risk students and optimizing educational outcomes in online learning environments.

Keywords: Machine learning, Student engagement, Online education, Predictive modeling, Learning analytics, Learning management system, Student performance.

1. Introduction

Student engagement is one of the most crucial factors that determine the success of a student in their academic endeavors. In recent years, with the emergence of machine learning technology, it has become possible to predict student engagement using various data sources. The application of machine learning techniques can help educators identify students who are at risk of disengagement and take proactive measures to prevent it. This chapter discusses the various approaches to predicting student engagement using machine learning technology, the data sources that are used, and the challenges involved.

The advent of online education has transformed the learning landscape, enhancing the accessibility and affordability of education for people worldwide. Despite the benefits and growing enthusiasm for online and distance learning, educational institutions are showing increasing concerns regarding students' academic performance and their ability to stay enrolled, especially when facing low rates of certification/graduation and high rates of dropout/completion.

With the growing interest in online education and the substantial volume of data generated through learners' interactions with online platforms, researchers have put forth methodologies to analyze learners' behavioral data, aiming to predict and enhance educational outcomes. The field of learning analytics (LA), often referred to as educational data mining (EDM), involves the analysis and identification of patterns within learners' data to inform decision-making, and it has garnered significant attention from researchers in recent times (Xavier & Meneses, 2020).

2. Student Engagement

Student engagement refers to the level of involvement, interest, and enthusiasm that a student has toward their academic pursuits. It involves both behavioral and emotional components, such as attendance, participation in class, completion of assignments, and overall motivation to learn (Fredricks *et al.*, 2004).

Predicting student engagement is crucial for educators because it allows them to identify students who are at risk of disengagement and take proactive measures to prevent it. Disengagement can lead to poor academic performance, increased dropout rates, and a lack of motivation to continue with education. By predicting student engagement, educators can intervene early and provide personalized support to help students stay engaged and achieve academic success.

3. Machine Learning

Machine learning aims to extract insights from data, forming a strong connection with fields such as statistics, artificial intelligence, and computer science. The three primary categories of machine learning methods are supervised learning, unsupervised learning, and reinforcement learning. (Müller & Guido, 2017).

Numerous machine learning algorithms have been put into practice within the research sphere. The data science literature highlights several crucial and renowned methods including (Russell, 2018):

- Decision trees
- Logistic regression
- Naïve Bayes
- Support vector machines
- Deep Learning
- K-nearest neighbors
- Random forests

3.1. Decision Trees

The structure of a decision tree is reminiscent of a tree, wherein each node represents an attribute, every connection signifies a decision (rule), and each terminal point depicts a result. It finds utility in analyzing both continuous and discrete datasets (Patel & Prajapati, 2018). The initiation of a decision tree involves a root node, from which nodes are progressively divided using a decision tree learning algorithm that relies on conditional inquiries. This division process follows a recursive pattern (Yadav & Pal, 2012).

3.2. Logistic Regression

Essentially, linear regression is conducted to establish the connections between two or multiple interrelated variables, aiming to predict outcomes through an examination of the changes or discrepancies (Uyanık & Güler, 2013).

3.3. Naïve Bayes

It utilizes a straightforward probabilistic formula for categorization. It evaluates a range of probabilities by determining the occurrence and arrangement of values within a dataset. It permits all characteristics to equally influence the ultimate determination (Wibawa et al., 2019).

3.4. Support Vector Machines

The fundamental concept of Support Vector Machines (SVM) involves mapping data into an n-dimensional space, where n represents the features, and then employing a hyperplane to separate the classes, serving the purpose of both classification and regression tasks (Deepa & Senthil, 2020).

3.5. Deep Learning

Deep learning is a subset of artificial neural networks (ANNs) referred to as such because it employs neural networks with multiple layers to handle data. The concept involves incorporating intermediate layers (referred to as "hidden" because they don't directly receive the initial data) to aggregate the values from the preceding layer, enabling the acquisition of more intricate patterns from the input (Sungkur & Maharaj, 2021).

3.6. K-Nearest Neighbors

It ranks among the simplest and uncomplicated methods for classification. This approach is applicable when there's limited knowledge about the data's distribution. K-Nearest Neighbors (KNN) was formulated at a time when dependable parameters for probability estimation were uncertain or challenging to define (Hall et al., 2008). A parameter referred to as "k" dictates the number of neighbors chosen by the algorithm. The effectiveness primarily relies on the selection of "k" and the distance measurement employed. When "k" is small, the prediction quality can suffer due to the data's sparsity. Conversely, higher "k" values result in excessive smoothing, leading to reduced performance and the potential to overlook crucial patterns (Zhang, 2016).

3.7. Random Forests

Random forest is considered an expert solution for the majority of problems and falls under the ensemble learning classifiers whereby weak models are combined to create a powerful one. Ensemble methods are among the most promising areas for research. It is defined as a set of classifiers whose predictions are brought together to forecast new instances. Ensemble learning algorithms have shown to be an efficient technique to improve predictive accuracy and dampen learning problem complexities into sub-problems (numerous decision trees are produced in random forests). To classify an object having attributes, every one of the trees gives a classification which is also considered as a vote.

4. Student Interaction by Using Machine Learning Technique Approaches

Raj & Renumol (2020) used a Massive Open Online Course (MOOCs) model for using a learning pathway that allows learners to learn by themselves in their own time, by using video lectures and learning materials that are available online. Unfortunately, the number of students who dropped out was high due to a lack of engagement. They also mentioned that another technique is used to predict students at risk by using a learning anadataset (OULAD), which is curranty used at Open University UK, is called VLE. This system logs students' interaction and their learning behaviors. By storing these data in the vast data repository and by using machine learning techniques such as KNN, CART, and Naïve Bayes network the outcome of the Bayes network is better than the other type of machine learning algorithm.

There is another way to work on university data by using a decision tree algorithm to build a model that can predict student engagement by extracting data in a real-time manner which can help to notify students at risk at the very early stage (Baradwaj & Pal, 2011). Hassan *et al.* (2019) suggested that the clustering algorithm can adjust to incoming data, including data from e-learning logs and alternative sources such as social media. They found out that students who watched the video of the assessment before the class were more likely to be engaged in the classroom. Based on the 8-year data collected in the study, they identified a better and more effective classification model. There are two main objectives to select the best candidates for classification to predict student engagement. The first one is maximizing the classification accuracy and the second one is dimensionality reduction.

The research (Ladha & Deepa, 2011) found that the best selection algorithms for data classifications are Chi-Square and Euclidean distance by better testing divergence from the distribution among independent class values. Open University Learning Analytics Dataset (OULAD) used the VLE technique by applying an anonymized dataset that focused on three attributes: courses, students, and their interactions with the course. They developed an optimal predictive model based on student engagement.

An earlier study by Rajabalee *et al.* (2020) found that three factors can directly affect student engagement: (1) The amount of completed activity by the student, (2) the importance of the activity which can add to the student's scores, and (3) activities with active interactions such as games or class discussions. Rajabalee *et al.* (2020) used diverse sets of machine learning algorithms to find out what was the best algorithm to give more accurate predictions regarding student engagement in a VLE. Among the various classification algorithms, the Random Forest algorithm exhibits superior performance. In contrast to the alternative models, Random Forest operates as an ensemble model where each tree contributes an output, and the prediction of the model is based on the class with the highest number of votes. The Random Forest algorithm achieves an accuracy rate of 94.1% in classification. The classifier's precision stands at 94.93%, reflecting a robust recall of 97.4%. In the context of the ongoing challenge of identifying low-engaged students, the classifier's recall performance holds significant importance.

It can be said that the Random Forest classifier has the highest precision and accuracy among the other algorithms. By using this methodology, we can identify the students who have lower engagement in their studies at a very early stage of their studies.

Lohman (2021) suggested that for better outcomes in machine learning algorithms for students' engagement, two factors need to be looked at: the efficiency of the evaluation process and the careful choice of parameters. Meanwhile, rating techniques and data analysis techniques can impact the outcome of the evaluation. Pramod and Ramakrishnan (2022) applied a text analytics-based analysis and looked at students' views about the quality of faculty and the factors influencing their opinions, and they used word classification in students' feedback and polarity score to evaluate and predict faculty effectiveness in the teaching and learning techniques. The data were collected via an online questionnaire survey, the questionnaire included questions on student profiles (such as gender, age, academic background, and prior work experience) and course-related and teaching-related information. The research additionally generated an emotional valence graph based on student feedback about faculty members and investigated the trends for faculty members possessing distinct attributes. Notably, faculty members who engaged students by utilizing case studies, practical experiments, and real-time examples exhibited high emotional valence graphs. Conversely, factors contributing to low emotional valence graphs comprised monotonous lectures, slow pacing, and strict, unclear assessments.

Their research also unveiled that students worry about their performance and grades in assessments and are not in favor of intricate evaluation methods. The level of difficulty and various aspects of evaluations, such as the evaluation format, question types, and question familiarity, were also deemed important by students when expressing their preferences for instructors. In addition, the findings of their study also suggested that the way of teaching influences how effective it is perceived to be and students did not prioritize factors like critical thinking and soft skills when rating educators (i.e., students prioritize their learning experience and exam results over the skills from a course). The significance of this research's findings can be comprehended through multiple lenses, spanning fields like technology, engineering, and management. It is possible to expand this study's scope by adapting the measurement of faculty effectiveness to various academic subjects, tailoring the indicators to suit each specific area. For example, in technology or engineering domains, indicators like fostering critical and analytical abilities could hold more significance. On the other hand, in management and business domains, skills related to problem-solving and decision-making might be more fitting. Such tailoring would improve the applicability of the model across diverse contexts.

5. E-learning and Online Learning Platforms

E-learning involves providing education and associated tasks through online platforms. This approach has yielded advantages such as flexibility for learners and enhanced engagement, achieved through both real-time and separate interactions using digital methods facilitated by a Learning Management System (LMS) (Coman et al., 2020).

One of the forms of teaching and learning is asynchronous e-learning and LMS is using this technique by using different learning objects such as video, documents, presentation, and audio (Cohen & Nycz, 2006). Dewan et al. (2019) mentioned that techniques regarding student engagement in online learning environments can be divided into three categories: automatic, semi-automatic, and manual techniques. In the automatic technique, the data obtained from log files and logs generated by the HTML-tutor could be analyzed by machine learning algorithms (Jayashree & Priya, 2019). Meanwhile, a bottom-up approach could be an effective approach for educational institutions (Kimball & Ross, 2013). This approach uses single data storage to make the queries easier.

Adnan et al. (2021) went which different machine learning techniques for student evaluation and student engagement in online learning, and they found out that the forest technique has 91% accuracy for the prediction of students' engagement in the online platform. The outcomes of their study indicated that attributes such as online quizzes, videos, and forums can enhance student engagement. On the other hand, Liu et al. (2022a) emphasized that the effectiveness of emotional and cognitive engagement should be considered.

Meanwhile, the temporal emotion-aspect model "TEAM" can be a useful unsupervised model. Social interaction and cognitive processing can be another effective factor for student engagement. The LMS data is not easily accessible to the public, they used a web scraper to retrieve data from discussion forums, and then a CSV file can be generated and fed a tabular dataset to the model.

The last step of this technique is using this dataset to create a report regarding student performance and engagement report. A web-based program was created to implement optimal machine learning algorithms. The purpose behind this is to establish a user-friendly web interface, allowing individuals to upload a file containing student information. Subsequently, the interface will forecast student achievement and involvement.

After applying different machine learning algorithms, it was realized that Random Forests has the best results with the highest accuracy rate. There are other studies looking at the online learning environment, student dropout rate, and student performance (students at risk, student grade, and student certificate acquisition). For example, Alhothali et al. (2022) came up with a dropout prediction approach with two features:

Statistical Features and Temporal Features. MonllaÃ *et al.* (2020) introduced a structure that investigated various prediction analyzers (students, users, courses), classification objectives (students at risk, course efficacy), indicative attributes (such as the student's click count), and machine-learning algorithms (like ANN or LR). To forecast student attrition, behavioral cues related to learning were extracted and employed to train the ANN model, resulting in a favorable outcome in terms of performance. The research findings about the frequency of student engagement are in direct relation to dropout outcomes.

6. Conclusion

Student engagement and interaction are the biggest challenges for the education sector. From online platforms to face-to-face, there are many challenges to keep students engaged and make their journey more pleasant. Through applying machine learning tools and algorithms, we can find the gap and make better decisions for those students who are at risk of dropout or lack of engagement, and things such as pre-class videos, online quizzes and forums as well as asking student questions and Interacting with students could enhance student engagement.

References

Alhothali, A., Albsisi, M., Assalahi, H. & Aldosemani, T. (2022). Predicting student outcomes in online courses using machine learning techniques: A review. *Sustainability*, 14(10), 6199.

Adnan, M., Habib, A., Ashraf, J., Mussadiq, S., Raza, A.A., Abid, M., Bashir, M. & Khan, S.U. (2021). Predicting at-risk students at different percentages of course length for early intervention using machine learning models. *IEEE Access*, 9, 7519–7539. Accessed on December 10, 2021. Available at https://ieeexplore.ieee.org/document/9314000.

Baradwaj B.K. & Pal, S. (2011). Mining educational data to analyze students' performance. *International Journal of Advanced Computer Science and Applications*, 2(6), 63–69. Accessed on August 20, 2023. Available at https://arxiv.org/ftp/arxiv/papers/1201/1201.3417.pdf.

Coman, C., Țîru, L.G., Meseșan-Schmitz, L., Stanciu, C. & Bularca, M.C. (2020). Online teaching and learning in higher education during the coronavirus pandemic: Students' perspective. *Sustainability*, 12(24), 10367.

Cohen, E. & Nycz, M. (2006). Learning objects and e-learning: An informing science perspective. *Interdisciplinary Journal of e-Skills and Lifelong Learning*, 2, 23–34.

Dewan, M.A.A., Murshed, M. & Lin, F. (2019). Engagement detection in online learning: A review. *Smart Learning Environments*, 6(1). https://doi.org/10.1186/s40561-018-0080-z.

Deepa, B.G. & Senthil, S. (2020). Constructive effect of ranking optimal features using random forest, support vector machine and naïve Bayes for breast cancer diagnosis. In *Big Data Analytics and Intelligence: A Perspective for Health Care*, 1st edn. Emerald Insight.

Fredricks, J.A., Blumenfeld, P.C. & Paris, A.H. (2004). School engagement: Potential of the concept, state of the evidence. *Review of Educational Research*, 74(1), 59–109.

Feng, J., Heffernan, N.T. & Koedinger, K.R. (2020). Predicting student engagement in an online course through automatic analysis of their recorded behaviours. *Journal of Educational Data Mining*, 12(1), 1–22.

Hafeez, M.A., Rashid, M., Tariq, H., Abideen, Z.U., Alotaibi, S.S. & Sinky, M.H. (2021). Performance improvement of the decision tree: A robust classifier using the Tabu search algorithm. *Applied Sciences*, 11(15), 6728.

Hall, P., Park, B. & Samworth, R. (2008). Choice of neighbour order in nearest-neighbor classification. *The Annals of Statistics*, 36(5), 2135–2152.

Jayashree, G. & Priya, C. (2019). Design of visibility for order lifecycle using the data warehouse. *International Journal of Engineering and Advanced Technology*, 8(6), 1–8.

Joksimović, S., Gašević, D. & Dawson, S. (2017). Learning analytics to unveil learning strategies in a flipped classroom. *The Internet and Higher Education*, 33, 74–85.

Krawczyk, B., Minku, L.L., Gama, J., Stefanowski, J. & Woźniak, M. (2017). Ensemble learning for Data stream analysis: A survey. *Information Fusion*, 37, 132–156.

Kimball, R. & Ross, M. (2013). *The Data Warehouse Toolkit*, 3rd edn. Hoboken, NJ: Wiley.

Ko, C.Y. & Leu, F.-Y. (2021). Examining successful attributes for undergraduate students by applying machine learning techniques. *IEEE Transactions on Education*, 64(1), 50–57.

Ladha, L. & Deepa, T. (2011). Feature selection methods and algorithms. *International Journal on Computer Science and Engineering*, 3(5), 1787–1797.

Liu, S., Liu, S., Liu, Z., Peng, X. & Yang, Z. (2022a). Automated detection of emotional and cognitive engagement in MOOC discussions to predict learning achievement. *Computers & Education*, 181. https://doi.org/10.1016/j.compedu.2022.104461.

Liu, Z., Zhang, N., Peng, X., Liu, S., Yang, Z., Peng, J., Su, Z. & Chen, J. (2022b). Exploring the relationship between social interaction, cognitive processing and learning achievements in a MOOC discussion forum. *Journal of Educational Computing Research*, 60(1), 132–169.

Liu, Z., Kong, X. & Liu, S.(2022c). Looking at MOOC discussion data to uncover the relationship between discussion pacings, learners' cognitive presence and learning achievements. *Education and Information Technologies*, 27, 8256–8288.

Lohman, L. (2021). Evaluation of university teaching as sound performance appraisal. *Studies in Educational Evaluation*, 70, 1–11.

MonllaÃ¸s OlivÃl', D.; Huynh, D., Reynolds, M., Dougiamas, M. & Wiese, D.A. (2020). A supervised learning framework: Using assessment to identify students at risk of dropping out of a MOOC. *Journal of Computing in Higher Education*, 32(1), 9–26.

Müller, A.C. & Guido, S. (2017). *Introduction to Machine Learning with Python: A Guide for Data Scientists*. California: O'Reilly.

Patel, H.H. & Prajapati, P. (2018). Study and analysis of decision tree-based classification algorithms. *International Journal of Computer Science and Engineering*, 6(10), 74–78.

Pramod, D. & Ramakrishnan, R. (2022). Faculty effectiveness prediction using machine learning and text analytics. In *IEEE Technology and Engineering Management Conference*, 25–29 April 2022, Izmir, Turkey.

Russell, R. (2018). *Machine Learning Step-By-Step Guide to Implementing Machine Learning Algorithms with Python*. Carolina: CreateSpace Independent Publishing Platform.

Rajabalee B.Y., Santally M.I. & Rennie, F. (2020). A study of the relationship between students' engagement and their academic performances in an eLearning environment. *E-learning and Digital Media*, 17(1), 1–20.

Raj, N.S. & Renumol, V.G. (2020). Early prediction of student engagement in virtual learning environments using machine learning techniques. *E-Learning and Digital Media*, 19(6), 537–554.

Sungkur, Y.T. (2022) *Predictive Modelling and Analytics of Students' Grades Using Machine Learning Algorithms*. Berlin: Springer Science+Business Media.

Sungkur, R.K. & Maharaj, M.S. (2021). Design and implementation of a SMART Learning environment for the upskilling of cybersecurity professionals in Mauritius. *Education and Information Technologies*, 26, 3175–3201.

Uyanık, G.K. & Güler, N. (2013). A study on multiple linear regression analysis. *Procedia — Social and Behavioral Sciences*, 106. Accessed on November 20, 2021. Available at https://www.sciencedirect.com/science/article/pii/S1877042813046429.

Wibawa, A.P., Kurniawan, A.C., Murti, D.M.P., Adiperkasa, R.P., Putra, S.M., Kurniawan, S.A. & Nugraha, Y.R. (2019). Naïve Bayes classifer for journal quartile classification. *International Journal of Recent Contributions from Engineering, Science & IT*, 7(2), 91–99.

Xavier, M. & Meneses, J. (2020). *Dropout in Online Higher Education: A Scoping Review from 2014 to 2018*. Barcelona: ELearn Center, Universitat Obertade Catalunya.

Yadav, S.K. & Pal, S. (2012). Data mining: A prediction for performance improvement of engineering students using classification. *World of Computer Science and Information Technology Journal*, 2(2), 51–56.

Zhang, Z. (2016). Introduction to machine learning: K-nearest neighbours. *Annals of Translational Medicine*, 4(11), 1–7.

© 2024 World Scientific Publishing Company
https://doi.org/10.1142/9789811285622_0012

Chapter 12

Application of Big Data in Curriculum Development

Farzaneh Mayabadi[*], Sweta Thakur[*], Shaleeza Sohail[†], and Fariza Sabrina[‡]

[*]*King's Own Institute, Australia*

[†]*University of Newcastle, Australia*

[‡]*Central Queensland University, Australia*

Abstract

While Learning Analytics has been widely used to improve learning experiences such as course content, activities, and assessments, it plays a significant role in providing data-driven insight into the efficacy of a program. This chapter sheds light on how big data can be used in curriculum development to ensure that the skills and competencies students learn at educational institutions align with those required in the current and future job market. By exploring three case studies in which big data has been utilized to revise and update curricula in different fields, this chapter suggests that big data allows curriculum designers to make data-driven decisions which leads to a higher rate of employability and satisfaction among students. This chapter also discusses the limitations and challenges of using big data in education.

Keywords: Big data, Education, Curriculum development, Data mining, Learning analytics, Data-driven decision.

1. Introduction

1.1. *Definition of Big Data*

Big data refers to large and diversified data sets that are generated, captured, and processed at high velocity (Laney, 2001). It also encompasses the development of mobile networks and cloud computing (Bollier *et al.*, 2010). Due to their compounded structure, it can be strenuous to store, anticipate, and analyze them to derive results. YouTube videos viewed, mobile phone location data, data shared on the Internet every day, transaction processing systems, and medical records are examples of big data (Drigas *et al.*, 2014).

Big data has gained considerable momentum as a technological development (Fichman *et al.*, 2014) in academic and business communities (Chen *et al.*, 2012). Despite the significant strategic and functional benefits of big data, and its potential to transform the field of management, there is a lack of empirical research to evaluate its academic and business values. This chapter aims to illustrate the value of big data in education by focusing on scholars' approaches in utilizing it to design and redesign curricula.

1.2. *Big Data in Education*

The use of big data, especially Educational Data Mining and Learning Analytics, is expanding significantly. Sin and Muthu (2015) believe that Educational Data Mining will transform the way in which the forthcoming generations will attain knowledge and acquire skills in the learning process. At the same time, there is an ongoing debate on how to use big data effectively to enhance the quality of education (Bienkowsk *et al.*, 2012; Günther *et al.*, 2017).

In education, the use of Learning Management Systems (LMS) has been increasing in the last few years. This is perhaps because of the convenience of accessing these platforms from mobile devices such as smartphones, laptops, and tablets. Like LMS, Massive Open Online Courses (MOOCs), open access web-based learning environments that allow unlimited participants, produce an expansive quantity of educational data. As traditional learning analytics do not have the potential to process and manage big data properly, the application of big data technologies and tools is increasingly imperative to make valuable use of this massive data for educational purposes. Drigas *et al.* (2014) argue that integration of big data into the education system can transform it in a modern and dynamic manner. This is advantageous not only for individual students but also presents educators with invaluable tools that allow them to make distinct decisions. This will help the education system to enhance its approach to learning and teaching in a more systematic and targeted way (Drigas *et al.*, 2014).

1.3. Big Data in Education and Curriculum Development

The main objective of curriculum development is to "guide the experiences of students toward predetermined educational goals" (Ornstein & Hukins, 2018: 3). It provides a framework for expected objectives, what students learn, in what manner they learn, and how to determine if the objectives are attained.

There are various approaches to curriculum development, among which Tyler's (1949) model, despite its age, is the most influential and commonly used by all fields. Four principles of Tylor's model are the purposes of the school, content, educational experiences, and evaluation. Tylor based these principles on four fundamental questions:

- What are the "educational purposes" of the school?
- What "educational experiences" should be provided to achieve these purposes?
- What is the most effective way to organize these educational experiences?
- How can we decide if these purposes are achieved? (Tyler, 2013: 15)

Given the dynamic nature of industries in the 21st century, it is crucial to consider the alignment of the program learning outcomes with the skills required by the professionals working in that area. In other words, attainment of skills required by relevant industry should be set as one of the "educational purposes" of a program. The program outcomes define what students should be able to know, do, or understand by the end of the program. A start with well-defined industry-specific learning objectives guides the entire curriculum design process, from "educational experiences" or content of the program to students' learning experience and the ways that attainment of learning objectives are assessed. By doing so, educators can ensure that program graduates are job-ready and equipped with the required skills to face the challenges of the dynamic industry environment.

To identify the ever-evolving skill sets sought by professionals today and predict those that will be vital in the future, big data can prove to be highly effective by identifying emerging trends, patterns, and requirements from industry reports, recent surveys, and market data. Curriculum designers can use big data not only at the initial stages of curriculum development but also to continuously enhance and refine curricula based on changing environments and needs. This iterative approach to curriculum development is responsive to the ever-changing demands of the job market and bridges the gap between academia and industry by equipping students with cutting-edge and in-demand industry skills. This chapter aims to discuss how big data can facilitate a seamless connection between the required competencies by industry and the acquired ones by reviewing three case studies using this approach.

2. Bridging the Gap Between Education and Industry

Referring to the importance of alignment between competencies learned at universities and those required in the computing industry, Hassan *et al.* (2023) suggest a framework for mapping these competencies. This framework helps academics to improve their computing curriculum to meet the requirements of industry which would ultimately lead to higher student satisfaction rates and employability. The data for this framework consists of candidates' resumes and job listings from prominent online job portals. At the preprocessing stage, image-based text detection is used to extract acquired skills from candidates' resumes. After cleansing, at the second stage, case-based reasoning is applied to map the candidates' skills to the required skills of the job postings.

Understanding and analyzing the discrepancy between the skills required by the computing industry and those set in the educational curriculum is crucial in creating a data-driven alignment between "acquired skills" and "required skills" (Hassan *et al.* 2023: 2). At the same time, it contributes significantly to students' "engagement and retention" as well as their career development (Hassan *et al.* 2023: 2). After comparing these two sets of competencies, Hassan *et al.* argued that big data and deep learning can be used to revise and enhance the curriculum to maximize the coverage of the skills required by industry. Modifications to the computing curriculum are provided to bridge the gap between the acquired and required skills as the final output using a feedback loop. Recommendations are provided for the required skills for data science and software engineering jobs using the proposed curriculum enhancement framework. The recommendations are around industry certifications, programming frameworks and programming languages for these two roles.

After improving the curriculum by using these technologies, the data set will be updated, and this mapping can be done continuously to ensure that the competencies covered in the curriculums are updated. Hence, the framework employs big data to provide a relationship between academia and industry for breeding IT graduates tailored to fulfill the ever-changing demands of the IT job market. Although real-world exploration of the framework is performed for the Norwegian technology sector, this framework can be used to enhance curricula in other fields.

Ketamo *et al.* (2019) conducted a case study on how AI and big data can be utilized to design and improve curricula to bridge the gap between the competencies and skills students attain at universities and those required by industry. For their experiment, Ketamo *et al.* needed two sets of data. One was the competencies required by the industry which were publicly available and collected from online job ads, companies' blog articles, websites, and their social media posts. These platforms provide curriculum designers with massive open data sets from which they can gain insight into the industry's demands. The other set of data was related to skills embedded in curricula offered by the three universities of applied science in the Helsinki Metropolitan area in Finland.

The collected data were prepared, organized, and analyzed and the results were reported. They used Headai's cognitive artificial intelligence platform which converted the analytics results to a visualized map. This visualized map provided academics an insight into future competence needs and social changes and helped them prioritize those competencies in their curricula to minimize the gap between acquired skills at educational institutes and required industry skills (Ketamo *et al.*, 2019).

A comparison between these two sets of data showed that some skills are required in industry but are not covered in the curricula. They found that there are many jobs available for graduates that they may not be aware of because of their unfamiliarity with the job titles and terminologies used in the industry. Academics can make use of this information to enhance their curricula or offer new programs to meet the demands of industry. Furthermore, the visualized map was able to distinguish the core skills required for master's and bachelor's levels separately which can help curriculum designers to revise and design curricula for different levels of their programs and define clear learning pathways (Ketamo et al., 2019).

They argue that big data describes the concept of "large-scale automated data processing" which was first introduced in the 1980s (Ketamo et al., 2019: 147). Compared to manual research, AI-based data analytics deals with a higher volume of data collected from multiple sources. This increases the reliability and validity of the research findings and provides a broader picture of the (discrepancy between) competencies required and those learned. Another advantage of using big data analytics is that it provides real-time access to various issues which helps curriculum developers revise and improve curricula in the light of real-time competence demand in industry (Ketamo et al., 2019).

In another case study, Hyun et al. analyze the context in which new nursing graduates have to work, and refer to the challenges they face in the transition from universities to the nursing industry. They argue that although nursing schools are trying to prepare graduates for industry, employers are concerned about the effectiveness of these programs and believe that the nursing graduates are not ready for real-world situations which may impact public safety and quality care for patients; "a systematic review of nursing graduate competencies reported that only a small proportion of experienced nurses and nurse managers believed that nursing graduates were competent on completion of their undergraduate education" (Hyun et al., 2022: 1).

By using the big data software Leximancer, a total of 325 international article abstracts, with a focus on contemporary issues related to the competencies of newly graduated nurses, were collected and analyzed. The key trait of Leximancer is that it converts information to a visual map that provides a broader picture of key concepts. From this analysis, some key concerns regarding nursing competency arose: the need for standardization of competencies in nursing, the need for appropriate assessment to measure levels of competencies, expectations vs. achievements of nursing graduates, and lack of high-quality and safe practice especially in collaborative and teamwork tasks. While these findings indicate the gap between nursing education and the nursing workplace, they facilitate data-driven decision-making in implementing educational strategies to address these issues.

Hyun *et al.* argue that curriculum designers should constantly revise and improve their programs and decide on which core competence to prioritize in their curricula and what type of assessments should be implemented to prepare graduates for the challenges they may face in nursing jobs in the present and the future. By having graduates who are competent enough to address the challenges of the modern world and provide high-quality care, we can protect our society and ensure the quality of the education system.

3. Challenges in Using Big Data

Integrating big data into curriculum development holds immense promise for enriching students' learning outcomes. This potential is realized through refined assessment designs, personalized learning journeys, and the delivery of precision education (Luan *et al.*, 2020). By tapping into diverse data sources encompassing educational activities and interactions, this approach has the capacity to tailor learning experiences to the unique needs and preferences of each learner. However, the integration of extensive and heterogeneous data into curriculum design is not without its challenges.

A notable hurdle comes from the sheer volume and huge complexity of this multifaceted data landscape as mentioned by Stefanowski *et al.* (2017). Processing, analyzing, and making sense of such extensive datasets necessitates specialized skills and tools that often transcend the traditional expertise of educators. This requires collaborative efforts between educational experts and data scientists, bridging the technical gap and translating data-driven insights into meaningful curriculum enhancements. This calls for dedicated professional development and concerted collaboration among data scientists, educational researchers, and curriculum designers. Adding to this challenge is the reality that many universities lack the analytics capacity and internal resources to fully leverage the wealth of data-driven insights (Attaran *et al.*, 2018).

The utilization of big data faces an additional barrier — challenges coming from organizational behavior, including resistance to change and a lack of vision. These obstacles are compounded by limited financial resources and inadequate computing power (Attaran *et al.*, 2018).

Within the context of harnessing big data, a prominent challenge emerges, particularly in today's educational landscape — ensuring the privacy and security of data. Educational data often contain sensitive information about students, teachers, and institutions, requiring robust measures to prevent breaches and inappropriate use. The maintenance of trust within the education community hinges on this. Balancing the application of data-driven insights with the preservation of privacy rights poses an ongoing and intricate challenge (Florea & Florea, 2020).

The substantial potential of big data goes hand in hand with concerns surrounding personal privacy and the requisite tools and methodologies for safeguarding it (Fischer *et al.*, 2020). These challenges have arisen alongside technologies capable of gathering extensive data and efficiently processing it through methods like data mining and diverse analytics, revealing the limitations of conventional technological approaches in preserving privacy adequately. As a result, it is important to thoroughly review the privacy protection rules. We need to think about what technology can do now and see how it all fits together.

The core of successful curriculum development lies in high-quality and pertinent data. Inaccurate or biased data can lead to flawed decisions that exacerbate educational quality. Challenges that keep coming up are about making data better and selecting the right data. Also, we need to develop algorithms that can be adapted for all kinds of learning situations (Hurley, 2016). Moreover, customizing curriculum to cater to individual student needs using big data can be complex. Every student's learning journey is distinct, necessitating algorithms that can adeptly adapt and personalize content. Striking the delicate equilibrium between data-driven personalization and the comprehensive nurturing of students' skills and capacities is a nuanced task (Macfadyen, 2014).

Another hurdle arises from the rapid evolution of technology and data sources. As the educational landscape evolves, new forms of data emerge — think data from online learning platforms or educational apps. Adapting curriculum development processes to harness the potential of these evolving data sources calls for agility and a culture of continuous learning (Naeem *et al.*, 2022).

Ethically, there's a significant challenge inherent in utilizing big data, and that is the potential risk of data privacy breaches (Herschel *et al.*, 2017). The accumulation and analysis of vast amounts of personal information introduce the risk of compromising individuals' privacy. The data collected might encompass sensitive details that individuals didn't intend to divulge, generating concerns about surveillance, unauthorized access, and potential misuse. Striking the right balance between the benefits of data analysis and the protection of individuals' privacy rights poses a complex ethical challenge.

4. Conclusion

Effective use of big data tools and technology to collect and analyze data can produce reliable results that allow scholars to make data-driven decisions in different stages of curriculum design and redesign, from identifying "educational purposes" to the program content, learning experiences, and assessments. These results can be used to devise personalized curricula based on individual needs and define clear learning pathways for different levels of education. They give scholars an insight into what terminologies should be used and what competencies should be prioritized in curricula in light of the real-time competence demand of the industry. All of these efforts ultimately facilitate a seamless connection between education and industry.

This approach to curriculum enhancement presents advantages to students and graduates as it increases the employability rate. By providing students with a better understanding of the market demands and equipping them with cutting-edge skills and competencies, they will be ready enough to deal with the changes they may face in workplaces in the present and the future. At the same time, we can ensure that work standards are not compromised, and the public receives quality services.

References

Attaran, M., Stark, J. & Stotler, D. (2018). Opportunities and challenges for big data analytics in US higher education: A conceptual model for implementation. *Industry & Higher Education*, 32(3), 169–182.

Bienkowski, M., Feng, M. & Means, B. (2012). Enhancing teaching and learning through educational data mining and learning analytics: An issue brief. Office of Educational Technology, US Department of Education.

Bollier, D. & Firestone, C.M. (2010). The promise and peril of big data. Accessed on August 31, 2023. Available at https://www.aspeninstitute.org/wp-content/uploads/files/content/docs/pubs/The_Promise_and_Peril_of_Big_Data.pdf.

Chen, H., Chiang, R.H.L. & Storey, V.C. (2012). Business intelligence and analytics: From big data to big impact. *MIS Quarterly*, 36(4), 1165–1188.

Drigas, A.S. & Leliopoulos, P. (2014). The use of big data in education. *International Journal of Computer Science Issues*, 11(5), 58–58.

Fichman, R.G., Dos Santos, B.L. & Zheng, Z.E. (2014). Digital innovation as a fundamental and powerful concept in the information systems curriculum. *MIS Quarterly*, 38(2), 329–A15.

Fischer, C., Pardos, Z.A., Baker, R.S., Williams, J.J., Smyth, P., Yu, R., Slater, S., Baker, R. & Warschauer, M. (2020). Mining big data in education: Affordances and challenges. *Review of Research in Education*, 44(1), 130–160.

Florea, D. & Florea, S. (2020). Big data and the ethical implications of data privacy in higher education research. *Sustainability*, 12(20), 8744–.

Gandomi, A. & Haider, M. (2015). Beyond the hype: Big data concepts, methods, and analytics. *International Journal of Information Management*, 35(2), 137–144.

Günther, W.A., Rezazade Mehrizi, M.H., Huysman, M. & Feldberg, F. (2017). Debating big data: A literature review on realizing value from big data. *The Journal of Strategic Information Systems*, 26(3), 191–209.

Hassan, M.U., Alaliyat, S., Sarwar, R., Nawaz, R. & Hameed, I.A. (2023). Leveraging deep learning and big data to enhance computing curriculum for industry-relevant skills: A Norwegian case study. *Heliyon*, 9(4), e15407–e15407.

Herschel, R. & Miori, V.M. (2017). Ethics & big data. *Technology in Society*, 49, 31–36.

Hurley, M., & Adebayo, J. (2016). Credit scoring in the era of big data. Accessed on August 31, 2023. Available at https://yjolt.org/credit-scoring-era-big-data.

Hyun, A., Tower, M. & Turner, C. (2022). The current contexts of newly graduated nurses' competence: A content analysis. *Healthcare (Basel)*, 10(6), 1–9.

Ketamo, H., Moisio, A., Passi-Rauste, A. & Alamäki, A. (2019). Mapping the future curriculum: Adopting artificial intelligence and analytics in forecasting competence needs. *European Conference on Intangibles and Intellectual Capital, Academic Conferences International Limited, Kidmore End*, pp. 144–153.

Laney, D. (2001). 3D data management: Controlling data volume, velocity and variety. *META Group Research Note*, 6(70), 1.

Luan, H., Geczy, P., Lai, H., Gobert, J., Yang, S.J.H., Ogata, H., Baltes, J., Guerra, R., Li, P. & Tsai, C.-C. (2020). Challenges and future directions of big data and artificial intelligence in education. *Frontiers in Psychology*, 11, 580820.

Macfadyen, L.P., Dawson, S., Pardo, A. & Gasevic, D. (2014). Embracing big data in complex educational systems: The learning analytics imperative and the policy challenge. *Research & Practice in Assessment*, 9(2), 17–28.

Naeem, M., Jamal, T., Diaz-Martinez, J., Butt, S.A., Montesano, N., Tariq, M. I. et al. (2022). Trends and future perspective challenges in big data. In *Advances in Intelligent Data Analysis and Applications, Sixth Euro-China Conference on Intelligent Data Analysis and Applications*. Singapore: Springer, pp. 309–325.

Ornstein, A.C. & Hunkins, F.P. (2013). *Curriculum: Foundations, Principles, and Issues*, 6th ed. Boston, MA: Pearson.

Sin, K. & Muthu, L. (2015). Application of big data in education data mining and learning analytics — A literature review. *ICTACT Journal on Soft Computing*, 5(4), 1035–1049.

Stefanowski, J., Krawiec, K. & Wrembel, R. (2017). Exploring complex and big data. *International Journal of Applied Mathematics and Computer Science*, 27(4), 669–679.

Tyler, R.W. (2013). *Basic Principles of Curriculum and Instruction*. Chicago, IL: University of Chicago Press.

© 2024 World Scientific Publishing Company
https://doi.org/10.1142/9789811285622_0013

Chapter 13

ICT Programs in China: A Case Study of Shanxi Universities

Xin Gu[*], Fareed Ud Din[†], and Robert M.X. Wu[‡]

[*]*King's Own Institute, Australia*
[†]*The University of New England, Australia*
[‡]*University of Technology Sydney, Australia*

Abstract

Presently, Information and Communication Technology (ICT) education holds substantial importance within higher education institutions worldwide. This research compiles and examines 51 ICT programs and 1,251 associated ICT courses from 11 universities in China's Shanxi province. The micro-level analysis aims to disclose insights about the macro-level scenario, delving into the course design of ICT education in China and potentially on a global scale. This case study discovers that the most sought-after ICT programs primarily center around Information and Computing Science, as well as Computer Science and Technology. Mathematic and Programming-related courses lay the foundation for ICT programs, while Programming is the most frequently offered course in ICT programs at Shanxi universities. Through the data analysis, a suggestion is made to include courses in the context of Cloud Computing and Cybersecurity for the ICT programs offered by Shanxi universities.

Keywords: ICT programs, ICT courses, Course structure, Shanxi universities, Case study.

1. Introduction

In recent decades, the advent of Information and Communication Technology (ICT), has profoundly influenced the global economy through various channels (Zafar *et al.*, 2022), and has revolutionized the way human beings live (Wang & Zhao, 2021). The rapid development in ICT and the pervasive use of digital devices have brought about its transformation at all levels and sectors of life that transform the way of working and learning at an impressive rate (Afari, 2023; Latorre-Cosculluela, 2023; Peciuliauskiene *et al.*, 2022). ICT tools, such as Zoom, Microsoft Meetings, have streamlined communication. Cloud has made global reach and collaboration possible. IoT has made smart cities and smart homes available. The widespread adoption of ICT has led to increased efficiency and productivity across various industries, therefore fostering economic growth on a global scale.

Indeed, numerous nations have invested substantially toward advancing ICT research and ICT education. These days, ICT programs play a significant role in higher education institutions across the globe (Ünal *et al.*, 2022). Specifically, ICT programs have emerged as central pillars within academia, shaping not only the skills of future professionals but also the very structure of courses and curricula. Furthermore, ICT has paved the path for interdisciplinary studies, enabling the convergence of various areas such as engineering, business, geography, and healthcare. Courses now integrate ICT skills to address real-world challenges, fostering cross-disciplinary problem-solving abilities.

This chapter aims to shed light on the diverse range of ICT programs that have emerged across Chinese universities recently and understand the current situations of ICT programs in China's higher education sectors. The case study is adopted as the research methodology for this study. Universities in Shanxi province are selected as the data source for this case study. Specifically, the Research Objectives (RQs) for this study are:

- RQ1: What are the most sought-after programs in ICT?
- RQ2: What are the key courses in ICT programs?
- RQ3: What are the key contents of ICT courses?

The following sections focus on the literature, methodology, results, discussion, and conclusion.

2. Background

In the past 40 years, China's higher education has transitioned from elite-focused education to popular and mass education. The enrolment rate of China's universities is estimated to reach over 60% by 2035, a remarkable growth in the development of China's higher education compared to the enrolment rate (5%) in the 1970s (Hou *et al.*, 2020). China's recent policy focuses on cultivating talent through specialized education and training programs to meet the rising need for competent ICT workers (Ministry of Education of the People's Republic of China, 2023).

In terms of the widespread adoption of ICT, China has been at the forefront by making considerable progress in initiating ICT projects and programs (Wang & Zhao, 2021). With the cross-border collaboration, China emphasizes the acceleration of basic infrastructure construction of digital facilities (Xu & Zhu, 2023) and also strengthens China's ICT excellence in the popularization of ICT courses (Wei *et al.*, 2023; Xu & Zhu, 2023). The universities in China are required to pave a path for students to succeed in the digital age and help the country's technological advancement by providing them with relevant and cutting-edge education in these fields. It requires China's ICT education providers to gain much more attention to higher education worldwide and catch up with world-class education as students desire to obtain up-to-date academic training to improve their competitive capacities and increase career opportunities over the past two decades (Hou *et al.*, 2020), such as research on China's e-commerce program (Gide & Wu, 2004) and the internationalization of China's higher education (Wu & Yu, 2006). With the advent of the information age and knowledge economy, society's learner requirements are gradually increasing (Sun *et al.*, 2022). China's central government released that ICT is crucial to the government's effort to improve technical capabilities (Ministry of Education People's Republic of China, 2023) so that China issues China's Educational Modernization 2035 to accelerate the progress of educational modernization (Zeng, 2022) and plans to strengthen the development of digital technologies that can be widely used in traditional businesses by 2035 (Gov, 2021). This effort has also received significant attention in China's government institutions. ICT programs have therefore been implemented at most higher education institutions in China. ICT programs have been incorporated into the academic curriculum at China's universities in response to the goal of providing students with essential digital skills and producing workforces to support the nation's economic development (Ali, 2020). Among them, four emerging programs have drawn the interest of the general public in China's educational institutions and are considered to be the favorites in terms of student intake, including AI, cybersecurity, cloud computing, image recognition, machine learning (ML), and the Internet of Things (IoT) (Burov et al., 2020; Huang, 2021; Toddy et al., 2022).

These prevalent and sought-after ICT education programs and courses in China represent the nation's dedication to technical development and the changing demands of the sector. Government agencies, financial institutions, and IT enterprises in China highly value graduates with cybersecurity experience. With cloud computing's ongoing transformation of the IT landscape, a greater demand is being felt for professionals who can develop, build, and manage cloud-based systems (Huang et al., 2022). IoT is the third focused program for careers in IoT development, solutions architecture, and project management (Wambuaa & Oduorb, 2022).

However, several issues are challenging ICT higher education in China. The biggest challenge is the narrowness of ICT education focus compared to global ICT education. Literature summarizes global ICT education into AI, big data, blockchains, cloud computing, data mining, Internet+, IoT, computer programming, learning management system, machine learning (ML), mobile applications, online learning, streaming media, social networking, e-learning, virtual reality, and web-based service (Hassan, 2021; Pham et al., 2021; Sun et al., 2022). Differences in curricular emphasis, instructional approaches, and exposure to cutting-edge technology cause the gap and slight disparity between ICT education in China and worldwide ICT education.

3. Methodology

Case study methodology is a qualitative research approach widely employed in diverse academic disciplines to investigate complex and contextually embedded phenomena (Johansson, 2007). Rooted in a holistic and in-depth exploration, case studies illuminate intricate real-world situations, offering a nuanced understanding of multifaceted issues within their natural environment. In this study, the ICT programs from Shanxi universities are considered the subject of the case study.

3.1. *Data Source and Data Collection*

There are 11 universities located in Shanxi Province, which are North University of China (UNC), Shanxi Agricultural University (SXAU), Shanxi Datong University (SXDTU), Shanxi Medical University (SXMU), Shanxi Normal University (SXNU), Shanxi University (SXU), Shanxi University of Chinese Medicine (SXUCM), Shanxi University of Finance and Economics (SXUFE), Taiyuan Normal University (TYNU), Taiyuan University of Technology (TYUT), and Taiyuan University of Science and Technology (TYUST). The universities and their abbreviations are listed in the alphabetic order in Table 1.

To achieve our research objectives, we conducted our searches over the official websites of each university. The searches conducted from March to May 2023 are from the official websites of these 11 universities. The data collection on each website requires three information: university names, program names, and course names.

Table 1: Eleven universities and their abbreviations.

University	Abbreviation
North University of China	NUC
Shanxi Agricultural University	SXAU
Shanxi Datong University	SXDTU
Shanxi Medical University	SXMU
Shanxi Normal University	SXNU
Shanxi University	SXU
Shanxi University of Chinese Medicine	SXUCM
Shanxi University of Finance and Economics	SXUFE
Taiyuan Normal University	TYNU
Taiyuan University of Technology	TYUT
Taiyuan University of Science and Technology	TYUST

Note: Developed for this study.

As a result, a data set of 51 programs and 1,251 courses from the above 11 universities are collected. The programs and number of courses from these 11 universities are listed in Table 2.

Table 2: Eleven universities, their ICT programs, and number of courses.

University	Program	Number of Courses
NUC	Artificial Intelligence	39
	Computer Science and Technology	34
	Data Science and Big Data Technology	34
	Information and Computing Science	24
	Information Countermeasure Technology	39
	Information Engineering	27
	Software Engineering	48
SXAU	Computer Science and Technology	23
	Data Science and Big Data Technology	16
	Electronic Information Science and Technology	19
	Geographic Information Science	18
	Information and Computing Science	22
	Information Management and Information System	17
	Internet of Things Engineering	14
	Network Engineering	19
	Intelligence Science and Technology	24
	Software Engineering	14
SXDTU	Computer Science and Technology	21
SXMU	Information Management and Information System	17
	Intelligence Medical Engineering	17
SXNU	Computer Science and Technology	27
	Geographic Information Science	44
	Information and Computing Science	21
SXU	Computer Science and Technology	26
	Data Science and Big Data Technology	35
	E-commerce	18
	Information and Computing Science	14

Table 2: (Continued)

University	Program	Number of Courses
	Information Management and Information System	19
	Software Engineering	13
SXUCM	Information Management and Information System	32
SXUFE	Data Science and Big Data Technology	32
	E-commerce	22
	Information and Computing Science	19
TYNU	Computer Science and Technology	26
	Geographical Science	36
	Information and Computing Science	24
	Internet of Things Engineering	25
TYUST	Computer Science and Technology	22
	Data Science and Big Data Technology	36
	E-commerce	10
	Geographic Information Science	13
	Information and Computing Science	15
	Internet of Things Engineering	22
	Intelligence Medical Engineering	20
	Software Engineering	45
TYUT	Computer Science and Technology	30
	Data Computing and Application	32
	Information Management	10
	E-commerce	16
	Information and Computing Science	31
	Software Engineering	30

Note: Developed for this study.

4. Results and Discussion

This section focuses on three RQs to explore the most sought-after programs in ICT, the key courses in ICT programs, and the key contents of ICT courses.

4.1. What Are the Most Sought-After Programs in ICT?

In order to identify the most sought-after programs and the novel programs within the field of ICT, an analysis is undertaken by aggregating the programs based on their respective names. The resulting count of the programs is illustrated on a count plot shown in Figure 1.

From Figure 1, it is obvious to identify that ICT and Computer Science and Technology are the most sought-after programs. Among all ICT programs, they are taking the leading positions. A total of 8 programs in Information and Computing Science and a total of 8 programs in Computer Science and Technology are provided at Shanxi universities. Data Science and Big Data Technology (5), and Software Engineering (5) are following, the second-leading programs in ICT education.

From Figure 1, it can be recognized that a set of novel art programs has emerged, namely Intelligent Science and Technology (1), Intelligent Medical Engineering (1), Geographical Science (1), and Artificial Intelligence (1). These programs have transitioned from individual courses to independent and standalone programs in recent years.

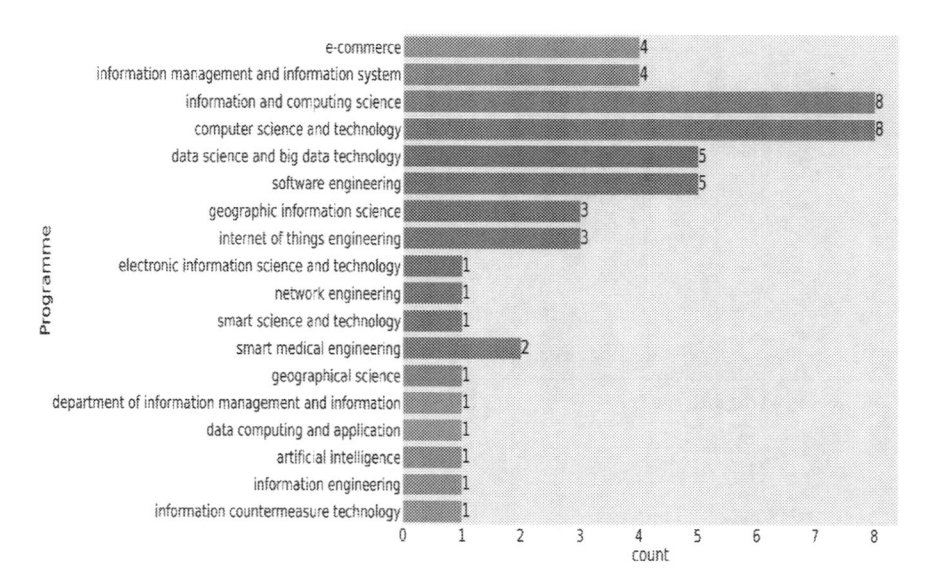

Figure 1: All ICT programs at Shanxi universities.

Note: Developed for this study.

This development signifies the growth and recognition of artificial intelligence not only in the real world (Davenport & Ronanki, 2018) but also within ICT education. Additionally, the second sign of the novel programs is that ICT has merged with other disciplines, such as medical science (Malik *et al.*, 2019), and geographical science (Janowicz *et al.*, 2020).

4.2. What Are the Key Courses in ICT Programs?

Courses are offered under ICT programs. Various programs offer a diverse range of courses. To explore what are the key courses within the realm of ICT, an analysis is conducted in two steps. In the first step, the examination of the key courses is conducted. In the second step, an investigation is carried out on the programs that provide these key courses.

To determine the essential courses within the realm of ICT, the first-step analysis is conducted by encompassing the aggregation of courses based on their names. From this research, the top 20 courses are identified and visualized on a plot, as presented in Figure 2.

Course	Count
discrete mathematics	25
data structure	24
computer network	22
operating system	21
advanced mathematics	19
probability theory and mathematical statistics	15
database system principle	13
data structure and algorithm	13
college physics	12
python programming	11
software engineering	11
object-oriented programming	11
linear algebra	11
algorithm analysis and design	10
java programming	9
digital image processing	9
computer composition principle	9
mathematical analysis	9
advanced algebra	8
database system	8

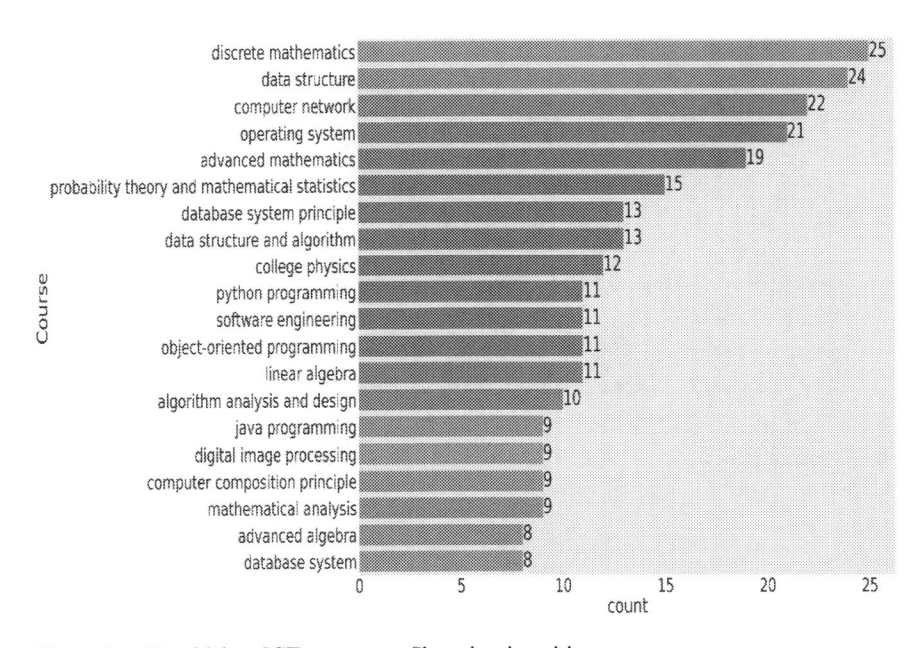

Figure 2: Top 20 key ICT courses at Shanxi universities.
Note: Developed for this study.

This plot offers a clear visualization of the distribution and prominence of these key courses in the field of ICT.

Figure 2 shows the strong position of Discrete Mathematics in all ICT courses at Shanxi universities. Discrete Mathematics is the most frequently taught among all 1,251 ICT courses. It is obvious to detect that quite a few courses in the top 20 key courses are related to mathematics. Besides Discrete Mathematics (25), Advanced Mathematics (19), *Probability Theory and Mathematical Statistics* (15), *Linear Algebra* (11), *Mathematical Analysis* (9), and *Advanced Algebra* (8) are all mathematics-related courses. A total of 87 records are *Mathematic* related courses, with 68 courses containing Mathematic in names.

Programming has long served as the cornerstone of ICT education (Urban-Lurain & Weinshank, 2000). At Shanxi universities, the programming-related courses cover Python Programming (11), Software Engineering (11), Object-Oriented Programming (11), Java Programming (9), and Algorithm Analysis and Design (10). A total of 52 programming-related courses are offered in ICT programs at Shanxi universities.

Data Structure (24) and Data Structure and Algorithm (13) are both data structure-related courses. In total, there are 37 courses out of 1,251 in ICT education at Shanxi universities.

Among the top 10 key ICT courses at Shanxi universities, database-related courses include Database System Principle (13) and Database System (8). The sum of all the database-related courses amounts to 21.

The other key courses from Figure 2 are Computer Network (22), Operating System (21), College Physics (12), Digital Image Processing (9), and Computer Composition Principle (9).

In summary, Mathematic, Programming, Data Structure, Database, Computer Network, Operating System, College Physics, Digital Image Processing, and Computer Composition Principle are the key courses of ICT programs. It is worth noting that, due to the different naming, not all courses belonging to these nine areas are reported visually on this figure. However, Figure 2 containing 270 records effectively captures the key ICT courses from Shanxi universities.

4.3. *What Are the Key Contents of ICT Courses?*

In the second-step analysis, further investigation is carried out on the programs that offer these key courses. Built on the foundation of key courses, analyses are undertaken by aggregating programs by their respective names. This study finds nine courses that serve as the key contents in most of the ICT courses, including Mathematics, Data Structure, Computer Networks, Operating System, Database, Physics, Programming, Digital Image Processing, and Computer Composition.

4.3.1. *Mathematics in ICT Programs*

Mathematics performs a crucial role in ICT programs. It provides critical thinking and problem-solving skills to ICT. *Discrete mathematics* is essential in the areas of network theory and cryptography. *Statistics and Probability* are applicable for data analysis and decision-making. The knowledge of *Applied Mathematics* is required in computer graphics, image processing, and optimization. *Mathematics* provides the foundation for algorithm design and analysis, enabling the development of efficient solutions. These determine the importance of *Mathematics* in the ICT discipline.

All the programs that provide the courses named with Mathematics are investigated. In all ICT courses from Shanxi universities, the Mathematics courses encompass a wide range of mathematical courses, including but not limited to Discrete Mathematics, Advanced Mathematics, Mathematical Statistics, and Mathematical Analysis. Linear Algebra and Advanced Algebra also belong to the Mathematics field. However, the results are distributed on a count plot, as illustrated in Figure 3, including all courses with Mathematic in their names.

Only 25 courses on Discrete Mathematics, 19 courses on Advanced Mathematics, 15 courses on Probability Theory and Mathematical

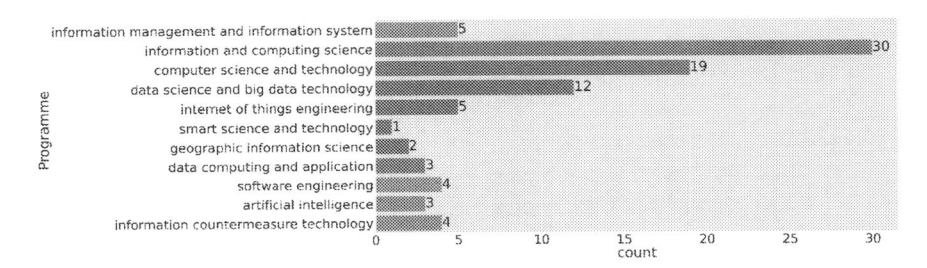

Figure 3: Key course: MATHEMATIC — in ICT programs at Shanxi universities.
Note: Developed for this study.

314 *Teaching and Learning in the Digital Era: Issues and Studies*

Statistics, and 9 in Mathematical Analysis are presented in Figure 2. That is 68 Mathematics courses in total. However, due to the variety of course names, there are 20 additional courses covering topics related to Mathematics, such as College Mathematics, University Mathematics, etc. Figure 3 presents 88 courses on Mathematics.

4.3.2. *Data Structure in ICT Programs*

Data structures enable efficient organization and manipulation of data, and provide the foundation for storing, retrieving, and managing information effectively. Appropriate design of data structure optimizes operations such as searching, sorting, and inserting data. Optimal design of data structures allows large datasets to perform complex computations efficiently. Understanding Data Structures is vital for developing robust and scalable ICT systems.

The programs that provide courses named with *Data Structure* are plotted in Figure 4.

Besides the 24 courses on Data Structure and 13 courses on Data Structure and Algorithms as shown in Figure 2, there are 8 extra

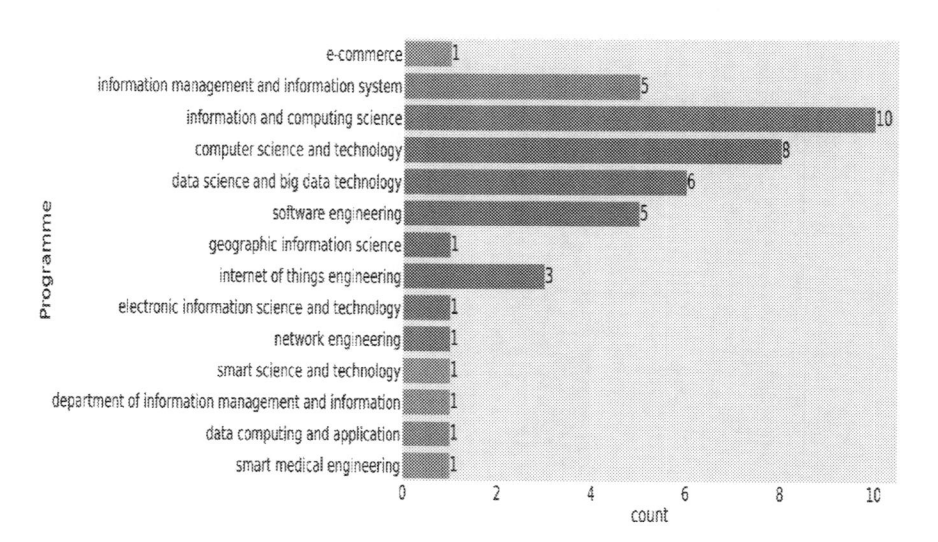

Figure 4:   Key course: DATA STRUCTURE — in ICT programs at Shanxi universities.
Note: Developed for this study.

courses covering topics related to Data Structure, such as Data Structure Principles out of 1,251 ICT courses offered at Shanxi universities. Figure 4 illustrates 45 courses on Data Structure.

4.3.3. Computer Network in ICT Programs

Computer Networking is about how computer systems connect and communicate. *Computer Networking* covers the concepts of network protocols, data transmission, routing, and network security. The knowledge of *Computer Networking* is essential for designing, implementing, and managing network infrastructures. Efficient data transfer and seamless communication among different devices and platforms also require computer networking knowledge. It is a crucial part of the ICT education.

The programs that provide courses named *Computer Network* are visualized in Figure 5.

From Figure 5, there are in total 37 Computer Network courses, including 22 courses referred to as Computer Network (Figure 2), and 15 Computer Network-related courses equipped with various names, such as Computer Network Principles, Computer Network Design, etc. Figure 5 reports 37 courses on Computer Networks.

4.3.4. Operating System in ICT Programs

The operating system provides a platform for software applications to run and manage hardware resources efficiently. The programming concepts of process management, memory management, multitasking, and multithreading are built on top of the operating system. The operating system

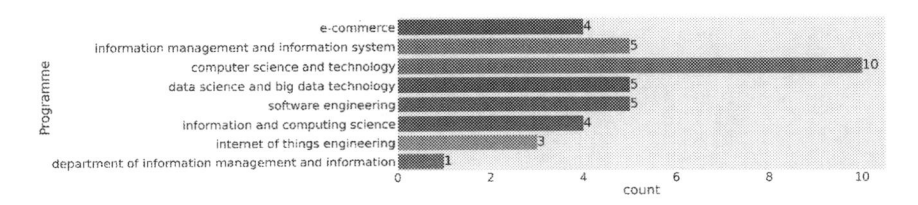

Figure 5: Key course: COMPUTER NETWORK — in ICT programs at Shanxi universities.

Note: Developed for this study.

316 *Teaching and Learning in the Digital Era: Issues and Studies*

```
Programme
  computer science and technology |████████████████████ 10
  data science and big data technology |██████████ 5
  software engineering |████████████ 6
  internet of things engineering |████████ 4
  information management and information system |██ 1
  information and computing science |██ 1
  data computing and application |██ 1
                                 0    2    4    6    8    10
                                          count
```

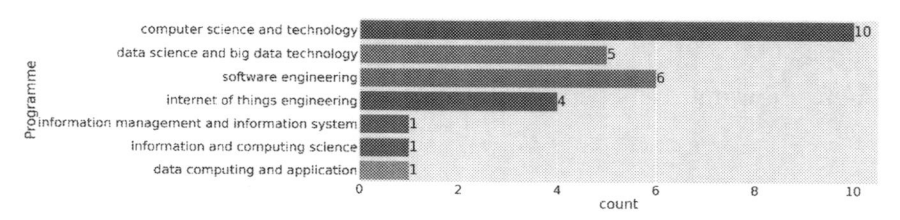

Figure 6: Key course: OPERATING SYSTEM — in ICT programs at Shanxi universities.

Note: Developed for this study.

also forms the base for understanding emerging technologies such as virtualization, cloud computing, and distributed systems. The *Operating System* serves as the foundation course for ICT programs.

The programs that provide courses named with *Operating System* are plotted in Figure 6.

In all programs, 21 courses are under the name of Operating System, and there are also 7 courses on Operating System that go by different names, such as Operating Systems, Operating System Principles, and so on.

Figure 6 reports 28 courses on *Computer Networks*.

4.3.5. *Database in ICT Programs*

Databases store, organize, and manage vast amounts of data. The database system course covers topics such as data modeling, relational database management systems (RDBMS), query languages, and database administration. The knowledge of database is vital for programmers and data analysts, including database design, query, and data manipulation. The *Database System* course is essential in ICT programs due to its critical role.

The programs that provide courses named with *Database* are plotted in Figure 7.

There are 56 database-related courses offered in ICT Programs at Shanxi universities. In addition to the 13 courses named as Database as illustrated in Figure 2, there are 39 additional courses covering the topic of Database, such as Database System Principle, Database Design, Database Analysis and Design, etc. Figure 7 reports 56 courses on the Database.

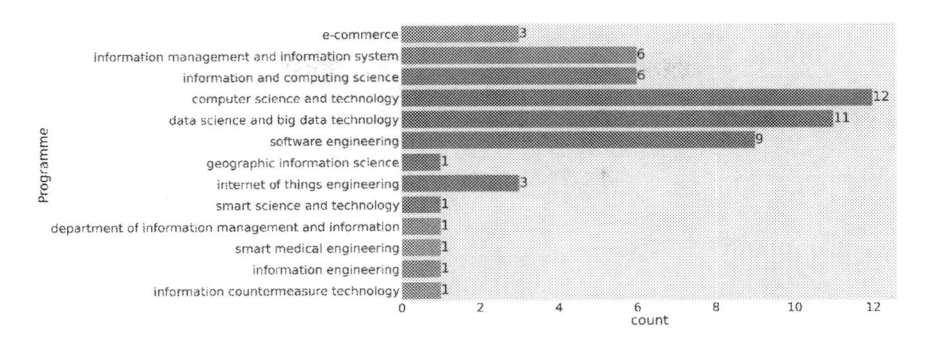

```
                              e-commerce ▓▓▓ 3
    information management and information system ▓▓▓▓▓▓ 6
                 information and computing science ▓▓▓▓▓▓ 6
                    computer science and technology ▓▓▓▓▓▓▓▓▓▓▓▓ 12
                data science and big data technology ▓▓▓▓▓▓▓▓▓▓▓ 11
                               software engineering ▓▓▓▓▓▓▓▓▓ 9
                      geographic information science ▓ 1
                       internet of things engineering ▓▓▓ 3
                        smart science and technology ▓ 1
  department of information management and information ▓ 1
                         smart medical engineering ▓ 1
                            information engineering ▓ 1
                 information countermeasure technology ▓ 1
                                                     0    2    4    6    8    10   12
                                                               count
```

Figure 7:   Key course: DATABASE — in ICT programs at Shanxi universities.
Note: Developed for this study.

4.3.6. *Physics in ICT Programs*

Although ICT is primarily about information and communication technologies, knowledge of Physics enhances comprehension of underlying concepts and phenomena. Physics contributes to ICT in various ways. By incorporating physics, ICT programs offer students a better understanding of the principles of electricity and magnetism, and in comprehending the behavior of waves, optics, and signal propagation, crucial in areas like networking and wireless communication.

The top 20 key ICT courses at Shanxi universities (Figure 2) itemize 12 College Physics courses. Physics is a broader term compared to College Physics in the context of course titles. Therefore, Physics courses are investigated in this section. The programs that provide courses named with *Physics* are plotted in Figure 8.

There is a total of 32 Physics-related courses as shown in Figure 8. They are named as College Physics, University Physics, College Physics Experiment, University Physics Experiment, Introduction to General Physics, and Mathematical Physics Equation.

4.3.7. *Programming in ICT Programs*

Programming has been always an integral and fundamental component of ICT education due to its indispensable role in developing software, applications, and systems. It allows students to transform ideas into tangible solutions, bridging the gap between concepts and implementation. Proficiency in Programming equips students with the skills to develop

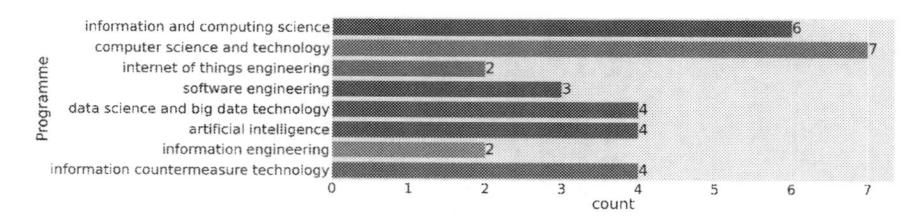

318 Teaching and Learning in the Digital Era: Issues and Studies

Figure 8: Key course: Physics — in ICT programs at Shanxi universities.
Note: Developed for this study.

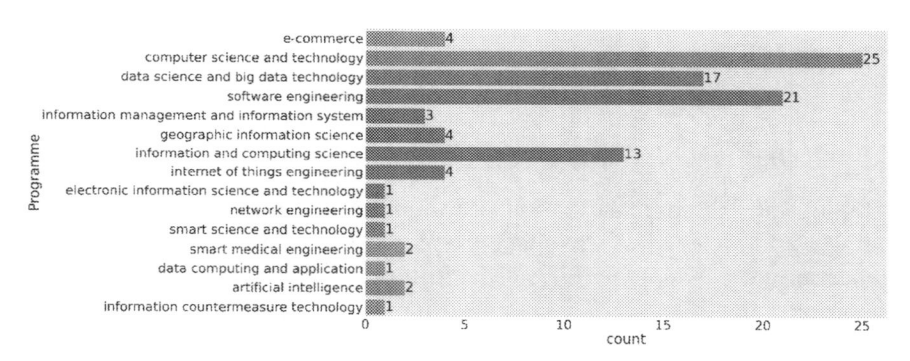

Figure 9: Key course: Programing — in ICT programs at Shanxi universities.
Note: Developed for this study.

websites, mobile apps, algorithms, and automation scripts. Programming can be called the backbone of ICT, empowering students to become effective problem solvers and creators of technological solutions. The findings in Figure 2 showcase a similar outcome. Python, Java, and Object-Oriented are the three major taught Programming courses in ICT programs at Shanxi universities. Through the visualized report in Figure 2, there are in total 31 Programming courses including 11 in Python Programming, 9 in Java Programming, and 11 in Object-Oriented Programming.

Programming is a much broader term in the context of course titles. The programs that provide Programming courses are illustrated in Figure 9.

There are 101 Programming courses out of 1,251 ICT courses as visually plotted in Figure 9. Among the 101 Programming courses available, 19 of them are focused on Java Programming, 17 are dedicated to Python Programming, and the remaining 23 cover Object-Oriented Programming.

Certain Object-Oriented Programming courses explicitly mention a specific programming language in their course names, while others are simply titled "Object-Oriented Programming" without specifying a particular language. The language could be Python, Java, C, or C++. The programs that provide Java, Python, and Object-Oriented are visually presented in Figures 10–12.

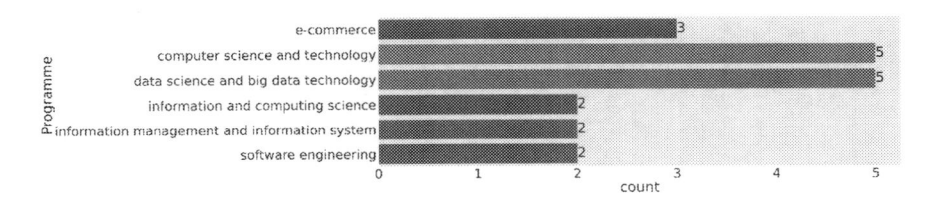

Figure 10: Key course: JAVA — in ICT programs at Shanxi universities.
Note: Developed for this study.

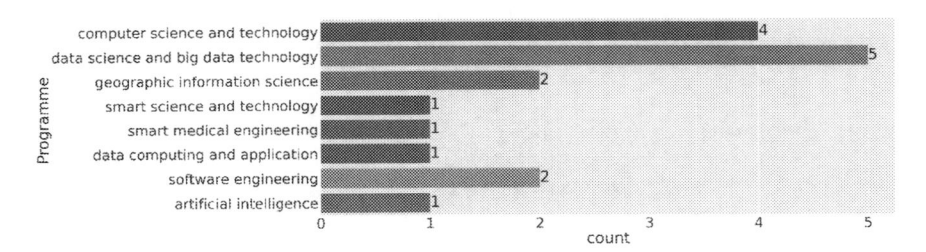

- e-commerce: 3
- computer science and technology: 5
- data science and big data technology: 5
- information and computing science: 2
- information management and information system: 2
- software engineering: 2

Figure 11: Key course: PYTHON — in ICT programs at Shanxi universities.
Note: Developed for this study.

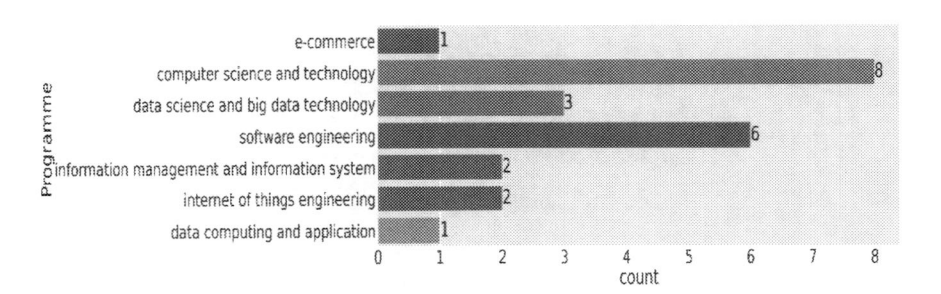

- computer science and technology: 4
- data science and big data technology: 5
- geographic information science: 2
- smart science and technology: 1
- smart medical engineering: 1
- data computing and application: 1
- software engineering: 2
- artificial intelligence: 1

Figure 12: Key course: OBJECT-ORIENTED — in ICT programs at Shanxi universities.
Note: Developed for this study.

- e-commerce: 1
- computer science and technology: 8
- data science and big data technology: 3
- software engineering: 6
- information management and information system: 2
- internet of things engineering: 2
- data computing and application: 1

4.3.8. Digital Image Processing in ICT Program

Digital Image Processing enables the manipulation, analysis, and enhancement of digital images using computational techniques. In today's visually driven world, computer vision, medical imaging, remote sensing, and multimedia systems require the knowledge of Digital Image Processing. Digital Image Processing course teaches students how to extract meaningful information from images, detect patterns, and perform image restoration and enhancement. Proficiency in Digital Image Processing empowers students to develop image-based solutions.

Image Processing is a broader name than Digital Image Processing in terms of course titles. Therefore, in this section, Image Processing is under examination. The programs providing Image Processing-related courses are visually plotted on a count plot (Figure 13).

There are nine courses registered under the name of Digital Image Processing. However, a total of 19 courses are related to Image Processing, such as Image Processing and Pattern Recognition, Remote Sensing and Image Processing, Computer Vision and Image Processing, etc. These 19 courses are provided by 14 ICT programs illustrated in Figure 13.

4.3.9. Principles of Computer Composition in ICT Programs

The Principles of Computer Composition is a fundamental core course in ICT education. It introduces the logical composition and working

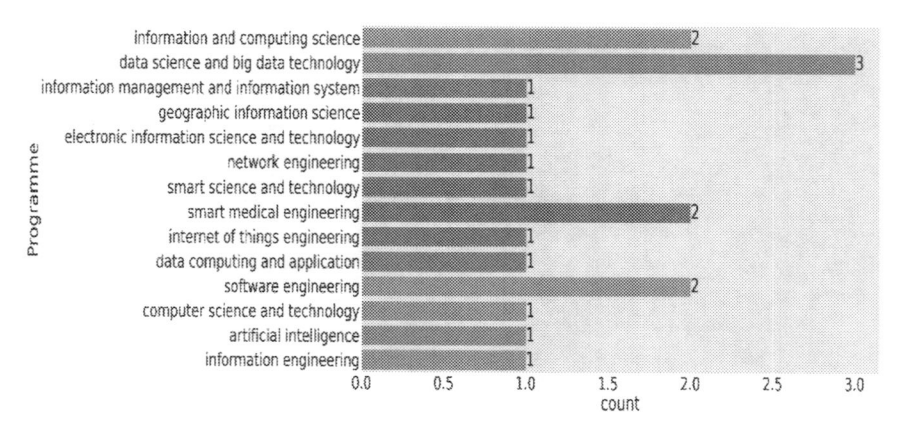

Figure 13: Key course: Image processing — in ICT programs at Shanxi universities.
Note: Developed for this study.

```
                  computer science and technology ████████████████████████████ 8
                 data science and big data technology ████ 2
                      information and computing science ████ 2
                            internet of things engineering ██████ 3
   information management and information system ██ 1
                                  software engineering ██ 1
                                                      0    1    2    3    4    5    6    7    8
                                                                       count
```

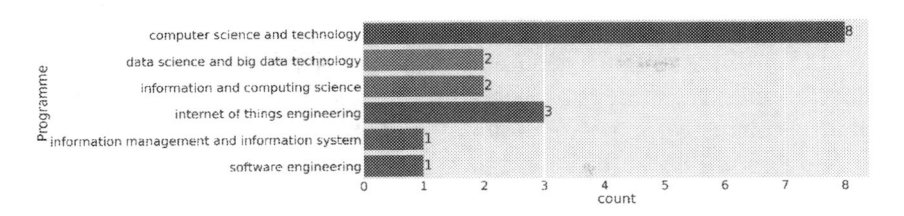

Figure 14: Key course: Computer composition — in ICT programs at Shanxi universities.
Note: Developed for this study.

mechanism of each function of a computer and it helps students to understand digital logic and computer systems.

In this study, Computer Composition is a more encompassing term compared to Principles of Computer Composition. Therefore, in this section, Computer Composition is investigated. The programs providing Computer Composition-related courses are graphically presented on a count plot (Figure 14).

In addition to nine courses in the title of Computer Composition Principle (Figure 2), there are extra eight courses providing Computer Composition-related courses. There is a total of 17 Computer Composition-related courses illustrated in Figure 14, including Computer Composition, Computer Composition and Structure, Computer Composition and Architecture, etc. These courses are provided by six ICT programs.

5. Conclusion

In this study, 51 ICT programs and 1,251 related ICT courses from 11 Shanxi universities in China are collected and analyzed. These universities are the North University of China (UNC), Shanxi Agricultural University (SXAU), Shanxi Datong University (SXDTU), Shanxi Medical University (SXMU), Shanxi Normal University (SXNU), Shanxi University (SXU), Shanxi University of Chinese Medicine (SXUCM), Shanxi University of Finance and Economics (SXUFE), Taiyuan Normal University (TYNU), Taiyuan University of Technology (TYUT), and Taiyuan University of Science and Technology (TYUST). The analysis is conducted based on the downloaded programs and courses to identify the most sought-after ICT programs and the novel ICT programs, and the key courses in the ICT discipline.

Currently, the most sought-after ICT programs primarily center around Information and Computing Science, as well as Computer Science and Technology. These established programs continue to obtain immense popularity among students. In addition, the ever-evolving nature of the ICT field has given rise to novel programs. Two AI-driven programs, including Artificial intelligence, and Intelligence Science and Technology, have emerged in ICT programs. And cross-discipline-oriented AI-driven programs, such as Intelligent Medical Engineering, Intelligent Geographic Science, have also emerged in ICT programs.

In terms of key courses, Mathematics and Programming related courses lay the foundation for ICT programs. Mathematics serves as the essential keystone for ICT programs, encompassing a diverse range of subjects such as Discrete Mathematics, Probability Theory, Advanced Mathematics, Mathematical Statistics, Linear Algebra, Mathematical Analysis, and Advanced Algebra. Mathematical knowledge builds a robust foundation in ICT.

Programming is the most frequently offered course in ICT programs at Shanxi universities. Programming languages, taught at Shanxi universities, are mainly focused on traditional object-oriented languages including Java, Python, C, and C++. Programming courses are not delivered alone. Database-related courses are frequently offered in parallel with programming courses.

In the realm of ICT course design, the significance of the Data Structure course positions a close second to none. It is prioritized as important as Database and Computer Network courses in almost all ICT programs.

Besides the traditional courses such as Operating System, Computer Composition, Physics, Mathematics, Database, and Programming, machine learning-based Digital Image Processing oriented from artificial intelligence is increasingly becoming a crucial component in the modern ICT course design.

This research is limited to the ICT progs in Shanxi universities in China. This research provides an overview of medium-level understanding of ICT education in China's universities. There is a need to conduct further research to understand the top level of ICT education in China. The second limitation is that not all ICT programs or courses are analyzed as not all Shanxi universities display all courses for their ICT programs. For example, e-commerce from TYUST only published 10 courses on the university website.

In today's digital landscape, cloud computing plays a vital role. It allows individuals, businesses, and organizations to store and use data and applications remotely. The cloud also allows the deployment of innovative technologies such as artificial intelligence, big data analytics, and the Internet of Things (IoT). Consequently, with the increased reliance on cloud computing comes the need for robust cybersecurity measures. It is also recommended that more courses in the context of Cloud Computing and Cybersecurity should be implemented for the ICT programs at Shanxi universities.

Comprehensive knowledge and skills are required in today's interconnected world. Future work lies in the investigation of the emerging ICT courses related to cloud computing, cyber security, virtualization, virtual reality, machine learning, and so forth. In addition, future work involves assessing differences between the ICT course design and the job market needs.

Acknowledgment

The authors would like to express their sincere gratitude to Huan Zhang for assisting with data collection.

References

Afari, E., Eksail, F.A.A., Khine, M.S. & Alaam, S.A. (2023). Computer self-efficacy and ICT integration in education: Structural relationship and mediating effects. *Education and Information Technologies*, 28, 12021–12037.

Ali, W. (2020). Online and remote learning in higher education institutes: A necessity in light of COVID-19 pandemic. *Higher Education Studies*, 10(3), 16–25.

Burov, O., Butnik-Siversky, O., Orliuk, O. & Horska, K. (2020). Cybersecurity and innovative digital educational environment. *Information Technologies and Learning Tools*, 80(6), 414–430.

Davenport, T.H. & Ronanki, R. (2018). Artificial intelligence for the real world. *Harvard Business Review*, 96(1), 108–116.

Gide, E. & Wu, M.X. (2004). Developing a framework of e-commerce program for higher educational institution. In *Proceedings on the 2nd Sino-America Advanced Workshop in Electronic Commerce & the 3rd Conference on E-Commerce Major Establishment in China's Universities*, pp. 633–637, June 20–24, 2004, Chengdu, China.

Gov (2021). The fourteenth five-year plan for national economic and social development and the vision 2035 in China. Accessed on June 21, 2023. Retrieved from https://www.gov.cn/xinwen/2021-03/13/content_5592681.htm.

Hassan, R.H., Hassan, M.T., Naseer, S., Khan, Z. & Jeon, M. (2021). ICT enabled TVET education: A systematic literature review. *IEEE Access*, 9, 81624–81650.

Hou, W.Y., Wu, M.X. & Soar, J. (2020). Internationalization of China's e-commerce higher education: A review between 2001 and 2019. In R.M.X. Wu & M. Mircea (ed.), *E-Business-Higher Education and Intelligence Applications*. London: IntechOpen.

Huang, F., Zuo, J. & Zhang, G. (2022). Application of cloud computing in applied undergraduate education and management. In *International Conference on Computer Science, Engineering and Education Applications*, pp. 462–474.

Huang, X. (2021). Aims for cultivating students' key competencies based on artificial intelligence education in China. *Education and Information Technologies*, 26(5), 5127–5147.

Janowicz, K., Gao, S., McKenzie, G., Hu, Y. & Bhaduri, B. (2020). GeoAI: Spatially explicit artificial intelligence techniques for geographic knowledge discovery and beyond. *International Journal of Geographical Information Science*, 34(4), 625–636.

Johansson, R. (2007). On case study methodology. *Open House International*, 32(3), 48–54.

Latorre-Cosculluela, C., Sierra-Sánchez, V., Rivera-Torres, P. & Liesa Orús, M. (2023). ICT efficacy and response to different needs in university classrooms: Effects on attitudes and active behaviour towards technology. *Journal of Computing in Higher Education*, 1–18.

Malik, P., Pathania, M. & Rathaur, V.K. (2019). Overview of artificial intelligence in medicine. *Journal of Family Medicine and Primary Care*, 8(7), 2328.

Ministry of Education of the People's Republic of China (2023). The guidelines for educational informatization. Accessed on June 27, 2023. Retrieved from http://www.moe.gov.cn/jyb_xwfb/gzdt_gzdt/s5987/201608/t20160816_274443.html.

Peciuliauskiene, P., Tamoliune, G. & Trepule, E. (2022). Exploring the roles of information search and information evaluation literacy and pre-service teachers' ICT self-efficacy in teaching. *International Journal of Educational Technology in Higher Education*, 19(1), 33–33.

Pham, Q.D., Dao, N.N., Nguyen, Thanh, T., Cho, S. & Pham, H.C. (2021). Detachable web-based learning framework to overcome immature ICT infrastructure toward smart education. *IEEE Access*, 9, 34951–34961.

Sun, H., Xie, Y. & Lavonen, J. (2022). Effects of the use of ICT in schools on students' science higher-order thinking skills: Comparative study of China and Finland. *Research in Science & Technological Education*, 1–18.

Toddy, P., Febrostti, D. & Rahgheanti (2020). Artificial intelligence for education policy in Wuhan City, China. *IOP Conf. Series: Earth and Environmental Science*, (717), 12037.

Ünal, E., Uzun, A.M. & Kilis, S. (2022). Does ICT involvement really matter? An investigation of Turkey's case in PISA 2018. *Education and Information Technologies*, 27(8), 11443–11465.

Urban-Lurain, M. & Weinshank, D.J. (2000, October). Is there a role for programming in non-major computer science courses? In *30th Annual Frontiers in Education Conference. Building on a Century of Progress in Engineering Education. Conference Proceedings*, IEEE Cat. No. 00CH37135, Vol. 1, pp. T2B-7. IEEE.

Wambuaa, M.R.N. & Oduorb, C. (2022). Implications of internet of things (IoT) on the education for students with disabilities. *A Systematic Literature Review*, 102(1), 30.

Wang, Q. & Zhao, G. (2021). ICT self-efficacy mediates most effects of university ICT support on preservice teachers' TPACK: Evidence from three normal universities in China. *British Journal of Educational Technology*, 52(6), 2319–2339.

Wei, G., Bi, M., Liu, X., Zhang, Z. & He, B.J. (2023). Investigating the impact of multi-dimensional urbanization and FDI on carbon emissions in the belt and road initiative region: Direct and spillover effects. *Journal of Cleaner Production*, 384, 135608.

Wu, M.X. & Yu, P. (2006). Challenges and opportunities facing Australian universities caused by the internationalisation of Chinese higher education. *International Education Journal*, 7(3), 211–221.

Xu, J. & Zhu, Y. (2023). Factors influencing the use of ICT to support students' self-regulated learning in digital environment: The role of teachers in lower secondary education of Shanghai, China. *Psychology in the Schools*. Doi.org/10.1002/pits.22938.

Zafar, M.W., Zaidi, S.A.H., Mansoor, S., Sinha, A. & Qin, Q. (2022). ICT and education as determinants of environmental quality: The role of financial development in selected Asian countries. *Technological Forecasting & Social Change*, 177, 121547.

Zeng, W. (2022). An empirical research on China's policy for ICT integration in Basic Education from 1988 to 2021. *Educational Technology Research and Development*, 70(3), 1059–1082.

Chapter 14

Technologies and Student Feedback Collection and Analysis

Gazi Farid Hossain, Deb Case, and Caitlin Smith

King's Own Institute, Australia

Abstract

Technology-enabled feedback encompasses many significant features including AI. It also allows students greater flexibility in providing feedback, and the university/institute enables them to make data-driven decisions as the collected data are free from bias and data analyses are accurate. There are different technology-centric feedback collections such as Open edX Insight, speech-to-text, Kahoot, Dialogflow, and so on. These technology-centric feedback collections mean collecting more realistic data from the students. Both qualitative and quantitative data could be analyzed by applying technology-centric data analyses tools. AMOS, LABLEAU, SAS, SPSS, Stata, Statista, XLSTAT, and ROOT are a few of the quantitative data analyses software, and Atlas, Airtable, Coda, Condens, MaxQDA, Notion, and NVivo are a few of the qualitative data analyses software. To make the students' feedback and survey more successful we recommend sharing survey methods/survey questions with other educational institutions, conducting broader surveys, broad topics to ask questions on, technology-based analysis of qualitative feedback comments, and including skills development-focused questions.

Keywords: Student survey, Student feedback, Survey, Data analysis, KOI, Best practices.

1. Introduction

Student feedback can provide higher education institutions with new insights and help to identify improvements in course delivery and teaching methods. Student feedback collects students' views and can assess student satisfaction and engagement with their studies. The purpose of student feedback is to improve the quality of teaching and improve student outcomes. There are numerous significant aspects of students' feedback. Students are the main recipients in the classroom. The intellectual level, depth of knowledge, resources, and other circumstances could vary in the classroom. Therefore, the same teaching strategies may not be effective in every place. Student feedback can assist teachers to customize according to the needs of the students. Based on the specific needs of the concerned students, the teaching strategies could be modified and improved. In addition, the institution could provide the supporting resources according to the concerned students' needs. This feedback not only yields useful insights for university administrators and instructors but also plays a key role in influencing student decisions on which universities to attend or courses to take. Usually, the feedback is collected during the course or at the end of the course to analyze teachers' performance and other factors (Rani & Kumar, 2017).

However, not all student feedback is effective and may, in some cases, provide inconsistent or inaccurate information. In many cases either the student feedback questionnaires are inappropriate or the feedback given by the students is inconsistent or inaccurate. Technological advances have led to significant changes in the way student feedback is collected and analyzed. It's important to continue to examine the effects of applying new technologies to the task of collecting student feedback. The merits and consequences of adopting new developments, such as artificial intelligence, need to be analyzed.

2. KOI's Survey Process

Student Experience Surveys typically aim to capture student feedback about the quality of teaching students, as well as information about whether students feel supported, are engaged with the study process, and what their opinions are about their learning resources and the overall learning experience.

King's Own Institute (KOI) is a tertiary-level institution offering high-quality accredited degree courses in Sydney and Newcastle, Australia. At KOI, an online survey is emailed to all students every trimester requesting feedback about the teaching performance of their lecturers and their study experience at KOI. It's important to distinguish this survey from feedback provided by teachers about students — their study progress and performance — which is not under discussion here.

The internal KOI survey, called the Student Evaluation of Teaching and Subjects (SETS), is conducted online each trimester through the Moodle Learning Management System (LMS) using the feedback activity. The feedback activity used to conduct the survey allows for the setup of customized questions covering topics regarding teaching, subjects, online learning, and learning resources, with students providing feedback for each of their subjects and teachers.

The survey is voluntary and conducted toward the end of the trimester after most major assessments have been completed, as this allows for more accurate data to be collected about opinions on subject assessments. Requests and reminders are sent out before and after the surveys, and an extension of one week is granted if the overall response rate is low. The response rate to this survey is currently 40%–50%.

Data is extracted from the surveys and individual student responses are collated and totaled to produce an overall rating for each subject and teacher. Quantitative data is processed using spreadsheets.

Qualitative data, in the form of student free-form comments, is manually reviewed and summarized. The data can be analyzed and assessed by the school, with an average total for each question.

The survey process used at KOI is described in a publicly available Student Feedback Policy.

Staff at KOI also leverage national standards and sample questions when reviewing and formulating new survey questions.

2.1. *KOI's Survey Questions*

The KOI Student Evaluation of Teaching and Subjects survey questions focus on four areas; teaching, subject, online learning, and learning resources. The questions are periodically reviewed and updated. Below are two examples of question sets used at KOI.

The following question set shown in Sample A was used to collect students' feedback up until May 2023.

Sample A. "Student Evaluation of Teaching and Subjects" Survey Questions

---

Section 1: Teaching
Ratings: 1 (Strongly disagree) to 5 (strongly agree)
(Q1) This teacher communicated well with the class
(Q2) This teacher seemed enthusiastic about teaching the class
(Q3) This teacher created a good environment for learning
(Q4) This teacher used methods and techniques that were effective in helping me to learn
(Q5) The feedback I received from this teacher helped my learning
(Q6) This teacher showed genuine interest in assisting students' learning

Section 2: Subject
Ratings: 1 (Strongly disagree) to 5 (strongly agree)
(Q7) The learning outcomes in this subject were made clear
(Q8) I am satisfied with the assessment tasks in this subject
(Q9) The workload demands of the subject are about right
(Q10) This subject helped me to develop some valuable skills/attributes
(Q11) I am satisfied with the way this subject was taught/delivered
(Q12) Overall, I am satisfied with this subject
(Optional) Any other comments about the teacher or the subject?

Section 3: Online Learning
(Optional) What were the best things about online learning?
(Optional) What aspects of online learning could be improved?

Section 4: Learning Resources
(Q13) Have you used any of the following databases within the last trimester? (Multiple answers)

- *EBSCO Databases*
- *Emerald Insight*
- *IBISWorld*
- *IGI Global*
- *ProQuest eBooks*
- *O'Reilly Learning*
- *None of the above*

Thinking of this trimester, overall how would you rate the following learning resources?
Ratings: 1 (Poor) to 5 (excellent)
(Q14) Teaching spaces (e.g., lecture theatres, tutorial rooms, laboratories)
(Q15) Student spaces and common areas
(Q16) Online learning materials
(Q17) Computing/IT resources
(Q18) Assigned books, notes and resources
(Q19) Library resources and facilities
(Q20) How would you rate the accessibility (easy to find and/or obtain) of our current collection of textbooks and learning resources to this subject
(Q21) Would you prefer print or online text resources for this subject?

2.2. KOI's Current Survey

The question set shown in sample B has been used to collect the students' feedback since September 2023.

Sample B. Current Survey Question Set

Section 1: Teaching
Ratings: 1 (Strongly disagree) to 5 (strongly agree)
(Q1) This teacher communicated well with the class and made it clear what I am expected to accomplish in this subject
(Q2) This teacher seemed enthusiastic about teaching the class
(Q3) This teacher created a good environment for learning
(Q4) This teacher used methods, technologies, and techniques that were effective in helping me to learn
(Q5) The feedback I received from this teacher was timely and helped my learning
(Q6) This teacher showed genuine interest in assisting students' learning
(Q7) The teacher encouraged students to ask questions and express opinions
(Q8) This teacher was well-prepared for the class
(Q9) This teacher had a good knowledge of the subject area
(Q10) Overall, I am satisfied with the teaching of this teacher

Section 2: Subject
Ratings: 1 (Strongly disagree) to 5 (strongly agree)
(Q11) The learning outcomes and performance requirements in this subject were made clear
(Q12) I am satisfied with the assessment tasks in this subject
(Q13) The workload demands of the subject are about right

(Q14) This subject helped me to develop some valuable skills/attributes and enhance my learning and/or contribute to my future career
(Q15) There were opportunities for students to collaborate and work as a team
(Q16) I am satisfied with the way this subject was taught/delivered
(Q17) I feel engaged in my learning experience at KOI
(Q18) Overall, I am satisfied with this subject
(Q19) Any other comments about the teacher or the subject?

Section 3: Online Learning
(Q20) What were the best things about Online Learning? (Optional)
(Q21) What aspects of Online Learning could be improved? (Optional)
(Q22) What were the best things about Hybrid Learning? (Optional)
(Q23) What aspects of Hybrid Learning could be improved. (Optional)

Section 4: Learning Resources
(Q24) Have you used any of the following databases within the last trimester? (Multiple answers)

- EBSCO Databases
- Emerald Insight
- IBISWorld
- IGI Global
- ProQuest eBooks
- O'Reilly Learning
- None of the above

Thinking of this trimester, overall how would you rate the following learning resources?
Ratings: 1 (Poor) to 5 (excellent)
(Q25) Teaching spaces (e.g., lecture theatres, tutorial rooms, laboratories)
(Q26) Student spaces and common areas
(Q27) IT support
(Q28) Student services
(Q29) Academic services
(Q30) Online learning materials
(Q31) Computing/IT resources
(Q32) Assigned books, notes and resources
(Q33) Library resources and facilities
(Q34) How would you rate the accessibility (easy to find and/or obtain) of our current collection of textbooks and learning resources for this subject
(Q35) Would you prefer print or online text resources for this subject?

2.3. KOI Survey Method

A mix of qualitative and quantitative methods works best for online surveys. Quantitative research relates to collating statistics whilst the aim of qualitative research is to gather opinions and comments in detail. At KOI a number of the survey questions put to students are rated on a numerical scale; 1 (Strongly disagree) to 5 (strongly agree), and the results are then collated to give an overall tally for a specific teacher or class. In addition, students are invited to provide free-form comments about some topics, should they choose to do so.

A few examples of qualitative questions are: "Any other comments about the teacher or the subject?", "What were the best things about online learning?", and "What aspects of online learning could be improved?"

2.4. Drawbacks of Current KOI Practice

2.4.1. Lacks in Software to Analyze Quantitative Data

There are many sophisticated and technology-based software to analyze quantitative data. AMOS and TABLEAU are a few of them. Some universities and non-university higher degree institutes including KOI apply Excel to analyze the quantitative data. Due to its limitations Excel is not fully useful and effective in every quantitative data analysis.

2.4.2. Manual Analysis of Qualitative Feedback Comments

Although the students' survey is conducted online using KOI's LMS, Moodle, the students' qualitative comments are analyzed manually. This is not only time-consuming but also expensive. There may also be some doubts about the reliability and acceptability of such manual analysis.

2.4.3. Skills Development-Focused Questions Are Missing

As discussed earlier, KOI students' survey questions have four areas: teaching-focused, subject-focused, online learning-focused, and learning resources-focused, while the Australian national survey encompasses five types of questions including skills development-focused questions. As the current business success and employment opportunities are skill-based, it is tremendously important to include skills development-focused questions in the student survey.

3. Australian National Survey

In Australia, the government provides survey formats for higher education institutions called Quality Indicators for Learning and Teaching (QILT). These are government-endorsed surveys that university and non-university institutions can use to conduct their own student surveys. This practice helps to promote best practices throughout Australia.

In addition, the Social Research Centre conducts surveys on behalf of the Department of Education. This data is collated and published to provide an annual snapshot of annual data. All higher education institutions are eligible to participate in this program, and approximately 42 Australian universities and 90 non-university higher education providers take part in the surveys. KOI participates in these surveys and is provided with summaries of the data.

Tableau software is used to generate spreadsheets containing quantitative data, as well as summary PowerPoint slides.

The Student Experience Survey (SES) measures:

- Skills development
- Learner engagement
- Teaching Quality
- Student Support
- Learning resources

In the most recent survey, "The main online survey took place in August 2022, with a secondary collection in September–October 2022 for trimester institutions. A broad range of promotional materials was provided to institutions to raise awareness of the SES and encourage participation amongst the target population."

4. Why Technology-Enabled Survey?

There is no doubt that not every students' survey is effective, especially the non-technology-based survey because of the inconsistencies in responses and/or poor analyses of data. The technology-enabled survey already demonstrated its abilities relating to consistencies in responses, accuracies in data analyses, greater accessibilities for the students, efficiencies in administering, and enhancing the response rates significantly because of the fun nature.

Technology-enabled survey ensures a consistent response from the students as it eliminates manual errors in data entry. Moreover, technology-enabled survey doesn't allow to skip the mandatory question. In other words, it makes sure that the respondent students answer all required questions, otherwise they can't proceed to the next question.

Technology-enabled survey also ensures accuracies in both qualitative and quantitative data analyses as it applies data analyses software. AMOS, LABLEAU, SAS, SPSS, Stata, Statista, XLSTAT, and ROOT are few of the quantitative data analyses software, and Atlas, Airtable, Coda, Condens, MaxQDA, Notion, and NVivo are few of the qualitative data analyses software. Accuracy in analyzing the data by applying the above-mentioned software is very high, almost every case it is 100%.

In addition to the consistencies in responses and accuracies in data analyses, technology-enabled survey is significant due to its greater accessibility. The respondent students could access to survey through Internet, LMS, mobile apps, and so on. Technology-enabled survey not only relies on formal students' survey once in a semester/trimester, it also may include discussion boards, quizzes, SurveyMonkey, Google forms, Microsoft forms, pools, quick survey, rating, and so on.

Moreover, the technology-enabled survey allows the university/institute to have access to the data-driven insights. Such data-driven insights aid the university/institute in making evidence-based decisions, especially to improve and develop their curriculum, classroom teaching strategies, and students' success and satisfaction.

5. Different AI Tools That Could Be Applied in Students' Survey

Uses of Artificial Intelligence (AI) in higher education institutes (HEIs) are being developed at an increasing pace (Rodway & Schepman, 2023). In recent years a significant number of AI has been developed which can be applied in HEIs. In addition to teaching and learning, AI's most transformative impact could be collecting and analyzing students' feedback on teaching.

Facial recognition cameras: Nowadays face recognition cameras are becoming more sophisticated and feature-rich. Artificial intelligence (AI) are built into cameras, hence it can now reliably tell the genuine survey and ingenuine survey. In other words, Artificial intelligence will examine the facial expressions of the students during the survey and their responses. For example, artificial intelligence will assess whether the facial expression of a particular student is normal or unusual. Unusual facial expressions could be angry, dull, or frustrated. It is obvious that while one student has an unusual or abnormal mood, his or her responses may not be very realistic.

Time taken: Artificial intelligence will assess the time taken by the students to complete the survey with the standard time. If the student took 30% or more less time than the standard time, then it could be concluded that the response is unrealistic. In some cases, the respondents do not read the questions, just pick any given answer to complete the survey as quickly as they can.

Knewton: It is an adaptive learning platform that can provide survey questions to students using learning management systems; such as Moodle or Blackboard. Knewton can assist in creating customized questions; both qualitative and quantitative. AI is at the core of Knewton's value proposition, as its ability to personalize content to students is dependent on its AI algorithm. Knewton trained its product with over 25,000 beta testers to identify knowledge gaps in users and figure out what content worked best at remediating those knowledge gaps (Knewton, 2023).

Dialogflow: A Google-powered chatbot development platform that can help universities or non-university higher degree institutions create their own students' survey platform. Dialogflow delivers more natural and genuine experiences for the students with virtual agents that support multi-turn conversations with supplemental questions and are built with deep learning technologies. Dialogflow prepares the survey once and deploys everywhere — via the contact centers and digital channels. Seamlessly it integrates the students across platforms, including web, mobile, and messenger (Dialogflow, 2023).

Open edX Insight: A free, open-source learning analytics platform that can help educators track student progress and engagement. Open edX

Insight can help universities or non-university higher degree institutions in monitoring how students are doing, and validate the choices course coordinators made in designing their courses. It can also help to re-evaluate choices and inform efforts to improve the courses and the experience of the students. Putting the data provided by edX Insights to work involves:

- Evaluating reported data against the expectations and hypotheses.
- Understanding the context of the survey run: the environmental factors and choices that make each run unique.
- Deciding whether action is called for.
- Selecting the action to take, and when (Open edX Insights, 2023).

Speech-to-text: A speech recognition API that can be used to develop voice-controlled students' surveys. Especially, to collect the qualitative data Speech-to-Text could be the best tool to apply. A significant number of students, particularly international students, skip the qualitative feedback to complete the survey quickly. For example, approximately 80% KOI students provide no information or make no comments relating to the open-ended qualitative questions. Speech-to-Text could be the motivator in this circumstance for providing adequate information and/or making comments (Speech-to-Text, 2023).

Classcraft: With access to high-fidelity early intervention data, the management can see how students are really progressing. Classcraft also assists in identifying the students who need assistance to progress. Lecturers and tutors can identify and manage how each and every student is achieving the assessment and overall in the classroom applying the Classcraft. It also helps Lecturers and tutors to engage students and promote positive behavior among the students (Classcraft, 2023).

OpenCV: An open-source computer vision library that can be used for a variety of educational purposes, such as object detection, face recognition, and tracking. It is discussed earlier that facial recognition cameras could be applied to gather correct feedback from the students. OpenCV could be another option (Mygreatlearning, 2023).

Kahoot!: A game-based learning platform that can be used to create quizzes to collect students feedback on teaching, courses, resources, and others. As Kahoot is a game-based quiz, students will love to participate because it's fun! (Kahoot, 2023).

These are just a few examples of the many free AI tools that educators and students can use to explore the applications of AI in education.

6. Technology Benefits for Analyzing Qualitative Feedback

Advanced technologies allow students to engage in a student-centered approach to learning (Rodway & Schepman, 2023). Colleges and universities that provide access to engage with these technologies offer their students a world of connection, inspiration, and a leg up upon entering the job market. Student access to classroom technology fosters a stronger sense of self-worth and motivation. Feeling a sense of connection to the real world allows students to build confidence in their abilities to engage in professional settings upon graduation. High-tech colleges prepare students for professional opportunities, making it easier for them to enter workplace environments. In addition to feeling more confident, students develop the skills to use new technologies applicable to various employment opportunities.

While positive student experiences involve many factors — such as individualized support, and regular reassessments of whether courses are designed to achieve learning objectives — studies have found that effective use of educational technology is an important component of student-centric learning experiences (Zitter, 2021). A 2019 study published in the *International Journal of Action Research* found that digital tools promote "interactive learning, timely feedback, and better engagement with students." In a similar vein, a recent Promethean survey found that 86% of educators believe technology is a powerful way to engage students.

At KOI all comments in student survey feedback are manually reviewed. They are classified as good, bad, or neutral comments, and a summary is created.

Using an online survey to capture data is faster than using manual forms, not least because it's not necessary to transcribe all the comments. The comments typed into the survey by the students are automatically captured.

The current rise of artificial intelligence technologies raises the question of whether it may be possible in the future to use artificial intelligence to classify, analyze, or summarize qualitative review feedback. There is currently some experimentation with ChatGPT and qualitative analysis.

During analysis of survey feedback comments, it may turn out that using artificial intelligence tools may be faster, more efficient, more objective, and help maintain the anonymity of survey participants.

On the other hand, data privacy issues may need to be considered, in terms of protecting the data once it has been collected.

7. Best Practices

Not all institutions conduct institution-wide surveys and of those that do, not all provide feedback. There was, therefore, not a wide enough sample from which to draw conclusions on what might be considered best practices. The "best" style of presentation and issues that should be presented depends upon an institution's size, students, the facilities available, and the courses and aspects of student experiences that were surveyed. For example, a small college with a fairly homogeneous group of students may only need to provide feedback using one method, whereas an institution with a large number of faculties and a diverse student body would be wise to use a variety of methods to ensure that as many students as possible are aware of the results and actions of the survey (Watson, 2003).

8. Applying AI Tools for More Complex Data Analysis

A useful avenue for future research will be the question of whether artificial intelligence tools can be applied to larger amounts of data to gain deeper insights, perhaps beyond the actual survey response data. For example, is it possible to investigate and establish a correlation between survey responses and other student characteristics, such as class attendance statistics? Other information sources already held by the academic institution may be usefully harvested to further support the insights gleaned from student surveys.

Existing and newly emerging technologies, such as exam proctoring tools, may have some application in the field of conducting student surveys. While not discounting important privacy and ethical concerns, useful insights may be gained from observing student facial expressions when they are completing surveys.

There has been some research into whether feedback comments are affected by the nature of the survey format, for example, online survey formats have been shown to elicit an 'online disinhibition effect' where students are more likely to write frank or negative comments because they feel less inhibited online (Gakhal & Wilson, 2019).

9. Recommendations

Sharing survey methods/survey questions with other educational institutions: Survey methods and/or survey questions; such as technology used, actual findings and results applied by the other universities and non-university higher degree institutes could be shared. Especially, the technology-based methods could be shared among the universities and non-university higher degree institutes. This will enable the universities and non-university higher degree institutes to adopt the best practices with technologies.

Conduct broader surveys: It is really important for the universities and non-university higher degree institutes to add more questions and more varied topics in the students' survey. For example, additional questions for 3rd year students — asking them to reflect on their study experience/knowledge gained, and skill development compared to the experience and knowledge they had as first year students.

Broad topics to ask questions on: It is also important for the universities and non-university higher degree institutes to include questions on sports or other social opportunities, internship, the experience of being an international student, or just open-ended questions asking what further resources students would like to see at KOI.

Technology based analysis of qualitative feedback comments: As discussed earlier, the manual analysis of qualitative data is time consuming and expensive, and there may be doubts about the reliability of the interpreted data. Current and future developments in artificial intelligence will facilitate more technology-based analyses of qualitative feedback comments in the future.

Include skills development focused questions: Skills, both practical and theoretical, are the main indicator of graduate to be successful in the job market. As a result, skills development-focused questions should be included in the students' survey.

10. Conclusions

Students' survey is one of the significant tools not only gathering students' feedback on teaching, learning and resources but also improving the teaching qualities, advancing students' knowledge, skills, and experience, as well as increasing university/institute's reputations and acceptancy in the society. The main challenge in students' survey is the effectiveness of survey. There is no doubt that not all students' surveys have equal consequences in terms of improvements. Technology-enabled survey has specific innovative features what makes it successful in every aspect. One of the significant features of technology-enabled survey is the AI. AI makes the survey questions interactive, interesting and fun oriented what attract more students to complete the survey. In addition, technology-enabled survey offers more options and flexibilities to take part in the survey. It also enables the administrators to determine the real and unreal responses using the facial recognition system and assessing the time taken to complete the survey.

References

Australian Government Department of Education (2023). Quality Indicators for Learning and Teaching. Accessed on August 30, 2023. Available at https://www.qilt.edu.au/#surveys.

Classcraft (2023). Classcraft for teachers. Available at: https://www.classcraft.com/ (Accessed 28 July 2023).

Dialogflow (2023). Chatbots for B2C conversations. Available at: https://cloud.google.com/dialogflow (Accessed 20 June 2023).

Gakhal, S. & Wilson, C. (2019). Is students' qualitative feedback changing, now it is online? *Assessment & Evaluation in Higher Education*, 44(3), 476–488.

Kahoot, 2023. Kahoot! Academy. Available at: https://kahoot.com/academy/study/ (Accessed 19 July 2023).

King's Own Institute (2023). Student feedback policy. Accessed on August 30, 2023. Available at https://koi.edu.au/wp-content/uploads/2023/05/KOI_StudentFeedbackPolicy_15May2023.pdf.

Knewton, 2023. Pathways to a Just Digital Futurere. Available at: https://d3.harvard.edu/platform-digit/submission/knewton-personalizes-learning-with-the-power-of-ai/ (Accessed 2 June 2023).

Moodle (2023). Feedback activity. — MoodleDocs. Accessed on August 30, 2023. Available at https://docs.moodle.org/311/en/Feedback_activity.

Mygreatlearning 2023. A Guide to Learn OpenCV in Python. Available at: https://www.mygreatlearning.com/blog/opencv-tutorial-in-python/ (Accessed 17 July 2023).

Rani, S. & Kumar, P. (2017). A sentiment analysis system to improve teaching and learning. *Computer*, 50(5), 36–43.

Rodway, P. & Schepman, A. (2023). The impact of adopting AI educational technologies on projected course satisfaction in university students. *Computers and Education: Artificial Intelligence*, 5 (100150), 1–12.

Watson, S. (2003). Closing the feedback loop: Ensuring effective action from student feedback. *Tertiary Education and Management*, 9(2), 145–157.

Zitter, L. (2021). *What Technologies Do Colleges Need to Support Modern Students?* Washington: EdTech Focus on Higher Education.

Index

A
academic dishonesty, 194
academic integrity, 139, 194–195
academic integrity in the age of digital era, 65
academic misconduct, 173
achieving better results, 216
actions taken by education providers to minimize instances of plagiarism/cheating included, 170
active learning, 25
active learning strategies, 227
adaptive learning, 25
adoption of AI, 36
AI capabilities in the organization, 35
AI-powered adaptive learning, 129
AI tools for identifying suitable candidates, 30
AI tools for writing job requirements and providing services to candidates, 31
AI tools that could be applied in students' survey, 335
Alice, 251
All ICT programs at Shanxi universities, 310
analyzing collected information and providing forecasting, 30
applications/systems supporting personalized learning, 68
ARCS Model of Motivational Design Theories, 219
artificial intelligence (AI), 5, 35
artificial intelligence (AI) in higher education institutes (HEIs), 335
assessment
    fraud, 142
    integrity, 139
    reform to accommodate online learning, 170
    security, 139
    in an online education, 139
    types, 166
asynchronous discussion forums, 227
augmented Reality (AR), 57
Australian National Survey, 334
authentic assessments, 175
authentication, 140
automation, AI and Robotics future impact on employment and job safety, 19

B
barriers/challenges/issues of e-learning, 12
behaviorism, 238

benefits, 88
benefits of creating engaging lessons, 215
benefits of GBL in programming, 242
benefits of online learning, 217
best selection algorithms for data classifications, 284
big data, 292
    in Education, 292
    in Education and Curriculum Development, 293
    software Leximancer, 296
blended learning, 65
business strategy, 31

C
CART, 283
case studies on GBL for programming courses, 246
challenge of creating engaging lessons, 216
challenge of online learning, 218
challenges faced during the implementation of GBL, 243
challenges in addressing assessment integrity, 145
challenges in the use of AI-based digital proctoring tools, 156
challenges in using big data, 297
challenges of personalized learning, 69
changing student demographics and unstable student enrolment, 7
ChatGPT, 87
ChatGPT 3.5, 88
Chat-GPT-4, 88
ChatGPT benefits to higher education, 89
ChatGPT implementation strategies/ success factors for higher education providers, 95
ChatGPT limitations, concerns and issues related to higher education, 91
cheating, 194, 196
China's educational institutions, 306
Chi-Square, 284
Classcraft, 337
Cloud, 56
CodeCombat 9, 251
cognitive load, 54
cognitivism, 238
collaborate and communicate with each other and teachers, 53
collaborative and social learning, 131
collaborative projects, 228
collusion, 197
common forms of academic dishonesty, 142
common types of academic misconduct include, 196
communication and collaboration tools, 125
competence-based learning, 27
competence-based learning vs. traditional classroom learning, 10
competition for talent, 11
concentrating on technological infrastructure and standards deployment, 32
connectivity and community building, 31
constructivism, 238
contract cheating, 144, 196
control of circumstances, 141
corporate e-learning, 22
course management, 124
course signals, 266
COVID-19, 40, 137, 168, 216
creating learning experiences and resources, 32
curated content, 230

current academic integrity practices, 203
current practices for online assignments at KOI, 203
current practices for online exams at KOI, 205

D

data analytics for personalization, 131
data mining, 268
data privacy breaches, 298
dealing with automation/digitization issues, 9
dealing with inquiries and provide 24/7 personalized services, 30
decentralized learning, 28
deciding learning/delivery models, 7
decision tree algorithm, 283
decision trees, 281
deep learning, 282
demanded citizens skills for future work, 39
demand for better learning experiences, 9
detecting content generated by ChatGPT and other AI tools, 98
determinants of student retention, 261
developing marketing materials, 30
developing strong academic integrity policies, 199
Dialogflow, 336
different skills needed, 10
digital assessment tools, 149
digital citizenship, 74
digital skills, 5
digital technology types used in higher education, 56
digital technologies, 3–4
disparity between ICT education in China and worldwide ICT education, 306
disruptions to the education sector, 6
drawbacks of current KOI practice, 333

E

early detection learning analytic tool, 266
easy access to information, 67
EDMODO, 60
education organizations' changes and challenges, 6
education systems in the digital age, 138
educational data mining (EDM), 280
educational data mining and learning, 292
educational learning analytics, 267
effective online assessment design, 172
effective questioning, 227
E-learning and Online Learning Platforms, 285
e-learning, 11, 122
emerging trends in learning management system (LMS), 128
emerging trends in online education, 128
engaged learning, 219
engagement — maintaining attention, 226
engaging presentations, 230
engaging, 215
enhancing classroom learning experiences, 24
enjoying class, 216
ethical considerations in the use of digital tools, 158
Euclidean distance, 284
evaluation of teaching and learning, 29

examples of games to teach programming, 251
ExamRoom.AI, 154
ExamSoft, 155
Examus, 154
experiential learning, 27
exploring additional education market, 9
external environment issues, 11

F

Fabrication, 196
facial recognition cameras, 336
facilitators of academic misconduct that are enabled in the age of digital era, 67
factors can directly affect student engagement, 284
factors need to be considered when education providers embark on learning analytics, 73
Fast-growing operating costs, 8
financial viability issues, 7
finding student study patterns and footprints on LMS, 269
first impressions, 220
focusing on access and equity, 10
focusing on internal capabilities and needs, 32
formative assessment, 138, 166
fostering a culture of academic integrity, 200
fundamental goal of education, 138
future skills, future trends, and opportunities, 24
future trends and opportunities in the teaching and learning areas, 24

G

game-based learning/gamification, 26
game-based learning (GBL), 237

games to learn programming concepts, 249
gamification, 56, 228, 237
gamification for engagement, 130
gamification in education, 58
gap between education and industry, 294
GBL for programming courses, 239
GBL for teaching programming, 241
generative AI, 35
generative pre-trained transformer, 87
getting attention in an online class, 224
getting the online learning right, 9
global shortages of teachers, 42
Google forms, 149
governance and organization, 32
Gradescope, 126
guest speakers and industry experts, 229

H

Headai's cognitive artificial intelligence platform, 295
higher education institutions, 328
highly demanded skills by business function, 34
high-quality and pertinent data, 298
Honorlock, 155
host virtual office hours, 229
humanism, 238
human resource machine, 251
Hurix, 149
hybrid classroom, 17
hybrid Learning, 16, 26

I

ICT education, 304
ICT education programs and courses in China represent, 306
ICT higher education in China, 306
ICT programs, 304

immersive learning/situation learning/ scenario learning, 26
impacts of digital technologies on education, 10
implementation of GBL, 244
important skills thought by teachers vs. important skills perceived by students, 10
improved student achievement, 215
in-class discussion, 227
increasing academic integrity issues arising from ChatGPT and other artificial intelligence applications and systems, 7
informal learning, 28
Information and Communication Technology (ICT), 304
integrating artificial intelligence (AI) into technical infrastructure, 30
integrating big data into curriculum development, 297
integrating learners' own devices into learning platforms, 30
interactive tutorial activities, 228
Interactive Whiteboards (IWB), 56
Internet of Things (IoT), 57
intricate evaluation methods, 285
investigate cheating, 175
IT support/services, 30

K
Kahoot, 149, 337
key tools for online education, 124
King's Own Institute (KOI), 203, 329
K-Nearest Neighbors (KNN), 282–283
Knewton, 336
Kodable, 251
KOI's current survey, 331
KOI's survey process, 328
KOI's survey questions, 329

KOI student evaluation of teaching and subjects survey, 329
KOI survey method, 333

L
large-scale automated data processing, 296
leadership, talent and culture, 32
learners' interactions with online platforms, 280
learning analytic dataset (OULAD), 283
learning (analytics for better understanding students' needs and learning performance and thus enhancing teaching quality), 29
learning analytics (LA), 71, 267, 280
learning behaviors, 283
learning management system (LMS), 54, 56, 63, 260, 262, 286, 292
learning theories for GBL, 238
learning/training in the organization, 22
lecture-focused teaching, 236
lifelong learning, 27
LMS activity, 262
logistic regression, 281
long-lasting impact of COVID-19, 8

M
machine learning, 281
machine learning algorithms, 284
machine learning technique approaches, 283
main difficulties in the development and delivery of online exams, 172
MapleLMS, 154
massive open online courses (MOOCs), 62, 283
measures for maintaining academic integrity, 199

Mentimeter, 149
MeriTrac (CodeTrack, Pariksha, and SmartTest), 155
Metaverse learning, 28
Mettl, 153
micro-learning, 28
mobile learning, 26
Mondly, 59
Moodle, 149
Moodle logs, 268
multimedia tools and content creation, 125

N
Naïve Bayes, 282
Naïve Bayes network, 283
(negative) impacts of digital technologies on humanity and society, 19
non-generative (traditional) AI, 35
nudge learning, 28

O
online academic integrity, 27
online assessment, 139, 169, 195
  emotions, 183
  students' view, 181
online assessment, evaluation, and feedback tools, 125
online collaboration spaces, 56
online education, 122, 168, 280
online education introduction, 122
online education platforms, 61
online examination, 179
  advantages, 179
  limitations, 180
  types, 181
online exam proctoring tools, 153
online learning, 11, 26
online learning platforms, 53
online paper mills, 67
online peer assessment, 176
online peer assessments: advantages, 178
online peer assessments: requisites, 178
online portals for HR related matters, 30
online quizzes and polls, 228
online safety, 74
OpenAI, 87
OpenCV, 337
open educational resources (OER), 70
Open edX Insight, 336
open learning, 27
open university learning analytics dataset (OULAD), 284
opportunities and challenges of online education, 123
opportunities arising from future skills and future trends, 33
opportunities in the teaching and learning areas, 24

P
panic-gogy, 216
partnership development, 31
passive learning, 229
passive traditional style of teaching, 55
pedagogical re-engineering, 216
peer learning/collaborative learning, 25
personalized learning, 24, 68
plagiarism, 196
plagiarism detection tools, 67
platforms and Systems for centrally managing student information, 31
Podcasting, 56
popular LMS, 64
predicting student engagement, 280
predictive learning analytic, 266

presentation length, 230
pressure on return of capital and asset investment, 8
pressure on securing research funding, 8
pressure on student success, 8
private higher education, 260
ProctorEdu, 154
ProctorExam, 153
Proctorio, 155
Proctortrack, 153
progress in digital technologies for education, 54
promoting products, 30
providing academic integrity training and education, 201

Q

quality indicators for learning and teaching (QILT), 334
Quizlet, 149

R

random forests, 283
rapid evolution of technology and data sources, 298
real-time student feedback, 29
reasons for committing academic misconduct, 197
reducing cognitive load and promoting efficient learning, 54
relevance of education, 7
reliable exams, 175
remote learning, 11
remote learning challenges, 67
remote learning continuing after COVID-19, 27
Robocode, 251
role of the government in the digital era, 39
role of teacher in the digital era, 41

S

Screeps, 251
security and privacy issues, 11
selecting tools for deterring academic misconduct, 202
self-learning, 25
sharing answers, 67
significant challenge inherent in utilizing big data, 298
social learning, 28
socio-psychological theories, 263
Socrative, 149
spatial computing, 57
speech-to-text, 337
strategies and tools for detecting academic cheating, 150
strategies and tools for redesigning online assessments, 146
strategies and tools to improve assessment integrity and security, 146
student attrition, 261
student-centered learning environments (SCLEs), 55
student engagement, 219, 280
student engagement and learning, 57
student experience, services and information management, 31
student feedback, 328
student generated content, 229
student Interaction, 283
student progress monitoring and at-risk alerts, 31
student recruitment, 30
student retention, 260
student retention models, 263
students' interaction, 283
student's trajectory, 41
success factors of e-learning, 14
successful AI implementation, 37

successful curriculum development, 298
success of OER initiative, 71
suggestions for effectively learning/ training in the organization, 23
suggestions for helping ensure academic integrity, 185
summary of the European Commission framework for the digital competence of educators, 157
summative assessment, 138, 167
support vector machines, 282

T
teacher shortages around the world, 7
teaching staff and professional staff recruitment and other HR matters, 30
tech-driven and behavioral threats to assessment integrity, 144
technology and online teaching, 231
technology and operations, 32
technology-based teaching and learning support to increase student engagement, 52
technology-enabled survey, 335
Tertiary Education Quality and Standards Agency (TEQSA), 65, 261
test invite, 154
textbook-centric learning, 236
The Society for Learning Analytics Research (SoLAR), 265
The Student Experience Survey (SES), 334
Thinglink, 149

threats and challenges to maintaining assessment integrity in the digital era, 144
time taken, 336
tools for evaluation and feedback, 126
top 20 key ICT courses at Shanxi universities, 311
trustworthy technology, 175
Tyler's model, 293
types of games, 250
types of interactions that can enhance students' engagement using educational technology, 59

U
Universities Australia (2017), 65
using digital technology to facilitate learners' lifelong learning journey, 31

V
video-based learning, 130
video learning, 28
video platforms, 61
virtual
　field trips, 228
　reality (VR), 57
　simulations, 228
　teaching assistants, 42
visualized learning, 26
VLE, 283

W
working on factors shaping future digital education, 31
working on quality of course and assignment design, 201
written assessments, 236

Printed in the United States
by Baker & Taylor Publisher Services